Also by William A. Hoisington, Jr.

The Casablanca Connection: French Colonial Policy, 1936–1943

Taxpayer Revolt in France: The National Taxpayers' Federation, 1928–1939

LYAUTEY

AND THE FRENCH CONQUEST OF MOROCCO

William A. Hoisington, Jr.

St. Martin's Press
New York

ISBN 0-312-12529-1

Library of Congress Cataloging-in-Publication Data

Hoisington, William A., Jr. 1941-
    Lyautey and the French conquest of Morocco / William A.
Hoisington, Jr. — 1st ed.
        p. cm.
    Includes bibliographical references (p.   ) and index.
    ISBN 0-312-12529-1
    1. Morocco—History—20th century.   2. Lyautey, Louis Hubert
Gonzalve, 1854-1934.   I. Title.
    DT326.H56 1995
    964—dc20   94-41987
                                                              CIP

First Edition: August 1995
10   9   8   7   6   5   4   3   2   1

INTERIOR DESIGN BY DIGITAL TYPE & DESIGN

CONTENTS

To Sharon Leigh Hoisington
and our daughters

PREFACE

This book describes and analyzes the method of colonial conquest and rule linked to the name of Marshal Louis-Hubert Lyautey (1854-1934), France's first resident general in Morocco and the most famous of France's overseas soldier-administrators. Lyautey popularized the notions of "peaceful penetration" and "indirect rule" (even though he did not invent them) and promoted the protectorate over Morocco as the highest form of French imperialism and the truest expression of "association"—the e6ffort to link diverse peoples with France while preserving their historical and cultural identity, their political and social structures.

When Lyautey was enshrined in Les Invalides over thirty years ago, General Charles de Gaulle insisted that what had made him a great colonizer (and thus a fitting representative of France in the twentieth century) was his humanity. It was Lyautey's sensitivity and desire for understanding; his concern for social, moral, and economic improvement; his respect for native customs and traditions; his constructive and generous action that shaped his colonial method.[1] At the same time Lyautey's method of pacification in Morocco differed in practice from what he proclaimed it to be and indirect rule failed to live up to its name. Neither succeeded in ending Moroccan resistance to France and neither achieved the Franco-Moroccan partnership that Lyautey said was his goal.

In the pages that follow I trace the development of the Lyautey method and assess the influences at home and abroad that fashioned Lyautey's ideas on conquest and rule. I follow pacification in the Algerian-Moroccan borderlands, the Middle Atlas, and Morocco's south and test the realities of indirect rule in the cities of Rabat and Casablanca, the most important urban centers of Franco-Moroccan communication and contact, and in the Chaouïa countryside around Settat. A final chapter on the Rif rebellion describes the collapse of the Lyautey method, in deed if not in word.

I am grateful to all who assisted me in France and Morocco with this project, especially Edward H. Thomas, executive secretary of the Moroccan-American Commission for Educational and Cultural Exchange; Mohammed

El Mansour, chairman of the Department of History of Mohammed V University; Hassan Mekouar, former dean of the Faculté des Lettres et des Sciences Humaines of Mohammed V University; and Abdelmajid Ben Youssef, archivist at the Bibliothèque Générale et Archives du Maroc. I acknowledge as well the generous support of the American Council of Learned Societies, the American Philosophical Society, the National Endowment for the Humanities, the Fulbright Program, the Rotary Foundation of Rotary International, and the Institute for the Humanities at the University of Illinois at Chicago.

The maps were prepared by Raymond M. Brod, cartographer in the Department of Geography at the University of Illinois at Chicago.

Throughout the text, the translations from the French are my own; italics have been maintained from the original, not added.

I dedicate this book to Sharon Leigh Hoisington and our three daughters—Anne, Sarah, and Kate—who shared all the pleasures and challenges of a long research and writing project with me.

LIST OF MAPS

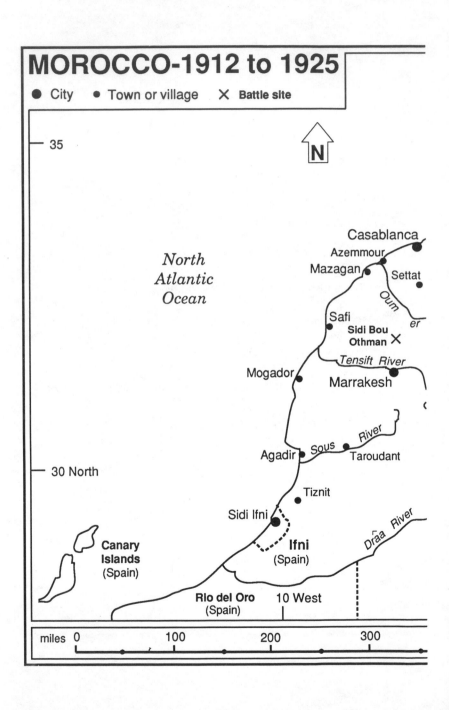

MOROCCO-1912 to 1925

● City ● Town or village ✕ Battle site

35

N

*North
Atlantic
Ocean*

Casablanca
Azemmour
Mazagan
Settat
Oum
er
Safi
Sidi Bou
Othman ✕
Tensift River
Mogador
Marrakesh

River
Sous
Agadir
Taroudant

30 North

Tiznit

Sidi Ifni

Canary
Islands
(Spain)

Ifni
(Spain)

Drâa River

Rio del Oro
(Spain)

10 West

miles 0   100   200   300

CHAPTER 1

Colonial Mission

■ ■ ■ ■

orn in Nancy in 1854, Louis-Hubert-Gonzalve Lyautey was from an upper middle-class family with aristocratic connections, royalist sympathies, and a military past.[1] Although Lyautey chose to enter the military academy of Saint-Cyr in 1873 for family and patriotic reasons, he said he wanted nothing of the horsemanship of the parade ground, nor the camaraderie of the barracks, nor the paperwork and routine of a staff appointment.[2] His early life as a soldier was, more than anything else, a personal test to demonstrate his physical recovery from a childhood fall from a second-story window that had kept him bedridden for two years. Lyautey was serious, idealistic, and endowed with a talent for writing; his letters and notebooks reveal a young man more interested in the social and literary world around him than in the arts of war. At the same time, he was never the "compleat" army outsider that he later claimed to be. He was ambitious. As a result, he mastered his professional tasks with intelligence, determination, and energy; he assiduously cultivated his superiors; and he always kept one eye on the promotion roster. Lyautey was a "good soldier," albeit an officer with a decidedly unmilitary bent.

Lyautey's introduction to overseas France came in the late 1870s when as a young first lieutenant he travelled from east to west across Algeria, which by then had been in French hands for almost half a century. He had known Algeria from his grandfather's war stories, but it still surprised him. From the first he recognized it as a "new world" that got "better and better" the longer he stayed.[3] He loved the desert and especially the light and the heat of the Algerian sun, which had an animating and therapeutic effect on him, banishing the pain in his bones that lingered from his childhood accident.[4]

For Lyautey Algeria was *The Arabian Nights* come to life and it stimulated his imagination much as it inspired other Frenchmen of artistic and literary sensibilities. Like a discriminating collector he sought out authentic Algeria, the Algeria that had resisted European domination. "The Arab at prayer is wonderful" he noted in his journal at a time when anti-Arab sentiment was on the rise among the European colonial population. "I definitely respect these people more and more, so unconcerned with what others may say, so proud and dignified in their faith."[5] But the real Algeria was not easy to find. In Algiers everything was too "affected," too studied. There was no way "to surprise" the Arab, to observe his life, to experience his color.[6] Constantine, in eastern Algeria, away from the coast and perched high on a massive outcropping of rock was better. Here was "a strange, noisy, and pungent world," so close to Europe and yet so far.[7]

Lyautey returned to Algeria in October 1880, this time for a stay of almost two years with his cavalry regiment at Orléansville, a small European town on the Chélif River in central Algeria. His search for "local color" now became a serious preoccupation with the language and culture of the Arab population.[8] This was in part a diversion from the routine of army life. If he conceded to the purveyors of local prejudice that the Arab was "dirty and stinking," he realized that he was "much more besides."[9] And that "much more" intrigued him. At the offices of the French military administrators, the Bureaux Arabes, he followed the "continual comings and goings" of the high and low in the native population and began to study Arabic in order to assess this human parade for himself.

> Sometimes I station myself near the interpreter, increasing my Arabic vocabulary day by day, or I sit in the Moorish café. . . . I watch and listen. Sometimes I hole up in the corner of the captain's office and play dead, never opening my mouth, but keeping my eyes and ears open to experience this procession of individuals who complain, beg, protest, accuse and defend themselves.[10]

On occasion Lyautey rode with the Bureaux officers into the countryside and he soon boasted to his parents that he was the friend of all the *caïds,* the native tribal governors, in the area.[11]

While celebrating these friendships, Lyautey recognized the unease, even hostility that existed among the native population because of the relentless European advance. He worried about the Mzabites of south-central Algeria: "Here is a happy, honest, faithful, patriarchal people for whom until now the desert has served as a life preserver, saving its oases from all agitation. After ten years of the railroad and the infusion of European ideas, what will become of them?"[12] Of Si Anni Ben Ahmed, the proud and intelligent caïd of the Ouled Si Anni, whom Lyautey counted as a friend, he noted simply: he "hates and scorns us."[13] With regret Lyautey concluded that the Arab could never really be "at peace with himself regarding his dealings with us."[14]

In March 1881 Lyautey was transferred to Algiers to serve as chief of staff of the subdivision of Algiers. He resisted the move without success. Not only was he now immobilized behind a desk, but he was cut off from the Arab population. "The more I see of Algiers, the more my impression of three years ago, of three months ago, of yesterday holds true: I abhor this city." Algiers was packed with European tourists, crowded with shops and the branch stores of the "big Paris houses," crisscrossed by wide avenues and boulevards, and polluted by the noise and dust of traffic and construction.[15] Moreover, the Arabs of the European city were "impenetrable, unapproachable, and, moreover, completely corrupted by our contact."[16]

Over time Lyautey was befriended by a handful of French officers interested in the life and culture of the Arab population and they became his guides to the city. On his own he walked for hours in the Casbah of upper Algiers with his sketchbook. He rented a small villa with a garden and palm trees overlooking the bay, which he decorated with the rugs, pillows, and accessories—"mes araberies" he called them—similar to those in the Arab dwellings he had visited. At "home" he even dressed the part, putting on an Arab shirt and burnoose to fit in with his surroundings.[17] He continued his study of Arabic and announced to his family that he had even begun to write the language. "Pronunciation, writing, reading, rules, nothing resembles what we know, but it is very interesting."[18] Moreover, as Lyautey would later point out to his father, language—"causé arabe"—was the "great means of action" through which one might gain the understanding and perhaps even the goodwill of all those with whom one spoke.[19]

Despite his initial anxiety at leaving the great out-of-doors for an office, Lyautey did become acquainted with members of an Arab "elite" of Algiers, the educated sons of a well-off commercial and professional class that had advanced and prospered by accepting French rule. He soon began spending some of his afternoons in his "dear casbah," admiring "the old city in its integrity" with a small circle of his "native friends," discussing theology and metaphysics, listening to the storytellers, and sometimes even talking politics.[20] These personal contacts caused him to question France's policy of assimilation—making Algerians French—which gave scant attention to Algeria's notables, their culture, or their political and social institutions. It smacked of a rude cultural and racial superiority that offended Arab feelings, provoking anger and at times outright resistance. In letters home, he warned that until France developed a "more civilized, more humane, more polite system of rule," insurrections—such as the Bou Amama revolt of 1881 in the South Oranais, which resulted from French expulsions of tribal groups from their lands—would occur "at regular intervals."[21] Algeria, he argued, should be placed in the hands of a "firm and competent" leader who would give a "vigorous push to economic, industrial, financial, and commercial projects" and yet not neglect the human side.[22] For Lyautey the road toward that sort of rule centered on contact with the native population, specifically with those leaders of society willing to commit themselves to the French. Generous and calculated, these notions would shape Lyautey's attitudes on colonial policy and the methods for implementing it.

In November 1882 Lyautey's promotion to captain took him to a new posting in France and for the next twelve years he would make the rounds of garrisons in the Metropole. Enjoying remarkable luck in his assignments as well as the support and encouragement of his commanding officers, Lyautey at last put to rest any lingering doubts he may have had about an army career. He was now convinced that he could maintain his complete freedom of thought and expression while under the flag. This was important to him, for in these years he aspired to become someone esteemed in Paris society for his literary talent and his ideas on military reform.[23] In addition, he sought a "total independence" from bourgeois social conventions which, he hoped, acceptance by a socially prominent "upper crust" would ensure.[24] In these calculations he was mistaken.

Lyautey published his first piece of writing in the March 1891 number of the prestigious *Revue des deux mondes.* "The Social Role of the Officer" suggested a "social duty" for the French army officer that emphasized social concord and national union, an unlikely target for an army that traditionally had little concern for anything beyond the military arts. Inspired by Albert de Mun, a retired army captain and influential conservative deputy who preached a patriotic gospel of national strength through social service, Lyautey proposed the army as a vast field of social action. What convinced him, aside from his own anxieties over the limitations and narrowness of army life, was the 1889 law on conscription. As a result of this "revolutionary act," which established a two-year period of compulsory military service for all Frenchmen between the ages of twenty and twenty-three, the entire male population of the nation "without exception" would pass through the army. This was a unique opportunity to influence all of France's young men, living clay that Lyautey assumed yearned to be molded through tough but useful national service.[25]

As Lyautey explained it, this task required a "new officer," prepared to link military training and military values—discipline, respect, and self-sacrifice—to a larger social mission. In the process the officer would become an "apostle" or "agent" of social change and ultimately the "teacher" of the entire nation. Lyautey insisted, however, that only by conquering his soldiers' hearts through acts of fraternity, mutual respect, and affection ("they love whoever loves them" was one of his startling phrases) could the officer hope to make a lasting impact. Disciplining the mind, shaping the soul, inspiring the heart—the army officer would not only ready his men for the tests of combat but also for living the rest of their lives.[26]

Senior army officers dismissed Lyautey's essay as childish nonsense or socialist prattle. In literary and political circles, however, "The Social Role of the Officer" marked Lyautey as an independent-minded soldier willing to speak hard truths about army life and to suggest needed reforms to an institution that all of France's sons would soon experience first hand. Nevertheless, if Lyautey had "conquered" Paris, where for a time he was in demand as a speaker and as a participant in discussion groups, it was not the Paris of the liberated "upper crust," but the Paris of the conservative and solidly republican middle class, intrigued at ways of utilizing the army as an instrument of social reform.[27]

In spring 1893 Lyautey left Paris for the small town of Gray at the edge of the Franche-Comté. This was the post he said he had wanted for personal and professional reasons. It distanced him from a woman whom he admired, but whom he had no intention of marrying and it was staffed by self-reliant officers. But Lyautey felt isolated. He was half-frightened, half-angered by the negative impression his article had made on the army high command—although it had not blocked his promotion to major—and demoralized by endless petty administrative tasks that drove him to despair.[28] Three and a half months later he was named chief of staff of the Seventh Cavalry Division at Meaux, near Paris, but here too he found no relief. After six months on the job, he wrote: "I am sick with loneliness, with sadness, and, above all, with horror at my duties and with soldiers in general. What else is there to do, however, but to wait until retirement."[29]

Trapped and discouraged, Lyautey languished in harness until September 1894 when he was suddenly shipped off to Indochina. This was less the favor from the general staff that it turned out to be than a delayed reprimand. Nevertheless, the escape overseas freed him from metropolitan disapproval, entanglements, and restraints as well as from the treadmill of military life in France. It was a way out. It ended, however, whatever hope he may have had of becoming an apostle of military reform in France, for the colonies, distant and unpopular, were the army's dumping grounds for troublemakers and misfits.[30]

Lyautey's introduction to the colonial life—what he called his "first colonial chapter" and which he said came after "having never, or scarcely ever left France"—began in October 1894.[31] He was attached to the headquarters staff of the French army of occupation in Tonkin, the northernmost province of the Empire of Annam, which had been under French protection for a decade. Lyautey desperately hoped his passage to Tonkin would be a "resurrection" from the "mummification of our idle, routine, and hidebound army."[32] But, as he worried in a letter to his sister when his ship entered the estuary of the Saigon River, it also might have been the beginning of "a dismal life, one of thankless and sterile effort, paltry and artificial."[33]

What changed things for Lyautey was his interim appointment as army chief of staff at Hanoi. He soon had the confidence of Governor-General Jean de Lanessan and Colonel Joseph Gallieni, commander of the second military territory in northeastern Tonkin. The ideas of these two men on colonial conquest and rule were compelling. De Lanessan believed that a protectorate, governed firmly but indirectly by France, rather than outright colonial annexation and direct French rule was the best way to establish quick, effective, and inexpensive colonial control. Although his critics charged that leaving a native regime in power perpetuated abuses, encouraged double-dealing, and at the slightest hint of French weakness invited resistance, de Lanessan argued the opposite, convinced of the powerful and positive impact of the French example.[34] Lyautey was soon won over. "To explain it once and for all," he told his sister,

> it comes down to this: to aim for a protectorate and not direct rule.
> Instead of abolishing the traditional systems, make use of them:
> Rule with the mandarin and not against him. It follows that, since
> we are—and are always destined to be—a very small minority
> here, we ought not aspire to substitute ourselves for the man-
> darins, but at best to guide and oversee them. Therefore, offend no
> tradition, change no custom, remind ourselves that in all human
> society there is a ruling class, born to rule, without which nothing
> can be done, and a class to be ruled: Enlist the ruling class in our
> service. Once the mandarins are our friends, certain of us and
> needing us, they have only to say the word and the country will be
> pacified, and at far less cost and with greater certainty than by all
> the military expeditions we could send there.[35]

De Lanessan's indirect rule—using a native ruling class as both an instrument and a screen—responded perfectly to Lyautey's negative impressions of colonial Algeria where direct French rule reigned with a vengeance. It paralleled his personal attraction to the elites among a native population, his real interest in indigenous culture and institutions, and his high estimate of the value of close human relations in colonial affairs. In a deceptively simple manner de Lanessan had employed all of this as part of a grander scheme to ease colonial conquest and facilitate colonial rule.

The attention of de Lanessan to the political side of things was matched by Gallieni's elaboration of a military "collaboration strategy" that relied on cooperation with groups in the native population to pacify the countryside and break any resistance to the French presence.[36] As the senior field commander in Tonkin, Gallieni's task was to eliminate the "brigands" who, often in complicity with both Chinese and Tonkinese authorities, terrorized the area from the Sino-Tonkinese frontier in the north to the edges of the pacified delta region in the south.

Gallieni used light, mobile columns to give his soldiers a freedom of movement somewhat akin to that of the bands of brigands that opposed them, adapting his military instrument to the jungle fighting environment. From different directions his columns converged simultaneously on the brigands' strongholds, destroying them methodically one by one. This differed from what had been done before, dispatching heavy columns helter-skelter, like "projectiles," first at one group of brigands, then at another. Next, he constructed blockhouses along the frontier as observation points, linked to one another by optical signaling devices. Behind this line, he established a network of military posts to control the local population and oppose any enemy infiltration; these were commanded by officers with both civil and military authority and garrisoned by strong reserve forces. Finally, in a stunning display of confidence in himself and his Tonkinese partners, he armed the native villagers and told them to defend themselves. "To this military work," Lyautey explained admiringly, "Colonel Gallieni combines the simultaneous organization of roads, telegraphs, markets, and European and native concessions, so that with pacification a great band of civilization advances like a spot of oil [*une tache d'huile*]."[37]

Everything did not move as slickly as Lyautey claimed. The military collaboration with native villagers, which Gallieni always touted as a permanent victory for French pacification, was in many cases only a temporary and unholy alliance against a common foe. And the organized brigandage—although Lyautey refused to admit it—was itself sometimes a genuine act of local native resistance to the French presence. In addition, Gallieni's strategy of converging columns was never completely successful. The columns proved difficult to coordinate in rough terrain and if the element of surprise was lost or if the brigands escaped his trap, Gallieni was forced to give chase, running the risk of ambush and frequently pushing his soldiers to the limits of their endurance.[38] Finally, as Lyautey seemed to have forgotten in the intervening fifteen years, the march of European "civilization" was a mixed blessing.

None of this dampened Lyautey's enthusiasm. In the field as Gallieni's chief of staff from March to May 1895, he witnessed what he called "the triumph of the Gallieni method, colonial rule and conquest linked together, the latter having no other objective than the former."[39] Admiration for the method went hand in hand with admiration for the man—"this magnificent specimen of a complete man," "this example of an absolute leader, soldier and administrator, tough and intelligent."[40] What marked him so clearly as a great leader, Lyautey decided, was "the boundless confidence with which he inspires all around him."[41] Gallieni, too, was contemptuous of routine, of rules and regulations, and of the entire "gold-braided bureaucracy." He was a soldier who had pushed himself and his authority to the limits, growing, developing his "complete personality," and expanding his military role just as Lyautey had hoped metropolitan officers would do. "Conqueror, explorer, military commander par excellence, he is the very opposite of the militarist [caporal], and I might even say of the military man [militaire] in the official and bureaucratic sense of this word in France."[42] To the author of "The Social Role of the Officer," Gallieni—the "linchpin" of Tonkin's "security, pacification, and progress"—had become the beau idéal, and he, Lyautey, had become "Gallieni-ed" (Gallienisé), transformed into a Gallieni disciple of the art of colonial conquest and rule.[43]

In July Lyautey returned to Hanoi for a second interim as army chief of staff where he was involved with the planning of the next campaign. Surprisingly, even after the time with Gallieni in the field, Hanoi was not drudgery. "I have never had a life more usefully spent and interesting," he admitted, "more in conformity with my tastes and where I believe my abilities lie, since my objective has always been the union of policy and action, of the bivouac and diplomacy."[44] For the first time Lyautey experienced the satisfaction that could come through administration and policy making at a top level. "I am like a fish in water, for these are important matters, the handling of affairs and of men, in a word, power, everything that I love."[45] "Instead of being prime minister in France," he conceded somewhat matter-of-factly, "I will at least have exercised similar authority for some days in Indochina and the taste will remain on my lips. And I would not give up these sleepless nights of work, this maximum exertion of my brain, this supreme joy of conscious authority for all the peaceful pleasures of this world."[46] In January 1896 Lyautey joined Colonel Jean Vallière, commander of the third military territory, for the winter campaign in northern Tonkin, ready to put what he had learned with Gallieni into practice. Lyautey told his brother that Vallière's effort could only really be successful if colonial rule went hand in hand with the military advance. The link between these two activities, "united under one authority with full freedom of action," was the "essential reason" for the results that Gallieni had achieved.[47] After Vallière's operations drove the brigands to the Chinese border, Lyautey was twice convinced:

> Oppose the brigands with the best of all deterrents— *organization*. . . . To accomplish this make the people our chief allies and over time take great care to show them only the benefits of our occupation. Do away with all fiscal dues. Substitute taxes in kind, so lightly felt by primitive peoples, for money taxes which weigh so heavily. Avoid all administrative complications in the reestablishment of native markets and villages. Pattern our conduct on native traditions and habits. Show generosity. And all this is Gallieni.[48]

It is no wonder that, as Gallieni prepared to return to France in late 1895, Lyautey could write of the "grief" he felt at the imminent separation from the leader "to whom I owe everything since I came here." Gallieni had "opened horizons which I never imagined existed, associated me with stirring work, and gave me an objective in life once more."[49] This was more than affection for a man and a method. It was testimony to an encounter with a lifework, made more ardent since it came at age forty, when Lyautey feared that time had already passed him by.[50]

This self-discovery continued after Gallieni's departure, spurred by Lyautey's fear, as a result of a political shake-up in Hanoi, that his own days in Indochina might be numbered. He fretted to his boyhood companion, Antonin de Margerie:

> I am definitely an "animal of action." I have always believed it, events have finally confirmed it, and, after twenty years of pawing the ground, I finally thought that I had found the "action" I wanted. Fortunate circumstances had at last put me in a position to do some "Cecil Rhodes," and I thought that maybe I would leave my mark here on something productive and durable. I thought perhaps I was going to be one of those in whom men believe, in whose eyes thousands seek command, at whose voice and with whose pen roads are opened, lands populated, cities built. I am committed to all of this. And if it eludes me now, it will be a bitter disappointment. More than ever before, I feel that without productive, decisive, and immediate action, I am at loose ends, I languish, and my talents are wasted.[51]

Fortunately for Lyautey his field of action was about to be widened, not narrowed. Gallieni had been sent to Madagascar in summer 1896 and in November he asked Lyautey to join him.[52] Gallieni's invitation was decisive. Lyautey told his sister that henceforth he was orienting his life toward the colonies. Based on his experience in Tonkin, he had decided that he was "someone [un monsieur] made to direct very important matters."[53] Now he would have the chance to prove it. He said that eventually he wanted to return to France, where there might yet be some important national "mission" for him to fulfill, but only after he had found his "place in the sun" and was recognized for his own abilities and his own accomplishments. A military career in France had failed to provide the opportunity for him to influence events or to do great things. "The only chance which remains for me is in the colonies where there is still room for some of my ambitions and where up until now the circumstances have served me very well."[54]

Of the value of empire Lyautey never had any doubt. Like the colonial economist Joseph Chailley-Bert, Lyautey believed that a colonial empire would provide France with "the most solid element of power and growth" in a world transformed by modern communications and new economic realities.[55] In consequence, French colonial policy ought to aim at securing those markets "indispensable to the smooth operation" of the French national economy.[56] In Lyautey's scheme of things Tonkin itself had no intrinsic economic value, but it was vitally important as a "jumping-off place" for the commercial penetration of China as well as a buffer state, "a sort of protective, but indispensable Savoy," to shelter the rest of the rich, rice-producing Indochinese peninsula from Chinese interference.[57] Since this was empire measured by the economic yardstick, not surprisingly Lyautey believed that Jules Ferry, the much-maligned champion of the Third Republic's economic imperium, was the "most farsighted colonial leader" that France had produced in the last thirty years.[58]

Economics aside, Lyautey believed in the positive social impact that empire could have on France and Frenchmen just as he had witnessed it at work on himself. He had found his way and so could France. Parroting the fin de siècle concern over French "decadence," Lyautey proposed the colonies as an overseas field of action to rescue France from "decomposition and ruin."[59] After two and a half years abroad he was filled with hope and admiration for the colonial Frenchman—ambitious, talented, selfless, and inspired by a sense of duty. "This is why I have become a convinced colonialist," he told de Margerie.

> Above all, it is because our colonial expansion enlarges this marvelous nursery of will and energy. It is because from Tonkin to

Madagascar and in the Sudan an entire generation is growing up purified by hard work; it is because the atmosphere of France is unhealthy, destructive of will and confidence . . . while the atmosphere here is just the opposite.[60]

Lyautey hoped the colonies would form an ever-increasing number of "the creative, the strong, the selfless, the high-minded" who through "a continuous and life-restoring connection" between France "outside" and France "inside" would have a "violent impact" on French attitudes. The result would be "an increase in the birth rate, in economic activity, in worldwide commerce, in entrepreneurial zeal, and in generous thoughts, vast desires, and broad judgments on the world and the nations which people it."[61] In addition to serving France's "immediate, practical, and essential interests," empire would be a "school for social action," teaching lessons to all French society.[62] The task that Lyautey had once tried to press on the metropolitan army had been reassigned to the colonies.

At first Lyautey justified empire solely because of its importance to France, not because it brought benefit to native populations overseas. Empire was both an economic necessity and a psychological cure for a French crisis. Moreover, the prescription had developed from his individual commitment to social action in France and his personal need to find a vocation that could give direction and purpose to his life. Over time, however, Lyautey came to believe that imperialism was morally justified only if it contributed to the economic well-being and happiness of all mankind.[63] And this was based on his understanding of the task of human beings in the world:

Even if France derives nothing from this, we would not have been less the workers for providence on this earth, if we brought back life, cultivation, and humanity to regions given over to brigands and barrenness, if we made these rivers the paths of communication which are their part in the economic scheme of things, if we exploited these forests and restored these fertile and uncultivated valleys. The most important thing is to leave on this earth some useful trace of one's passage. Man has only been put here to till the soil by the sweat of his brow and in the sight of God it makes little difference whether this cultivation, which is man's reason for existence on this earth, profits one or another national group, which sooner or later is destined to disappear.[64]

En route to Madagascar in January 1897 Lyautey was already planning to write an article about his colonial experience in Tonkin, focusing either on the "colonial role" of the military officer or on "military colonization" as he had come to understand it.[65] In the months after Gallieni's leave taking he had continued to reflect on the nature of the Gallieni method. He acknowledged that Colonel Théophile Pennequin, the military commander in northwestern Tonkin and Gallieni's alter ego as a colonial innovator, had been the first to shape pacification to the ethnic environment in what was called the "policy of races" (politique des races). Recognizing how different the peoples of the mountains and valleys of the north were from the Annamites (or Vietnamese) of the delta, he instituted administrative practices that fit in with their own customs and traditions. By so doing Pennequin took the "collaboration strategy" a step further, moving it beyond a simple partnership with the traditional Annamite elite to a multiple partnership with ethnic minorities as well. This permitted the French to use the ethnic divisions in Tonkin to their advantage, but at the same time it weakened the cohesive force of the Empire of Annam, the authority they had come to protect. In addition, Pennequin was the first to arm the native villagers and to employ them as part of the pacification process. Yet even if Gallieni had not always been the originator of pacification policy—and in some cases had merely "followed and developed" Pennequin's ideas—Lyautey celebrated him as its "most brilliant practitioner."[66]

Lyautey also denied the mechanical in the Gallieni method. When twitted that the "method" was not always a surefire success, even in the hands of a Gallieni or a Pennequin, Lyautey retorted: "There is no method, there is no 'cliché Gallieni,' there are ten of them, there are twenty of them, or rather, there is only one method and it is called flexibility, elasticity, adaptation to time, place, and circumstance." What counted most of all—and Lyautey wrote this phrase in English, for he thought Englishmen understood it better than his own countrymen—was getting the "right man for the right place" and then giving him "carte blanche" to get the job done.[67]

Lyautey arrived in Madagascar in March 1897 and was greeted with a situation far different from that in Tonkin. The imposition of a French protectorate had been resisted by Malagasy leaders for over a decade and even after a French expeditionary force captured Tananarive, the capital of the Merina kingdom, in September 1895 and forced the queen to sign a protectorate treaty, the fighting continued. In desperation, the French junked the protectorate formula and any pretense of indirect rule and annexed the island in August 1896. In these unpromising circumstances Gallieni was named governor-general (and promoted to the rank of brigadier general) with full political and military authority. His mission was to quell the resistance—now called a "native insurrection"—by whatever means possible. He concentrated on breaking the power of the Merina elite, which he considered feudal, oppressive, and untrustworthy—it was also Anglophile and Protestant—by tough and brutal methods. He exiled the Merina queen, executed two of her chief ministers, removed the Merina aristocracy from all positions of political authority, and undercut the Merina economic and social domination of the island's interior by ending slavery and redistributing land.[68] This was direct French rule with a punch.

Gallieni did what he felt had to be done in a political and military situation that was out of control. There was even a dark twist to his actions. The Merina elite was not the chief instigator of the anti-French insurrection—and Gallieni knew this—but its demise permitted him to install a completely pro-French regime.[69] This, to be sure, was the point: The Gallieni method of military pacification and indirect rule was only possible with native leaders who were willing to cooperate with the French. Lyautey got the message. In fact, he may have been the messenger in Gallieni's attempt to secure faked evidence from Malagasy leaders to buttress the general's official version of events.[70] In spite of all this—in fact, perhaps because of it—Lyautey continued to promote Gallieni as the "most marvelous specimen" of the colonial man of action that turn-of-the-century France had produced and stiff competition for the "Anglo-Saxons," the eternal overseas rivals. Adapting sporting language to empire, he wrote: "Madagascar versus South Africa, Gallieni versus Cecil Rhodes. What a good match!"[71]

Lyautey was given a field command in the northwestern part of the island. Unlike Tonkin where he was always someone else's chief of staff, he found himself on his own, the "absolute leader" of a vast territory.[72] He was delighted with his military and political responsibilities and his energetic life. "I was created and placed into the world only for this!" he proclaimed.

> After twenty years of a routine career in France, after having felt so often the anguish of a destiny that passed me by, in these past three years I have found myself at last in the wind at full sail, certain of myself, of what I am doing, guiding my own life, directing men, and steering events. I thought myself born to create and I am creating, to lead and I am leading, to introduce new ideas, projects, and enterprises and I am doing just that.

He asked his sister to send him a ring engraved with "a bit of verse" that he said he had found in Shelley—"The soul's joy lies in doing" *(La joie de l'âme est dans l'action)*.[73] Over time it became a line of Lyautey.

Not everything was perfect. Lyautey used force and persuasion to bring Rabezavana, a former Merina royal governor, to terms and with Rabezavana as his *ad latus* he quickly ended the insurgency in the northwest. But the experiment in military collaboration and indirect rule did not last; in the end Rabezavana, like the Merina queen, was exiled to Réunion.[74] He tried to make his command post at Ankazobé an urban hub and economic link on the road between Tananarive in the center and Majunga on the northwest coast. However, because of the greater interest of French colonists in developing the line between Tananarive and Tamatave on the east coast, Ankazobé wound up as a ghost town in the tropics.[75]

Lyautey also complained to Gallieni that turning over so much of the island so quickly to civilian rule, as the Metropole demanded, denied soldiers the chance to prove themselves at peacetime government.

> By always stripping us of the pacified territories as soon as the shooting stops and restricting us to the role of "penetrators" and leaders of the advance guard, we risk perfecting only our aptitude for trailblazing—which no one doubts that we can do—while wasting the organizational and administrative ability so well developed in some of us, yet so unknown to the public.

He wanted to delay the transfer from military to civilian rule as long as possible. All authority in a newly pacified territory would first rest with a single military officer, who would create civil or military commands under him as the circumstances required. This would show that soldiers and civilians could work together and demonstrate as well that the "real colonial of tomorrow" was a mixture of the two types.[76] But Gallieni was under pressure to move as quickly as possible to civilian rule. There was no time for colonial trial runs along the way.

Despite Lyautey's disappointment that Madagascar did not become the forcing ground for more colonial theory, more colonial method with "very important and general consequences," in little over eighteen months he would become the interpreter of Gallieni to France—explaining the colonel's method in Tonkin, polishing the general's reputation in Madagascar—as well as an advocate for the "colonial" leader of the future.[77] While in Paris for discussions with the government on Madagascar, Gallieni asked Lyautey, whom he now recognized as a colonial promoter-in-the-making, to speak to the Union Coloniale Française, one of the most influential of the colonial interest groups, on the "major points" of his "method of colonial occupation."[78] From this talk in December 1899 came Lyautey's second article for the *Revue des deux mondes.*

"The Colonial Role of the Army" argued that it made little difference whether civilians or soldiers governed in the colonies. What mattered was that whoever ruled be "colonial"—"the right man in the right place" accord-ing to the Gallieni formula—and that he combine the best qualities of mili-tary and civilian leadership. A "natural gift" for command, decisiveness, and coolness in the face of danger had to be paired with initiative and common sense, a "thirst" for responsibility and a "passion" for improvement, a broad interpretation of rules and regulations and a willingness to stress the spirit over the letter of the law. This union of virtues in a single individual would result in the ideal "colonial" able to handle the special tasks of overseas con-quest and rule.[79]

Lyautey described how Gallieni and his "school" had used the army in the pacification of Tonkin and then in the "normal life of the pacified country." He explained Gallieni's rejection of the "classic and traditional" military col-umn as an instrument of war and the adoption in its place of the method of "progressive occupation" that in a brilliant formulation Lyautey defined as less a matter of a series of military operations than of "an organization on the march" (une organisation qui marche). This army would fight, then stay put. Once in place its soldiers became governors, dividing the land into adminis-trative sectors, circles, and territories. And everywhere the colonial soldier-administrator used the "combined action of force and politics" to maintain the peace and begin the process of social and economic reconstruction.[80]

Gallieni's insistence that the military occupation be presided over by offi-cers who had both military and administrative responsibility went a step beyond the officers of the Algerian Bureaux Arabes, who had administrative, but not military authority. He believed that the "unity of action" made pos-sible by a single command was essential in "immense colonial countries" where the "constant and direct use of armed force is obligatory" and where a handful of men were required to keep the peace among whole populations. Here, more than anywhere else, the "right man" was essential, particularly at the level of the territorial command.[81]

Gallieni's "organization" preceded rather than followed the military occu-pation. Each soldier knew what his task would be on the day after the shooting stopped, when the army instantly became responsible for the social rebuilding and economic development of the occupied territory. This "colonial" obligation transformed the army from a fighting force bent on sheer destruction into a troop determined to shelter and protect its new pat-rimony. In this way colonial war was indeed something different from war on the European continent and it demanded more from its leaders and its soldiers. Gallieni insisted that a colonial expedition had to be directed by the man selected to be the first administrator of the country after the period of conquest was over. This was in order to guarantee that conquest and rule would be interpreted as part of the same process. And just as he believed that the use of "political action" was "much more important" than the use of force, Gallieni considered administration or government to be "the true role of the colonial officer." At the same time, the men in the ranks on whom Gallieni relied for their "inexhaustible qualities of dedication and inventiveness" were to be a reservoir of talent, endlessly tapped to provide agricultural experts, technical advisers, and teachers.[82]

There was a new language of conquest to describe the army's colonial mission. In Lyautey's words an "invasion route" or a "line of operations" now became an "avenue of commercial penetration." A strategic or tactical position became a "center of economic relations." The countryside was no longer "a source of military provisions," but "a center of resources and cultivation."[83] And, according to Lyautey, the "greatness" of colonial conquest was that, alone of all warfare, it created life—*"Et c'est la grandeur de la guerre coloniale ainsi comprise, c'est qu'elle seule fait de la vie."* Through colonial war France could fulfill its "providential mission" to bring agricultural, industrial, and economic development—"and, yes, it must also be said, a higher moral life, a more complete life"—to peoples who did not have it. To this civilizing mission Lyautey added his own personal testimony on the importance of the individual Frenchman abroad—the colonist, the administrator, the soldier, the missionary—with his conviction that this "colonial endeavor" would provide France with an "incomparable school of energy and will."[84]

The Gallieni method of colonial conquest and rule, the "providential mission," and the "colonial endeavor" promoted an expanded French presence abroad. In fact, Lyautey's essay was an attempt to counter the "colonial anti-militarism" that had emerged as part of the French colonial movement in the 1890s among those at home and in the colonies who rejected both the high costs of military expansion and the heavy-handedness of military rule.[85] Justified as more productive, more efficient, more beneficent, more patriotic, and less expensive than the empire building of the past, this was a "new imperialism" and Lyautey was on his way to becoming its chief spokesman and wordsmith. To carry out this overseas mission Lyautey also argued for a new colonial army and later in the year the *Troupes de Marine,* until then attached to the Ministry of the Navy, were transformed into the *Troupes coloniales (La Coloniale)* under the Ministry of War. This provided much of the autonomy that Lyautey had hoped for, but it fell short of what he called "the most logical, fruitful and truly colonial conception" of independent armies for each colony, the design that the English had chosen.[86]

With this article Lyautey not only boosted Gallieni, but he became a public figure in his own right in the *monde colonial,* which in the 1890s stretched far beyond explorers, soldiers, and missionaries. Lyautey's commitment to colonial service coincided with the emergence of a "colonial lobby" in France of academics, lawyers, businessmen, journalists, diplomats, and civil servants whose ideas on empire—its purpose, its organization, and even its economic importance to France—tallied with his own. The colonial lobby—and particularly the determined *parti colonial* in the Chamber of Deputies and the Senate—provided Lyautey another way to advance his own career. He in turn helped French colonialism define a mission and decide on a method for overseas conquest and rule.[87]

After a year in France, Gallieni returned to Madagascar (in June 1900) with Lyautey as his chief of staff. Three months later he named Lyautey the political and military commander of the southern third of the island, an area equal to a third of France.[88] Five provinces, eighty officers, four thousand soldiers, and one million Malagasy fell under his authority, including both civil provinces and military circles, precisely the "mixed" administrative regime to which Lyautey had insisted the real colonial officer was suited. For the next twenty months he experienced pacification as a colonial leader on his own, living out the precepts of the "colonial role" of the army.[89]

More certain of himself than he had been at any other time in his life, Lyautey began to measure himself against Gallieni. "I am forty-six years old tonight," he wrote on 17 November 1900.

> This was Colonel Gallieni's age when I met him six years ago. He was a colonel. I am a colonel. He commanded the most important of the territories of Indochina. I command a third of Madagascar. He was known and talked about, and either detested or passionately admired. The same is true of me. He had faith in his star. I have faith in mine. All is well.[90]

Lyautey began by asking Gallieni's approval to establish a protectorate among the 30,000 Baras-Imamonos in the Cercle de Tuléar to the southwest of Fianarantsoa, the capital of the southern command. Although Madagascar was officially a colony under direct French rule, Lyautey justified this request for an "interior protectorate" in the familiar language of the Tonkin school. "To reduce the costs of our administration by using the native population as much as possible, preserving the established groups, and leaving the traditional leaders in charge," he recited,

> is one of the most desirable goals to seek in colonial policy. . . . Each time we find ethnic groups already organized and local institutions

in place, our first concern ought to be to safeguard and make use of them. To be sure, we economize on personnel, but more than that, we save time. Whenever, as a result of ignorance, blundering, or prejudice, we have destroyed these traditional structures and find ourselves with nothing to work with [en face d'une poussière sociale], it will take us years, if not centuries, to reestablish a solid base for our government.[91]

Gallieni approved the Baras protectorate (and others in the south), based on Lyautey's assessment of the viability of their institutions and, more important than anything else, the willingness of their leaders to collaborate with France.

Lyautey's military task was to clear the forests east of Fianarantsoa of "rebel" groups who regularly attacked French convoys, raided native villages, and threatened French coastal trading stations. Unlike in Tonkin where the brigands had supposedly come from China and the objective had been to chase them away and prevent their return, in Madagascar the "unvanquished" were island natives. French policy had to aim at their transformation rather than their eradication. Thus, even as Lyautey's field commanders swept through the forests destroying rebel outposts, Lyautey warned against doing anything that might make reconciliation impossible. "That is the heart of the question and it should be pointed out that it has too often been neglected." Lyautey insisted that contact with the enemy remain open, that the olive branch remain ever extended, and that, despite the intensity and anger of combat, the enemy never be reduced to desperation. What is more, in no case should there be reprisals on a defeated population. This was the "most delicate" and surely the most difficult aspect of colonial warfare because it ruled out using the full force of one's military might and forbade meting out brutal retribution.[92]

Lyautey later insisted that military success had come because the unity and coordination of the southern command had produced "a superior efficiency" that had enabled him to track and trap rebel groups in a net of "chain mail." Once the area had been effectively pacified, he had disarmed the population, believing this to be "the only absolutely complete and effective sanction of pacification" in a country where the French were outnumbered and where the possession of arms would always be a "permanent temptation" to revolt.[93]

Farther south in the area west of Fort Dauphin where an extensive cactus forest provided an "almost impenetrable shelter" for native tribesmen, Lyautey planned for a slower, yet equally irresistible occupation, based on the construction of a series of permanent military posts.[94] At Behara he remarked that the solidity of a legionnaires' fort was one of the "best elements" of pacification policy. "The natives living nearby see it and read into it our force, our resolve, and our plans for the future, and submit."[95] What is more, these posts provided a point for economic contact with the native population. Once French merchants began to trade cloth for Malagasy cattle, the Malagasy would move from a "prehistoric" economic situation, where the collection of cattle was an end in itself, into the colonial marketplace. "The only trading post that I consider really colonial," Lyautey told his sister, "is one which under the protection of our rifles and cannon offers our products and attracts local goods. Militarily this is what we call: 'the tactic of economic penetration.' And it is worth far more for national prosperity than all the other tactics that are taught at the École de Guerre."[96] This was a new definition of the role of the military post in the pacification process. The "surest test of pacification," Lyautey insisted, was the renewal of the natives' confidence, the resumption of economic exchanges, and the creation of a "harmonious relationship" between French soldiers and the indigenous population—in short, "the transformation of our posts from the *poles of repulsion* that they are today into *centers of attraction*."[97] Pacification had an economic objective and at the same time, according to Lyautey, peace could be hurried along by economic incentives.

Lyautey justified his decision for the total military "penetration" of the south as a strategic necessity, although at first he had been against it. Even when an area seemed to pose little threat, he had decided that, as a general rule, unpacified regions would always upset pacified ones. And any halt in the French advance for whatever reason would be interpreted by the native population as a sign of weakness. The only sure answer was a complete military take over. In this way the work of political organization and economic development could begin at full speed and any "second conquest" at some later date and perhaps in less favorable circumstances would be avoided.[98]

The southern command was dissolved in May 1902. Lyautey spent a month and a half at Tananarive putting his dossiers in order and preparing for his return to France. In his letters home and in his final report, published the following year, Lyautey dutifully attributed his success to the methods of his "colonial mentor."[99] He emphasized the victory of politics, economics, and military restraint over brute force in the south. And he underscored the value of the "protectorate idea" and the virtue of indirect rule to the accomplishment of France's colonial mission. Here alone was the perfect union of continuity and change, of past and future. Everything should continue as before—all native institutions and practices should be preserved; all the native rulers should be left in place, invested with their traditional authority and power—under the "mere supervision" of a French official.

> It is through this officer in permanent contact with the native leader that little by little the latter's horizons will expand and through him those of his people. And it is through him as an intermediary that bit by bit we will introduce our ideas of justice, humanity, and progress, that is to say, we will involve ourselves in all that is beneficial and legitimate and stay away from all that is annoying and unacceptable to people for whom our intervention disturbs all customs and all traditions. This set-up has two characteristics which should make it incontestable: it is the only one that conforms to the reality of the situation and it is the most economical.

Yet, as his disarming of the southern Malagasy tribesmen made clear, Lyautey was always ready to acknowledge that "[r]egardless of the results obtained through the economic and moral conquest of the native population, regardless of the degree of their submission and that of their leaders, we must never mislead ourselves into thinking that our domination will ever be acceptable to them."[100]

In October 1902 Colonel Lyautey was posted to the Fourteenth Hussards at Alençon. Apprehensive at being separated from the colonial work to which he had given himself so completely—those years of life "really lived," as he had told Gallieni—he contemplated early retirement.[101] The next twelve months in France, amidst the ongoing upset of the Dreyfus crisis, reinforced his sense of desperation. "In the present disarray," he told Chailley-Bert,

> in this internal dissolution it is more and more apparent to me that in the colonial life alone is concentrated all the vitality of our country. It is only there that one finds disinterested, healthy, and, in consequence fruitful efforts. I grasp for it like a shipwrecked person who does not want to drown. It is the only workshop of French energy that exists.[102]

CHAPTER 2

The Road to Morocco

■ ■ ■ ■

Within weeks of his words to Chailley-Bert, Lyautey was thrown a life preserver. Charles Jonnart, the governor-general of Algeria and a prominent member of the colonial lobby, narrowly escaped being killed by Moroccan tribesmen at Zenaga Pass during a tour of inspection near Figuig in May 1903. The incident, which some suspected had been staged to draw attention to the deteriorating situation along the Algerian-Moroccan border, forced Paris to take Algerian security seriously. Jonnart demanded and got Lyautey's appointment as commander of the Subdivision of Aïn Sefra, a tribute to the power of the colonial lobby and to the growing prestige of the Gallieni "school." Lyautey (now promoted to the rank of brigadier general) was granted privileged access to Jonnart and permitted to mount small operations and to respond to unexpected situations without waiting for the approval of higher-ups.[1] This proclaimed the true urgency of the military situation: In mid-August the French post at Taghit came under the vigorous assault of eight thousand Moroccan tribesmen, and in early September a supply convoy was attacked and pillaged at El Moungar, leaving thirty-eight soldiers dead and forty-seven wounded. "Gallieni and only Gallieni is needed here," Lyautey wrote his mentor, adding with a characteristic note of self-doubt, "I need your touch and I don't have it."[2]

Turn-of-the-century Morocco was a country struggling to survive a slow but persistent European penetration that had begun decades before. Soon after the proclamation of the French protectorate in Tunisia in 1881, France showed a keen interest in Morocco, if only for the strategic purpose of defending Algeria's western flank. English opposition to every French design, however, kept France from achieving any quick political or military advantage in northwest Africa and, in fact, for years Anglo-French competition preserved the semblance of Moroccan independence. Morocco's sultans, who claimed descent from the Prophet Mohammed (and at times even sneered at the less exalted lineage of the Ottoman sultans), ruled over a society dominated by tribalism in which, more often than not, powerful Arab or Berber chieftains successfully challenged the authority of the central government (the Makhzen). The integrating factors of religion and trade, politics and force—as well as the talents of the sultan, who headed the community of the faithful and was chief arbiter and mediator in the secular world—kept this "sharifian empire" (from *sharif,* descendent of the Prophet) in existence. To Europeans at the beginning of the twentieth century, however, Morocco appeared to be a ramshackle state—medieval in aspect, in organization, and in savage brutality—whose days were numbered.[3]

When Lyautey arrived in the Algerian-Moroccan borderlands at the end of 1903 the prestige of Sultan Abd el-Aziz (1894-1908) was at an all-time low. After France had seized the Touat oasis in the north-central Sahara three years before—revealing in a dramatic way Morocco's internal weakness, for this was the first loss of territory to any Christian power—Abd el-Aziz requested English support for a program of domestic reforms. This desperate and belated attempt to use the West against the West did not succeed. Rejected by all those in Morocco who stood to lose power or privileges or who opposed European intervention of any sort, the reforms provoked widespread discontent and contributed to a revolt of the tribes around Taza under the leadership of a pretender to the throne, who claimed to be the sultan's older brother. At the same time there was a stiffening of tribal resistance to the French along the southeastern frontier—Lyautey's new command—at variance with the sultan's long-standing practice of negotiating border problems. In each case, Abd el-Aziz's subjects seemed to be serving notice that he had failed in his primary task of defending the patrimony of Islam and that they were taking matters into their own hands.[4]

Lyautey's appointment was a victory for those who desired pacification along the Algerian-Moroccan border of the active and aggressive sort that had marked Tonkin and Madagascar. This was what animated Eugène Étienne, the deputy from Oran, a passionate advocate of the commercial interests of western Algeria, and the leading spokesman for the colonial lobby in the Chamber of Deputies. For years Gallieni's chief political backer in Paris, Étienne, championed a "forward policy" in the South Oranais, pushing French troops into disputed borderland oases and nibbling away at Moroccan territorial integrity tribe by tribe, regardless of the consequences to Franco-Moroccan relations or to France's connections with the other European powers. Étienne's immediate concern was for Algerian security. His ultimate goal was to make Morocco French.[5]

This frontier saber rattling went counter to the notions of Foreign Minister Théophile Delcassé, who, while taking a backseat to no one on imperial issues, disputed Étienne's methods. Delcassé sought to secure Morocco for France by working through the sultan and his government in what was called the "Makhzen policy" and by negotiating with the European states one by one, beginning with Italy and Spain. This course was too slow for Étienne and his small band of Morocco enthusiasts who had little regard for the sultan's sovereignty and who had for years urged Delcassé to deal directly with England and Germany. Delcassé's reluctance to do this, grounded in his stubbornness to admit the permanence of the English occupation of Egypt and his fear of German ambitions in the Mediterranean, pushed Étienne to move on Morocco by other means. Étienne's position as the leader of the *groupe colonial* and of a republican faction critical to the government's majority in parliament permitted him considerable freedom of maneuver. As a result, over Delcassé's opposition Jonnart could have his way, which meant he could have Lyautey.[6]

Lyautey immediately occupied the Béchar oasis southwest of Aïn Sefra that had served as a staging area for the Moroccan tribesmen who had come from the direction of the Tafilalet oasis. He baptized the post Colomb (later known as Colomb-Béchar) to disguise its precise whereabouts from those in Paris who were squeamish about violations of Moroccan territory.[7] His strategic purpose was to move the French line of defense farther west to ensure the safety of his lines of communication and supply as well as to situate himself among tribes that he thought could act as a "protective mattress" between Tafilalet and Algeria. As in Tonkin, he planned to use force adapted to the surroundings, in this case lightly armed, mobile Saharan companies on camels or horses, backed up by the mounted *tirailleurs* and spahis of the Algerian army and units of the Foreign Legion. At the same time he promised peace, security, and economic benefits to the tribes in return for their cooperation.[8]

Although Lyautey had a significant military advantage over his adversaries in weapons and organization and used it, he emphasized the nonmilitary side of his method in his letters and reports. He said that he favored a step-by-step process of political "disassociation" on those tribes that resisted the *pax Gallia,* exploiting their divisions and rivalries to secure his desired ends. And with care and method he suggested that Béchar would soon become a "pole of attraction," the center for political and economic action on Tafilalet itself. In all of this Lyautey pledged cooperation with the sultan's government and its representatives, as Delcassé's 1901-1902 Franco-Moroccan accords on the borderlands specified. But he was convinced that the sultan had not kept—in fact could not keep—the peace in this region, so he planned "to use" the Makhzen wherever possible and to go it alone everywhere else.[9]

To give himself the maneuvering room he wanted, Lyautey asked Paris for "carte blanche" to use force against Bou Amama, the old Algerian rebel who had taken refuge in Morocco after the collapse of the revolt of the early 1880s. Although two decades earlier Lyautey had expressed some sympathy for the motives behind that rebellion, he now depicted the retired "warrior-saint emeritus" as the "eternal enemy" behind every French setback in the borderlands.[10] Settling the Bou Amama problem, he insisted, would put an end to "*almost* all the difficulties of our South Oranais frontier." To his friends in the colonial lobby, however, he revealed that Fez, the seat of the sultan's government, was the real direction of his thinking. He mused wistfully on the not-too-distant time when all Morocco might fall under the command of "our future Lord Croner [*sic*]," disclosing his ambition to be the one to make Morocco the Egypt of France.[11]

Paris did not rise to the Bou Amama bait. French financial influence had reasserted itself at Fez in early 1904, which would lead to an important public loan to the Moroccan treasury in midyear. This was a substantial success for Delcassé's "Makhzen policy." Moreover, finally convinced of the virtue of an Egypt-for-Morocco "barter," the foreign minister concluded an agreement with England, the April 1904 Anglo-French Entente Cordiale, which put to rest this debilitating imperial competition.[12] In short, as long as bankers and diplomats were bringing Morocco closer to France, Lyautey and his soldiers were unnecessary.

Once again Lyautey acted on his own. In June 1904 he ordered the occupation of the Ras-el-Aïn oasis. On the Charef River, Ras-el-Aïn was directly south of Oujda and squarely within Moroccan territory. Again, he called the French camp by another name: Berguent. Lyautey insisted that the column under the command of Major Paul Henrÿs, his military chief of staff, was only there to shield the frontier tribes from the trouble that Bou Amama intended and to keep him under observation. "In no way are we conquering Morocco," he wrote his sister, "and I am handling this matter with the prudence of a snake." But he admitted that he had made an advance of one hundred kilometers and that Berguent was "a perfect base of operations for the day when we do decide to do something." In the meantime it would be an ideal setting for Franco-Moroccan military cooperation (since a small Makhzen detachment from Oujda had joined the 800-man French force) and, as Berguent developed into a market center, an important site for political and economic pacification. "In short, I will make Ras-el-Aïn into another Béchar under the banner of this joint police force and of cooperation with the Makhzen." Within six months he promised tranquility all along the frontier.[13]

The advance to Ras-el-Aïn stunned Paris. Lyautey blamed the journalists and some of his too-zealous friends for turning what had been a "discrete penetration" of Morocco into a public "affair."[14] The truth was that he had engaged the government in a matter of some seriousness without having the authority to do so. The Quai d'Orsay's man at Tangier, Georges Saint-René Taillandier, standard-bearer for Delcassé's "Makhzen policy," demanded that Lyautey be ordered to quit Moroccan soil. This sudden military move gave the lie to France's commitment to peaceful change in Morocco, complicating Saint-René's relations with the sultan as well as with the representatives of the other European powers. Delcassé, too, at the moment engaged in sensitive negotiations with Spain on the division of Moroccan territory, resented the untimely appearance of a French column at Ras-el-Aïn. Although Lyautey undoubtedly had the approval of Jonnart and the military authorities in Algeria for what he did, both the civilians and soldiers in Paris were understandably furious at this flagrant disregard of metropolitan control.[15]

At the end of July the Council of Ministers ordered Lyautey to pull up stakes and withdraw "from Moroccan territory."[16] Amazed at the rebuke, he claimed that this would go down in the history books as a "second Fashoda," only now France's adversary was not England, but a Morocco that was more fiction than reality. He telegraphed the Ministry of War that any sudden evacuation of Berguent would also be interpreted by the native population as flight before Bou Amama and cause a "real disaster" throughout the borderlands. It would deal a "mortal blow" to French influence and break all the commitments that he had made to the loyal tribes concerning their security and well-being. He said he would not carry out such an order. Should it be maintained, he "respectfully" asked to be relieved of his command, but in such a way as to make it clear to the native population that it was he who had overstepped the bounds of his authority and not the government of France that had broken its word.[17]

Despite the melodramatic phrases, Lyautey counted on his friends in high places to intercede for him. In his letters he maintained that he was correct to have done what he did at Berguent. What is more, he told Étienne that had he not been hobbled by the timorousness of the diplomats, he would have taken possession of all the territory up to the Moulouya River "in the name of the sultan." Occupied and organized; that is, conquered and ruled indirectly by Frenchmen, it would cease to be the haven of Bou Amama or any other agitator.[18] This sterner program aside, Lyautey repeated that evacuating Berguent would be a step backward for regional peace and security, positively an encouragement to insurrection, and, not the least of all, a blow to the colonial doctrine that he represented. Everything that had been accomplished up to now with little bloodshed was in jeopardy, only to have to be won back later at swordpoint.[19]

With Étienne, Jonnart, and most of the Algerian lobby in Lyautey's camp, Premier Émile Combes overruled the Ministry of Foreign Affairs. To save face and cabinet solidarity he maintained the evacuation order, but decided to let Jonnart determine both the time and the circumstances under which the evacuation would take place. Jonnart was absolutely opposed to a withdrawal. At the height of the crisis he had sent an amazing telegram to Paris: "Lyautey acted on my orders. I approve of what he did. If the evacuation order is maintained, I will go myself to this post to stand by him." Lyautey was confident that it would never happen.[20] Still, while rejoicing at the victory, Lyautey was stopped in his tracks, forced to recognize Berguent as a dead end rather than another step forward. And in comic-opera fashion he had to turn over the Ras-el-Aïn casbah to the sultan's troops, while moving his own post just 500 meters eastward across an agreed-upon imaginary dividing line between Morocco and Algeria.[21]

More than anything else, Morocco boosted Lyautey to national attention. The "Berguent incident" moved the debate on policy from the Council of Ministers to the Chamber of Deputies. Aggressively defended by Étienne and Gaston Thomson, who represented the settler interests of Bône, Lyautey now had the public support of forceful patrons who were willing to run the considerable military and diplomatic risks in Morocco and Europe of his action.[22] At the same time it exposed the division in the colonial camp, for Delcassé openly worried about the growing power of "Étienne's clique" on foreign policy and the unfortunate consequences at home and abroad of any "military conquest" of Morocco.[23]

As a matter of principle, Lyautey found it offensive to be pegged the "frightful soldier," the advocate of brute force in Morocco, since the full scope of his colonial method was lost in the shuffle. And he was astonished to find himself at odds with those who preferred nonmilitary means of action, since he was the most "unmilitary" of all the soldiers he knew.[24] He complained that no one in Paris had read him or followed his career. If they had, he insisted, the discussion on policy would have been cast in different terms. It was never a question of either sending an army into Morocco or not, but of doing something quite unconventional based on the "new and complete doctrine" he had formulated in "The Colonial Role of the Army" and *Dans le sud de Madagascar*. Here there was no dilemma over war or peace, force or negotiations, military conquest or economic penetration. The answer was to employ both according to the moment and the circumstances. He never intended to be a "hammer" pounding away at Morocco, he told his friend, the writer and social critic Eugène-Melchior de Vogüé, but "the drill which penetrates slowly but irresistibly."[25]

Nevertheless, Lyautey's aggressive moves in the borderlands—as much as the European diplomatic accords on Morocco and the elaborate French plans-in-the-making for Moroccan military, economic, and financial reform—stiffened the sultan's resolve to oppose France. As if to make the point, Abd el-Aziz dismissed the members of the French military mission in December 1904. In fact, the emergence of a real Makhzen resistance soon brought Germany to the Moroccan side. Lyautey might dismiss Quai d'Orsay concerns over German rumblings as the nightmare stuff of the permanently sleepless Rhine-watchers, but he was wrong. Pushed by the German foreign ministry, which now saw an occasion to block French designs in North Africa, the kaiser interrupted his annual Mediterranean cruise in order to pay a visit to Tangier at the end of March 1905. At the German legation he voiced his concern for the sultan's sovereignty, Morocco's integrity, and Germany's commercial interests. This public challenge to France—immortalized as the "coup de Tanger"—not only encouraged the sultan to reject the French reform proposals, but the war scare it created in France ultimately brought about Delcassé's resignation. At the moment of truth no one in the French cabinet, except perhaps Delcassé himself, was willing to face a duel with Germany over Morocco.[26] By pressing so hard in the borderlands Lyautey had played a part in the making of the crisis and thus in the unmaking of Delcassé.

Acknowledging "the setback to [French] diplomacy on the entire Moroccan question" if not his own role in it, Lyautey now argued that allowing him to pursue military action up to the Moulouya River could alone reestablish France's diminished standing in the eyes of the native population.[27] And he asserted to Jonnart that the "defensive protection" of the railroad under construction from Beni Ounif to Colomb-Béchar still required the use of light, mobile patrols for both political and military action among the tribes.[28] Indeed, despite the European crisis—in fact, because of it—Lyautey contended somewhat implausibly that his method was still the only correct one for the borderlands. If allowed to do so, he would intervene with force all along the frontier *"as an arbiter"* among the tribes to support and protect the "elements of order and peace"—that is, those groups willing to side with the French—

regardless of whether they were for or against the sultan and his Makhzen. This was "a policy exclusively of interests and of practical and tangible results, no longer a policy of principles and sentiments."[29] As far as Lyautey was concerned, with Delcassé gone so was working with the Makhzen.

As the Franco-German crisis continued, compelling France to agree to an international conference at Algeciras on the question of Moroccan reforms, Lyautey complained of the Makhzen's support for resistance in the borderlands. He urged the use of force—the "decisive argument"—to curb it, for only when France showed itself to be "the most powerful and the most resolute" could it prevail against the talk of holy war.[30] By implicating the sultan and his government in activities that imperiled Algerian security, without a nod to the sultan's sovereign right or religious duty to defend the edges of his empire, Lyautey hoped to put the final nail in the coffin of the "Makhzen policy."

> This idea of building a strong state adjacent to your own, *unless you hold all the strings,* of creating unity where there was only division, of establishing an entity conscious of itself and its strength where before there had been only something nebulous, is in sum nothing more than the policy for which Napoleon III was so often and so justly reproached—the nationalities policy.

Just as Napoleon III had "constructed" Italy and Germany on France's flanks, Lyautey argued, so the Quai d'Orsay had tried to invent Morocco on Algeria's frontier. This policy, which in Lyautey's biased rendering reduced the sultan's empire to the realm of fancy, had worked to France's disadvantage, Lyautey maintained, and he wanted to bury it once and for all.[31]

The French diplomatic victory at Algeciras (January-April 1906), confirming France's primacy in Morocco and damaging German prestige, broke the sultan's resistance and ended any fear of a Makhzen-inspired insurrection. With great reluctance Abd el-Aziz signed the final act of the conference in June 1906, giving France wide authority to intervene in Morocco's political and economic affairs, especially in the port cities where police units under French and Spanish control ensured the safety of European interests. The newly established Banque d'État du Maroc, dominated by the Paris banks, effectively placed the financial destiny of the country in French hands.[32] Algeciras resurrected the "Makhzen policy" and in consequence Lyautey was once again held on a tight leash. However hard he tugged and in whatever direction—either to respond to a direct provocation or to display French force among the tribes—he was pulled back.[33] How unfortunate it was, Lyautey grumbled privately to his sister, to have such a fine military tool

at the ready and yet not be permitted to extend its use to the "natural frontier" of the Moulouya or, better, all the way to Fez. And he admitted to de
Vogüé that his dream of "penetrating Morocco gradually, sure of my instrument and my method" had now vanished.[34]

How successful the method had been was put to the test in midyear
1906. The merchants of Tafilalet, the largest oasis center in the Moroccan
southeast, suddenly advocated a trading embargo against the French. And
the Doui Menia and Oulad Djerir, nomadic tribes who had made peace little
by little with the French and were currently engaged in highly profitable commerce at Lyautey's marketplaces in Colomb-Béchar and Beni Ounif, began
withdrawing from French contact and moving their tents closer to Tafilalet.
The successful French commercial penetration of Tafilalet was part of the reason for this change in attitude, for here Lyautey's economic strategy had
repelled as well as attracted. Religious and national sentiments were also of
real importance. As a consequence of Algeciras and the recognition of the
sultan's powerlessness to halt the seemingly relentless French advance,
Tafilalet again became a turbulent center of political and military resistance
as at the time of the attack on Taghit. Now Tafilalet's leaders spearheaded a
drive for a mass movement to oust the French from Colomb-Béchar and ultimately to replace Abd el-Aziz with a sultan who would defend the faith mil-
itantly. It was this agitation that compelled the Doui Menia and Oulad Djerir
to choose between Tafilalet and the French. And after having made their
choice, they scurried toward Tafilalet.[35]

Caught by surprise, Lyautey imagined that he would soon be confronted
by thousands of holy warriors, bringing "a real tempest" with them.[36] He
requested permission for a "purely defensive action," a series of "simple
threats": the occupation of the Guir River, the pursuit of marauders on the
right bank, and several unspecified "energetic acts."[37] This was not to be a
military expedition against Tafilalet, he assured Jonnart, but the continuation
of "the slow infiltration, the progressive penetration, the covert break-up" of
hostile forces that he had practiced all along.[38]

The occupation of the upper Guir, however, meant an advance to the
Bou Denib oasis, the "strategic objective" between Colomb-Béchar and
Tafilalet, and would require a significant military effort. Even Lyautey recognized that such a move might well provoke a German response and even
become the pretext for a European conflict.[39] Still, Tafilalet crowded everything else out of his mind. It was "absolutely incandescent" and rather than
wait for the expected explosion, he wanted to run the risk of taking Bou
Denib in order to capture his adversaries' base of supply and split their
forces in two.[40] He emphasized to Jonnart that the quick occupation of Bou

Denib might stop the agitation "point-blank," ending the danger for some time to come.[41]

Paris ruled out any preventive action against Bou Denib, convinced that all this was trumped up by Lyautey just to put more troops on the march and resolved as well to avoid any new international incident over Morocco. And in the end, in spite of Lyautey's dire predictions, nothing happened. Everything seemed to indicate that Lyautey had lied about the danger or at the very least overreacted. In fact, the march on Colomb-Béchar had come close to taking place. It failed, however, because of the lack of strong political and military leadership in the pan-tribal coalition.[42] Nevertheless, at Tafilalet, where the Lyautey method had come up against the stiff resistance of Moroccans who were moved by careful considerations about their own political and economic future, it had been of no use at all.

As the situation at Tafilalet showed, relations between Frenchmen and Moroccans worsened after Algeciras. Individual Frenchmen in Tangier, Fez, and Marrakesh became the targets of mob violence, and these incidents, more than Lyautey's call for military action in the borderlands, convinced Paris to use force. After the murder of a French medical missionary at Marrakesh in March 1907, Prime Minister Georges Clemenceau ordered the occupation of Oujda, the most important Moroccan city in the east and just kilometers from the Algerian border. Oujda would be held as ransom until the sultan's government had made good on a tough list of demands. This was a severe blow to Moroccan sovereignty, to the standing of the sultan among his people, and perhaps the final blow to the "Makhzen policy" Delcassé-style.

All this should have delighted Lyautey. But, although he was technically in charge of the military operation—he had been promoted to interim commander of the Oran division in December 1906—he still complained that nothing was being done in the proper manner. He was under strict instructions not to meddle in the political or economic affairs of Oujda or the region, and even forbidden to budge outside the city except to protect his lines of supply and communications. Lyautey hinted that he, not the inhabitants of Oujda, was the real hostage.[43]

Lyautey contended that the dramatic military advance in the east had created the impression among Moroccans that the French were at Oujda to stay and would soon begin patrolling the surrounding countryside. Local caïds had come spontaneously to the city to talk and submit. But French immobility was transforming the situation to the advantage of France's opponents, in particular the neighboring tribes of the Beni Snassen, who respected only force. By sending mixed signals to the native population, the

French occupation actually compromised French security.[44] "Our situation at Oujda is ineffective and becoming ridiculous," he lamented to de Vogüé. "We are paralyzed right and left from doing tasks that are so simple, so logical. We are stopped dead in our tracks by mirages."[45] In a summary to higher-ups he called Oujda "the most beautiful display of powerlessness that we have had on our frontier. It would have been better not to go there at all than to go there under these circumstances."[46] In sum, Oujda had become a messy "chamber pot." Irritated at Lyautey's insolent barbs, alarmist talk, and endless tirades, Paris simply turned a deaf ear.[47]

At the end of July anti-French sentiment in Casablanca resulted in the deaths of eight Europeans employed on a port construction project. The ensuing wave of killing and looting in the city triggered an abrupt landing of French sailors from the gunboat *Galilée,* which made matters only worse. The *Galilée*'s subsequent shelling of the native city, which caused hundreds of deaths, provoked new rioting that raised fears for the safety of the entire European community. Following a logic that had created many another colonial beachhead, Clemenceau, whose instincts to that time had been decidedly anticolonial and antimilitary, dispatched a two thousand-man expeditionary force to Casablanca to restore order.[48]

All the tribes of the Chaouïa—the territory around Casablanca—now rose to expel the invader, transforming the French task from a quick offshore rescue mission to a long-term defense of the city. Like Lyautey at Oujda, however, General Antoine Drude, who led the expeditionary force, was prohibited from venturing into the surrounding countryside to pursue his attackers. This made it impossible for him to quell the uprising quickly, for his adversaries, who by the end of August numbered more than ten thousand, believed that he had neither the will nor the strength to chase them away.[49] To the military problem was added a political one. With French soldiers now at Oujda and Casablanca, Abd el-Aziz's authority as commander of the faithful and defender of Islam collapsed. At Marrakesh a more powerful champion stepped forth. Moulay Abd el-Hafid, the sultan's real brother, was proclaimed sultan in mid-August and he vowed to push the French back into the sea. What made his call to arms more troubling than that of the other pretender, north of Taza, was its startling nationwide resonance. Astride a coalition of tribes from the Chaouïa to the western High Atlas, which linked the ruling Alaoui dynasty with the Berber "lords" of the Atlas for the first time in Morocco's history and encompassed almost all the cities of the south, Abd el-Hafid announced a struggle that would lead Morocco into civil war.[50]

Surrounded by the debris of the sharifian state, wrecked in ample measure by a French force under his own command, Lyautey affected a pose of

Olympian detachment. None of this would have happened—not the "hornet's nest" of the Chaouïa, nor the new sultan at Marrakesh—had his method to "finish off" Morocco been employed. Forgetting the spirited resistance at Tafilalet, he still talked only of the need for a "police action" under the cover of the sultan that in a tribe-by-tribe fashion would move slowly but surely from east to west toward Fez. Despite the mounting evidence that this could not work without encountering crushing opposition, he offered it again as "the rational, simple, and elegant solution" to the Moroccan problem.[51]

Paris ignored the Lyautey solution as well as the equally adventurous suggestion that went with it, made in concert with the French minister at Tangier, that France stick with Abd el-Aziz come what may.[52] Insisting that any resolute French government could still draw considerable benefits from the treaties already signed with the sultan and perhaps even "new advantages," such as the immediate establishment of a French protectorate, Lyautey advocated continued reliance on Abd el-Aziz as the chief instrument of French policy. Advised, directed, and supported with firmness and skill, Abd el-Aziz might yet become "the best agent" to secure at long last "the privileged situation in Morocco which we cannot renounce."[53] This was precisely the course of action that he had opposed since 1903. Now, of course, the circumstances had changed. In the sultan's darkest hour as his influence dwindled from moment to moment with his subjects, Lyautey incongruously judged him a fit candidate to advance French aims.

Choosing to remain neutral in the civil war between the two sultans, Paris also refused Lyautey's "repeated and urgent requests" to counter the uneasiness among the Beni Snassen by occupying Cherraa and Aghbal, strategic dots on the map that would deny these tribesmen access to the plains north of Oujda.[54] To make certain that Lyautey got the message, Minister of War General Georges Picquart, who believed that Lyautey had cried wolf once too often, tightened the reins. He separated the Oujda column from Lyautey's command, placing it under the direct authority of the Ministry of War, as was the case with Drude's expeditionary force in Casablanca. Although there was an undeniable symmetry to this approach, Lyautey was sure that Picquart was out "to muzzle" him, describing the new command situation as "monstrous and revolting." To make the humiliation complete, in the end the Oujda column was given the green light to coerce the Beni Snassen. For months, Lyautey said, he had recommended "the most harmless preventive measures" against the Beni Snassen, guaranteed to avoid any shots being fired. Now, he complained, Paris authorized an action that would ensure a fight. Did Picquart prefer to create "incidents" under the leadership of others, rather than to avoid them under him? Things had stepped "beyond the limits of the paradoxical."[55]

A series of sudden Beni Snassen attacks around Oujda and the nearby coastal towns in Algeria frightened Paris into restoring Lyautey's freedom of action. Pressed by Jonnart, who feared the collapse of all that had been accomplished in the borderlands, the government ordered Lyautey to occupy the mountainous refuge of the Beni Snassen. Lyautey relished the turnabout. From early December to the second week of January 1908 he subdued the tribes by surrounding the Beni Snassen massif, cutting the tribesmen off from their sources of food and supplies, then advancing into the mountains from both the north and the south. As he summed it up to de Margerie, the campaign was "a mathematician's joy," a masterpiece of method, even though a tight economic blockade and the overwhelming use of force had been responsible for the quick victory.[56] "This time I have been left royally in peace," he told de Vogüé, "and from the very beginning I have not been bothered by anyone or anything."[57] Best of all, Lyautey finally reached the right bank of the lower Moulouya River.[58]

Lyautey used this success to urge his friends in Paris to intervene again on his behalf. "I know I have the right formula for what remains to be done here," he lobbied Chailley, but the government would "rather risk the worse than use me of its own accord."[59] He restated the case for his method to de Mun, who had asked him to answer honestly if France could really expect to avoid a burdensome conquest of Morocco and set up a protectorate "à la tunisienne" through local operations and small nibbles at Moroccan territory. Lyautey responded that this was precisely what he had done in the South Oranais. In four years he had penetrated 200 kilometers in the south "without noise, without incident, without loss of life" through "a continuous and intense exercise of politics and force," exploiting tribal divisions, pitting one group against another, capitalizing on material interests, and intervening as an arbiter in disputes, but acting only when he was strong—in fact "the strongest"—on the playing field. From Colomb-Béchar to Tafilalet, from Aïn Sefra to the middle Moulouya he said that he had respected the letter of the treaties and ever buttressed "the façade of sharifian authority." If he had been free to do exactly as he pleased, he told de Mun that "today we would be the masters at Taza, bearing down on Fez, the arbiters of the situation in indirect and discreet ways, our troops barely visible, so that neither Spain, nor Germany, nor Europe would have had anything to say."[60]

Politics was the heart of his method, Lyautey lectured de Mun, and there was no country or race of people more susceptible to political action than Morocco or the Arabs.

> Do you think that I could have resolved the Beni Snassen matter—
> for which I am given credit—as I did by military means alone?
> Certainly not, or at least not unless I had thirty thousand men
> instead of six thousand. I only succeeded because I had worked the
> terrain for a year. By acting simultaneously on Bou Amama, the
> pretender [at Taza], and the native groups already linked to us by
> material interests, I was able to divide our adversaries and exploit
> old rivalries in order to neutralize the western part of the confed-
> eration. This kept the number of our opponents to a minimum and
> reduced our costs.

With time, the means, and above all carte blanche, Lyautey assured de Mun that his method could carry France all the way to Fez.[61]

This was a creative retelling of history. From the moment he set foot in the borderlands Lyautey had willfully broken every rule and wiggled between the lines of every treaty, producing a string of "incidents" for the Quai d'Orsay and the Ministry of War to explain away to the sultan, to the Chamber of Deputies, and to the European powers. He had helped to under-mine France's "Makhzen policy," and by stimulating Moroccan resistance on the southeastern fringes of the empire he had encouraged German involve-ment in Morocco. His play of politics and economic interests among the tribes did have some notable short-term successes, such as with the Doui Menia and Oulad Djerir between 1904 and 1906.[62] It also generated oppo-sition of one sort or another by interfering with traditional relationships, frus-trating local or regional political ambitions, upsetting existing patterns of trade, and, perhaps more than anything else, violating the patrimony of Islam. The disruptive nature of the Lyautey method as well as the far-reaching con-sequences of its goals called forth Moroccan resistance. And resistance required the use of force.

Unfortunately, the spare, tight, efficient "organization" that had marched from the pages of Lyautey's writings to Colomb-Béchar and Berguent— including the lightly armed, mobile units of native troops, drawn from the local population—had only limited peacekeeping success against the hit-and-run tactics of small bands of desert guerrillas. And when confronted by any tribal population willing to make a stand or faced with a pan-tribal coalition fused together by a commitment to holy war, Lyautey had to rely on large numbers of regular troops, supplied with the modern weapons of war.[63] In Morocco's borderlands the reality of colonial warfare was quite different from the version of it that Lyautey supplied to his correspondents at home.

The resistance to Lyautey in the southeast gained new momentum in spring 1908 when tribes of the eastern High Atlas, spurred by the calls to holy war of Abd el-Hafid and a local spiritual leader, organized an expedition of 3,000 to 4,000 thousand warriors determined to oust the French from Colomb-Béchar. Surprising the French at Menabha, some distance from Colomb-Béchar, they dealt the worst blow to a French column—nineteen dead—of any single borderlands fight in the past five years. A second French column, rushed from Colomb-Béchar, pursued the tribesmen to the Bou Denib oasis where under the devastating fire of French artillery the pan-tribal coalition disintegrated.[64]

The French remained at Bou Denib. The occupation of this oasis, only sixty kilometers from Tafilalet and precisely where seventeen months earlier Lyautey had been told he could not go, provoked an even broader pan-tribal coalition, enrolling tribesmen from throughout the region as well as from the more distant middle and western High Atlas. In September 1908, 20,000 warriors marched against the French at Bou Denib, but to no avail. French artillery—as well as reinforcements from Colomb-Béchar—shattered the coalition's army in two decisive battles, ending all further resistance in the southeast. This was a victory, but not for Lyautey's method.[65]

Although Lyautey continued to urge Paris to unleash him toward Fez, French attention was riveted on Casablanca and the Chaouïa. In August 1908 Abd el-Aziz abdicated, clearing the way for the accession of his brother to the sharifian throne. This did not mean, however, that the holy war against the French had triumphed. As in the east, the French expeditionary corps at Casablanca, now transformed into a virtual army of occupation, had exhausted the local resistance. Far from being master in his own house, the new sultan had to deal with tenants whom he could not evict. The arrangements that Abd el-Hafid finally worked out with the French in March 1910, which tightened France's stranglehold on Morocco, took the fire from the sultan's early pronouncements as the "sultan of the jihad." Compromised in the eyes of his people by the inexorable French advance just as his brother had been, Abd el-Hafid watched glumly as his countrymen began to reject his leadership.[66]

Frustrated by the Quai d'Orsay's tortuous negotiations with Abd el-Hafid—whom Lyautey called "a fiction and a phantom"—and the missed opportunities for declaring a protectorate over Morocco, Lyautey resigned himself to returning to a command in France.[67] His last hurrah came in June 1910 when the government finally allowed him complete freedom of movement along the Moulouya and where, after minor skirmishes with the Middle Atlas tribes, he established a firm French presence. With great satisfaction he announced to Jonnart that the 1845 Franco-Moroccan treaty defining the boundaries of Algeria and Morocco was "virtually abolished" and that France would "forever" hold the Moulouya.[68] By the end of the year when Lyautey left the borderlands for Brittany as commander of the Tenth Army Corps at Rennes, almost all of Morocco east of the Moulouya was under French control.

In spring 1911 the tribes around Fez and Meknès rose against Abd el-Hafid. This played into the hands of the Morocco activists in the colonial lobby in Paris as well as French hard-liners in Tangier and Fez, who, like Lyautey, were tired of the slow-paced "charade" with the sultan and yearned for a dramatic incident to help slip Morocco into the French pocket. Under the cover of aiding the besieged sultan and saving European lives, a French "relief force" from Casablanca of nearly 7,500 men marched from the coast to Fez in mid-May. Intended to confront Morocco and all Europe (including France itself, where at this moment public opinion was decidedly cool to Moroccan adventures) with a fait accompli, the "rescue mission" produced an international crisis—a German gunboat anchored off Agadir in July as a sign of Germany's determination to stand up for its own claims in Morocco— that moved Europe to the brink of war.[69] When tensions eased as a result of the Franco-German agreement of 4 November 1911—which made a French protectorate over Morocco only a matter of paperwork—Lyautey wrote the obituary for his own lifework. "The Gallieni-Lyautey school is dead," he announced to Chailley-Bert, for General Charles Moinier's trek to Fez had accomplished in weeks what Lyautey had tried for years to do.[70]

The death notice was dramatic but somewhat premature. Although French troops were at Fez, rural unrest persisted in northern Morocco owing to the inconsistency of French "native affairs" policies among the tribes as well as to the certainty that France would now dominate the sultan. For these matters Lyautey still had life and breath—as well as pen and ink. He worried that Morocco, like Algeria, would soon become home to a cumbersome civil administration and a large army bureaucracy. This would divide the responsibility for decision making in an unfortunate and dangerous way, particularly in a "dense and war-like country" where unity of action alone made sense.[71] What he meant was made clear by the French consul at Fez, the manager of relations with the sultan and the Makhzen, who complained that heavy-handed military rule among the tribes along the road between Casablanca and Fez was eroding the sultan's sovereignty, quite the opposite of what the Quai d'Orsay desired as it edged toward a protectorate. The soldiers, on the other hand, insisted that security interests overrode everything else and that working with the sultan's men usually meant capitulating to native leaders who were despotic and untrustworthy.[72] The Lyautey solution, of course, was to put the matter in the hands of a military administrator of the "colonial" sort, equally skilled in the arts of politics and war and ready to employ the system of indirect rule that a protectorate demanded.

The Treaty of Fez of 30 March 1912, "inspired" by the Franco-Tunisian conventions of 1881 and 1883, formally established the French protectorate over Morocco. Its announced purpose was "to establish in Morocco a proper government based on internal order and general security" that would permit "the introduction of reforms" and ensure "the economic development of the country." The "new regime" would initiate the administrative, judicial, educational, economic, financial, and military reforms that the French government deemed "useful" to Morocco, including the organization of a "reformed sharifian government." It would safeguard the sultan's "religious position" and "traditional prestige" (as well as the exercise of the Muslim religion and the functioning of religious institutions throughout the country) and support him "against any danger which might threaten his person or his throne or which might compromise the tranquility of his domain."[73]

For his part the sultan accepted the military occupation of whatever territory France judged necessary for the maintenance of order and "the security of commercial transactions," the proclamation in his name of whatever edicts France required for the establishment of the protectorate regime, and the complete surrender to France of all independence in foreign and financial matters. The sultan could sign no international agreement, contract no public or private loan, grant no commercial concession without the prior consent of the French government.

France would henceforth be represented in Morocco by a commissioner resident general who with all the powers of the republic at his disposal would execute the terms of the treaty. As the "sole intermediary" between the sultan and foreign representatives and with the authority to approve and promulgate all the sultan's decrees, he became the sultan's first minister and foreign minister rolled into one.

Morocco was "protected" in a novel way. According to agreements among the European powers, the sultan remained sovereign everywhere, France his lone protector. As a condition of England's approval of the protectorate set up, however, France immediately turned over the mountainous northeast of Morocco to Spain in the Franco-Spanish treaty of 27 November 1912. England would only accept a weak European power across from Gibraltar—certainly not France—and thus Spanish Morocco became England's Belgium in the western Mediterranean. The sultan's delegate (khalifa) at Tetouan, headquarters of the Spanish zone, represented sharifian authority in the north. In addition, the city of Tangier became a "special zone" under international administration, carved out of land that in terms of colonial geography and economics ought to have belonged to Spain.[74]

Like the Act of Algeciras, the Treaty of Fez embittered relations between Moroccans and Europeans, contributing to violence at Fez and later to the proclamation of a new holy war in Morocco's south. When French reforms were introduced into the sultan's army in mid-April, the native troops in Fez mutinied, killing their French officers and other Europeans. Then, joined by the civilian population of the city, they attacked European offices and businesses and sacked the Jewish quarter. Only with some difficulty were French troops able to restore order and keep the peace until Moinier, now back at Casablanca, returned to Fez with reinforcements. Unlike his first march, however, this time there was no question of a trumped-up threat. Moinier was faced with putting down an "urban uprising" after a "massacre" had actually taken place.[75]

These unsettling events worked to Lyautey's advantage. Following the lead of Prime Minister and Minister of Foreign Affairs Raymond Poincaré, who now believed it was "indispensable" to have a soldier with both civil and military authority as resident general, a majority in the French cabinet backed Lyautey. He was the candidate of Poincaré and Minister of War Alexandre Millerand, both committed to national expansion and France's world mission and convinced by what they knew of Lyautey themselves and by what they had heard from others. When Lyautey was later called from Rennes to Versailles to speak for himself, Poincaré remembered "a brilliant exposé, sometimes tumultuous and redundant, sometimes verbose and filled with digressions, but always ending up by shining a concentrated light on the essential points and offering a practical and ingenious solution to the most serious and complex problems."[76]

"The task to be undertaken [in Morocco]," wrote Poincaré in his formal proposal to the president of the republic, "is one of civilization and progress." But no productive or lasting measures could be ventured in regions that were not already pacified. To prepare for this "necessary pacification" and to extend it "in a methodical way," it was "indispensable" that the man entrusted with the government's confidence have concentrated in his hands—"under the sultan's sovereignty" to be sure—both civil and military powers. These were Lyautey's sentiments written by another's hand. The job was "difficult and complex," Poincaré continued. The resident general had to set up a protectorate in accord with France's international commitments, including the promise to respect economic equality among all the nations engaged in trade with the sharifian empire. He had to remain faithful to the protectorate concept that forbade "direct rule." Finally, through the "expedient disposition" of French troops, the "effective use" of military intelligence officers, and the "rational execution" of a political, economic, and strategic program, he had to induce Morocco's tribes to accept the protectorate and to maintain their commitment to it. This "important mission," Poincaré concluded, matched the "experience and patriotism" of General Lyautey. On 28 April 1912 President Armand Fallières named Lyautey France's first resident general of Morocco.[77]

This abrupt resuscitation of Lyautey's colonial career might seem a surprising reversal of fortune, given the mixed record of his aggressively interventionist method in the borderlands, a string of questionable political and military judgments, and a history of reckless disobedience of truly calamitous potential. Still, Lyautey had conquered eastern Morocco even if his method had not and, best of all, he had managed to avoid disaster. With the help of friends in Paris and Algiers Lyautey at last had the field of action he wanted and the authority he desired. He assumed that this would be his final chance to put his ideas on colonial conquest and rule into practice and he grabbed it. At age fifty-seven, still tottering between brash confidence and paralyzing self-doubt, Lyautey packed his bags for Fez.

CHAPTER 3

A Method for Morocco?

■ ■ ■ ■

A s Edmund Burke III and Daniel Rivet have shown, French conquest and rule did not come easily in Morocco. From the first Lyautey was confronted with a situation not unlike that which Gallieni had faced in Madagascar. Fez was in turmoil and the tribes of the surrounding region had risen to liberate the sultan, now considered the prisoner of the foreigner. Terrified at the rural uprising on his behalf and depressed at his new role as "sultan of the French," Abd el-Hafid spoke only of abdication.[1] In the south the Saharan pretender, Ahmed el-Hiba, responding to the events of the north, had put himself at the head of a popular revolution, which proclaimed the need to reform society, to purify Islam, and to oust the French. By mid-May his "holy war" had begun to shake the Sous from Agadir to Taroudant. Taken together, all this amounted to a "national insurrection" against France, hardly an auspicious moment for the Lyautey method of peaceful penetration and indirect rule.[2]

Lyautey acknowledged that Morocco would be a voyage into the difficult "unknown." En route to Casablanca he confided to his sister that moment by moment the situation seemed to become "more and more serious and unwieldy."[3] He landed in Casablanca on 13 May 1912, greeted with the ceremony befitting his new status as resident general. Eleven days later he entered Fez where he found himself in quite another world, an "empty void" of closed doors and people who turned away or cursed when he passed.[4] Even he was taken by surprise at the extent and intensity of anti-French sentiment. The day after his arrival Fez was besieged by tribal forces that quickly overran parts of the city. For twelve hours on 25-26 May the French engaged in tough house by house, garden by garden fighting before dispersing the attackers. Far from the line of fire, *L'Afrique française* admitted that this was certainly a "unique" welcome. In response Lyautey immediately requested reinforcements for what he now called this life on a "tightrope."[5]

Despite the fear of losing his balance, Lyautey began his official duties with an audience with the sultan, his first face-to-face meeting with Abd el-Hafid, and his first chance to describe aloud his hopes for the future. With words that surely terrified rather than comforted, Lyautey remarked that the "collaboration" with the Moroccan government that he had "inaugurated and practiced" for seven years in the Algerian-Moroccan borderlands would now be pursued on a larger scale and at a higher level. (In truth, only now that he was inside Morocco would Lyautey embrace the "Makhzen policy" that he had done so much to undermine.) France would remain at the sultan's side to help establish a regime of order, justice, and prosperity. The "serious and unfortunate" events they were both witnessing in Fez, Lyautey insisted, would "in no way" constitute an obstacle to the work about to be undertaken by the two governments. Respectful of the "traditional prerogatives" of sharifian authority, of the Muslim religion, and of the accomplishments of the sultan's subjects, Lyautey affirmed France's commitment to give the sultan "the most effective support" in the move toward a future of civilization and progress.[6]

The sultan's response was positive, but his deep, bitter feelings not hard to fathom. He acknowledged the "important and difficult" task that lay ahead, but he had no doubt of Lyautey's "ultimate success," given his "eminent qualifications," his expertise in things Moroccan, and his work in the borderlands. "You are not unknown to the Makhzen, Monsieur le Commissaire Résident Général," he announced in the manner of a dismal oracle. "We know your feelings with regard to this empire and the respect you have for the Muslim religion and the ways and customs of our subjects." The "confidence" that he said he had up until then placed in other advisers, he now placed in Lyautey. "You can, therefore, count on our friendship and the sincerity of our sentiments."[7] But apparently nothing more. Throughout the "second" siege of Fez, a crisis that Lyautey slowly downgraded from "most critical" to "very serious" to "serious," Abd el-Hafid was of no help at all. Henri Gaillard, the French consul at Fez, had to hold the sultan by the hand to keep him from escaping into the native city. Lyautey was left alone to do what he could to restore a semblance of sharifian government—a "Makhzen façade"—with whatever local leaders still had some authority and influence.[8]

When the overall defense of the city was finally assured, Colonel Henri Gouraud—a veteran of Sudan, Chad, Mauretania, Senegal, and, most recently, of the relief column to Fez—was sent on the offensive. He defeated the main force of the tribal coalition on 1 June, and the day after, as a measure of his success and of the seriousness of the situation he had handled, he was promoted to brigadier general. This was hardly a good omen for peaceful penetration.[9] What is more, Fez continued to remain unsettled. Lyautey attributed this in part to mistakes made by the French command before his arrival. In the aftermath of the mutiny the soldiers had failed to recognize that there existed a "peaceful, hard-working, commercial middle class" that had little to do with the disorder and that desperately wanted the return of quiet. Worse, they had ignored the city's aristocracy—the influential and educated urban elite; the doctors of law and the religious authorities; and the *sharifs,* those "highest" of Fez's aristocrats "without whom nothing effective can be done here." From these mistakes, Lyautey maintained, had come a French regime of "suspicion and terror" that rivaled the worst moments of the Committee of Public Safety during the French Revolution.[10]

Lyautey inaugurated his method in Morocco with intense political contacts with the Fassi elite to buck up those "healthy and influential elements which have an interest in solidarity with us."[11] "Every day I see the native notables, either individually or as a group," he recounted to de Mun.

> I restore their confidence. I listen to their grievances. Most often I decide in their favor, for almost all of their complaints are justified. Through them I have begun to find some links with the tribes and it is thanks to them that at this very moment Gouraud is accompanied by several native leaders who are cooperating with us.[12]

By mid-June he could report to Paris that the situation at Fez was "satisfactory." He had made substantial progress with the urban leadership that was concerned about protecting, even expanding its autonomy under the new regime. And he trusted that the "principal native merchants," once convinced that France was solidly entrenched in Morocco, would also become firm supporters of the protectorate. What they wanted for starters, he added, was a secure link between Fez and the coast, for that was where the commercial action was. Lyautey concluded that the negotiations for a political accommodation, something for which the Fassis had a proverbial reputation, had now begun in earnest.[13] Respect and consideration for the native elite (if he felt he could pull their strings), always part of Lyautey's method, seemed to have produced a positive political payoff.

Still, the scent of "holy war" remained so heavy in the Moroccan air that Lyautey guessed it would take only the appearance of a "junior Abd el-Kader" for France to be "submerged" by the Muslim faithful.[14] But what some saw as mindless fanaticism and xenophobia, Lyautey described as the expression of an inchoate national consciousness (which he likened to the Spanish resistance to Napoleon), profoundly shocked by the imposition of the protectorate regime. According to Lyautey, the events leading up to the Treaty of Fez (as well as the treaty itself) had created a great divide in Morocco's history, a "historic abyss" that separated the Morocco that was from the Morocco that would be.[15] This explanation gave a coherence, an historic dimension, and ultimately a nobility to Moroccan resistance. It also marked a change in the way that Lyautey himself interpreted the kind of opposition that he was up against, for he had earlier told Poincaré that in Morocco there was neither holy war to fear nor national feeling to offend.[16] Lyautey now realized that something fundamental had changed in the nature of Moroccan resistance to France between 1911 and 1912. Or perhaps this was nothing more than a simple shift in perspective. In the borderlands Lyautey had seen "holy warriors" up close and experienced firsthand the terror of pan-tribal coalitions where traditional factionalism had been put asunder for the common cause. What was different? At that time he had been a critic of France's Moroccan policy, arguing that he could do things faster, better, and cheaper. Now he was the one in charge of getting the job done. Suddenly everything may have seemed more complicated than before.

Lyautey's first decision on pacification strategy after the "liberation" of Fez was to limit his activity to those areas of Morocco already under French military occupation—only the Chaouïa and the Rabat-Fez corridor—in order to ensure "in an absolute fashion" their security, followed by their political, social, and economic organization. The military tasks at Fez and Meknès— search and destroy operations against rebel groups, the establishment and expansion of secure zones around the cities, military and political action on those tribes likely to lay down their arms—Lyautey assigned to Gouraud, who had impressed him with his commanding use of force and his nimble political abilities in and around Fez. The political responsibilities, including all dealings with the sultan and his Makhzen at Fez, he kept for himself and Gaillard.[17] Backed by French force, politics would now hold sway.

Lyautey's most pressing chore was the restoration of Makhzen authority "to the extent that it was possible" throughout the occupied zone.[18] This was the only way, he told Poincaré, to handle the "multiple difficulties" of the Moroccan situation.[19] According to Lyautey, the sultan was the key to the success of the protectorate and to the method of indirect rule. Without the sultan the protectorate would be exposed as a "simple fiction"—the phrase was Henri Gaillard's—and rejected by Moroccans and world opinion.[20] With him it would succeed. Unfortunately for Lyautey, his greatest opponent was Abd el-Hafid himself, who, depressed at the advent of the new order, rejected collaboration with France by what he did and by what he refused to do. With the same scant regard for Morocco's sultan that Gallieni had shown for Madagascar's queen, Lyautey quickly negotiated Abd el-Hafid's abdication and exile, proving again that indirect rule would only succeed with native leaders willing to cooperate with France. Lyautey explained all this matter-of-factly. "We are in a protectorate situation [*pays de protectorat*] where nothing can be done without cooperation. Cooperation requires two parties. Five days ago there was only one party, or to tell the truth, there were two of us, but we were not cooperating." Given the sultan's "absolute obstructionism" ("going on strike" was another phrase Lyautey used to describe it), forcing Abd el-Hafid to abdicate was the only possibility.[21] At the moment of his leave-taking and fully conscious of the fact that he would be the last independent sultan, Abd el-Hafid broke the parasol that symbolized sharifian dignity and destroyed the imperial seal, signifying the end of Moroccan sovereignty.

To make the protectorate work Lyautey chose the thirty-one-year-old brother of Abd el-Hafid to be the next sultan. Dignified and loyal, moderate and pious, Moulay Youssef had long demonstrated his friendship with France. As the sultan's representative (*khalifa*) at Fez since June 1912, he had worked closely with Lyautey and Gouraud, both of whom had been won over by his personal qualities, his intelligence, and his cooperative spirit.[22] Although Lyautey conceded that it was not possible to imagine a sultan taking power in a "more troubled and serious situation," he was sure of Moulay Youssef's "loyal cooperation" and that was what mattered most. "At last we are all going to be able to work," Lyautey told the French community at Rabat, "and it is truly a relief for me to be able to utter those words."[23] They were repeated by every French official from the president of the republic on down. *L'Afrique française* went a step further and in French revolutionary fashion counted the beginning of the French protectorate—Year One—from day one of Moulay Youssef's reign.[24] For his part Moulay Youssef pledged "to complete the entente and perfect the friendly cooperation with France in the work of peace and progress in the sharifian empire."[25]

Two days after Moulay Youssef was designated sultan in Rabat "according to all the traditional forms," el-Hiba was proclaimed sultan at Marrakesh.[26] Lyautey was jolted by the appearance of a rebel sultan in this most important southern imperial city, for he had tried to neutralize the south in nonmilitary ways by working through the Makhzen *grands caïds*: Madani and Thami el-Glaouï at Marrakesh, Mohamed Anflous at Mogador, and Aïssa Ben Omar at Safi.[27] Apparently he had placed too much faith in his dealings with them and in their ability to handle el-Hiba, whose challenge was not only to the French and "their" sultan, but to the entire collaborationist regime.[28]

Although admitting the "great inconvenience" of opening a new theater of military operations, Lyautey had no choice. After Hibist probes toward Casablanca and the Chaouïa, he ordered Colonel Charles Mangin, responsible for the security of the coast, to respond with menacing displays of force. To make matters worse, nine Frenchmen were trapped in Marrakesh, including Lyautey's personal representative on mission. At first when the hostages were in the relatively safe custody of *grand caïd* Thami el-Glaouï, who was himself caught uncomfortably between el-Hiba and the French, Lyautey considered a "rapid *coup de main*" to liberate them, hoping to catch el-Hiba off guard. If successful, the sheer daring of the mission might have turned some of el-Hiba's erstwhile allies against him. But when Lyautey learned that el-Glaouï had been forced to hand the prisoners over to el-Hiba, he began negotiations in earnest for their release. Only after he was convinced that the negotiations could never succeed—el-Hiba demanded the withdrawal of French troops beyond the Oum er Rebia River, then from all Morocco—and that waiting much longer might actually further endanger their lives, did Lyautey give Mangin the go-ahead for a march on Marrakesh.[29]

The "famous telegram" of 2 September 1912, which began "Allez-y carrément" was precisely what Mangin, a veteran of the killing fields of the western Sudan, the Marchand march to Fashoda, and Indochina, had been waiting to read.[30] En route to Marrakesh at Sidi Bou Othman he engaged and defeated a Hibist army two to three times the size of his own 5,000-man force. In what was, according to Douglas Porch, "the worst single defeat" inflicted on Moroccans in the history of the conquest of their country, el-Hiba lost thousands of his followers to the artillery, machine guns, rifles, and sabers of the French, while Mangin mourned only two dead and twenty-three wounded.[31] It was one of those lopsided victories that made instant heroes of colonial soldiers. Still some distance from Marrakesh with a battle-tired army, Mangin sent a flying column to the gates of the city under his second in command, Major Henri Simon. Luck followed Simon as it had Mangin. El-Hiba and his army were now in full flight across the Atlas—a "real rout" Lyautey later called it—and Simon reached Marrakesh without mishap. Despite some anxious moments, the prisoners were released unharmed and the city placed under the double protection of Mangin and Thami el-Glaouï, now back in the sultan's fold as the city's governor.[32]

In spite of the popular discontent that el-Hiba's jihad had revealed in such a dramatic and dangerous way, the *grands caïds* remained the cornerstone of Lyautey's method of conquest and rule in the south. Admitting that "their rivalries, their disputes, their constant switching from one camp to another" had been "at the base of all the troubles of this region," Lyautey still wanted "to use" them by maintaining a balance among them—never favoring one over another nor getting involved in their personal quarrels—yet on occasion neutralizing one by working through the others.[33] He told Mangin, now charged with the Région de Marrakech, that for the time being Marrakesh was to be an "end point" of French military activity. In consequence, the colonel was instructed to concentrate on the vast territory from the Oum er Rebia River to the Atlas Mountains and not to venture beyond it. His mission was to restore law and order to the region, bringing it again firmly under the Makhzen's political and administrative authority. At the same time Mangin was to oversee the native authorities in a discreet, yet consistent and strict way to ensure that there would be no return to the abuses of the past that had brought the local populations to the brink of revolt and in many cases over its edge.[34]

The action of Mangin at Marrakesh did more than fire the imagination of the armchair colonials in France. To Lyautey's great relief it "considerably altered" the political and military situation throughout Morocco, as had the French military victory at Bou Denib in 1908, by halting the coalescence of anti-French forces. But it had come after peaceful penetration, including delicate political negotiations with el-Hiba that had gone beyond the question of the hostages, had failed. At the same time it did not diminish the dangers of the problem that Lyautey now defined in terms of two Moroccos—"the one that we occupy, which is militarily weak and governed by a Makhzen without force or prestige, and the other, much more important, which is comprised of the Berber masses who are deeply agitated, fanaticized, and militarily strong, and who under influences beyond our control stand united against us."[35] Described in this fashion, all Morocco was still up for grabs.

In occupied Morocco Lyautey continued to promote Moulay Youssef as the best agent of the protectorate, even though each sultan backed by France had ultimately been rejected by his own people. Could there ever be a "viable sultan" under the protectorate? Whoever shaded under the imperial umbrella might always be considered "a puppet, the shadow of a shadow, the creature of the infidels," forever without prestige or religious authority. Yet, as Lyautey saw it and as he explained it to his political friends in Paris, by the end of 1912 Moulay Youssef had emerged as a "real sultan," accepted at least by the Moroccans in the zone under French military control. Surrounded by "old ritualistic Moroccans," denied Europe's vices, and tutored by Gouraud with "consummate intelligence, tact and reserve,"

Moulay Youssef had passed Lyautey's test.[36] "Your approach to Moulay Youssef has worked a miracle," he told Gouraud. "You are the principal instrument of his education and, thanks to you, perhaps we will be able to make him the most traditional, the most Muslim sultan that Morocco has known for a long time."[37] The sultan's own qualities as a "good Muslim and an honest man" figured into all of this. Yet Lyautey rightly called Moulay Youssef his "greatest success" for in truth he had fashioned the sultan into the partner he required.[38] This was good politics, good method, and the beginning of indirect rule in Morocco even if in the eyes of many Moroccans Moulay Youssef always remained the sultan of the French.

As Daniel Rivet has shown, the making of the sultan and the reconstruction of his Makhzen went hand in hand with the construction of the protectorate. He is surely correct that Lyautey's insistence on rebuilding a Makhzen with a "vieux Maroc" patina did much to accommodate Moroccans to the French presence and to associate them with the new protectorate regime. It was a wager on the traditional social and political order that paid off. This was a victory for Lyautey's "Makhzen policy," his policy of respect for the native elite, and his *politique des grands caïds* for all of which Rivet gives Lyautey very high marks.[39] At the same time, however, the Makhzen was rebuilt by French hands and stripped of much of its real power and authority, for even if the sultan and the native leaders were not humiliated nor "Algerianized," they were never again masters in their own house. How could it have been otherwise in a Morocco under French military occupation and under a protectorate regime that promised social improvement, political betterment, and economic progress?

Before Lyautey the sultan had ruled through five ministers, who were appointed by him and served at his pleasure: the *grand vizir* (the sultan's chief adviser with responsibility for the domestic affairs of the empire, including the nomination of the most important local officials: the pashas [city governors], the *caïds* [tribal governors], the *cadis* [religious judges], and the *mohtasebs* [market inspectors]), the foreign minister, the minister of finance, the minister of war, and the minister of administrative appeals and supervision. As resident general of the French protectorate and commander in chief of French troops, Lyautey served as both foreign minister and minister of war to the sultan; therefore, these sharifian ministries were abolished. So were the Ministry of Administrative Appeals and Supervision and the Ministry of Finance (in 1914); their functions were transferred to protectorate administrators. In the "reformed" Makhzen (and reform continued throughout the Lyautey years), the sultan ultimately presided over four officials of ministerial rank: the *grand vizir,* who was the solitary holdover from the ancien régime, and the ministers of Muslim justice, state property, and religious property, whose ministries had been created by the French. The purpose of these reforms was to reshape the Makhzen to allow the sultan authority over what might be called the "Muslim affairs" of the empire and the French control over everything else. In Alan Scham's summing-up, the French reforms "swept away almost the entire administrative structure of the empire, at least at the ministerial level."[40]

Separate from the Makhzen hierarchy and operating largely without the aid or advice of Moroccan authorities was a French protectorate administration of modern "neo-sharifian" departments under the authority of the resident general and directly responsible to the protectorate's secretary-general, the most important protectorate official after Lyautey. In 1912 there were only two major departments—the Department of Finance and the Department of Public Works—and several minor services. By 1925, as a result of expansion and reorganization, there were eight departments (almost all with multiple services) to deal with the needs of any twentieth-century government—agriculture, commerce, communications, education, and health—as well as departments and services to handle the special concerns of the protectorate, chiefly, native affairs and colonization.[41] This was the setup for direct French rule.

For indirect rule at the top—advising, guiding, informing, and overseeing the sultan and his ministers—Lyautey first relied on a secretary-general attached to the sharifian government (secrétaire général du gouvernement chérifien), then on a counsellor to the sharifian government (conseiller du gouvernement chérifien), and finally on a full-fledged Direction des Affaires Chérifiennes (Department of Sharifian Affairs), established in 1920.[42] Henri Gaillard was the first (and last) secretary-general of the sharifian government. The former French consul at Fez, Gaillard was the ideal middleman between the Makhzen and the protectorate administration; talented, hard-working, expansive, assured, well connected in colonial and Moroccan society, and knowledgeable in the workings of both French and Moroccan government. He developed his office into a real protectorate powerhouse, but it was abolished in May 1917—and Gaillard was appointed French consul in Cairo—as a result of a high-level reorganization that tightened and centralized the protectorate bureaucracy. Gaillard's successor, Raoul Marc, the former French consul at Mogador, was named counsellor to the sharifian government, a position of less influence and standing. What is more, he unfortunately had neither Gaillard's urbanity nor his style. Solitary and somewhat mysterious, Marc never had the full trust of the sultan nor the complete confidence of Lyautey, an anomalous situation for an important banner-carrier of indirect rule.[43]

For indirect rule in the cities and among the tribes in the areas of Morocco designated as "military regions," Lyautey employed the military officers *(officiers de renseignements)* of the Service des Renseignements (intelligence service), which had been established in 1907 to aid the French occupation of Casablanca and the Chaouïa. Reflections of Lyautey's colonial "ideal type," these soldier-administrators—the heirs of the military administrators of the Algerian Bureaux Arabes and the Tunisian Service des Renseignements— were to use force and persuasion to pacify and organize the areas under their authority. They provided the military command with the information needed for military action, overseeing the local systems of government and justice, supervising the collection of taxes, instituting social and economic improvements, and in general counseling and monitoring the pashas, *caïds,* and *cadis* in the performance of their duties. In January 1913 Lyautey counted 194 *officiers de renseignements* and 64 bureau posts, 47 in western Morocco, 17 in eastern Morocco.[44] This was the front line of indirect rule.

As pacification progressed and military regions became "civil regions," Lyautey turned over the chief responsibility for indirect rule to the civilian supervisory corps (Corps du Contrôle Civil), which was established in July 1913. Although Lyautey patterned the Contrôle Civil on the Tunisian service, he aspired to make it into the French counterpart of England's elite colonial service through selective recruitment by competitive examinations, specialized training (including the essential requirement of knowing Arabic), and attractive pay and advancement possibilities. Because of the disruptions of the First World War, however, the first exams were not held until 1920; until that time the supervisory agents *(contrôleurs civils)*—sixty-three in all—were recruited in the main directly from the civil staff of the protectorate administration or the cadres of the *officiers de renseignements* and interpreters with a scattering of recruits from other overseas colonial administrations (especially Algeria and Tunisia), the Ministry of Foreign Affairs, and the Institute of Oriental Languages in Paris.[45]

At first the Contrôle Civil was under Lyautey's personal authority, but in 1917 it was transferred to a newly established Department of Civil Affairs (Direction des Affaires Civiles). Three years later it was placed under the direction of the protectorate's secretary-general and in 1922 renamed the Service des Contrôles Civils et du Contrôle des Municipalités. Its mission remained the same. "The *contrôleur civil* cannot administer anything by himself," Lyautey wrote in 1914,

> but he is the representative of the government of the protectorate to the local native authorities and, at the same time, the guide, the coun-

sellor, and the supervisor of these authorities. They are not prepared for our methods of administration nor for our stage of administrative development. They receive instructions from a higher authority, the Makhzen, but these instructions, prepared upon the advice or the initiative of protectorate officials, are not always well understood by the local native authorities. It is up to the agents in charge of supervising them to explain the meaning of these instructions and to guide and oversee the native authorities in their execution.[46]

Over and over again Lyautey repeated that the essential mission of the *contrôleur civil* was "to supervise" much more than to administer directly, "to make use of" the native authorities rather than to act for them in the accomplishment of their administrative tasks.[47] Supervision meant many things. Lyautey made this clear to the Ministry of Foreign Affairs in October 1917.

[T]he functions of supervision are in fact much more extensive than the word seems to indicate. In effect, the *contrôleurs civils* not only have the mission of supervising the systems of native justice and government per se; they are in truth the real administrators of the country, charged with centralizing and coordinating in all matters . . . the action of the government in their circumscription.[48]

Even if Lyautey meant only to justify the high salaries of the *contrôleurs civils* to the penny-pinching Quai d'Orsay that paid them, what he said was no exaggeration.

Lyautey prized teamwork, so it is no surprise that one of his innovations in local administration in Morocco was to insist that the *officiers de renseignements* and the *contrôleurs civils* work together as harmoniously as possible. This was part of his method for colonial rule, the search for the colonial as opposed to the military or civilian "right man," and it tallied as well with the needs of Moroccan pacification. By and large he succeeded in creating a unified "Moroccan administration" for colonial rule, rather than two rival systems of the sort that marked Tunisia.[49] Nevertheless, as will be seen later at Casablanca and in the Chaouïa, civil-military competition for sway over the native leadership and disagreements between military and civilian administrators on the nature of indirect rule were significant, and in the end perhaps unavoidable.

Teamwork would mark the Lyautey method throughout Morocco. For the protectorate's most important leadership tasks Lyautey selected a handful of experienced and energetic soldiers and civil administrators. After some changes and false starts he confided to the minister of war in June 1914:

> I have never had my instrument better in hand than at present with men of whom I am absolutely certain: Humbert as my adjutant who thinks as I do *[qui est absolument dans ma peau]*, Baumgarten who puts my mind at ease in eastern Morocco, and my team of Gouraud, Henrÿs, Blondlat, Brulard who march as one.[50]

He relied as well on his "faithful" colonels from Aïn Sefra: Henri Berriau, Jean Delmas, and Joseph Poeymirau, all members of his military staff.[51] On the civil side Lyautey recruited Paul Tirard from the administrative elite of the Conseil d'État to be the protectorate's secretary-general, Gaillard from the Ministry of Foreign Affairs to serve as secretary-general of the sharifian government, Charles Gallut from the financial services of Indochina to act as director of finance, and Gaston Delure from the Corps des Ponts et Chaussées to be director of public works. All were top-notch professionals in their respective fields, but Lyautey made it clear that was not enough. "In order to attend to the difficult birth of this country, I don't want to be assisted by any Molière-type doctors in pointed caps speaking Latin, but by sturdy practitioners who roll up their sleeves and get down to work."[52]

What set the Lyautey team apart from the military clans or political networks of the Metropole was the unifying purpose of the method and the mission coupled with Lyautey's intense concern for those under his command. As ever, Lyautey's moral sermons to the highest (as well as the lowest) on his team linked the value of hard work and the joy of accomplishment to a promised spiritual renewal that would alter the individual and transform France. Morocco was to be the crucible for all of this.

At the beginning of December 1912 Lyautey reported on the progress of his mission to the Foreign and Colonial Affairs Committee of the Chamber of Deputies. He reviewed the events of Fez and the continuing improvement in the region; he described his initial pacification plans and their abrupt modification as a result of the taking of Marrakesh; he explained the abdication crisis and the new sultan's importance to French policy; he repeated his principles and outlined his methods for conquest and rule. He insisted that even with the 57,000 troops he now commanded in Morocco—45,000 in the west, 12,000 in the east—pacification would be a slow process. There would be no grand expeditions, but only the steady penetration of the country as both circumstances and opportunities presented themselves. "It is a matter of patience and of feeling one's way. This is why, when looking to the future, it is impossible to say what the next step will be."[53]

This was hardly the brash confidence of the borderlands. In fact, Daniel Rivet believes that whatever there was of method throughout Lyautey's colonial career was abandoned when he took command in Morocco. According to Rivet, Lyautey fashioned his "native policy"—or better, his Moroccan policy—from the realities he encountered on a day-to-day basis. And in many cases—as at Fez and Marrakesh—a policy was forced upon him by events. In the end, only the notion of "the right man in the right spot" remained of a method of colonial conquest and rule.[54] Douglas Porch goes a step further. For Porch the Lyautey method was ever and always a clever exercise in public relations aimed at Frenchmen who were uninterested in costly colonial expansion. Lyautey first convinced them that he could acquire an empire on the cheap, then, as the expenses mounted, that everything was being spent for a truly noble cause. This was a salesman with the right pitch, but no method at all.[55]

There is some truth in both of these views. At the same time the method continued to provide a purpose to empire building that forever captivated the idealist, the romantic, the humanist, and the missionary in Lyautey and, as important, in his audience. In addition, it satisfied the materialist and the modernizer in him, ever fascinated by the power as well as the progress inherent in the development and control of trade and communications. Finally, as a soldier, Lyautey clung to the method that promised to transform the army's task—and, to be sure, the army itself—overseas. As a result, despite surprises and setbacks, Lyautey never gave up the method nor exploited it solely for its public relations value. He believed in it and justified it honestly and unblinkingly as the only "rational" method. "This country must not be dealt with by force alone," he told de Mun in October 1912. "The rational method, the only one, the right one—and the one for which I was sent here and not someone else—is the continuous and combined exercise of politics and force."[56] Lyautey tried to practice what he preached, pushed by faith, self-confidence, ambition, and the realization that in a very real way it was the method that bound his team together. Nevertheless, as will be seen, it failed to disarm Moroccan resistance to France or to create the real partnership between Moroccans and Frenchmen that was always Lyautey's chief objective.

CHAPTER 4

Pacifying the Middle Atlas

■ ■ ■ ■

According to Lyautey's method, pacification was both goal and process. It meant an end to the fighting, but also the manner by which enemy territory might be transformed into a productive area of peace under French supervision. Lyautey spoke of three "zones of action." The first and most important zone was that which had been completely pacified and in which the work of administrative and economic organization had begun in earnest. This required a tight "collaboration" with "native agents at all levels in the hierarchy" and might include encouragement to European colonization. The second zone, which acted as a "cover" for the first, extended to the edge of unoccupied territory. In this zone the "repressive action" of French troops, constant political activity, and a never-ending surveillance worked hand in hand.[1] The third zone was the war zone where advancing French troops met any belligerent native population in combat. The zones of war and peace were intimately connected to one another in a forward dynamic. Since the transformation of the second zone into a completely pacified zone required another "cover," this meant a further move into hitherto unoccupied territory.

The French advance into the Middle Atlas in spring 1913 was the expected outcome of pacification theory. The timing, however, resulted from two French mistakes: the occupation of the Beni Mguild Plateau south of Meknès and the establishment of a post at Oued Zem in the Tadla. The first was the consequence of unrest among the Beni Mtir, a cover zone tribe, which the French blamed on the neighboring Beni Mguild, who lived beyond the zone of French occupation. The disturbance might also have been the result of the brutal methods of Colonel Charles Reibell, who had little sympathy for Berber tribesmen, dead or alive.[2]

To tighten French control Lyautey created a Cercle des Beni Mtir within the Région de Meknès and put it in the hands of Colonel Paul Henrÿs, one of his "most expert officers" in matters of native policy. Henrÿs was a veteran of the South Oranais where he had been Lyautey's chief of staff and a prime mover on the Lyautey team. He was to reestablish the "cover" of the hinterland toward Meknès and restore order among the Beni Mtir through "a skillful policy backed up by a show of force." This would demonstrate to the Beni Mtir—and particularly those tribal fractions "in a state of complete revolt against us"—precisely where their security and true interests lay. At that moment there was no plan for an invasion of the Beni Mguild. Their territory was to be respected and concerted efforts made "to attract them to us without compelling us to go to them." By concentrating both political and military authority in Henrÿs's command Lyautey hoped that the "intolerable insecurity" around Meknès would be quickly ended.[3]

The Cercle des Beni Mtir refused to rest. Beni Mtir and Beni Mguild tribesmen surprised Henrÿs by attacking El Hajeb, southeast of Meknès, on 17 and 20 March and despite a Henrÿs victory at the end of the month that broke the cooperation between the two tribes, the colonel could not finish off the resistance.[4] Defying French military superiority, the Beni Mtir moved farther south toward the foothills of the Middle Atlas, drawing Henrÿs after them. Henrÿs concluded that only "the toughest measures" would bring the Beni Mtir to heel and that it would take time. "These tribal fractions have been in constant revolt against the Makhzen," he reported to his superior, General Denis Dalbiez, "and have never submitted to any real authority. They constitute the most warlike element in the entire Région."[5] In addition, he decided that negotiations with tribal leaders would not work and might even encourage further resistance by making them think that the French had given up on the use of force.[6]

Henrÿs's pursuit of the Beni Mtir led him straight to the Beni Mguild. He marched to Ifrane, whose fortified casbah he destroyed on 23 April, and then moved southwest through a dense cedar forest to Azrou, the "principal center" of the Beni Mguild tribe, which he occupied at the end of April. For the next two months Henrÿs chased hostile Beni Mguild and Beni Mtir groups to and fro. Finally at the end of June he announced in triumph that most of the Beni Mtir had laid down their arms and returned to the area around Meknès. Lyautey praised him (and arranged his promotion to the rank of brigadier general) for his "excellent political action" with the Beni Mtir, even if success had really come out of the barrel of a gun. This was a setback for Lyautey's method. In addition, to do what he did Henrÿs had had to expand his zone of activity. He was now "solidly established" on the Beni Mguild

Plateau. This not only brought the French into direct contact with the Beni Mguild, but closer than they had ever been to the Zaïan tribes, the belligerent nomadic confederation that roamed from the plains of the Oum er Rebia to the slopes of the Middle Atlas.[7]

To the south the French also stumbled by establishing a post at Oued Zem. This was the work of Colonel Charles Mangin, already well known for his heroics in the Sudan and his capture of Marrakesh in 1912, who revelled in dash and indiscipline. It was perfectly in character for him to have staked out Oued Zem without permission, and in fact it was probably what Lyautey would have done in Mangin's place. Nevertheless, the residency complained that the post had been installed "prematurely" among tribes "in no way yet disposed to submit to our influence." It had been set up "too quickly, without sufficient political preparation [and] in conditions absolutely contrary to the doctrines that the Resident General has always insisted upon." The combined effect had been to encourage an aggressiveness and a cohesion among hostile groups whose attacks on the post had created "a growing danger" that was now impossible to ignore and that had to be dealt with "without delay."[8]

To calm the situation General Louis Franchet d'Espérey, commander of the French occupation forces in western Morocco, increased troop strength in the Oued Zem-El Boroudj area and ordered Colonel Henri Simon, the military commander of the Chaouïa region, to take "prudent" yet "energetic" action to disperse all enemy groups. In no case, however, was he to yield to the temptation of heading for the Oum er Rebia River (which magnetized colonial officers much as the Rhine did their metropolitan counterparts) because any contact with the "bellicose tribes" of the southern Tadla risked a "general conflagration" that Franchet d'Espérey wanted to avoid "at all costs."[9] Simon carried out his orders to the letter. In mid-March he scattered a force of 5,000 Beni Amir, Beni Zemmour, Smaala, and Zaïan tribesmen bent on severing the communications link between Oued Zem and Kasbah Ben Ahmed. But the enemy harassment persisted and Simon could not quell it.[10]

To deliver the knockout blow to a budding tribal combination Lyautey was forced to call on Mangin. He put the colonel in charge of all the troops in the Oued Zem-El Boroudj area on 18 March, but bound him to the same instructions given to Simon.[11] Mangin immediately moved against a Zaïan military contingent (harka) led by Moha ou Hammou El Zaïani, then raided the Zaïan camp on 26 March in an encounter that army historians later labelled the battle of Botmat Aïssaoua. "Bravo," applauded Lyautey. "All my congratulations for the vigor of your punch and your brilliant success *and* for not having gotten carried away. You understood how necessary it was to force Moha ou Hammou back into Zaïan country without entering it yourself."[12]

With Lyautey's approval Mangin next turned southeast against the Aït Roboas and the Beni Amir, clearing the area from Oued Zem to Boujad and from Boujad to Kasbah Tadla on the right bank of the Oum er Rebia. Mangin also proposed a joint action with Henrÿs against the Zaïan in the direction of Khénifra. If successful, this would reopen the old "Makhzen road" between Fez and Marrakesh, a not-insignificant military and political objective. But Lyautey was not ready to take on the Zaïan confederation. When Mangin continued to talk about the Fez-Marrakesh road and the need to transfer his post from Oued Zem to Kasbah Tadla, closer to Khénifra, Lyautey laid down the law. He dismissed any thought of a move against Khénifra and reminded the colonel that his goal was to seek "a stable political situation" in the region. For the moment he was to concentrate on the Beni Amir, the Beni Moussa, and the Aït Roboas. Only later would he be authorized to challenge the Zaïan and then in order to assist Henrÿs by advancing toward Moulay Bou Azza, not Khénifra. And Mangin was not to set up (nor even think about setting up) any "new permanent installation" at Kasbah Tadla that would make a French withdrawal difficult or bring the Berber tribes of the mountains "down on our backs."[13] Although Lyautey had taken one risky step after another in the South Oranais, he now tried to harness his colonels to a cautious pacification plan that squared with Berber realities.

Events worked to Mangin's advantage. Attacked by a Chleuh *harka* of the Aït Attab and Aït Bouzid tribes, the colonel gave pursuit across the river and won stunning victories at Aïn Zerga and Sidi Ali Bou Brahim at the end of April. In addition, he made Kasbah Tadla his headquarters in all but name.[14] This clearly violated the orders from Lyautey and the resident general reminded him of this: "I absolutely refuse to sanction any permanent installation at Kasbah Tadla or at any other point along the Oum er Rebia." He explained that he had received "the most serious news" about the chance of war in Europe and that this had placed him under the "formal obligation" of limiting his military effort in Morocco. As a result, he could not open up any "new questions" and certainly could not allow any territorial expansion. "It is more important than ever not to get involved in the mountains, so as not to risk getting caught up—in spite of what you may intend—in dangerous incidents of war."[15]

With some humor Mangin argued that the Tadla question had already been opened up by the creation of the post at Oued Zem and that it could only be closed by establishing a post at Kasbah Tadla. He insisted that the new post was "indispensable" to protect Boujad, Oued Zem, and the right bank territory, to hold on to the "single" bridge at this point across the Oum er Rebia (which for half of the year could not be forded), and to exercise a positive influence on the left bank tribes. Moreover, it would give all the land currently under French occupation "a very solid eastern border" behind which the "so very mobile" population of the Tadla region could settle.[16]

In the end Lyautey reluctantly condoned the establishment of Kasbah Tadla, but only as "an advance post and end-point" to be outfitted inexpensively and garrisoned by as small a force as possible. He wanted there to be no "misunderstanding" about what he was approving. Kasbah Tadla would not be the "bait" for an enemy attack in order to spin out another French advance.[17] "Until further notice," Lyautey spelled out, "I consider the Oum er Rebia the limit of our activity in the south; I consider Kasbah Tadla as a simple flank guard on this frontier; I want no military involvement south of the Oum er Rebia." This time he said he needed to keep his hands free to work elsewhere.

> At this moment all my attention is focused on what is happening with the Zaïan. Colonel Henrÿs is in the process of establishing himself solidly on their northern flank. Lieutenant Colonel [Jean] Coudein is working on their center. The coming weeks will clarify many things on this score. I may have to strike a decisive blow or simply establish a balance of military force. This is why, more than anything else, I have to be liberated from all worry about the Tadla, which you are in the process of organizing and stabilizing, and the region south of the Oum er Rebia, which I ardently desire to see taken care of by means other than our own.[18]

Now was the moment for political action to hold sway in the Tadla. As ordered, Mangin began conversations with the Berber leader, Moha ou Saïd l'Irraoui, the "war chief" of the Aït Ouirah and the Aït Roboas, whose principal residence, Rhorm El Alem, was situated eighteen kilometers southeast of Kasbah Tadla. An old man of "great prestige" and "much authority" in the region and a former Makhzen caïd, he presented Lyautey with an opportunity for an "arrangement" of the sort worked out with the High Atlas caïds. With this in mind Lyautey despatched Colonel Simon (now head of the Service des Renseignements) and Si Mehdi el-Mennebhi, a well-connected high Makhzen official who often served as a go-between for the French, to second Mangin in the talks. Because of el-Mennebhi's friendship with Moha ou Saïd (Moha had served under el-Mennebhi in the campaign against the pretender at Taza) Lyautey hoped that "a solution of the most elegant and pleasant sort" might be worked out. In the end, it could not be. Perhaps this was because Mangin was such a poor political instrument. He found negotiations with native leaders—the essence of Lyautey's idea of "political action"—to be agonizingly drawn out and confused. More likely, it was because Moha ou Saïd, who at first showed interest in the conversations, had come under intense pressure from tribal leaders committed to all-out resistance and was forced to break them off. In any event, Foreign Minister Stéphen Pichon was probably wrong or being deliberately deceptive when he later told the Chamber of Deputies that at the very moment when Moha ou Saïd was speaking with Mangin, he was stirring up hostilities against the French.[19]

Confronted by an unyielding adversary, Mangin decided that force alone would do the trick. He asked Lyautey's permission for a "rapid action" against Moha ou Saïd's camp at El Ksiba, two hours east of Rhorm El Alem, pledging a "prompt return" to Kasbah Tadla.[20] Both Simon and el-Mennebhi agreed that this was a necessary first step on the road toward further negotiations. Lyautey approved the request, explaining to the Ministry of Foreign Affairs that the colonel was to teach Moha ou Saïd a lesson by hitting him hard. Hopefully this would deal a "decisive setback" to his fighting ability and prestige and bring him quickly back to the bargaining tent.[21]

Once again Mangin crossed to the left bank of the Oum er Rebia. But nothing went as planned. Although the French had the twin advantages of cannon and surprise, the battles of El Ksiba on 8 and 10 June were neither quick, decisive, nor beyond reproach. The enemy received "a terrible lesson," but so did the French. On his side Mangin counted 63 dead and 153 wounded. Much of this was his own fault. In the first encounter he engaged his cavalry "prematurely" and past the point where it could rely on the effective support of the infantry. By day's end twenty-five cavalrymen were dead, wounded, or missing. To erase the poor impression left by the cavalry's mishap and to retrieve the bodies of the fallen, Mangin remained in the field. His second day at El Ksiba was more successful. But on the return march to Kasbah Tadla, Moha ou Saïd's riflemen pinned down Mangin's rear guard, resulting in "cruel losses" and forcing the colonel to abandon the bodies of his dead and their equipment. As a result, even though Moroccan casualties in the two battles totalled almost eight times those of the French, it was difficult to tell the victors from the vanquished. Privately Lyautey admitted that this had been "the toughest battle yet fought in Morocco" on a terrain that was extremely difficult and against an enemy "whose spirit, firmness under fire, and tactical sense in the use of the terrain had not been matched in any previous encounter."[22]

At first Lyautey worried that Mangin's road back to Kasbah Tadla, scattered as it was with French dead and supplies, would be seen as a retreat and encourage Moha ou Saïd to take the offensive. This did not happen. After El Ksiba all "serious agitation" in the southern Tadla stopped. "Since then," according to French reports, "not a single dissident has ventured into the plain between the Atlas and the Oum er Rebia and not one shot has been fired at our troops."[23] On the other hand, Lyautey acknowledged that the Mangin strike had failed as a prod to bring Moha ou Saïd to terms, for now all contact with him and the tribes of the left bank had ended. Lyautey immediately had the sultan appoint Mohammed Bou Aouda as pasha of Kasbah Tadla, for Bou Aouda knew Moha ou Saïd personally and Lyautey believed he might be the one who "little by little and by spending all the time that is required [could] reestablish the contacts which had begun to form before the El Ksiba affair." But without doubt El Ksiba was a clear reverse for pacification Lyautey-style.[24]

Crossing the Oum er Rebia to fight at El Ksiba caused a furor in the Chamber of Deputies akin to the uproar over Lyautey's advance to Berguent nine years before. It was the event the anticolonial opposition needed to interpellate the government on the expanding Moroccan "adventure," made dramatic by the rumors of serious disagreements between Lyautey and Mangin. As in 1904, Socialist Jean Jaurès pressed for explanations on the discrepancy between the government's stated policy not to extend the field of military operations and Mangin's move across the river. Covering both Lyautey and Mangin, the foreign minister replied that the Oum er Rebia was no Moroccan Rubicon, nor its crossing Mangin's "whimsical disobedience." This was an action designed to protect both the French troops and the submitted tribes on the right bank of the river. It had been authorized by the government, approved by Lyautey, and executed by Mangin.[25] Although this was true, Lyautey's hand had been forced, raising questions as to who was in charge.

Even before the inquiry in the Chamber, Lyautey had sent Franchet d'Espérey to Kasbah Tadla to tell Mangin that henceforth the Oum er Rebia would be the "absolute limit" of French "direct action." He reported to the foreign ministry on 12 June that intervention on the left bank would be limited to "political means" and that on the right bank he would proceed to the installation of posts, the organization of supply stations, and the establishment of a command structure. "We shall limit ourselves to consolidating the results already achieved in this zone so as not to be dragged into active operations." This did not suit Mangin who was packed off to France where he later distinguished himself in the European war as a fighter of uncommon valor. For the record, however, Lyautey insisted somewhat disingenuously that if the "Tadla question" had been opened, it was

> because the tribes of this region rose up against us without any provocation on our part. Their furious attacks and their threats to

the approaches of the Chaouïa made it indispensable to respond to this offensive with vigorous operations and to make the Tadla a cover zone of the Chaouïa, whose pacification must be absolutely assured.[26]

The trouble in the Tadla interfered with the action against the Zaïan tribes, whose territory had long been targeted as the French entryway into the Middle Atlas. Until El Ksiba Henrÿs's activity in the north and Mangin's in the south had been described as coordinated moves. "What is being constructed progressively, methodically, and solidly," went the official version of April 1913, "is a real pincers around Zaïan country, the staging area for all the aggressions against us and the heart of all our difficulties in central Morocco."[27] But the El Ksiba "affair," caused in part by Mangin's refusal to play his assigned role in the Zaïan strategy, threatened to compromise what had already been done. When pressed, Lyautey asserted that neither Henrÿs nor Coudein, both so secure in the north and center, had been affected by El Ksiba. This may have been so. At the very least, however, El Ksiba showed the kind of resistance that the French might be up against around Khénifra and forced Lyautey to admit that any solution of the Zaïan question "in the near future" would require a serious military effort. This flew in the face of his earlier claim that with his method the Zaïan bloc might fall into French hands "almost without a shot being fired."[28]

With characteristic energy Lyautey began to work within the perimeter that "for the moment" marked off the French occupation west of the Atlas. From Sefrou in the north to the Atlantic on the south, this vast cover zone vibrated with intense activity—the organization of the Beni Mguild and the Tadla tribes, military rounds among the submitted Beni Mtir and Beni Zemmour, and political action on the tribes bordering the frontier.[29] By November 1913 the southern front of the occupied territories was secure from Sefrou to Kasbah Tadla and 2,500 Zaïan tents had submitted to French posts in the Régions de Rabat and Meknès. Along the border of the Cercle du Tadla, unsubmitted Zaïan tribes continued their commercial relations with the French-controlled Smaala and Beni Zemmour in return for the promise not to attack French posts or submitted tribes. This whittling away at the Zaïan bloc—textbook Lyautey in action—produced a new, more determined resistance. The people of the Middle Atlas, who had counted on the Zaïan as a "dike" to hold back the French, now gave the "Berber agitator" Sidi Ali Ben El Mekki Amhaouch a hearing.[30]

Ali Amhaouch was known to the French. Nine years earlier a mission sponsored by the colonial lobby's Comité du Maroc and headed by the

Marquis René de Segonzac had visited him in the holy city of Arbala, a small market town near the sources of the Moulouya and the El Abid Rivers, where he kept his residence. At that time de Segonzac described Ali Amhaouch as one of the "great spiritual leaders of Morocco" and "the most powerful religious personality of the Southeast" in part because he exercised an important influence within the Derkaoui religious brotherhood, a potent regional expression of popular Islam. Ali Amhaouch was called the "the sultan of the mountains" and de Segonzac warned: "It is only too certain that we have in this fanatical *sharif* a shrewd adversary, and that we will find him blocking all our efforts at the head of his mountaineers from the Atlas."[31]

Ali Amhaouch lived up to his advance billing. In 1913 he was still numbered among the "three great leaders" of the Middle Atlas (Moha ou Hammou and Moha ou Saïd were the other two), who commanded the mountain roads that connected eastern and western Morocco. And within this "powerful Berber trinity" only he remained uncompromised by traffic with, or defeat by, the French invader.[32] Contrôleur Civil Maurice Le Glay, the political officer who had won his spurs with Colonel Henrÿs among the Beni Mtir and Beni Mguild, feared that without swift action Ali Amhaouch would grow stronger. He recommended a move against the Zaïan, occupying El Hamman to cut Ali Amhaouch off from Mohamed Aguebli of the Aït Zgougou and taking Khénifra to separate him from Moha ou Hammou. The *contrôleur* predicted that this would "finish him off definitively." It also would have started a Zaïan war. Usually cautious in matters military, Le Glay advocated "a substantial military effort" of the sort that Lyautey had denied Mangin and the French government was pledged to avoid. "But, conditions have changed," he insisted, "and events are pushing us more than we are leading them. We cannot wait for them to overturn us."[33]

Given the active "centers of resistance" in the Middle Atlas apparently irreducible by French political action, Lyautey authorized a military advance in spring 1914 against the Tsoul east of Fez in preparation for a march on Taza. Taking Taza would join Morocco and Algeria and have "the most advantageous consequences from both the economic and strategic point of view and the most happy impact on the general political situation of all Morocco."[34] He proceeded as well with plans to invade Zaïan country, specifically to capture Khénifra, thereby detaching all the right bank territory from the control of the Zaïan confederation. Success in all this would give the military occupation of Morocco a rectangular shape on the map (if one connected the urban dots of Agadir, Marrakesh, Kelaa, Kasbah Tadla, Khénifra, Anoceur, and Guercif), covered by the "natural boundaries" of the High Atlas on the south and to the east of Marrakesh, the Oum er Rebia in the center, and the Middle Atlas in the north. Politically it would put the French in "yet more intimate contact" with the Berbers to facilitate the "future occupation of the Moroccan Atlas."[35]

Taza—the last stone of the French edifice in North Africa—was cemented into place in early May and celebrated as a triumph of the Lyautey method.

> The union of Morocco and Algeria marks the completion of a work of conquest, pacification, and organization of which France can be justifiably proud. In an incredibly short period of time we have accomplished a colonial endeavor in Morocco of which no people at any other time can provide an example.[36]

Lyautey credited success at Taza to the "patient and methodical preparation," the "prudent and clear-sighted political action," and the "meticulous organization" of the officers (especially Generals Maurice Baumgarten and Henri Gouraud) who directed the operations.[37] But L'Afrique française chalked up the progress of Moroccan pacification to the man at the top: "These results confirm in a stunning way General Lyautey's policy of penetration which consists, as we all know, of using *as a matter of course* the troops at his disposal as an effective aid in negotiation *by the sheer force* of their presence [and] only in *exceptional* circumstances in combat."[38] Contrary to the Taza hoopla, there were few parlays with native chiefs and many shots fired in anger.

The second step in the conquest of the Middle Atlas and the first "large scale" military operation among the mountain tribes would be the "dislocation" of the Zaïan bloc.[39] It, too, could not be achieved without a fight. In fact, the intellectual canon that now guided the Zaïan operations stressed the indispensability of combat to the conquest of the Berber tribes. "The Berber has never yielded to anything except force," wrote one of the L'Afrique française correspondents who rode with the French troops along the Zaïan frontier.

> Even those who most want to submit will not lay down their arms until they have been fired and only after we have begun to set up our posts in their country. No fraction will seek a reconciliation with us without first having had "the powder speak" and we must expect serious resistance from the most fanatical among them.[40]

French army ethnographers classified the Zaïan confederation into two branches. The first, the Aït Zgougou, was made up of the Mrabtin (on both sides of the Oum er Rebia north of El Bordj), the Aït Amar (around Oulmès), the Aït Ichkiken, the Aït Abdallah, and the Aït Abdous (all near El Hammán). Combined, their tents numbered between 3,350 and 3,600 and were under the command of Mohamed Aguebli. The second Zaïan branch was the Aït Yacoub, composed of the Bou Hassoussen (a submitted tribe around Moulay Bou Azza), the Aït Bou Haddou (on both sides of the Oum er Rebia and around Sidi Lamine), the Aït Krad (on both sides of the Oum er Rebia, but to the north and east of Khénifra) and the Aït Harkat (around Khénifra and Adersan on both the left and right banks of the Oum er Rebia). These tribes numbered between 4,000 and 4,200 tents and were commanded by Moha ou Hammou, since 1877 the acknowledged leader of the confederation, who through politics (one of his daughters was given in marriage first to Sultan Abd el-Aziz, then to Sultan Abd el-Hafid) and force had maintained Zaïan independence. All the tribes summered in the mountains and foothills of the Middle Atlas and wintered on the plains, transforming the landscape according to the season of the year with hundreds of chocolate-colored tents.[41]

From the start of France's intervention in Morocco, the Zaïan had demonstrated an "intransigent xenophobia." They had fought against the French in the Chaouïa in 1907 and 1908, harassed their march to Fez in 1911, and supplied arms and munitions to resistant Zaër, Beni Zemmour, Beni Mtir, and Beni Mguild tribesmen in 1912 and 1913. Political action had achieved only minor successes on the confederation's periphery (for example with the Bou Hassoussen) and no "serious fissure" had been opened up at its "core," despite repeated efforts to get Mohamed Aguebli, often at odds with Moha ou Hammou, to side with France. As the French moved closer to Moha, he intensified his resistance, calling for a holy war, multiplying his contacts with other Berber leaders, and stepping up his raids on the submitted tribes and French convoys. As so many times in the past, Lyautey concluded that powerful military action alone would bring about the "serious results" that pacification required.[42]

At the beginning of May 1914 Lyautey gave Henrÿs, whom he called a "past master" of both political and military action, the overall command of the Zaïan operations. He explained that the independent activities of the Meknès, Rabat, and Tadla commands had reached the limit of their effectiveness. The time had come for a "single authority" to assume full control for the conquest and rule of Zaïan territory. Lyautey described Zaïan country as a wedge, jutting between the northern and southern zones of the French occupation of western Morocco. It interrupted the "direct, natural, and normal" communication between Marrakesh and Fez via the Oum er Rebia and Khénifra and served as a "base of operations" for all the dissidents of central Morocco. Its continued existence "at the very heart of our occupation," he concluded, was "a permanent danger, and not just a passive danger, but an active one." Henrÿs's task was "to make this wedge disappear" by splitting off all the Zaïans on the right bank from the Berber bloc and establishing a line of posts "parallel to the crests of the Atlas."[43] Mangin's dream had become Henrÿs's next assignment.

Henrÿs planned to send three columns against Khénifra—one from the Région de Meknès under Lieutenant Colonel Henri Claudel, a second from the Région de Rabat under Lieutenant Colonel Guillaume Cros, and the third from the Territoire du Tadla under Colonel Noël Garnier-Duplessis. In touch with each other by wireless radio and informed by reconnaissance planes, these converging columns (with a total of 14,000 men) were to move across a terrain "marked by deep and difficult ravines" of which Henrÿs had little firsthand geographical knowledge and pass through tribal groups about which he had only skimpy political intelligence. It was a risky business.[44]

Henrÿs anticipated stiff resistance to his advance, yet he counted on tribal disagreements and the early defection of Mohamed Aguebli to work in his favor.[45] To weaken his enemy's resolve he spread the word that the French assault would come from three directions but remain under a single, unified command. In addition, he made it clear that the conditions for submission would be generous: the surrender of all rapid-fire rifles, the return of whatever goods or supplies had been taken from raids on French troops, and the payment of a small per-tent tax. The longer the tribe held out, however, the stiffer the penalty. Finally, Henrÿs authorized the liberal use of "political funds" for bribes and payoffs to informants and tribal leaders. There were thus material incentives to coming over quickly to the French.[46]

On the other hand, Henrÿs worried about Zaïan unity and Berber solidarity. Would the confederation shatter or stick together? And what stand would the Berbers of the mountains take?[47] "Given their grudges and jealousies, will Ali Amhaouch and Moha ou Saïd lend their rivals the support of their forces," a columnist for L'Afrique française wondered aloud, "or will they be satisfied to remain on the sidelines in the mountains, leaving the Zaïan on their own, quite content to see the authority of Moha ou Hammou founder on the field of battle?"[48] By month's end Henrÿs had some answers. He was sure that Ali Amhaouch and Moha ou Saïd were working in liaison with Moha ou Hammou. But he also knew that they had mistakenly targeted the Tadla column as the only one poised at Khénifra.[49] Although bothered by the prospect of Berber cooperation, Henrÿs seemed firmly in the saddle (or in this case the seat of his armored car) to direct events.

The three columns stepped off for Khénifra from their advance bases on 10 June on roads "that no Christian had ever walked" to reach a city "that no unbeliever had ever defiled." Henrÿs travelled with the Claudel column, the strongest of the three and the one intended to draw fire away from the other two. Even before Claudel set out from Aït Lias, however, Zaïan tribesmen, well armed with rapid-fire Lebel rifles and well supplied with ammunition, attacked him on three separate nights. On the second night French losses were "appreciable"—five killed, including one officer, and nineteen wounded.[50] To Henrÿs this confirmed Moha ou Hammou's "aggressive intent," a somewhat strange description of the motives of a Moroccan leader about to be set upon. He also noted somewhat apprehensively that Moha had the ability to move his forces against one or another of the French columns within the space of a single day.[51]

In the end the French strategy succeeded. Drawn north by the strength of the Claudel column, Moha ou Hammou allowed Cros and Garnier-Duplessis to advance without impediment. And Claudel's sudden move on the morning of the 10th caught Moha in the midst of making preparations for what would have been the fourth attack on the French camp in six nights. With a "vigorous offensive" supported by artillery, Claudel quickly overcame the hastily readied Zaïan defense, dispersing the Mrabtin toward the upper Oum er Rebia Valley, the rest of the Aït Zgougou toward El Hamman, and the Aït Yacoub toward the Mriret Plateau. On the 11th Claudel traversed the barley fields of Mriret without incident. In the narrow, rocky valley called the Teguet Pass, however, he encountered "sustained" sniper fire from Mrabtin sharpshooters, which delayed his arrival at El Bordj. From El Bordj the cavalry immediately crossed to the left bank of the Oum er Rebia and rode to within cannon shot of Khénifra. The rest of the column followed at daybreak on the 12th, fighting off Zaïan attacks from the mountains as it moved closer to the city. By positioning himself between the city and the mountains, Claudel hoped to cut off any Zaïan retreat so as to engage and defeat Moha ou Hammou decisively. But Khénifra had already been evacuated, prompting *L'Afrique française* to ask if the Zaïan were consciously making their capital a "new Moscow."[52]

By mid-morning on 12 June the three French columns had joined up on the left bank and were operating together. All day Zaïan and Chleuh tribesmen (from the Aït Ischak, Aït Youdi, and Aït Ichkern tribes) attacked the French vigorously and repeatedly. Despite "their tenacity and scorn for death," however, the Moroccans were repulsed by late afternoon. At day's end there were only five French killed and nineteen wounded, bringing to seven the number of dead on the two-day march into Zaïan country.[53] With slight injury Henrÿs had achieved his objective. He had eradicated the Zaïan wedge and firmly established himself all along the right bank of the Oum er Rebia. The French flag now billowed from the highest crenellation in Khénifra. But Henrÿs found himself in possession of a city and a land

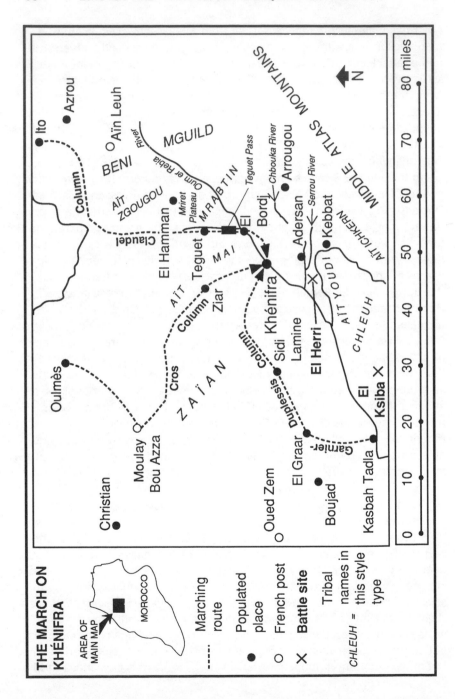

THE MARCH ON KHÉNIFRA

AREA OF MAIN MAP

MOROCCO

Marching route

Populated place

French post

Battle site

Tribal names in this style type

CHLEUH = this style type

emptied of people. All the tribes and their leaders with whom he had hoped to enter into relations "so easily" had fled before him, remaining "clearly hostile" to the foreign presence. This was a bitter disappointment for Henrÿs, although it should have come as no surprise.[54]

Khénifra was far from secure. During the night of 14-15 June the French camp was attacked on all sides. Although the enemy was driven back by artillery and machine-gun fire guided by searchlights, the next day Henrÿs was prompted to display his strength in an even more dramatic manner. Making good on his promise to respond to every pin prick with a punch, he marched two columns southwest toward Adersan, a Zaïan stronghold and one of the historic casbahs of Sultan Moulay Ismaïl, cannonading the villages *(dechras)* and casbahs of the Aït Harkat along the way.[55] Explaining Adersan, Henrÿs reminded Lyautey that they were now "masters" of more than 5,000 square kilometers of territory. "We must not only protect this land and its people against the attacks of Moha ou Hammou and his regulars, who have taken refuge towards Arrougou, but also against Ali Amhaouch's Berbers and the Chleuh of Moha ou Saïd." The march to Adersan proved that Henrÿs could strike in whatever direction he wanted on the left bank to bring confidence and security to the submitted tribes and frustrate any combined Berber action. Moreover, he could do all of this without getting caught up in a mountain war.[56]

Nevertheless, to and from Adersan Henrÿs sought decisive combat with the Zaïan without success. By retreating into the Middle Atlas they had brought pacification to a halt, perhaps, complained *L'Afrique française,* "for long months," while at the same time keeping up a determined pressure on the French through skirmishes, night attacks, and ambushes—guerrilla tactics that were deadly effective.[57] Given the ambiguity of this situation, Henrÿs did what he could while he waited. He ordered all markets under French control closed to the Zaïan and their allies, and all convoys going to or coming from these tribes halted and their goods confiscated.[58] For the time being Khénifra would be a pole of repulsion to France's enemies rather than a pole of attraction. And Henrÿs sent Professor Émile Laoust, his specialist in Berber languages, back to Rabat because for the moment he had no "influential Zaïan chiefs" with whom to talk.[59]

On the last day of June Henrÿs suddenly got the chance he wanted. Alerted to a gathering of Zaïan tribesmen near El Bordj, he marched north from Khénifra along the left bank of the Oum er Rebia. Just south of El Bordj he was attacked by "very numerous forces, armed with rapid-fire rifles and demonstrating much daring and audacity." Neither artillery nor machine-gun fire stopped them; they were turned back only after the French resorted to "vigorous bayonet charges." The "extraordinary stubbornness and tenacity" of the enemy stunned the French, even though Henrÿs soon realized that these troops were protecting the approaches to an important Zaïan encampment. The encounter was chalked up as a French victory, for the Zaïan dead numbered nine times those of the French, but French losses were high: seventeen killed (one officer) and seventy-seven wounded (two officers). It was Henrÿs's "first serious engagement" with the Zaïan, and although he had been unable to deliver the demoralizing blow—which L'Afrique française insisted did more for pacification than anything else—he expected a pause in Zaïan activity.[60]

The "irrepressible" Moha ou Hammou became even more audacious. Four days after El Bordj he sent 500 horsemen against a supply convoy escorted by Claudel's column. Following "several hours of combat and vigorous bayonet charges," the attackers were driven off, but French casualties—eleven killed (one officer) and thirty wounded—were significant. Henrÿs counted this as an act of desperation. He explained to Lyautey that despite the certainty of withering losses, Moha battled on to maintain his prestige and thus his hold over those tribes who were tottering on the brink of defecting to the French. This may have been wishful thinking. Even though the Mrabtins were indeed discouraged by the number of their casualties, Moha ou Hammou, unconquered in the field, still commanded the confederation's allegiance.[61]

Based on Zaïan realities, Henrÿs strengthened the safety of the right bank by posting a mobile group of four battalions at Khénifra under Lieutenant Colonel René Laverdure, a second to the east under Claudel, and a third to the west under Garnier-Duplessis. He further tightened the internal security of the occupied zone by using the troops at already-established posts as a second line of defense and ordering native irregulars and partisans (goums and groupes francs) to rove between two newly created posts (at Sidi Lamine and Mriret) to protect convoys and the submitted tribes from "bands of pillagers" and other stray dissidents. This defensive system, Henrÿs claimed, would hold the Berbers in check from the Guigou River in the Région de Fez to Beni Mellal in the Région de Marrakech until such time as Lyautey decided to continue the French expansion in the Middle Atlas.[62]

Henrÿs was clearly discouraged by the continued hostility of Moha ou Hammou whom he seemed to hold personally responsible for the Zaïan retreat into the mountains. According to Henrÿs, by terror and force Moha had pushed all those tribal fractions disposed to peace back into the hinterland, "interrupting all communication between them and us" and creating a barrier that French emissaries were unable to cross. What Moha had done, however, Mother Nature would undo, for at the onset of winter the Zaïan would be compelled to return to the lowland pastures of the valley of the Oum er Rebia. More than anything else, Henrÿs believed that this forced trek would weaken Moha's grip on the confederation and act as the prelude to its submission. Given his experience with the Beni Mtir and Beni Mguild the previous year, Henrÿs predicted that after a taste of winter's hardships it would take only "a matter of days" for the Zaïan to give up.[63]

Once the Zaïan confederation was subdued, Henrÿs thought it should be partitioned, ending forever its dominant place in the Middle Atlas. As far as he was concerned, the confederation's unity was only "artificial," forged by the violence and power of the "House of Hammou."[64] "I have always considered these family dictatorships in Berber territory to be temporary historical mistakes," he told Lyautey, "weighing heavily on peoples whose traditional social organization is completely opposed to them." To permit Moha ou Hammou to hold onto his "fief" after the Zaïan war was over would deny the Middle Atlas "the moral benefit of our liberating action." Perhaps of equal significance to the genesis of Henrÿs's partition plan was Moha's stubborn resistance. Henrÿs firmly believed that this—despite all Lyautey's talk about transforming adversaries into allies—ruled out any "future dealings" with him or his family.[65] Had Moha cooperated, everything might have been different.

To divide the Zaïan tribes Henrÿs recommended attaching the Aït Bou Haddou to the Territoire du Tadla; the Mrabtin and the other Aït Zgougou tribes to the Cercle des Beni Mguild in the Région de Meknès; the Aït Harkat (including the Aït Mai fraction) and the Aït Krad to a newly created Cercle de Khénifra; and the Aït Amar and the Bou Hassoussen to the Annexe d'Oulmès.[66] As important to the leadership and governance of the tribes was Henrÿs's "Berber policy" that would fashion their inner workings. Since the Berbers of the Middle Atlas were "so different in customs and mentality" from the tribesmen of the plains, Henrÿs decided in good *politique des races* fashion that they required distinct administrative regimes. He believed it would be a mistake to impose Makhzen institutions and their pashas, *caïds,* and judges *(cadis)*—what he called "the Makhzen patina"—on peoples who did not know or want them. To do this would repeat one of the errors of the Algerian conquest where a fixed set of rules had been applied everywhere without discrimination. For Henrÿs the success of French expansion in Morocco depended "a great deal" on the response of the tribes to the administrative organization they were given. And he was sure that the Berbers would react positively to the affirmation of their own institutions.[67]

Some of this Henrÿs had said before. In the "political instructions" to his field commanders, issued at the beginning of June, he warned against doing anything to upset Berber "customary law" by introducing either French or Muslim practices. "We will study the local institutions in order to make use of them, either by reinforcing them or by modifying them in a prudent way, without feeling ourselves bound in whatever we change by the Muslim forms that are in use elsewhere."[68] For example, Henrÿs considered the Berber village or tribal council (djemaa) as the authentic expression of Berber political life. It was thus a "convenient and appropriate" instrument through which to exercise French supervision and implement reforms—the elimination of all that was "anarchic" and "cruel"—and by which to ensure French authority. Regardless of the djemaa's pedigree and past importance, there was no doubt who would now be in charge. At the tribal level Henrÿs intended to handpick the representatives of each fraction to guarantee "the execution of our orders."[69] And at Khénifra he replaced the pasha with a djemaa of his own creation and choice, mocking the notion that this was a "republican institution" in accord with the popular will and sustained by the principle of election.[70]

Henrÿs also told his officers not to rely too much on the Arab families among the Berber population or to give them "a privileged position at the expense of purely Berber persons," even though it would be easy to do, if the latter did not speak Arabic. French ignorance of the Berber languages was only a "temporary difficulty," he insisted, which everyone had to work hard to remedy, so that French policy among the Berbers would not be guided by the Arabs. Finally, Henrÿs counselled never to link French authority with that of the Makhzen. "The Makhzen has had only a very weak hold on these people. It means nothing to them except unsuccessful attempts at domination, violence, and exactions." To appeal to the Berbers the French effort needed to take a "new form," divorced from the "purely Moroccan and Muslim traditions of the plains."[71] All of this betrayed an ignorance or a willful disregard of the connectedness of Moroccan society in an attempt to seduce the Zaïan into submission. At the same time, as politique des races or divide to rule, it ran counter to Lyautey's partnership with the sultan. But, most significant of all, it failed to stop Berber resistance to France.

The "Berber trinity" of Moha ou Hammou, Ali Amhaouch, and Moha ou Saïd spoiled the realization of Henrÿs's grand design. Acting in concert, Berbers from several tribes attacked Khénifra all during the month of July, and although each assault was turned back by French machine-gun and cannon fire, Henrÿs warned that it was "always possible" that a combined force of real importance might appear. In addition, he worried that enemy raiding parties would soon fall upon the submitted tribes. Acknowledging that this intense resistance to the French was the terrified reaction of people who were confronted with "an unprecedented disarray in their existence" (and thus it was not just the work of a few tyrannical leaders) Henrÿs still promised the collapse of the Zaïan bloc with only a "reasonable minimum effort." A solid defensive line centered on the posts at Khénifra, Mriret, and Sidi Lamine was to be the first step. Here the action of the Claudel and Garnier-Duplessis columns would assume greater importance. They would not only patrol the right bank, but exert military force wherever they could to keep the hostile left bank confederations separated, what Henrÿs called "detatching" the Zaïan from the Chleuh, the Berbers of the south. The second step—and this was the giant one—was to be a straight advance into the Middle Atlas from the direction of the Guigou River through the territory of the Beni Mguild.[72] By any measure this was an ambitious scheme.

The outbreak of the European war pushed off Henrÿs's military projects. The French were badly overextended at Taza and Khénifra where both operations had opened up wide fronts requiring extensive activity. When the needs of the Metropole forced the repatriation of thirty-seven battalions, Lyautey was permitted to leave his armature of advance posts intact, rather than abandon the interior for the coast. Using his own metaphor, he hollowed out the lobster, but left its shell.[73] Emboldened by what they took to be an all-out evacuation, Zaïan tribesmen attacked Khénifra and the departing troops with fury. From 4 August until almost the end of the month Khénifra was under attack "without interruption," making its supply a harrowing, albeit heroic enterprise.[74] Lyautey called the city the protectorate's "bastion" against the hordes of "hostile Berber masses" and declared that on its shoulders alone rested "the maintenance of our occupation."[75]

To keep the Berber forces divided Henrÿs relied on Claudel and Garnier-Duplessis. In separate actions they engaged Moha ou Hammou and Ali Amhaouch at Mahajibat, Bou Moussa, and Bou Arar on 19, 20, and 22 August and inflicted "considerable casualties." The result was a relaxation in Berber activity that permitted Henrÿs to declare his situation "notably improved," much less "unsettling" than it had been at mid-month.[76] By 1 September new troops replaced those sent to France, and Khénifra became the somewhat less embattled "keystone" of the Middle Atlas.

Lyautey described his mission as holding the Taza-Khénifra-Kasbah Tadla-Marrakesh-Agadir line with its "living barricade" of troops against those "resistant and warlike populations" who had "never lost the hope of ousting us" and of recovering "the freedom of chaos, pillage, and oppression which have benefitted them for centuries."[77] From September to November Khénifra stood fast despite Zaïan assaults and by November the attacks had decreased to the point where the French could speak of an "armed peace" between the two sides. Henrÿs was convinced that the threat to the city was over. He had proven that the war in Europe would not force a French retreat nor weaken his defense of Khénifra. Now both time and the weather would work for him.[78]

As winter approached, Henrÿs again counted on disagreements among the tribes to erode their unity and will to resist. Most of the Zaïan, whose traditional wintering ground was on the right bank, were now squeezed into a small triangle of land bounded by the Oum er Rebia, the Serrou River, and the wooded foothills of the Middle Atlas. Disputes had already erupted between them and the Aït Harkat, Moha ou Hammou's tribe of origin, which held the major part of the land on the left bank suitable for winter quarters. In addition, the spot where Moha ou Hammou had set up his own winter camp—at El Herri, eleven kilometers south of Khénifra—had for years been the object of strife between the Zaïan and the Aït Ichkern. As a result, despite threats and even punishment from Moha ou Hammou, a number of tribes or tribal fractions (the Aït Abdel Aziz, the Aït Mai, the Aït Lhassen, the Aït Bou Haddou, and the Aït Ichkern) had begun to make peaceful overtures to the French: to trade at Khénifra, to send their sick to the post's infirmary, or to start conversations about the conditions for their submission and return to the right bank. All of this led Henrÿs to believe that the tribes were "on the verge of coming over to us." Once the snows filled the valleys, he thought the resistance on the left bank would collapse.[79]

Suddenly, on the morning of 13 November Colonel René Laverdure, commander of the Territoire de Khénifra, marched against the Zaïan at El Herri. He planned to take Moha's main encampment by surprise, delivering the elusive "decisive blow" against the Zaïan and serving up Moha's head on a platter to the high command. Twice before Laverdure had asked permission for such a left-bank strike and both times it had been denied, not because it was forever out of the question, but because his troop strength at Khénifra was too weak or the risk of military entanglement in the mountains too great. Laverdure was told to confine himself to "limited action" on the right bank, protecting supply convoys, wood-gathering parties, and road-building crews. Frustrated by these mundane housekeeping chores and convinced that a dramatic success against the Zaïan was within his reach, Laverdure acted without telling his superiors what he was up to. The only document revealing his intentions was an order to his own command that he left behind, announcing that the Khénifra garrison was off to "annihilate" Moha's camp.[80]

At daybreak Laverdure's detachment (six companies, two batteries of sixty-five and seventy-five cannons, and one squadron of cavalry) reached the encampment at El Herri, which was comprised of about one-hundred tents. The surprise was complete. The first the Zaïan knew of the attack came in the rain of artillery shells that exploded in their midst. After the guns had turned the camp into a field of chaos, the cavalry put its inhabitants to flight. Those who escaped armed and uninjured regrouped on a hilltop south of the camp and were able to inflict "numerous losses" on their pursuers on horseback, fighting with such energy that the French had to rout them with infantry attacks. Only then could the French return to the business of the day: the sacking of the camp, which included the capture of two of Moha ou Hammou's wives. Moha himself, however, eluded his would-be captors.[81]

The road back to Khénifra was deadly. From the start the infantry was unable to move in safety without the protection of the artillery, and the rear guard was constantly under fire. After the troops had crossed the Chbouka River mid-morning, the rear guard was suddenly surrounded and overwhelmed by the "repeated and furious attacks" of tribesmen who seemed to come from all directions at once. In quick succession both gun batteries were captured and their crews killed. Then "several thousand" Zaïan turned on the rest of the detachment. Despite a desperate struggle, the French were overcome. Six hundred and thirteen officers and men, including Laverdure himself, died on the battlefield. Only the convoy of the wounded, sent ahead while the fighting was in progress, straggled into Khénifra. Even then, it barely made it through the gates of the city. Henrÿs later asserted that had the tribesmen not stopped to loot the bodies of the dead, Khénifra itself might have been lost. And with Khénifra would have gone the entire defensive network of the Berber front.[82]

The command of Khénifra immediately passed to Captain Pierre Croll. Once he had secured the city's defenses, Croll telegraphed the news of the disaster to Lyautey at Rabat and to Henrÿs at Fez. He told them that on the return from El Herri Laverdure had been attacked by 5,000 tribesmen and that his detachment had been "almost entirely annihilated." He asked that reinforcements be sent to Khénifra by forced march, since his garrison, now reduced to only three companies, was extremely vulnerable.[83] This was the first that Lyautey or Henrÿs had heard of the Laverdure expedition. The next morning as Croll was still piecing together the full story of the tragedy, Zaïan horsemen appeared on the hillcrests to the south and east of Khénifra. Motionless and silhouetted by the sun, they symbolized to Croll the abrupt change in French and Zaïan fortunes.[84]

Henrÿs wired Garnier-Duplessis to move his mobile group from El Graar to Khénifra and ordered the formation of a second mobile group at Ito under Lieutenant Colonel Joseph Dérigoin.[85] Henrÿs then left Fez for

Meknès where he telegraphed Lyautey that he planned to strike "hard and fast" so that the "Laverdure disaster" would not compromise the French situation throughout Morocco. It would be "a rapid, energetic action," he explained, employing all the means he had at his disposal. "Everyone, everywhere must be aware of the fact that our forces are numerous, that strong columns are already on their way to Khénifra, and that the repression will be swift."[86]

Garnier-Duplessis reached Khénifra on the 16th after fighting his way through "numerous groups" of Mrabtin and Aït Mai tribesmen at Djebel Bou Arrar. Two days later Henrÿs and Dérigoin arrived at the city without having encountered any opposition. With evident surprise Henrÿs noted that the countryside between Lias (where he had joined Dérigoin) and Khénifra was "completely empty." So was the area around the city. Once Garnier-Duplessis had entered Khénifra, the Zaïan, Aït Ichkern, and Aït Ischak prudently moved their camps from the Chbouka and Serrou Valleys and around El Herri into the mountains along the forest edge. From here they watched as French troop strength at Khénifra climbed to an all-time high (after Henrÿs's arrival) of more than 7,000 men.[87]

To display French force Henrÿs tramped the area between Khénifra and El Herri on 19 and 20 November, surveying the battle sites and burying the dead. Far off he saw the smoke from "numerous" camp fires and toward Arrougou he glimpsed "important assemblages" of Moroccan tribesmen, but they kept their distance. Henrÿs spared Lyautey the grisly details of his reconnaissance. "I will not stop to describe to you the horror of this field of combat, covered with hundreds of bodies completely stripped of their clothing and having lain on the ground for six days." The statistics were difficult enough to report. Thirty-three French officers, 200 French soldiers, 218 Algerian or Tunisian soldiers, 37 Moroccan soldiers, and 125 Senegalese soldiers—a total of 613 officers and men—had died at El Herri. This was 49.8 percent of the detachment of 43 officers and 1,187 men that Laverdure had led out of Khénifra. When the wounded were added to the dead, Henrÿs tallied the losses as 90 percent of the officers, 71 percent of the French soldiers, 54 percent of the Algerian-Tunisian soldiers, 78 percent of the Moroccan soldiers, and 56 percent of the Senegalese soldiers. All but seven bodies were recovered. (The missing seven had been taken by Moha ou Hammou as trophies of war or as the medium for a future exchange.) None had been decapitated or otherwise mutilated, except, as Henrÿs clinically put it, "by numerous postmortem dagger wounds." To the charge in lives for that single "disastrous day" was appended the price in weapons (the artillery pieces, 4 machine guns, and 630 rifles, carbines, or muskets), animals (62 horses,

56 mules), equipment, and personal effects.[88] All told, Laverdure's expedition had cost France dearly in men, materiel, and prestige.

Lyautey blamed the "inexcusable imprudence" of the march to El Herri on sheer adventuring and the quest for personal glory. He did not doubt that Henrÿs would draw the proper lesson from the disaster and preach it to all who would listen. Discipline, self-restraint, and sacrifice alone marked the path of patriotic duty in Morocco where one false step might fatally compromise everything that those, like Henrÿs himself, had worked for so hard and so long.[89]

Henrÿs, too, was convinced that there was no political or military justification for Laverdure's "act of indiscipline." It was certainly not needed to break up an incipient tribal coalition, nor to punish the tribes, nor to provoke their submissions, which both he and his intelligence officers had concluded were "imminent" anyway. Moreover, the operation was "poorly prepared and poorly executed" with troop strength at Khénifra less than half of what it had been at the end of September when Laverdure had been denied permission for any left-bank action precisely because of the weakness of his forces.[90]

Although Laverdure had been skilful and energetic in the defense of Khénifra following the outbreak of the European war, Henrÿs believed that he had never fully appreciated "the extraordinary offensive capability of the Berbers of the mountains." Obsessed by the notion of a "daring strike" against Moha ou Hammou whom he apparently brushed off "as just another black chieftain," Laverdure unwittingly led his men into an "anthill" where all the Zaïan, a large number of the Mrabtin and Aït Ichkern, and more than half of the Aït Ischak were concentrated. In truth, he probably never detected an enemy force, but once the fighting started at El Herri the countryside swarmed with armed tribesmen ready to enter the fray. In short order he was surrounded, overpowered, and destroyed.[91]

Lyautey's final word on Laverdure, which he communicated privately to Minister of War Alexandre Millerand, was that had he not died on the field of battle, he would have deserved *"the most severe punishment"* at the hands of a military tribunal. But, even more than Laverdure and his personal indiscipline, Lyautey fingered the doctrines of a "certain school" among the colonial military as the "true cause" of the El Herri disaster. In articles in major journals and in books written for the general public, in the mass-circulation Paris newspapers and in speeches in the Chamber of Deputies, Lyautey recognized the arguments, repeated over and over again, by the members of this school. The theme was always the same: The conquest of Morocco was too slow and too costly and ought to be placed in more capable hands. Large numbers of troops were being employed in a "passive, inert, timorous method of occupation," disguised by phrases such as "spot of oil," "progressive penetration," "the combination of politics and force," and other such drivel. What Morocco needed, these critics concluded, was vigorous and aggressive war making, led by audacious commanders who were able and willing to use force as the first, not the last resort. Without government response or reprimand this drumbeat, Lyautey insisted, was impossible to silence. Even Laverdure in whom both Henrÿs and Lyautey had once expressed great confidence had succumbed to its sound.[92]

The heart of the matter was more than an approach to colonial conquest. It was a military system that rewarded only deeds of blood and glory. Lyautey urged the government to start recognizing the heroism and sacrifice of the defense as well as the offense and to compensate things other than "acts of war." He expressed his gratitude for the quick promotions of General Henrÿs, Colonel Garnier-Duplessis, and Captain Croll in the wake of the El Herri events, but insisted that others just as meritorious had been passed over because their labors had not been on the battlefield. The telling example was the stalled promotion of Colonel Henri Simon, head of the Service des Renseignements, who was charged with the delicate, but largely behind-the-lines mission of setting up and implementing "the entire native policy," which Lyautey considered "the most effective element" of French operations in Morocco. In short, Lyautey not only wanted punishment for those who sowed the seeds of indiscipline by preaching acts of war, but promotions for those who through "wisdom, strength, and discipline" had the courage to avoid them.[93]

In this letter to Millerand, Lyautey underscored as he had for years that force was not the first and best element in his "method" of colonial conquest. What he did not say was that since political and economic action—and surely not the "Berber policy"—had failed to bring the Berber tribes of the Middle Atlas to heel, force was the only element he could rely on. Unfortunately, despite his best efforts, Lyautey could not get the Zaïan to play their assigned role in the pacification process. Thus, although Lyautey's approach to the problem of Moroccan pacification differed markedly from that of his critics, his solution remained essentially the same. Laverdure's only mistake—but it was a deadly one—was to have used force irresponsibly.

In the aftermath of El Herri the residency emphasized its swift response to the disaster—the quick concentration of French forces at Khénifra, the immediate return to the El Herri battlefield, the victorious reengagement of Zaïan tribesmen. All this had reestablished "the prestige of our arms, momentarily compromised." "Thanks to the rapid action of General Henrÿs," went the official version, "the El Herri incident, however regrettable and unfortunate, will remain purely a local affair and will not have any negative impact on the whole of our political and military situation in Morocco."[94]

Privately Lyautey was less sanguine. Despite the brave communiqués designed to save face, he admitted that the consequences of El Herri were "deplorable." "I do not believe," he candidly told Millerand,

> that in our entire colonial history there has ever been a case of the destruction of such an important force, of the loss of all of its officers (except some wounded who had been evacuated at the very beginning of the fight), of the disappearance of so much materiel and booty of war.

And it could have been worse. For forty-eight hours after he learned of the disaster, Lyautey worried that Khénifra itself would fall, signalling "the total collapse of our establishment in Morocco." The French had held on, but only by the skin of their teeth.[95]

The failure of the tribes to follow up on their victory had alone saved Khénifra. Momentarily incredulous at their battlefield success and without a plan to capitalize on it, they were unprepared to go further. Moreover, Henrÿs reported that after the initial French attack on Moha ou Hammou's camp, the Aït Ichkern and other Zaïan fractions actually joined in its plunder, assuming that Moha was beaten and that what was left was theirs for the taking. Only when it became apparent that the French were not having an easy time on the road home did they become the sole target of the tribes. In sum, Henrÿs believed that the victory had been tart for Moha ou Hammou and the Aït Harkat, even though it had been sweet for the tribes.[96]

Nevertheless, in the days that followed Moha ou Hammou reasserted his leadership of the confederation by displaying the proofs of his triumph throughout the mountains. Rifles and cannon, swords and revolvers were difficult to deny. "One moment shaken by the attack and pillage of his camp and his own flight," Lyautey recounted with a mix of surprise and admiration, "the next his balance regained, his authority and his prestige increased." Whatever the real story of El Herri, Moha had fashioned his own tale of personal victory. And Lyautey felt compelled to point out again to Paris how these disastrous French dashes into battle aided all the Mohas of the Middle Atlas by perpetuating the "legend" of Berber invincibility.[97]

Lyautey still believed that he would be able to handle the situation along the Berber front even after the unfortunate change in circumstances. But there could be little hope of striking progress. He predicted continued resistance in the Middle Atlas until the war in Europe was over; then Morocco would need one more push. "It will be necessary to move into the mountains vigorously and simultaneously with well-organized, well-equipped, and strongly led columns from the south of the Région de Fez, from Khénifra, from the east of the Région de Marrakech, and probably from eastern Morocco and Bou Denib in order to converge on the Moulouya." This was really a small matter, Lyautey claimed with breezy and unjustified optimism, "neither long nor difficult," a business of "some months at the very most." And the result would be the "final liquidation of the conquest of Morocco."[98]

In the meantime throughout the Middle Atlas the call was sounded once more to expel the invader. The tribes in the Région de Marrakech around Azilal—the Aït Abbès, Aït Bouzid, Aït Attab, Aït Messat, Aït Atta d'Amalou, Beni Mellal, Krarza, and Beni Ayad—showed considerable interest in the task, and the Aït Mitrad, Aït Izdeg, and Ahel Khora (Aït Youssi) began to send warriors to Moha ou Hammou's camp. And there was renewed cooperation among Moha ou Hammou, Ali Amahouch, and Moha ou Saïd.[99] Coupled with unfavorable word about the French progress in the European war and Moroccan unease over Turkish intervention on the German side, which put a Muslim sultan at Constantinople in the enemy camp, El Herri caused "a great effervescence throughout the entire Berber bloc."[100] Still, there was no "combined movement," no general insurrection against the French. Henrÿs readied himself instead for smaller resistance activity, which he promised to stamp out vigorously, for he noted that like the fire under the ash, the flame could suddenly reappear and quickly set the countryside ablaze.[101]

Henrÿs reorganized his command into three regional military sectors: the Région de Fez (including the Territoire de Taza), the Région de Meknès (minus the Annexe des Cherada), and the Région du Tadla-Zaïan (comprising the Territoire du Tadla, the Cercle d'Oulmès, and the Cercle de Khénifra). As before, his overall goal was to keep up a constant pressure on the hostile tribes while shielding the submitted tribes from unsettling outside interference. To do this Henrÿs relied on the two mobile groups from Ito and Kasbah Tadla that would also cover Khénifra, still the keystone of the Tadla-Zaïan front, but now protected by only a defense garrison, making any repetition of Laverdure's "reckless initiative" impossible.[102]

Garnier-Duplessis was put in command of the Région du Tadla-Zaïan and instructed to maintain a "rigorous and just authority" over the submitted tribes that alone would prevent the spirit of revolt from touching them. Henrÿs warned him of possible attacks from the left bank by the Zaïan and Aït Ichkern, but he also predicted a series of new submissions, given the French rebound from El Herri and the onset of winter. To speed up the process Henrÿs ordered an economic blockade of the Middle Atlas, closing the markets of El Bekrit, Kebbat, and Beni Mellal to all but the submitted tribes. And convinced that submission was only lasting when paid for at a high price, he insisted on a "war penalty" of five douros per tent and one horse for every ten tents that crossed to the right bank of the Oum er Rebia. In addition, he specified the surrender of one rifle for every four tents and the return of all materiel taken from French troops at El Herri or elsewhere. Once agreed to, the conditions had to be fulfilled promptly or the war penalty doubled. For tribal fractions that had once submitted, then chosen dissidence, Henrÿs demanded repayment of the original submission price plus a fine of twenty douros and one rifle per tent.[103]

Henrÿs's peace package had few takers. Although the Zaïan were driven by snow and freezing temperatures to the pasture lands of the right bank, they refused to submit or to be permanently expelled from their lands at cannon point.[104] Month after month they moved back and forth across the Oum er Rebia, evading the French patrols as best they could and engaging them in combat whenever necessary. In March Dérigoin's mobile group swept the right bank and Garnier-Duplessis scoured the left bank north of Khénifra. Near Lias Dérigoin was attacked by a small band of Zaïan tribesmen whom he had little difficulty dispersing. Garnier-Duplessis had a tougher time. On his way out he found the countryside empty, but on the way back he was "assailed by numerous and aggressive groups" of horsemen. For a moment it may have seemed like a repetition of El Herri, but in the end he inflicted "serious losses" on the enemy, while sustaining only minor casualties (one dead, eight wounded) himself.[105]

Despite these incidents, Henrÿs remained convinced that the Mrabtin, the Zaïan, and the Chleuh had "exhausted their strength" and were unable to mount a real offensive against him. He still considered Moha ou Saïd "a very serious troublemaker," but, according to French reports, the Berber leader had "lost ground" with the Aït Ouirah, some of whom had opened conversations on the terms of their submission with the officers at Kasbah Tadla. Moha ou Hammou's resources were also dwindling and the moment was coming when Henrÿs believed that he, too, would no longer be listened to. Nevertheless, Henrÿs acknowledged Moha's continuing influence, admitting that "it would have been valuable to have had him attached to our cause, even secretly, from the very beginning."[106]

In truth, up to this point in time the Zaïan campaign had been a stunning example of the failure of political action to aid the military conquest. Neither Moha ou Saïd nor Moha ou Hammou had responded to the repeated French efforts to make contact. Only Mohamed Aguebli had helped and then just "a little bit" by staying neutral while Claudel's column marched on Khénifra.

On the other hand, Henrÿs wondered aloud what real help these "petty Berber chieftains" could be anyway. Unlike the powerful lords of the High Atlas, who commanded the obedience of their subjects, these Middle Atlas leaders were tethered to the tribal will. Unfortunately, Henrÿs had reached this conclusion rather late in the game. He began the Zaïan campaign believing that he soon would be negotiating peace terms with Moha ou Hammou and for this purpose he had brought both gold coin and a professor of Berber languages along with him. In the end, neither the money nor the linguist had been of any use.[107]

While Henrÿs continued to predict the collapse of Berber resistance, the attacks persisted. The general intensified his economic warfare, now determined that the tribes would either submit or starve. In May he ordered Garnier-Duplessis to cross to the left bank and confiscate or destroy the crops of the Aït Roboas. This deliberate provocation brought together a "large hostile force" of between 4,000-5,000 Chleuh from Beni Mellal and El Ksiba, which attacked Garnier-Duplessis south of Kasbah Tadla on 15 and 16 May at Sidi Sliman and Oued Bokhari. He broke their assaults (which were "especially violent" on the second day) with cannon fire, then went on the offensive and pursued them to Beni Mellal. The Chleuh counted 300 dead and 400 wounded compared with the 3 French dead and 5 wounded. This was the sort of one-sided victory that instantly restored credibility in French force and brought a flurry of submissions. "Wherever we wish," Garnier-Duplessis boasted, "we can strike with force and command obedience," even though he knew the mountains remained out of his reach. The action earned him promotion to the rank of brigadier general and *L'Afrique française* claimed that as a result of his *"action de force"* an "absolute calm" had returned to the Middle Atlas, discouraging even Moha ou Saïd who had quit Beni Mellal for a high mountain casbah. Once again, force—not politics or economics—had been decisive against the Berbers and had been rewarded in a substantial way.[108]

The quiet on the Zaïan front lasted six months. Then on 11 November 1,200 to 1,500 Zaïan, Aït Ichkern, Aït Ischak, and Aït Bou Haddou tribesmen attacked Garnier-Duplessis while he was escorting a convoy from Khénifra. It was a "short, but violent and bloody" encounter. The Moroccans fought with such a daring and determined fury, with such "an absolute scorn for death" that they came to within fifty meters of the French lines before being stopped. Only "vigorous bayonet charges" dispersed them. French casualties were insignificant (only three killed and twenty-two wounded), but once Henrÿs confirmed that "all the Zaïan fractions" had participated in the attack, indicating a renewed Zaïan solidarity, he responded with a powerful demonstration of force.[109] With both mobile groups under his command, he quickly moved southeast of Mriret toward the Oum er Rebia, sweeping the right bank of the river where Zaïan and Mrabtin tribesmen had pitched their tents. From a high point overlooking the valley his artillery pounded the enemy camps at will. The operation was lethal but it did not end Zaïan resistance.[110]

In January 1916 the Zaïan once again crossed the Oum er Rebia. They set up their winter camps inside French lines in the area between Sidi Lamine, Lias, and the Teguet Pass. There were small raids on the submitted tribes and rumors of sterner plans, fanned by reports that the Zaïan had chosen a new "young and ardent" war chief. The Zaïan camps were troublesome, but Henrÿs's persistent nightmare was the formation of a substantial war party that would cut French communications between Khénifra and Taza. To ensure Khénifra's supply he ordered both mobile groups to the city. En route from Sidi Lamine the Garnier-Duplessis group attacked 200 Chleuh warriors (on 16 January) and two days later was attacked in turn by Zaïan tribesmen who were driven off by "a vigorous bayonet attack by the Legion and a charge by the spahis." All the way to Khénifra "numerous enemy bands" also harassed the second group commanded by Colonel Pierre Thouvenel. Both groups reached Khénifra on 20 January and resupplied the city. However, when they returned to Mriret, they were both attacked in force by Zaïan and Mrabtin tribesmen. In the fight that followed the Moroccans lost 200 warriors, while the French had 25 killed (1 officer) and 56 wounded. Despite another encounter that the French insisted had made a "strong impression" on the enemy, there was no end to the resistance.[111]

Throughout 1916 Lyautey described his theater of operations as a trapezoid with corners at Taza, Beni Mellal, Gourrama, and Debdou whose western side (the Taza-Beni Mellal line) was dotted with French advance posts. Facing the Zaïan was the post at Aïn Leuh, which served as the operational center for the mobile group of Meknès, while farther south the post at Beni Mellal levelled French cannon on "the most important market of the left bank of the Oum er Rebia," ensuring the "strategic mastery" of the plain between the river and the mountains and contributing to the economic blockade of the Zaïan tribes. "The occupation of Beni Mellal marks an important phase in our methodical seizure of these complicated regions," noted L'Afrique française. "But at this time we cannot go farther without risking an extremely painful mountain war."[112]

In November Lyautey decided to take the risk. He authorized the occupation of the upper valley of the Moulouya in order to complete the isolation of the Zaïan. This time, however, Henrÿs would not be in charge. Eager to put in time on the European front, he had accepted a command in France.

His successor was Colonel Joseph Poeymirau, Henrÿs's second at Meknès and a long-time Lyautey disciple, drenched in the mentor's doctrine. From opposite sides of the mountains Poeymirau's mobile group from Meknès and Colonel Paul Doury's mobile group from Bou Denib were to link up on the Moulouya in spring 1917. In preparation for this transmountain venture Poeymirau first established a post at El Bekrit on the northeastern edge of Zaïan country, forcing the submission of the Aït Abdi, the Aït Zgougou of Mohamed Aguebli, and the Aït Lias. (Aguebli himself, long a fence-straddler when it came to cooperation with the French, was killed in the post's inaugural bombardment.) El Bekrit protected Poeymirau's right flank from any sudden Zaïan attack and split the Zaïan off from the hesitant or unsubmitted fractions of the Beni Mguild, ever ready to join a good fight. At the same time the mobile group from Debdou worked the middle Moulouya and the mobile group from Fez moved among the Aït Seghrouchen and the Marmoucha to distract or immobilize other potentially troublesome tribes. As a result, Poeymirau had no difficulty keeping his rendezvous with Doury in early June. Their march opened the first French path across the Atlas— "the biggest step taken in Morocco since the Taza link"—which Doury secured by establishing a camp at Kasbah El Makhzen and that won for Poeymirau his promotion to the rank of brigadier general.[113]

The paths into and across the Atlas were themselves signs of the end of Zaïan invulnerability. Despite the terrain, supplying El Bekrit proved no difficulty for the French and within three months the troops of the Meknès region had built a road that could manage truck traffic. On the other side of the Atlas the soldiers of Bou Denib opened a road to Rich and Colonel Doury promised that an automobile track over the Atlas through the Telremt Pass would be ready in spring 1918. By summer army engineers planned to have completed a motor road from Tafilalet to Meknès, bridging the Moulouya at Trik El Bab. (To demonstrate the speed of change in the Atlas Lyautey left Rabat by automobile on 10 October and reached Timhadit, southeast of Meknès, the same day. The following day at mid-afternoon he was at Trik El Bab.) Southeastern Morocco was moving closer to the rest of the protectorate, shifting its center of gravity from Bou Denib to Kasbah El Makhzen and its center of supply from Colomb-Béchar to Meknès. More important, there had been a successful separation or "compartmentalization" of the Moroccan resistance, which Lyautey hoped would lead inexorably to its destruction. A kind of political strangulation would now take place within the new boundaries in the Middle Atlas, tightened by the French ability to move more rapidly in the mountains than they ever had before.[114]

Lyautey targeted the upper Moulouya as the heart of all French political and military action in 1918 and predicted that resistance would "fritter away automatically" as more and more of the "peaceful populations" of the mountains, freed from the double terrors of chaos and war, began to support the French. The "spot of oil," Lyautey argued, would penetrate the Middle Atlas both politically and economically just as it had the plains.[115] This did not happen. The Zaïan did not challenge the new posts created along the Meknès-Tafilalet road: El Hamman and Itzer joined El Bekrit along the northeastern flank of Zaïan country, Kasbah El Makhzen (also called Ksabi Ech Cheurfa) was raised to post status, and Midelt was set up on the north face of the High Atlas. However, the tribes located to the east of these posts (the Aït Seghrouchen, the Aït Youssi, the Beni Alaham, and the Marmoucha) menaced their security in summer 1918 on rumors that the French would soon be forced to evacuate the mountains because of the worsening war situation in Europe. In mid-June one of Poeymirau's detachments was attacked at the Tarzeft Pass. He counterattacked successfully, but it took him three days and the full strength of his mobile group to regain complete control of the pass. When the fighting was over (and the French battle citations showed that it had been tough), Poeymirau claimed he had inflicted "severe losses" on the tribesmen, eliminating the threats to the posts and the fear of any union of tribal forces on either side of the French road. Lyautey called it another "brillant succès" for the mobile group of Meknès and undoubtedly it was, but it was not the kind of easy triumph that he had promised Paris. Ironically, the best news of spring and early summer 1918 was the death by natural causes of Ali Amhaouch.[116]

An uprising in the Tafilalet jeopardized the French position in the Middle Atlas. Although the French had long been interested in occupying the Tafilalet to ensure the "complete security" of the South Oranais, the upper Moulouya had rightly taken precedence.[117] Nevertheless, in December 1917 Colonel Doury marched to Tighmart and installed a resident French mission to counter a rumored German influence. Lyautey, who still remembered the incandescence of that desert oasis in 1906, warned against getting involved in any military action that might divert attention from the "principal objective" on the upper Moulouya and create any "new problem" that could be "particularly difficult to resolve."[118] What he feared might happen did. The Aït Atta, who occupied the territory between the Dadès, the Tafilalet, the High Atlas, and the desert, were so agitated by the tiny, but very visible, French presence that Lyautey was forced to send Doury extra troops just in case the situation got out of hand. "We are the ones," Lyautey complained to Doury, "who have deliberately provoked this difficulty, whereas it would have been so simple to stick with the status quo." Lyautey lectured him on how any trouble in the Tafilalet would compromise the overall military program in Morocco. And for what? The Algerian-Moroccan south was a land of "very seductive mirages," but little else, at least when compared with regions that did have an economic future, like the Moulouya Valley or the forests of the Atlas. His Horace Greeley-like advice to Doury and the young officers around him was to "look north," for there "and only there" was there any reason for an important French effort.[119]

Drawn back to the Tafilalet by the continued tribal "effervescence" coupled with the assassination of the mission's native interpreter, Doury marched the palm groves in force at the end of July, supported by artillery and aircraft. On 9 August he engaged a "powerful force" of 1,500 tribesmen in a "very hard fight" at Gaouz, which ended in hand-to-hand combat. He reported that he had "almost annihilated" the enemy, but in the process had lost 200 of his own men as well as equipment, horses, and mules.[120] This "bloody and glorious affair" put Lyautey in a tight spot. Again he was being diverted from the main task on the upper Moulouya. He told Doury that Gaouz had seriously affected his overall program, forcing its modification at the precise moment when events in France and Morocco favored action in the north. He hoped that the predicament in this "most peripheral of zones" could be handled quickly so as not to continue to weigh heavily on the situation elsewhere.[121]

It could not be. Once fully apprised of the action at Gaouz, Lyautey decided that the "decisive defeat" of the enemy was the only way to end the matter in the Tafilalet for good. This would take still more troops and more time. To ensure that Doury would not be suddenly overwhelmed Lyautey asked for military assistance from Algeria, explaining his temporary embarrassment by insisting that Doury had been caught by surprise amidst a religious uprising fueled by German propaganda.[122] For his part Doury added insult to injury by remaining cavalierly insensitive to the problems he had created. "It is inadmissible," Lyautey told the colonel, "that I am kept so poorly informed, particularly at this moment when all political and military action in Morocco is paralyzed by the Tafilalet question."[123]

To straighten things out Lyautey put Poeymirau in charge of subduing the Tafilalet, now joined to his command at Meknès. Lyautey confessed that the Tafilalet was having "the most serious and regretable consequences" everywhere and blamed Doury for "grave mistakes and errors of vision" before, during, and after the battle of Gaouz. Doury had had no right, Lyautey complained, to run the risk of attacking a strong war party with such a small force of his own, with troops that were exhausted, and without a line or base of supply. Gaouz could have easily turned into another "great disaster" for France. Lyautey wanted no more of these "adventurous side trips" into areas where there was no need to go. He ordered Poeymirau to settle on a "limited and practical program" to keep the Tafilalet from interfering with what was going on in the rest of Morocco and Algeria. Think of the Tafilalet as an "hors d'oeuvre," he suggested. Never mistake it for the main course.[124]

Getting out of the Tafilalet was difficult. From the beginning of September to the end of October Poeymirau battled enemy *harkas* with all the force he could muster. Lyautey urged him on—"bombardments, destruction of villages [*ksours*] and gardens, inexorable sanctions and reparations"—so that the Tafilalet would remember the touch of French force for a long time to come.[125] Yet two months after Poeymirau's return to Meknès, the Tafilalet erupted again in "a large wave of revolt" involving thousands of tribesmen. Poeymirau arrived with reinforcements in January 1919 and fought a series of battles throughout the month until he was seriously wounded in the chest by the accidental explosion of an artillery shell. The "complete destruction" of the enemy was left to Colonel Antoine Huré who finished the task on the last day of January. Finally and at great cost the Tafilalet seemed quiet.[126]

For a time the Tafilalet had been an "open wound"—a Moroccan Verdun —draining the protectorate's lifeblood. Lyautey correctly realized that whatever resources he spent there would not be replenished. The French government would support him at Taza and at Khénifra because the economic development of a "productive Morocco" was in the metropolitan interest. The Tafilalet was something else again for which even the specter of German agents among the date palms—whose ingenuity, Lyautey once admitted, could stump Sherlock Holmes or even Balzac's heroes—could not generate much enthusiasm in Paris. In addition, the Tafilalet trouble stiffened the Middle Atlas resistance. At one time or another each of the posts along the upper and middle Moulouya came under siege with relief arriving only bit by bit after the last shots had been fired in the Tafilalet.[127]

Eventually political quarrels among the Zaïan tribes contributed to the confederation's demise. One by one the sons of Moha ou Hammou began conversations with the French: Hassan in December 1917, Bouazza in January 1918, Amarok in February. To be sure this was not surrender, yet this "first sign of a spirit of conciliation," noted the commander at Khénifra, was "an event of capital importance."[128] Then in June 1918 Ou El Aïdi, a nephew of Moha ou Hammou and the bitter rival of his cousin, Hassan, presented himself at Khénifra and offered the submission of his fractions for guns and money. The French reasoned that he would use both against Hassan and, unwilling to play a "dangerous double game," refused to go along. The hope was that the sons of Moha would finally lead their father to Khénifra (if he did show up, Lyautey's standing orders were to treat him "with all the respect and etiquette owed to a leader who had fought valiantly") and no one wanted to do anything to spoil that chance.[129] In the end the submissions of the sons of Moha ou Hammou and Ou El Aïdi were still more than two years away, and that of the "old caïd" never came.[130]

Nevertheless, the connections with individual Zaïan leaders paid off. Based on the contacts and information of the brothers Hammou and Ou El Aïdi, the French decided to move against the Mrabtin and the Aït Bou Haddou in the spring of 1920. This action to the north and south of Khénifra came after almost six years of inactivity along the Oum er Rebia and therefore required some explanation. Poeymirau maintained that the posts on the Moulouya had not done what had been expected of them and in fact during the long Tafilalet crisis they had caused more grief than they were worth. During the best of times, the posts controlled only the territory within cannon shot of their defenses and during the worst, they were a "dead weight" because of the difficulties of supplying them when under siege. Like Henrÿs, Poeymirau believed that the "only really practical way" to force the Zaïan bloc to submit was to deny the tribes access to the pasture lands of the right bank of the Oum er Rebia. Although this had been tried before without great success by roving mobile groups on the right bank, Poeymirau now wanted to control the fording spots on the river by setting up posts or blockhouses on the left bank. Caught in the posts' crossfire or chased from the riverbank by mobile "police" units, the transhumant tribes would ultimately bow to the reality of French force and give in.[131]

Under Poeymirau's overall command, troops from Meknès and Tadla crossed the eastern line of French occupation in the Middle Atlas at two points. On 18 April the Meknès group marched five kilometers southeast of Mriret to Taka Ichian and two weeks later on 2 May the Tadla group crossed the Oum er Rebia fifteen kilometers south of Khénifra and advanced five kilometers to the Zaouïa des Aït Ischak. The equidistant marches brought forth equal responses: The French were resisted every step of the way. Nevertheless, once at Taka Ichian, the road to the Oulrès Plateau (where the French would set up a post at Amassin) was clear. Poeymirau called that short trek a "military promenade." The Aït Abdel Aziz fraction of the Mrabtin (580 tents or almost one-third of the Mrabtin tribe) quietly submitted and a second fraction, the Aït Sidi Ali, began negotiations in earnest. Similarly, after the French occupied Aït Ischak, the Aït Bou Haddou requested terms, and the Aït Yacoub ou Aïssa indicated their willingness to follow suit, if the French would guarantee them protection against the unsubmitted mountain tribes. In the end Poeymirau established three posts along the left bank of the Oum er Rebia—at Amassin, at El Bordj north of Khénifra, and at Tadjemout midway between Khénifra and the Aït Ischak—and predicted that this "nibbling away" at the Zaïan bloc would soon finish it off.[132]

The successful spring campaign culminated with the "official act" of submission by Hassan, his brothers, and their allies. Poeymirau met them in Khénifra on 2 June and accepted their capitulation in Lyautey's name. Within the year Hassan would be pasha of Khénifra and Amarok his *khalifa*, hailed as solid partisans of France. President Alexandre Millerand wired his congratulations and the "ardent thanks" of the republic to Poeymirau and his troops for their success in obtaining the surrender of "the sons of the Zaïani" and the restitution of the materiel taken at El Herri. The souvenirs, if not the memory of the November 1914 defeat, were no more. In six weeks Poeymirau had expanded the French zone of occupation to the left bank of the Oum er Rebia, bringing nearly 3,000 tents under French protection. He had ended Khénifra's isolation and established the Oum er Rebia as a "solid barrier," permitting the organization of the right bank in complete security at long last and making "inevitable" the submission of the rest of the Zaïan confederation. Only 2,500 Zaïan tents remained beyond the French grasp and some of their makers had already begun talking to the French.[133] The Zaïan future looked bleak.

In spring 1921 the Zaïan suffered another setback. Moha ou Hammou was killed in a skirmish between resistant and collaborating Zaïan tribesmen on the Mezghouchen Plateau. *L'Afrique française* recalled that for more than forty years Moha had "incarnated" the spirit of independence of one of the most important Berber federations of unsubmitted Morocco. Despite reverses, rivals, and defections from his cause, he had remained steadfast in his opposition to the French, had been an "implacable foe" who embodied the endurance and defiance of the Zaïan and, as a sort of Vercingetorix of the Middle Atlas, had become a hero of Berber independence, even national resistance. In the end he had lost everything to the French—his sons, his country, his life. They imagined that his death would cause "real despair" among the Zaïan and hurry their defeat.[134]

At the news of Moha's death the French slated the last bit of unconquered Zaïan territory for immediate conquest. The Bekrit massif (called the "Bekrit pocket" or the "Bekrit hernia") received both political and military attention. The sons of Moha ou Hammou brought an important tribal fraction over to the French in May, then in September Poeymirau coordinated a three-pronged attack on the massif to finish off the resistance. From El Bekrit, General Jean Théveney's mobile group marched west to the Arhoun

Plateau while Colonel Henri Freydenberg's mobile group moved east from Taka Ichian onto the Mazemma Plateau. Théveney encountered "stubborn opposition" but Freydenberg had an easy time of it. Coming at the target from different directions, the two groups made visual contact before noon, while a column of partisans, guided by Moha's sons, occupied the Tizza Plateau, menacing the defenders from behind. By nightfall all three units had achieved their military objectives and within days the submissions of tribal fractions began. The Bekrit pocket ceased to exist.[135]

The seven-years' Zaïan war was over. Winning it had proven more difficult than the French had ever expected. The Zaïan withdrawal into the mountains and their stubborn refusal to return "chez eux" had left the French in possession of a land emptied of people.[136] This was not, however, territory abjectly handed over to the conqueror. Khénifra and French forces on both sides of the Oum er Rebia remained the targets of furious Zaïan attacks for years. The "massacre" at El Herri was only the most dramatic sign of the fierce and constant Zaïan determination to oust the invader.

Zaïan resistance challenged Lyautey's notions about a peaceful, methodical, and inexpensive conquest of Morocco. Faced with metropolitan demands for budget cuts and troop reductions, he revised his plans and invented a new language. Lyautey insisted that his goal had never been the occupation nor even the pacification of "geographical Morocco," but only of "useful Morocco" (Maroc utile), the part of the country that had an evident economic, military, or political importance. Any region where French effort required a financial and military expenditure out of proportion to the return—"useless Morocco"—would obviously remain untouched. He promised that all Maroc utile would be in French hands by 1923.[137]

With this in mind the French continued their expansion in the Middle Atlas, from El Bekrit and Itzer west along both sides of the Middle Atlas peaks, from Rhorm El Alem northeast to El Ksiba, and from Aït Ischak southeast to Tinteghaline and Bou Tciouanine among the Aït Ichkern. By mid-June 1922 Poeymirau was in full control of the upper Moulouya River and both sides of the Middle Atlas from El Bekrit to the point where the headwaters of the Moulouya and the El Abid Rivers took their separate courses, one to the Mediterranean, the other to the Atlantic. He had also cut a "new, direct, and easy" passage across the Middle Atlas.[138]

On the military charts Poeymirau's accomplishment looked impressive, but the progress of tribal pacification was less sure. In April 1922 at El Ksiba (the site of the 1912 battle with Mangin) Colonel Freydenberg's mobile group confronted Moha ou Saïd, the single survivor of the once-potent Middle Atlas triumvirate and still the "apostle of resistance" to the Chleuh.

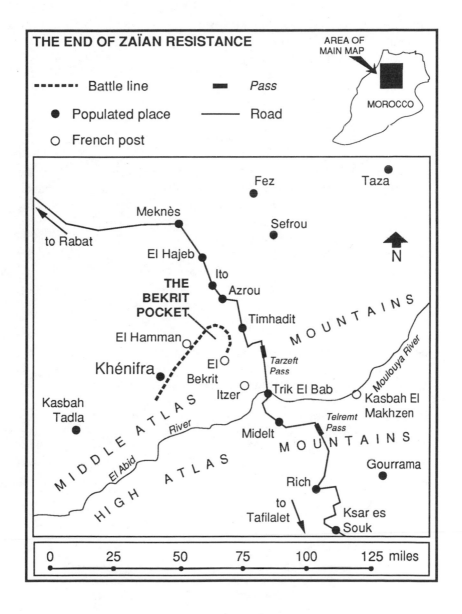

THE END OF ZAÏAN RESISTANCE

- - - - - - Battle line ▬ Pass
● Populated place ─── Road
○ French post

AREA OF MAIN MAP

MOROCCO

Fez
Taza
Meknès
Sefrou
to Rabat
El Hajeb
Ito
THE
BEKRIT
POCKET
Azrou
Timhadit
El Hamman
Khénifra
El Bekrit
Tarzeft Pass
Itzer
Trik El Bab
Kasbah El Makhzen
Kasbah Tadla
River
El Abid
Midelt
Telremt Pass
Gourrama
Rich
to Tafilalet
Ksar es Souk

MIDDLE ATLAS

HIGH ATLAS

MOUNTAINS

Moulouya River

MOUNTAINS

N

| 0 | 25 | 50 | 75 | 100 | 125 miles |

After defeating Moha's Aït Ouirah and the Aït Seri (Imihouache and Aït Brahim) in battle, Freydenberg occupied El Ksiba, Saarif, and Imihouache, closing the Oum er Rebia Valley, the road to Khénifra, and the Tadla Plain to the mountain tribes once and for all. So certain was Lyautey that "one of the thorniest questions of the pacification of the Middle Atlas" had finally been resolved that he made a special trip to El Ksiba to congratulate Freydenberg and his troops in person.[139]

The celebration was premature. Rather than submit (even though one of his sons was already on the French payroll), Moha ou Saïd fled to the upper reaches of the Middle Atlas. This happened over and over again. After the tough fighting at Tinteghaline, most of the Aït Ichkern retreated defiantly from Freydenberg to the High Atlas. Poeymirau encountered the same thing in his sweep westward from El Bekrit. The valleys and gorges of the western High Atlas now became the last refuge of an "important and substantial dissident population of all sorts" who showed no signs of giving up. All the French could do was hope that in time this seemingly eternal "guerilla war" would cease and the "dissidents" return to the fold.[140] For Moha ou Saïd— as for Ali Amhaouch and Moha ou Hammou—that time never came. He died in combat with the French in March 1924.[141]

"What is pacification in most cases anyway if not the end of a misunderstanding?"[142] In spite of Lyautey's gentle definition, the conquest of the Middle Atlas can hardly be dismissed so easily. The Berber tribesmen of the Middle Atlas recognized pacification as an alien intrusion and opposed it with every possible means. Their resistance scorned the Lyautey method of colonial conquest, for when pacification succeeded it did so only through the exercise of brute force, not through the peaceful penetration of the civilizing "organization on the march" nor through the lures of the "Berber policy." As elsewhere in Morocco, the French presence stimulated tribal unity, forged pan-tribal coalitions, and linked Moroccans together, at least until all hope of resistance against a more powerful foe disappeared.[143]

CHAPTER 5

Conquering Morocco's South

■ ■ ■ ■

U nlike the pacification of the Middle Atlas where Lyautey had few native leaders to talk to or to act upon, Lyautey's method of conquest and rule south of Marrakesh rested on collaboration with the Berber "lords" of the western High Atlas and on the lesser *caïds* south and west of the mountains. Patterned on the "collaboration strategy" of Tonkin, this *politique des grands caïds* was designed to continue the mutually beneficial relationship that the sultans had developed with the "great *caïds*" (whose power derived from their control of the high mountain passes) since the end of the nineteenth century. Now Lyautey guaranteed them a privileged place in the protectorate in return for the military and political services they would perform for France.

From the start Lyautey listened to the charges that the Berber "feudal barons" he dealt with were unreliable, that they mercilessly exploited the native population, and that they were insensitive to European interests. Ultimately, he was warned, they would compromise his liberating design of colonial conquest and rule.[1] He refused to give them up, however, because he needed them to show that working through a native elite was possible everywhere in Morocco and, most important, that it would keep French troops out of the line of fire. According to Lyautey, his *politique des grands caïds* spared French lives; it saved French money; it safeguarded French prestige. It minimized French involvement in a desolate land of little apparent economic value and avoided direct French participation in a political and military struggle in the south that often verged on a holy war to oust the unbeliever.[2] In truth, however, the *grands caïds* probably used Lyautey as much as he used them, in the end discrediting rather than justifying the partnership

with native leaders.[3] In addition, more French soldiers, supplies, and money
were engaged south of Marrakesh than Lyautey ever cared to admit.

The chief French ally south of the Atlas Mountains was Haïda ou Mouis,
the pasha of Taroudant, who first came to French notice through the reports
of Jacques Ladreit de Lacharrière in April 1911. Lacharrière identified Haïda,
then the *caïd* of the Menabha, one of the tribes of the Ras El Oued confederation, as the "principal personality" of the upper Sous region. At first, however, the emissary of the Comité du Maroc was unimpressed. Sixty years of
age, Haïda seemed to him, if not mentally "worn out," at the very least
unconcerned with the daily conduct of affairs, which he left to one of his
sons. But it soon became apparent to Lacharrière that Haïda's influence was
"paramount" in the political life of the countryside. Intelligent and a man of
"great common sense," he was also physically vigorous, taking part in all the
raids against rival groups or dissident tribal fractions. In addition, his moral
conduct was "relatively pure."[4] Perhaps decisive in Haïda's favor, however,
were his pro-French sentiments, built up by personal feelings toward individual Frenchmen, his admiration for things French, and his own shrewd
political sense. Since the then-current pasha of Taroudant, Si Mohammed el-
Kabba, leaned toward the Germans (who were influential in the Sous), it was
only natural that Haïda, anxious to preserve his own power and authority,
would find a European associate of his own.[5]

In the year after Ladreit de Lacharrière's trip, the Sous was transformed
by the presence of Ahmed el-Hiba, who rallied tribe after tribe to his explo-
sive brand of political, religious, and social reform on his progress from Tiznit
to Marrakesh. The Ras El Oued were no exception. To preserve his authority Haïda quickly threw in his lot with this radical popular movement that
pronounced the end of the regime of the Makhzen and the *grands caïds* in
the south, proclaimed a new Islamic society, and preached the imminent
destruction of the French protectorate.[6]

Haïda shared command of el-Hiba's forces that entered Marrakesh in triumph in July 1912. But after el-Hiba's defeat by Mangin at Sidi Bou Othman
in September, Haïda changed sides again, now joining with the other turn-
coats—*grands caïds* Madani and Thami el-Glaouï, Abdesselem M'Touguí, and
El Hadj Taïeb Ben Mohamed el-Goundafi—to chase el-Hiba back to Taroudant.
In May 1913 they laid siege to the city and secured it for the Makhzen.[7]

Rewarded by the sultan with appointment as pasha of Taroudant, Haïda
proved to be tenacious, aggressive, and loyal. He fended off all Hibist assaults
on the city in the spring and summer, then sallied forth in September to con-
quer Tiout, a Hibist stronghold southeast of Taroudant in the foothills of the
Anti Atlas.[8] With Tiout in his pocket he bombarded a second village south

of Taroudant into submission. Then on the strength of this growing reputation for toughness he occupied two Haouara villages located in the direction of Agadir in November without firing a shot.[9] Finally, Haïda took a share of the credit for the defection of the *caïd* of Mogador from the Hibist camp in January 1914, a giant step toward pacification along the coast. "We have noted the string of successes of Haïda ou Mouis," wrote the correspondent for *L'Afrique française*, who concluded that, as a result of all this, Haïda had emerged as "an important Moroccan personality."[10] Two months later Haïda proceeded from Taroudant to Agadir and back again, lording the authority of the Makhzen over all the fractions of the Haouara and demonstrating convincingly that the Sous Valley was secure.[11]

Lyautey's interest was aroused. He requested more information about Haïda from Lieutenant Colonel Maurice de Lamothe, his chief of intelligence on the southern military command. What de Lamothe reported back—that Haïda was tough, energetic, brave, decisive, sensible, respected, and both a good diplomat and a good administrator—convinced Lyautey that Haïda was a *grand caïd* in the making. More than that, de Lamothe told the resident general what he wanted to hear, that conquest and rule in the south "by exclusively native means" could succeed (and even produce positive results in the economic development of the country) with someone like Haïda in charge, *if* everything was overseen by French agents.[12]

With the start of the European war in August 1914 came a new outbreak of Hibist agitation in the Sous and Lyautey counted on Haïda to handle it. Haïda was told to prevent the unrest from spreading north of the Sous River "at whatever cost" by restoring order among the Chtouka, the confederation south of the Haouara that occupied the space between the Sous River in the north and the Massa River in the south and between the Atlantic on the west and the edge of the Anti Atlas in the east. He was directed to cooperate in all ways with the pasha of Tiznit, Mohamed Ben Dahan, without actually marching to Tiznit nor into the region south of that city, for the Hibist danger was thought to be so great that venturing too far from Taroudant might court disaster. For this enterprise Lyautey promised all the munitions and supplies that Haïda needed. However, he was on his own—"completely free" as the French put it—to choose both the time and the method of his action.[13]

Haïda ensured the loyalty of the Haouara by occupying their towns and executing those tribal notables compromised in the Hibist agitation. Then, alerted to the presence of a Chtouka war party *(harka)* southwest of Taroudant under the command of Nadjem, one of el-Hiba's brothers, Haïda quickly struck at Dar El Koudia, burning the dwellings of those tribesmen who were suspected of dealing with the enemy.[14] More than punishment, his serious intent was a union of the Anti Atlas tribes against the Chtouka. In early September he reached agreement with the leaders of the Oulad Iahia de Brahim, the Issendalen, the Ida ou Finis, the Ida ou Zattout, the Ida ou Zekri, and the Guettioua to form a *harka* and on the 23rd of the month Haïda attacked Chtouka forces at Oumdjerid. This "tough" battle, which lasted from dawn to dusk, ended with the "complete rout" of the enemy.[15] Lyautey took this as a preview of things to come from Haïda, celebrating his "character and energy," while admitting that the instruments of French policy still remained "precarious and uncertain" throughout the south. Thus, for the time being success could only be "relative and temporary."[16]

Haïda followed up by pursuing Nadjem to the Atlantic coast—closer to Tiznit than he had been told to go—where he defeated the remnants of the Chtouka *harka* at Kenibich and occupied the city of Aglou. The Chtouka immediately sent their delegates to negotiate with him, but perhaps aware that he had overstepped the bounds of his mission although a signal victory was now clearly within his grasp, Haïda let the occasion pass and returned to Taroudant.[17] As soon as he had gone, Nadjem reappeared with a thousand Chtouka tribesmen. With little hint of distress, Haïda announced that he would resume the campaign against Nadjem after celebrating the Aïd El Kébir.[18]

French intelligence reported that the Chtouka, worn out and having met with no great success as Hibists, now "bitterly" regretted their submission to "this brigand" Nadjem. At the first sign of the return of Haïda's troops they would abandon him for the Makhzen.[19] This is precisely what happened. The Ida ou Menou submitted on 16 December and the Aït Baha on the following day. Then followed a succession of Chtouka submissions; the Ida ou Mhamed, the Aït Amira, the Inchedhen, the Aït Boukko, and the Aït Yazza each asked for Haïda's terms in turn. Nadjem's departure farther south triggered new submissions, and at Nadjem's former campsite Haïda now received the gifts, the pledges, and the letters assuring him that the Chtouka tribes wanted only "the peace of the Makhzen." In a matter of days after Aïd El Kébir, Haïda had restored order among the Chtouka and firmed up the Makhzen's authority in the Tiznit region.[20] As evidence of Lyautey's high regard for Haïda's achievement, de Lamothe, now the military commander of the Région de Marrakech and the supervising architect of the *politique des grand caïds,* decorated the pasha with the cross of a chevalier of the Legion of Honor.[21]

Haïda continued to track Nadjem, following him into the foothills of the Anti Atlas where he had gathered "several thousand followers" from among the mountain tribesmen. Haïda attacked the villages of the Ikounka at the end of December, killing "a large number" of tribesmen and taking numerous prisoners, "a copious booty," and one hundred rifles of which twenty-five were rapid fire. This "bloody defeat" for Nadjem strengthened Haïda's control of the plains and propelled him into the mountains where he met Nadjem in a second "violent encounter" in mid-January. This time the losses on both sides were "quite considerable"—for Haïda, thirty killed and thirty-five wounded—yet the psychological advantage remained with the Makhzen.[22]

Defections from Nadjem's camp encouraged Haïda to make a final and brutal assault against the Hibists. He did this by concentrating all his force on the Ikounka villages that were systematically cannonaded and plundered one by one. The other resistant tribes were given twenty-four hours to submit or face the fate of the Ikounka. Few could hold out. With the Ikounka in the lead the Aït Mzal, the Aït Baha, the Mechguigla, and the Aït Ouadrim sent their delegates to receive Haïda's terms on 6 February.[23]

The French reported this as the "supreme blow" to el-Hiba's cause. It forced Nadjem—and el-Hiba himself—to flee farther south, abandoning both baggage and animals in a humiliating rout.[24] The "real" empire had struck back and now displayed its victory in imperial pageantry. At the beginning of April eighty notables representing the diverse fractions of the Chtouka confederation (including those from the Ahl Mader, the Resmouka, and the Massa tribes) arrived in Marrakesh to make their official act of submission before Khalifa Moulay Zine Ben Lahssan, the sultan's brother, who pardoned them in the name of the Makhzen. The ceremony, which in other times and in other courts might have inspired a Gobelins tapestry, was called the "consecration of the work of pacification of Pasha Haïda ou Mouis."[25] Gobelins or not, Lyautey began to count Haïda in the company of the *grands caïds:* "In the Atlas and the Sous from Taroudant to Agadir and Tiznit—that is, everywhere in the Moroccan far south—there reigns a peace and security that has been unknown for many years, thanks to the strength of Haïda ou Mouis, the pasha of Taroudant, and the four *grands caïds,* M'Tougui, el-Goundafi and the el-Glaouï, who have worked in close cooperation with Colonel de Lamothe."[26]

To be sure, de Lamothe deserved more than tag-end mention. Lyautey had earlier made it clear that the colonel had "organized and directed the pasha's mission" as indeed he had, supplying Haïda with money, equipment, and technical advice. "For several months" Lyautey pointed out

> he has dedicated himself with unflagging patience and perseverance to reestablishing order in the Sous, troubled by the agitation of el-Hiba, by using exclusively native forces. He did not hesitate to

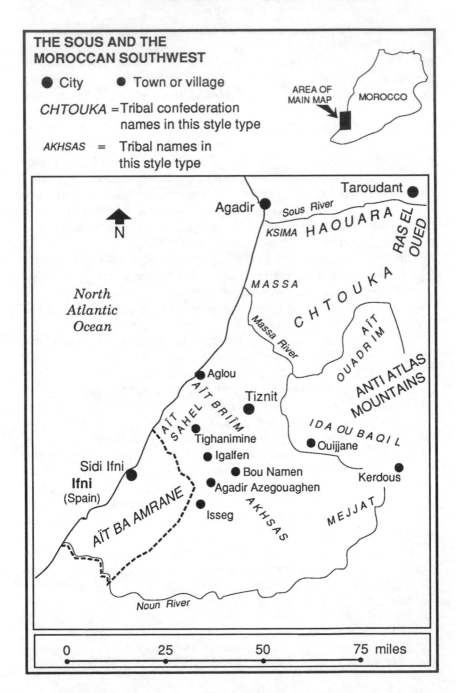

THE SOUS AND THE
MOROCCAN SOUTHWEST

● City   ● Town or village

CHTOUKA = Tribal confederation
names in this style type

AKHSAS = Tribal names in
this style type

AREA OF
MAIN MAP   MOROCCO

Taroudant ●

Agadir ●   Sous River

KSIMA   HAOUARA   RAS EL OUED

N

MASSA

CHTOUKA

North
Atlantic
Ocean

Massa River

AÏT OUADRIM

● Aglou

Tiznit ●

AÏT SAHEL   AÏT BRIÏM

ANTI ATLAS MOUNTAINS

Tighanimine
● Igalfen

IDA OU BAQIL

● Ouijjane

Sidi Ifni ●
Ifni
(Spain)

● Bou Namen
● Agadir Azegouaghen

AKHSAS

● Kerdous

AÏT BA AMRANE

● Isseg

MEJJAT

Noun River

| 0 | 25 | 50 | 75 miles |

go himself into the Sous with a small native escort to confirm first-hand the results achieved by the action of the pasha of Taroudant. He has succeeded in the south in protecting the security of the Région de Marrakech without military intervention.[27]

First as Chef du Service des Renseignements of the southern command, then as commandant of the Région de Marrakech, de Lamothe became the "great animator" of the politique des grands caïds. Although he acknowledged that working with the caïds was sometimes inconvenient, time-consuming, and indelicate, de Lamothe believed that this was the risk of indirect rule everywhere. On balance he judged that the advantages of working with the grands caïds far outweighed the disadvantages. In the Sous, for example, the overriding need was for a leader to overcome the conflicting interests and dominate the competing personalities of the region in order to weld together a coalition against el-Hiba. With Haïda in the saddle de Lamothe could promise Lyautey that such a coalition would be formed and, more impor-tantly, that it would stick together.[28]

The focus of Hibist activity now shifted south of Tiznit where three of el-Hiba's brothers—Nadjem, Merrebbi Rebbo, and Naama—had begun to orga-nize resistance among the Aït Briïm, the Akhsas, and the Aït Ouijjane. In a display of speed, organization, and force Haïda entered Tiznit with his troops in early September, making it the effective center of his military operations. He then marched into Aït Briïm and Akhsas territory where he attacked and defeated a force of 350 horsemen and several thousand foot soldiers. After this "brilliant success" Haïda moved southwest into the coun-try of the Aït Ba Amrane confederation where he received the submission of several tribal fractions.[29] He then turned toward Ouijjane, southeast of Tiznit, whose walls he breached with cannon fire. This victory was costly—the fight lasted two days and ended in hand-to-hand combat with "serious" losses on both sides—but important.[30] L'Afrique française admitted unblush-ingly that "without a single drop of French blood being shed" Haïda was opening up the Moroccan south for France's "peaceful possession" at the end of the European war.[31] And according to the protectorate's Rapport mensuel, Ouijjane demonstrated "once again the durability of the work of pacification pursued for two and one-half years with wisdom and good will by the old pasha of Taroudant [who] is and will remain for a long time to come the prin-cipal element of our force and the keystone of our entire policy."[32]

Haïda remained the keystone of French policy in the south throughout 1916 at a time when the promises of German money and military supplies in the area around the Drâa River sparked renewed interest in el-Hiba, never idle in his mountain retreat at Kerdous among the Ida ou Baqil, and spurred the anti-French resistance. Word that the Spanish planned to occupy Tarfaya at Cape Juby (where they were welcomed in August by a Hibist representative) and were negotiating for a port site on the Ifni coast also boosted el-Hiba's standing. In April and again in July Haïda intervened among the tribes most unsettled by this news, but it was not enough. To protect Haïda from shipments of German weapons by sea French cruisers patrolled the coast from Agadir to the mouth of the Drâa. To bolster him on land a "temporary" French mission was sent from Marrakesh headed by Captain Léopold Justinard. Justinard arrived at Tiznit in October and remained in the south for nearly four years.[33]

Justinard's orders were to help Haïda hold the Makhzen coalition together, to pursue contacts with tribal leaders outside the Makhzen circle from Tiznit to the Noun River, and to make Tiznit itself an "impregnable fortress," the first line of defense against the resurgent Hibist movement. Justinard's intervention was to take the form of suggestions or "advice" rather than direct orders, even though what he said would be reinforced by who he was, a French officer and the representative of both the commander of the Région de Marrakech and the resident general. He was told to steer clear of the quarrels among the Makhzen *caïds*—and there were titanic disputes between Haïda and the pasha of Tiznit, El Hadj Abderrahman Ben Mohammed el-Guellouli—and wherever possible to splash a "spot of oil" on troubled waters. He was to survey the resources of Tiznit and to make sure, "as discreetly as possible," that they were being put to best use. He was to supervise the recruitment and instruction of a troop of soldiers at Tiznit. He was to oversee the city's defenses—for which de Lamothe offered to send a cannon from Marrakesh—and to ensure Tiznit's safety from any attack "no matter how powerful." Finally, Justinard was instructed to send daily military and political reports via wireless telegraph to Agadir and Marrakesh.[34]

De Lamothe insisted that Justinard take special care in his relationship with Haïda ou Mouis, since it was "absolutely necessary" that he enjoy the pasha's friendship and confidence.

> He is an old soldier—blunt, rough, and stubborn, but loyal and sure. He is suspicious, touchy, and of a mind-set that grasps but poorly the subtleties of politics. He is an old man whose faculties are somewhat weakened and that only regain their full vigor on the battlefield, and who too often lets himself be influenced by his entourage.

Despite all this, de Lamothe stressed that Haïda was "the keystone of our policy and our power south of the Atlas."[35]

With regard to el-Hiba, de Lamothe was equally straightforward.

> You will fight against el-Hiba with every means at your disposal. Your objective is the submission, capture, or elimination of him and his family. His mere departure from the region would not be a completely satisfactory solution. If he should seek to open negotiations with you, do not refuse a priori, but refer the matter to me immediately.

As for el-Hiba's brothers and close lieutenants, Justinard could be "very generous" in his terms for their surrender. He could promise them their freedom and safety in a specified place of residence as well as the restitution of their possessions, except whatever had already been confiscated for the use of the public authorities.[36]

Justinard built a confident alliance with Haïda and the other Makhzen chiefs as he had been instructed to do, and he succeeded—with the help of the French navy—in blocking the shipment of German arms and ammunition to the Hibists. Justinard remembered it as a "little episode" in the history of the Great War. In November 1916 two Germans, a Turkish officer, and their Moroccan interpreter disembarked from a submarine near the mouth of the Drâa River, laden with letters and gifts for el-Hiba. Headed by Edgar Pröbster, the former German consul at Fez, the group explained to the local chiefs (who relayed the information to el-Hiba at Kerdous) that they would provide them with arms and ammunition for the holy war against the French. The weapons would soon arrive by submarine. For a while Pröbster and Justinard played a game of hide-and-seek among the sand dunes as each tried to outwit the other. In the end, however, Justinard was able to provide the navy with enough information on the whereabouts of the submarine to foil any landing. Pröbster and his party (who might have been turned over to Justinard, if he had had more than "meager political funds" at his disposal) moved south along the coast to the Spanish post at Cape Juby from whence they were transported to the Canary Islands, then repatriated.[37]

The "Pröbster affair," which came with pledges of solidarity from the German kaiser and the Ottoman sultan to the southern tribes, bucked up the Hibist cause once again. It assisted in the formation of a war party of Aït Ba Amrane, Aït Sahel, Akhsas, and Aït Briïm tribesmen at Isseg in December 1916. To calm the region de Lamothe instructed Haïda to march against them. He told him not to be content with a "vague submission" of the tribes, but to act in a "vigorous and thorough" way. This would establish "a durable organization" among the tribes, permitting them to police their own territory and ward off any future German contacts.[38] What de Lamothe failed to sense in what he often described solely in terms of a Franco-German contest, however, was the enduring power of the anti-French and anti-Makhzen resistance in the south.

Haïda left Tiznit at the head of a small army of 950 horsemen and 1,650 foot soldiers, equipped with rapid-fire rifles and 3 cannon, on 1 January and camped at Tighanimine among the Aït Sahel, gaining their submission. The Aït Briïm followed suit. He then opened negotiations with the Aït Ba Amrane, but after days of inconclusive talks, he determined that force alone would do the trick. He started toward Agadir Azegouaghen by a route that required backtracking to Bou Namen, a maneuver that he came to fear might signal "apprehension" to the resistant tribes. Reversing course, he followed the more direct, yet dangerous route to Igalfen, which took his *harka* through a "long and narrow pass" to be negotiated only in single file. As the *harka* emerged from the pass, it was greeted by a force of Akhsas, Mejjat, and Aït Ba Amrane tribesmen. Although the first elements of Haïda's *harka* held back the enemy for a while, the rest of his men, harassed by snipers in the pass, could not move fast enough to join the battle. And the supply convoy with much-needed ammunition lagged far behind.[39]

When he realized the danger, Haïda ordered his cannon to the front. Before they could be set in place, however, he was killed by unfriendly fire. Haïda's death precipitated a retreat that turned into a panic. The *harka* abandoned everything—weapons, supplies, and animals—in a mad dash to the rear and the ultimate safety of the walls of Tiznit. Although the *harka*'s casualties were a fraction of those the French had suffered at El Herri two years before—there were only fifty-one killed and fifty-six wounded—the consequences of the defeat were potentially as frightening. De Lamothe feared that anything could happen, including a general uprising that would sweep the south clean of everyone loyal to the sultan and France.[40]

At Tiznit Justinard picked up the pieces. He brought the Makhzen leaders together, restored their confidence, and began the task of regrouping, reorganizing, and resupplying the *harka*. This, he believed, was the only way of maintaining order until de Lamothe, who was then on an inspection tour with the resident general in the eastern part of the Région de Marrakech, had had a chance to assess the situation for himself. Lyautey later praised Justinard for his "clear notion" of his duty and of the necessities of the moment.

His determination, energy, and composure [*calme sang-froid*] greatly contributed to the safety of the city of Tiznit by restoring order and cohesiveness in the *harka* so that in short order it became a Makhzen force capable of resisting any and all attacks.[41]

El Hadj Houmad was designated his father's successor and was quickly described by the French as manifesting "a strength and a wisdom" that they did not know he possessed. More important, the Makhzen structure did not collapse, weathering the storm of Haïda's death "beyond all expectations." Part of the reason was that it had not been struck by gale-force winds. El-Hiba had been caught off guard by this unexpected success, which at first caused confusion in his own camp; he was quite unprepared to follow it up. After dividing the considerable booty from Haïda's *harka*, el-Hiba's partisans had simply gone home.[42] To be fair, this severe deficiency in military organization—which had come to the aid of the French on more than one occasion—was shared by all Moroccan tribesmen.

Haïda's obituary made clear the debt that France owed him.

> Unfortunately in the far south we have lost an active and precious collaborator. Haïda ou Mouis, pasha of Taroudant, left this city on 24 December for the Tiznit region to make contact with the principal leaders of the Anti Atlas devoted to the Makhzen. He had begun to get the submissions of the Aït Sahel. But at the beginning of January he was killed in an engagement during the course of which the enemy suffered huge losses. Since 1912 Haïda ou Mouis had been the heart and soul of Makhzen resistance to Hibist schemes in the Sous. Devoted to our cause, he led the struggle against el-Hiba and his partisans with a tenacity and energy which never disappointed us. After having definitively established the authority of the Makhzen in the Sous, Haïda ou Mouis proved himself to be an administrator of the highest order. Since 1914 he was an officer of the Legion of Honor. His son, El Hadj Houmad, was immediately recognized by all the Makhzen *caïds* and leaders in the Sous region.[43]

Despite the reassuring tone of *L'Afrique française,* de Lamothe judged the situation in the south to be "very serious and very threatening." Even with all of Justinard's good work, Houmad's *harka* at Tiznit had been reduced to 500 horsemen and 150 foot soldiers, one-fourth of the force his father had originally assembled. At Marrakesh de Lamothe called the High Atlas *caïds* together to announce that a French column of 4,000 regular troops would be sent south of the Atlas to operate with Houmad's *harka*; the *grands caïds* were asked to supply additional Makhzen forces. The immediate task was to restore the prestige of the Makhzen by avenging the death of Haïda ou Mouis, to recover the weapons lost (particularly the cannon), and to disperse what remained of the enemy *harkas.* In addition, de Lamothe spoke of the need to ensure the continuity of Makhzen leadership.[44]

In authorizing de Lamothe's dispatch of French troops to the south, Resident General *à titre intérimaire* Henri Gouraud (who substituted for Lyautey from December 1916 to May 1917 while Lyautey was in Paris to succeed Gallieni as minister of war) insisted that the general use French force only when it was "indispensable" to do so. In no case was he to create any new posts nor to station any garrisons of regular troops in the south.

> The involvement of regular troops that we have decided upon is not part of our general program of action. It is the result of an accident, the defeat of a native force, which obliges us to play the role—with the cooperation of the native forces assembled at Tiznit—originally assigned to Haïda ou Mouis.

As with Lyautey on the subject of Marrakesh in 1912, Gouraud made it plain that he was being compelled to suspend operations elsewhere to handle this emergency in the south and that he did not like it.

> I am asking you to conduct your military operations and political action in the Sous from the standpoint that it is eminently desirable for you to stay there as short a time as possible and that you leave no regular or auxiliary troops there, unless it is impossible to do otherwise.[45]

The native forces that marched with the French column were drawn proportionally from the troops of the *grands caïds* and the other Makhzen tribes close to the Tiznit region. This affirmed in a double way "the principles of collaboration between [the French] and the native population and that of Makhzen solidarity among all the Makhzen leaders and all the tribes." Thami el-Glaouï supplied 200 horsemen and 400 infantrymen to join the 50 horsemen and 600 foot soldiers he had sent ahead to Taroudant; Taïeb el-Goundafi provided 180 horsemen and 300 infantrymen in addition to the 100 horsemen and 300 foot soldiers from his troops already at Taroudant; Abdesselem M'Tougui contributed 200 horsemen and 300 infantrymen; and the Haha tribes, led by their *caïds* and *khalifas,* provided 100 horsemen and 200 foot soldiers. When added to the *harka* under Houmad at Tiznit, the total native contribution to the military expedition came just 520 short of parity with the

French. However, Lyautey's final report on the Sous column, addressed to the minister of war in August 1917, put the Makhzen contribution at 1,380 horsemen and 3,900 foot soldiers, which meant that the Makhzen contingent exceeded that of the French by 1,280.[46]

De Lamothe left Marrakesh on 14 February and reached Agadir on 3 March after an arduous first-time crossing of the High Atlas that took his troops to a light-headed altitude of 1,500 meters on paths that were little more than tracks for mules. Two weeks later he entered embattled Tiznit in what was an "emotional spectacle" for Justinard, who compared it to Moinier's relief of Fez in 1911. However, as he feared, de Lamothe found the political situation in Tiznit colored by tension, disagreements, and intrigue among the Makhzen *caïds*; marked by a resurgence of banditry among the Haouara and the Mesguina, stamped by unease and discontent among the Chtouka, and tinged with indiscipline and a lack of cohesiveness within the *harka* itself. In the two months since Haïda's death Makhzen leadership and authority in the south had begun to unravel.[47] There was no better indication of the importance of the leadership abilities of a *grand caïd* or of the vulnerability of any French policy based on individual native chiefs.

The mere presence of de Lamothe and French regulars did much to restore confidence at Tiznit, but a "movement of insurrection" had made "considerable progress" throughout the region. From the Aït Sahel in the southwest to the Aït Ouadrim in the northeast an arc of dissidence followed the slopes of the Anti Atlas with two major points of concentration, Isseg in the south, where the tribes had been most affected by German-Turkish propaganda, and Ouijjane in the north, which was again under el-Hiba's direct influence. Through prophetic exhortations to action el-Hiba had driven the tribes to a "state of extreme excitation," explained de Lamothe, binding them together in a sort of "pact of London," which forbid any separate peace with the Makhzen or the French. As a result, de Lamothe insisted that political action would be of no use at all.[48]

De Lamothe marched against Ouijjane on 25 March. After eight hours of combat the city was taken, el-Hiba's forces scattered, and the pretender sent in flight to Kerdous. Three weeks later de Lamothe captured Isseg, then engaged and dispersed war parties of Akhsas and Mejjat tribesmen on the road back to Tiznit. This "serious fighting," which involved French artillery and aerial bombardments, resulted in more than 1,200 killed among the Hibists, but fewer than 20 dead among the Makhzen's forces.[49]

It was "useless and even dangerous," de Lamothe decided, to pursue the remnants of the defeated *harkas* farther south toward the Noun River. Although the south was not completely pacified, he had avenged the death of Haïda ou Mouis, demonstrated French might, and cleared the area from the Séguia El Hamra in the south to the lands of the Aït Ouadrim in the north. Wherever de Lamothe marched, the tribes had denounced el-Hiba and proclaimed Moulay Youssef as sultan, disbanded their *harkas,* broken off their dealings with the Germans or the Spanish, and returned to the markets opened by the French. De Lamothe's greatest disappointment was his failure to capture or kill el-Hiba, which had figured large in his instructions to Justinard. It was not from lack of trying. A French air squadron bombed Kerdous for two days, destroying el-Hiba's residence, but touching not a hair on the pretender's head. El-Hiba would die of natural causes in Kerdous in 1919.[50]

De Lamothe's final chore was to establish a steadfast Makhzen command structure. He reminded Lyautey that in 1913 the sultan's authority had been delegated to the pashas of Taroudant and Tiznit, who were both named *naïbs* of the Makhzen. Haïda ou Mouis had quickly shown his worth, but neither Mohamed Ben Dahan at Tiznit nor his successor in 1915, Abderrahman el-Guellouli, had been up to the task. Pasha Abderrahman was intelligent and loyal, but rapacious and lacked both prestige and vision, a "second-stringer" rather than the first-rate player who was needed. When trouble had erupted around Tiznit, Haïda proved himself to be "the only real element of force" in the entire region and in the end he became the real "suzerain" of Tiznit. What de Lamothe needed was a new pasha at Tiznit, now "the most dangerous and delicate" sector of the Anti Atlas, to direct and coordinate the action of the Makhzen throughout the south.[51]

After reviewing several candidates, de Lamothe proposed Taïeb el-Goundafi as the sultan's *naïb* at Tiznit. In all things el-Goundafi was a *grand caïd:* proud (so proud in fact that the battle account of Ouijjane was rewritten so that he could be awarded the croix de guerre *avec palme*), powerful, rich, generous, well-connected, and most important, a man of diplomacy as well as force. Although el-Goundafi was an outsider to the Sous, de Lamothe counted this an advantage. El-Goundafi's own command in the High Atlas would provide the material resources he needed to govern at Tiznit, but it was distant enough to calm local fears of any permanent territorial annexation, which de Lamothe considered out of the question. Short-tempered and headstrong, el-Goundafi was also ambitious, and de Lamothe believed that his desire to succeed in the south would keep him honest and under control. As el-Goundafi's second, de Lamothe nominated Ahmed Boubka, the former *khalifa* of Pasha Abderrahman, intimately familiar with the tribes of the south and their leaders. And he asked that Captain Justinard's "temporary" mission at Tiznit be extended, so that he could advise el-Goundafi on political matters as well as oversee his administration. In de Lamothe's words Justinard would be "a sort of resident."[52]

At Taroudant de Lamothe modified Houmad's command, subtracting from it the Chtouka who were added to the tribes under el-Goundafi's authority. Although Houmad was a man of loyalty, goodwill, and real intelligence, he lacked the military experience (and the prestige that went with it) to handle the Chtouka confederation. De Lamothe also recommended increased, albeit "rather discreet" political control over Houmad to ensure that the French continued to "inspire" the decisions he made, yet never got directly involved in their execution. The result would be a "perfect collaboration" between the French and the Makhzen at Taroudant and "complete unity" between Taroudant and Tiznit.[53]

His mission finished, de Lamothe and his column returned to Marrakesh on 30 May after a second transmountain trek. He reported to Lyautey that the danger in the south was over, the "mahdist" coalition broken. The "stunning revenge" inflicted on the enemy for Haïda's defeat—the "great losses" in three major battles, the occupation of Ouijjane, the damage wreaked on Isseg, the air attacks on villages at the edge of the Sahara as well as those perched high in the Anti Atlas—would be remembered for some time to come. He pointed out that his column had travelled 450 kilometers from Marrakesh without having fired a shot, welcomed along the way "as suzerains and as friends," which could be no better proof of the wisdom of French policy and the solidity of the protectorate. As loyal comrades-in-arms and exemplary collaborators, de Lamothe saluted the *grands caïds* who deserved the praise and rewards of the protectorate.[54]

In his report to the minister of war Lyautey emphasized the importance of the *grands caïds* to the success of de Lamothe's mission and to the Moroccan policy he had followed since 1912. Whatever de Lamothe had asked of them, they had done. The *grands caïds* had defended Taroudant and Tiznit while the French column was en route from Marrakesh; they had secured the road back and forth across the mountains; they had protected and supplied the column and its convoy; and they had fought side by side the French. "At no point did they let us down," Lyautey asserted. "They made themselves the instruments of our policy. Over and over again in combat they demonstrated qualities beyond compare; they proved themselves to be clear-sighted as well as courageous leaders of men." In short, according to Lyautey, "a large part" of de Lamothe's success was owed to the loyalty and talent of the *grands caïds*.[55]

At Tiznit Lyautey and de Lamothe hoped that one *grand caïd* would simply replace another and the policy would continue as before. But just as the mountains and the far south had resisted the pacification of Haïda ou Mouis, they resisted el-Goundafi. Even after significant military progress among the Chtouka mountain tribes in 1918 and 1919, he was unable to put an end to the stubborn defiance of Makhzen rule. On the plains, Justinard noted, Muslims prayed in the name of Moulay Youssef, but in the mountains in the name of el-Hiba. (Between the mountains and the plains—at Ouijjane, for example—prayers were said in the name of "him whom God has chosen," proving, Justinard quipped, that the Chleuh must have had some Norman blood in their veins.) Confronted with revolts in 1920 and 1921, el-Goundafi was forced to retire in 1922, charged with "exactions and abuse of his authority." His successor was the brother of Sultan Moulay Youssef, Moulay Zine Ben Lahssan, the *khalifa* of Marrakesh.[56]

The flaw in the *politique des grands caïds* was expressed in Justinard's query, asked over and over again at Taroudant and Tiznit, "Qui gardera les gardiens?," for Frenchmen had no confidence in the actions of others unless they pulled the strings.[57] At the same time, recalling his experiences at Tiznit to the officers of the Marrakesh garrison in 1924, Justinard made it clear that setting off a

> purely native *harka* is always like a roll of the dice, even when it is strong and under a leader of great prestige, unless it is backed up by a regular force which can provide eventual material support and whose very presence maintains the cohesion of the diverse elements of the *harka*.[58]

Thus, the *politique des grands caïds* of relying on Morocco's "lords" of the Atlas as conquerors (or even as governors) was never really successful. Moreover, it was never the policy of first choice, although Lyautey often touted it as a triumph of both indirect conquest and rule, but employed only when France lacked the desire or the means to do anything else.[59]

CHAPTER 6

Remaking Rabat

■　■　■　■

Throughout his tenure as resident general Lyautey was challenged by the double task of preserving Morocco's cities from European disruption and of constructing twentieth-century towns for his European compatriots. In Rabat, which he chose as the administrative headquarters of the protectorate (as later in Fez, Meknès, and Marrakesh), Lyautey decided that two cities would exist side by side: the Muslim city (or *medina*) and the new European city. The former would be protected or restored, the latter built modern from the ground up. This "dual city" approach, which in a serendipitous fashion saved the *medinas* from destruction, left French urban policy open to charges of racial segregation, even "urban apartheid." French planners insisted to the contrary that this was not a "radical separation" *à l'anglaise* based on racial distance, but a "discreet separation" of two cities that remained tightly bound together.[1]

To be sure, separation did calm the fears of Europeans for their own health and safety at a time when Morocco's *medinas* were still the sites of epidemic diseases and anti-European violence. And it also expressed the European sense of racial and cultural superiority. Yet Lyautey himself was no white supremacist and although over time his urban plans may have transformed Rabat's *medina* into a Muslim ghetto, this was never his intention. What was clear from the start, however, despite the tale of two cities living different but connected lives, was that all Rabat would be remade according to French blueprints and ruled not very indirectly according to French designs. If this was an urban partnership, it was negotiated strictly on French terms.

Rabat stands on the left bank of the Bou Regreg River where the river joins the Atlantic Ocean. Surrounded by fawn-colored ramparts that accentuated the impressive fortified citadel of the Kasbah des Oudaïas, it offered the 1912 traveller by sea "one of the most beautiful frescos" imaginable.[2] From the river one glimpsed the Hassan tower, the unfinished minaret of a ruined twelfth-century mosque, a massive construction in reddish sandstone with spare, graceful decoration, a fitting companion to the Giralda in Seville and the Koutoubia in Marrakesh.[3] Rabat's "splendor" had been "contemporaneous" with that of Granada, Lyautey noted during his first visit to the city in 1907, and recognition of this rich cultural and architectural past guided all his efforts at remaking the city.[4]

Lyautey's Haussmann was Henri Prost, "the great urban planner . . . who was really the inspiration behind our new cities," Lyautey recalled, "and of the notion that they could be built next to the native cities without causing too much harm."[5] Prost had worked in Rome, Florence, and Constantinople, and his 1910 plan for the redevelopment of Antwerp had been a prizewinner. For a decade under Lyautey's direction he would oversee the physical transformation of Morocco's cities, paying special attention to Rabat.[6]

Within Rabat's *medina* (including the Jewish district or *mellah*) that was encircled by the city's "interior" walls, Prost worked carefully since he did not want "to spoil" old Rabat.[7] But beyond the Hassan tower within the greater perimeter of the "exterior" walls, he laid out a new Rabat of broad avenues and modern buildings amongst the gardens and orange groves that surrounded the sultan's palace.[8] Prost separated the old and new cities with Boulevard Gouraud on the western boundary of the *medina* and Boulevard Joffre-Gallieni on its southern boundary, yet tied them together with elegant laces by extending all the roads from the *medina* gates across the length and breadth of the new city. Along the western or Almohad wall of the *medina,* the El-Alou gate was the starting point for the Boulevard Front-de-Mer, the Avenue Marie-Feuillet, and the Avenue de Casablanca, all of which linked the old city with the new Ocean *(Océan)* district along the Atlantic. At the El-Had gate in the southwestern corner of the *medina* began the Avenue de Temara, which moved south and west toward the Temesna gate in the "exterior" wall and beyond to Casablanca. Along the southern or Andalusian wall of the *medina* three major north-south streets traversed the Hassan tower *(Tour Hassan)* and Residency *(Résidence)* districts of the new city. From the El-Chella gate, the *medina*'s most important entrance, the Avenue de Chella made its way to a point overlooking the walled Merinid necropolis and from a gate near the *mellah* Rue Henri-Popp stretched from Boulevard Joffre to Boulevard Front-de-l'Oued. From El-Teben gate began Rue (later Avenue) du Dar-El-Makhzen, designed to be the commercial and ceremonial axis of the French city. Lined with public buildings, banks, and businesses—the Poste Centrale, the Banque d'État du Maroc, the Palais de Justice—it climbed toward the Es-Sounna mosque, passing the gate of the sultan's palace, then branched to lead up to the offices of the protectorate administration and at the top of the hill to Lyautey's official residence. Since the palace compound and the residency were situated equidistant from the *medina* and parallel to each other on opposite sides of this central thoroughfare, Prost might have been using his city plan to emphasize the "dual rulership" of the nation. But the hilltop gave the symbolic advantage to the French, whose flag at the highest point in the city left no doubt as to who called the shots.[9]

Prost designed French Rabat as an *urbs in horto,* a "city in a garden" of bougainvillea and hibiscus, oleander and jacaranda. He built a modern administrative capital of spacious tree-lined streets, elegant arcaded public buildings, pleasant commercial establishments, and comfortable villas, all intended to project tranquility and repose; quite the opposite look and feel of rough-and-tumble, no-nonsense Casablanca, the protectorate's economic hub. The Prost plan mapped the French city into districts—administrative, commercial, residential, university, and military—where form followed function. But since housing the protectorate's offices was Rabat's "reason for being," there was understandable emphasis on the tasks of government.[10]

Everywhere the city was fashioned as a showcase for the best in French colonial urban design. The favored architecture was "Franco-Muslim," a French interpretation of Islamic forms done with considerable style and artistic sensitivity.[11] And at three points Prost engineered vistas: of the estuary (from the base of the Hassan tower), of the Moroccan city (from the residency), and of the entire city and its old walls (from the heights of Aguedal).[12] Guillaume de Tarde, a top protectorate administrator, insisted that, when the city was fully developed, it would stand as "one of the most original creations of modern civilization in the realm of urban planning."[13] And in 1936 Évariste Levi-Provençal, the historian of Moroccan Islam and Muslim Spain, proclaimed French Rabat famed throughout the world as a "masterpiece" of successful town planning and architecture.[14]

There were mistakes in the Prost plan that compromised the achievement. Prost failed to provide enough space for the increase of the native population, which would ultimately lead to overcrowding in the *medina.* Yet he provided too much land for the French, dispersing a European population that was never greater than one-third of the entire city population over an area ten times the size of the *medina.* Some of the European scattering had to do with the high cost of center-city land and the protectorate's delay in imposing stiff property tax and land-use laws. It also fit in with the notion

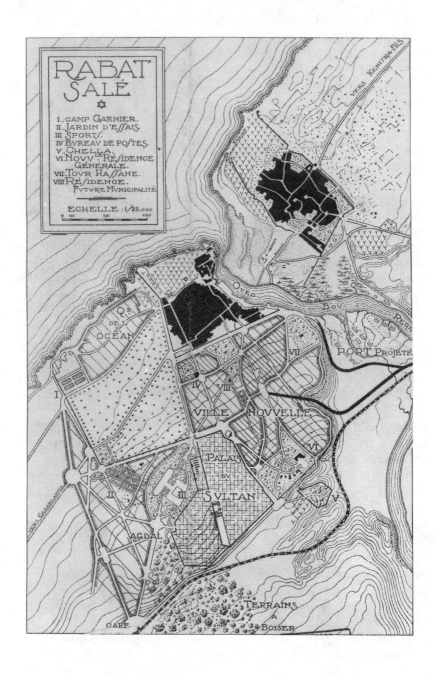

of a city of villas. In the end, however, it boosted the costs of development and services in the new city. Moreover, although all the land required for the French city was acquired legally from Moroccan owners through the introduction of modern urban planning laws, Moroccans were often cheated or dispossessed. It is difficult not to agree with Janet Abu-Lughod that the resources in land, labor, and money that Moroccans contributed to the building of French Rabat burdened them in an unfair and inequitable way.[15]

With the changes in wood, brick, and mortar there came a reorganization in Moroccan municipal government as well. For Frenchmen, who emphasized stagnation rather than movement in their accounts of Morocco's urban history, Rabat on the eve of the protectorate was a Muslim city frozen in time "with all its Oriental flavor" and all its "antique" local customs. Its city government was judged inadequate to handle the tasks of modern urban administration, particularly those of a municipality expected to encompass a significant European population. As a native government, it was "without authority" over Europeans and suffered from "the habits of sluggishness and of indifference common to Muslims." As a result, French administrators not only supervised the native authorities in their traditional tasks (as indirect rule required), but reshaped Moroccan urban life "from a European perspective."[16]

The French began by creating a municipal services administration (Services Municipaux) for Rabat with departments of finance, public works, police, health, public assistance, and architecture. This modernized some functions of city government and instituted new ones. The first municipal services director, Captain Robert Normand, admitted that all these changes had to take place behind a "native façade" and certainly the French were doing a lot of things behind the scenes. Still, Normand's goal was to move carefully between what was and what would be. This meant keeping in mind that the French were not "building on empty space." There existed in Rabat a "complete, organized public life" which, even when the French thought it "defective," could only be touched with "the greatest prudence" and then by counsel and advice rather than by fiat.[17] In practice the French found this hard to do.

Although the native structure of command was left in place, the alterations made in it amounted to an urban revolution. Si Seddik Bargach, Rabat's city governor *(caïd),* was the chief urban administrator, the head of the police force and sharifian army levies, the judge in all cases that did not involve Koranic law, the most important religious official, and a collector of local taxes. His powers were far-reaching, his rule autocratic. Under the French, however, even though Bargach's approval was needed for everything that affected the city, his powers were sharply reduced in all administrative and financial questions, restricted in legal affairs, and abolished (by 1924) in police and military matters. On the other hand, preferring unity of direction and clear lines of responsibility to the overlap and mutual surveillance that had been the Makhzen's hedge against corruption or abuse of power, the French demoted the sultan's representative in the city *(khalifa)*, Si Larbi Zebdi, who had once been the rival of the *caïd* in attributes and influence, to the *caïd*'s deputy. Regardless of their new job descriptions, however, both men were now compelled to work in tandem with the reigning director of municipal services, who had inherited much of their power and authority.[18]

The change from city autocrat to municipal figurehead was not easily made. Bargach was from an important and well-connected family that had provided the sultans with many high administrators. His father had been the sultan's representative in Tangier who had signed the 1856 Madrid Convention. Bargach himself was a former governor (pasha) of Tangier and had long and intimate knowledge of Rabat, for he had served first as customs officer in that city, then *khalifa* before becoming *caïd*. On his death in 1917 Bargach was eulogized by Municipal Services Director Maxime Revilliod as one of the first to comprehend "the great mission" that France had embarked on in Morocco and as one of the protectorate's most loyal and devoted collaborators. This was the standard fare of memorials. According to Normand, who admittedly had only worked with the *caïd* for a little over a year, Bargach had served France "with slowness and without enthusiasm." On occasion he had even blocked the implementation of certain measures that the French considered important, forcing them to maneuver around him and work through the *khalifa* instead.[19]

The roles of other Moroccan city officials were also transformed. The management of city finances (including the levying and collection of taxes and the payment of public officials), which had been the joint responsibility of the *caïd*, the chief customs officer *(amin el-diouana)*, and the collector of city market and gate taxes *(amin el-moustafad)* now rested with a municipal commission set up in 1913 and ultimately with the municipal services director. Makhzen property, public utilities, and public works—all formerly administered by the market and gate tax collector or the administrator of religious properties *(nadir des habous)*—also became the responsibility of the municipal commission. And the market inspector *(mohtaseb)* who set prices, checked on product standards, collected the property tax *(taxe urbaine)*, and oversaw the artisan corporations— and whom the French had often depicted as a *prévôt des marchands* out of the Middle Ages—was reduced to a "petty bureaucrat of little importance."[20] In short, although the French insisted that they only exercised "a sort of tutelage" over native administrators, this was far from the truth.[21]

The Services Municipaux of Rabat and nearby Salé as well as their suburban areas were initially put in the hands of army officers under the "pro-
visional" authority of the French consul in Rabat. Captain Normand of the
army corps of engineers was appointed director of municipal services of
Rabat in June 1912 and Lieutenant Marcel Rigot the municipal services
director of Salé.[22] The mix of civil-military control at the top, which was a
favored Lyautey device to emphasize talent over narrow professional expertise, was supposed to discourage the rivalries that had plagued Algeria, prevent duplication of effort, and present a united and harmonious French front
to the European community inside Morocco and to the outside world as well.
It was a balance difficult to maintain. Before the year was out, Lyautey reinforced the military presence by naming Major Édouard Brémond, who had
commanded the Rabat port police from 1907 to 1910, to assist the consul
at Rabat in the administration of Rabat and Salé. Brémond was "specifically
charged with the native policy of the cities and the tribes of the suburban
areas [and] of relations with the Makhzen and native administrators." He in
turn was seconded by Captain Pierre Coudert, responsible for Rabat's suburban region. For a time Lyautey was content to make a "military municipality" of Rabat. The sultan, the Makhzen, and the residency were all present
in the city; the surrounding area was large and unsettled; the native administration was not yet sufficiently dependable. The tasks of military security
and good government called for expertise and organization that at present
only the military could provide.[23]

At the same time Lyautey did not neglect the civil side. In June 1913 he
authorized the creation of a municipal commission. Presided over by Caïd
Bargach, who was assisted by two vice presidents (the French consul and the
municipal services director), the commission was a mix of French and
Moroccan administrators and handpicked notables, designed to give life to
Lyautey's policy of association with the native urban elite. Representatives
from the city departments of finance, public works, and health; a delegate
of the Administration du Contrôle de la Dette Marocaine (which represented
the French financial interests that had negotiated the 1904 and 1910 loans
to Morocco); the first vice president of the Chamber of Commerce of Rabat;
the market inspector; and the market and gate tax collector were all de jure
commission members. Twelve city notables (four Frenchmen, six Muslims,
two Jews), nominated by the residency and appointed by the sultan's chief
minister (grand vizir), served for one-year terms. (Since they could be re-
appointed any number of times, in practice they often remained on the
commission for several years.)[24] Voting was merely advisory to the caïd
or the director of municipal services, but because of the importance of the

commission members, whatever happened had some impact. No session of the commission was open to the public although a summary of each meeting was prepared for the press and a complete transcript sent to the residency.[25] This was the commission that would tend to much of Rabat's city business during the Lyautey years.

The French dominated the municipal commission in part because the meetings were conducted in their language. A photograph of the *grand vizir* taking one of his first French lessons under the watchful gaze of Maximilian Delphinus Berlitz in 1908 was worth more than a thousand words.[26] The statistics were equally eloquent. At the commission's first session in August 1913 the 4 French members "represented" 2,518 Frenchmen, the 6 Muslim members 22,906 Muslims, the 2 Jewish members 2,851 Jews. Moreover, since by sharifian decree only Frenchmen (and not other Europeans) could sit on the commission, Frenchmen spoke for all Europeans resident in Rabat.[27]

Within a year the commission's French membership was doubled from four to eight to keep pace with the increase of the European population in the city, its growing diversity, and the development of Rabat's peripheral districts. The effect was to give Frenchmen an equal voice with Moroccans and a louder voice than the Muslim representatives who continued to have six votes. Over the years—and by 1923 there were fifteen French and fifteen Moroccan members (twelve Muslims and three Jews)—this unequal formula for representation continued unchanged.[28]

The French members of the commission were representatives of major business, banking, or financial institutions (the Compagnie Générale du Maroc, the Compagnie de Navigation Paquet, the Comptoir Lyonnais, the Crédit Foncier d'Algérie et de Tunisie, the Union Commerciale Indo-Chinoise et Africaine), professionals (engineers, doctors, lawyers, pharmacists), merchants and landowners of all sorts, and small businessmen (masons, butchers, restaurant owners). Among their number Gaston Bernaudat, an inspector of the Compagnie Marocaine, the largest civil engineering firm in Morocco, and Léon Petit, an entrepreneur and civil engineer, gained citywide notoriety for their persistent and aggressive promotion of French Rabat's interests.[29]

On the Moroccan side there was an equal measure of talent—usually disguised by the ubiquitous occupational tags of merchant *(négociant)* or property owner and businessman *(propriétaire et commerçant)*—clout, and commitment. There was always a Bargach on or near the commission, either as *caïd* (Si Seddik until 1917, then Abderrahman Ben El Hadj Mohamed Ben Ahmed Bargach) or as one of the *caïd*'s two *khalifas* (Si M'Hamed Ould Si Seddik Bargach, then El Hadj Abdelaziz Bargach, and finally, Si Mohamed Ben Abderrahman Bargach, the *caïd*'s oldest son) or as a designated commission member (Si El Hadj Mustapha Ben Abdelmajid Bargach, beginning in 1920). The head of the clan, Caïd Abderrahman, was an honest and able administrator who had already been pasha of Casablanca and of Mogador. He was known for his fierce personal and family ambitions, his adeptness at keeping competitors off balance, and his adroit dealings with the French, for whom he apparently had little true regard.[30] A measure of his success was that he remained *caïd* of the city for three decades.

Surrounding the Bargach were the delegates of Rabat's principal families. *Khalifa* to both of the Bargach *caïds,* Si Abdennebi Souissi sat on the municipal commission until 1916. *Caïd* of Rabat in his own right under Sultan Abd el-Hafid, Souissi was considered a devoted and hardworking bureaucrat with a "very correct attitude" toward the protectorate authorities. Although a one-time rival of the Bargach clan, he had long since settled his differences with the Bargach *caïds.*[31] Souissi's replacement as *khalifa,* Si Ahmed Ben Mohammed Zebdi, was allied to all the major Rabat families and stayed on the municipal commission for decades. Thoughtful, intelligent, and discreet, he was of "great help" to the French administrators of the Services Municipaux who were constantly impressed by his industry and "excellent influence" on the commission. He was someone, they noted, with the talent to become *khalifa* or *mohtaseb.* In the mid-1930s the Chef de la Région still rated Zebdi "a personality of the first rank who enjoys a real influence with the pasha and the Moroccan population." His only fault was his "sympathy" for "the nationalist party," which in time would become yet another virtue.[32]

Si Mohammed Ben Naceur Ghennam was one of the first six Muslim members appointed to the municipal commission and he remained in that seat until 1920. Four years later he was named first *khalifa* to the *caïd,* a post he held into the 1940s. Never a leader of real force nor an administrator of talent (and later physically weakened by ill health), Ghennam belonged to a "party" opposed to the Bargach. His major qualification for office, then, was simply who he was; and his major responsibility was to do whatever he could to counter the sway of the Bargach.[33] In that task he needed all the aplomb he could muster.

Rabat's finances and economic well-being, its health and security, its food and water supply, its physical improvement and architectural embellishment were the stuff of the municipal commission's deliberations. And despite French dominance in the commission—and the determined steering of the municipal services director—there seemed to be real cooperation and progress. Eight months after the commission had begun its regular meetings, Consul Louis Rais reported to Lyautey that "up until now" the French and Muslim members had shown "the best spirit" in the discussion of city matters and that there would be some "benefit" in having them meet more frequently.[34] Not everyone was so enthusiastic. Normand complained that many of the commission's wishes were hard to satisfy "because of the lack of funds." Nevertheless, he acknowledged that in making and implementing the decisions affecting the city "nothing could be more precious than the combination of the understanding and good will of the natives with the authority and creative spirit of the Europeans."[35] Unwittingly Normand had revealed the true power relationships.

The 1913 decree *(dahir)* was only the first word on municipal organization. The second came in April 1917 when another *dahir*—considered the real "municipal charter" of Morocco—clarified the roles of the *caïd* and the director of municipal services (who became, in effect, "the true *mayor* of the city"), established a municipal perimeter in order to define the geographical limits of Rabat's taxing authority, and split the commission (now officially classified as a "mixed" municipal commission) into separate Moroccan and European sections for discussion and voting. This ended the difficulty of conversation in two languages (more disadvantageous to the Moroccan members than to the French), but emphasized in a stunning way the division of the city's population into two distinct and unequal halves. In truth, Lyautey would have preferred the creation of individual assemblies for the native and European parts of the city since this followed from his "twin-city" approach. The 1917 decree, however, attempting to juggle with unity and diversity, did not go that far.[36]

Raising revenue for Rabat, perhaps the most important task of the municipal commission, was a process complicated by the international controls on Morocco: the legacy of European maneuvering for economic advantage in the decades preceding the protectorate. In addition to the treaties protecting European trade and exempting Europeans (and their Moroccan protégés) from sharifian taxation, the Administration du Contrôle de la Dette Marocaine administered all Makhzen land and properties and collected all market and gate taxes through its delegates in the eight Moroccan ports open to foreign commerce. This unusual situation, which Frenchmen had helped to create, now worked against the financial reorganization of the city. "Perfectly natural at a time when the intent might have been to ruin Morocco to dominate it all the more," Normand confessed, "this institution has at present become a considerable obstacle, distorting the municipal budget and preventing all progress on the important question of market taxes."[37]

Despite Rabat's financial predicament, worse by far than that of any other Moroccan city, French authorities insisted that all urban reform had to begin with a municipal budget that balanced income against expenditures.

To raise money the municipal commission taxed whatever remained untaxed in the city and even contracted with the Contrôle de la Dette to collect taxes on its behalf. The city's accounts, however, could only be evened up as a result of generous protectorate subsidies.[38] To transform the old order of taxation the French persuaded most of the foreign powers (but not Great Britain or the United States) to renounce their capitulatory rights, bringing the "quasi-totality" of the Moroccan population under the tax laws. And in 1916 the Contrôle de la Dette surrendered its right to collect the gate and market taxes that permitted far-reaching tax reform the following year. Within twelve months the revenues from gate and market taxes doubled in all the port cities, henceforth making them the most productive source of municipal income. By 1917 all but three of the fifteen municipalities that had been receiving subsidies to cover their deficits were now able to balance their budgets on their own. With some justification French tax men patted themselves on the back for "quite a brilliant accomplishment" in the area of urban tax matters.[39]

Despite this budget-balancing success, Rabat alone in 1918 still showed a budget shortfall. Rabat's municipal commissioners complained that their city had been saddled with a permanent budget deficit because of Lyautey's "Prostian" plans that were out of proportion to the costs involved. Rabat's expenses regularly exceeded its revenues by more than one-half, meaning that the city budget could only be balanced by a protectorate subsidy equal to one-half of all the funds the city had raised on its own.[40] As Municipal Services Director Jean Truau freely acknowledged in 1920, Rabat would be burdened with "state expenses" for some time.

> Rabat is quite a special city, a spendthrift city through necessity. Its dual nature as both an imperial city and the seat of the residency forces it to spend more than it takes in. And that is indispensable if we wish our city to be worthy of the role that the resident general has destined for it in Moroccan life. When Rabat attains the level of development that the administration has planned for it, Rabat will be able to take care of all its needs just as the other cities of Morocco.[41]

This would have given no cause for alarm if Rabat could depend on Lyautey's constant generosity. The truth was, however, that the protectorate subsidies did not keep pace with the expenses of the new city.

To its horror the municipal commission was tethered to protectorate purse strings that drew tighter with time. To its credit it tried valiantly (but not always fairly or evenhandedly toward Moroccans) to seek new sources of revenue. It began to use the power of eminent domain to "create" city property and it established new fiscal perimeters as taxing areas to include the tribal lands of the Oudaïas, Haouzias, and Ouladas.[42] Municipal commissioner Léon Petit quickly recommended the expropriation, irrigation, and sale to colonists of 5,000 hectares of land between the Ykem River and Rabat. He estimated that the sale of water alone to these new colonial farms would cover Rabat's annual deficit. And taxes on the produce of the land (the *tertib*) and gate and market taxes would bring additional revenue to the public coffers. What Petit characterized as a "simple" operation—the dispossession of collective land that "produces nothing or almost nothing"—was in fact rather complicated. In addition, according to Municipal Services Director Revilliod (Truau's predecessor), colonizing the Oudaïas's land, which was *guich* land (Makhzen property that had been turned over to the tribes in return for the supply of troops to the sultan), was "an extremely important question" with ramifications throughout Morocco. It required further study by the residency before any action could be taken.[43] For the time being Petit's vision of instant riches for Rabat disappeared.

To make matters worse, the residency oftentimes increased the city's financial obligations without consulting (and sometimes without informing) the municipal commission. This was a constant irritant between the colonists who always wanted more political power and Lyautey who tended to act autocratically. In 1918 the residency signed a "most burdensome" contract with the Ministry of Religious Property *(habous)*, which controlled a city aqueduct, for the supply of water to the city after the commission had already negotiated its own less costly agreement with the Société Marocaine de Distribution d'Eau, de Gaz, et d'Électricité. How could the city attempt to balance its budget asked commissioners Bernaudat and Petit, if "abnormal charges" were imposed on it?[44] Some time later the commission noted sharply that the water it was being forced to buy from the Ministry of Religious Property was not even being delivered.[45]

In 1922 when the residency added the expense of maintaining Rabat's primary schools to the city budget—what commission members called a move down the road toward the "municipalization of education"—there was a sharper display of municipal temper. Petit called for a "parliament" that could vote school taxes should it wish to do so. Taxation without any representation apparently had gotten out of hand. The mere mention of a parliament was enough to cause a political flutter in the press, but nothing more.[46] There was certainly no move on the part of the protectorate to give greater authority to the municipal commissions. The municipal commission "has no power to make decisions that are binding on the city government,"

Truau reminded the commissioners at the end of 1924, "but only to give advice when it is asked to do so."[47]

Remaining on the financial sidelines was difficult for many commission members to accept and the protests continued. In 1925 when the residency reduced its subsidy to the city from 3 to 2.5 million francs, Gaston Bernaudat recalled that each year for the past three he had protested the decreases in the protectorate's annual contribution that had now apparently become routine. "We, the citizens of Rabat, did not ask for the creation of a city out of proportion to the size of its population," he insisted. "Let each one of us [the residency and the municipal commission] pay his own share of the expenses which have resulted." He proposed that the residency accept the "principle" of an annual subsidy to the city equal to "at least one-third of the total municipal budget." Pharmacist Paul Séguinaud seconded Bernaudat's complaints. He objected to the "unwarranted extension" of Rabat's municipal—but not fiscal—perimeter that had "considerably" augmented the city's expenses for road maintenance, the lighting of city streets, sewer construction, and police protection. He, too, asked that the full subsidy be restored, even increased.[48]

Bernaudat added that the members of the commission wanted their voices to be heard—especially in financial matters—because they ought to be.

> Since we are appointed by the government, there is perhaps too great an inclination on the part of the public authorities to disregard our opinions. In my view that diminishes this institution and, if that is the way it is going to be, it would be better to abolish [the municipal commission] and create something more effective.[49]

Understandably Frenchmen desired more self-government in Rabat, and the push for an elected municipal assembly, even if it remained consultative, seemed to most the right step toward municipal maturity and "emancipation."[50] But despite Lyautey's high regard for the talent and energy of the colonial Frenchman, which he had once hoped would transform the Metropole, he resisted the commission's every move in that direction.

Water and electricity, ancient and modern sources of Rabat's life and energy, rivaled money as a topic of conversation at the meetings of the municipal commission. And as with city finances, although they affected both Moroccans and Europeans in multiple ways, these matters were dealt with almost exclusively by the French commissioners. In 1912 two aqueducts entered Rabat from springs eighteen kilometers from the city. One came from Aïn Attig (near Temara along the coast); it served the *medina* and was administered by the Ministry of Religious Property. The second came from Aïn Reboula (south of Rabat); it served the sultan's palace and was administered by the Makhzen. Because all but 2,500 meters of the *medina* line was uncovered and above ground and was drawn off along the way for the watering of livestock and the irrigating of farms and gardens, the water reached the fountains of the *medina* impure and in insufficient quantity. Without any authority over this line the Services Municipaux could do little more than oversee its operation and make suggestions for improvement.[51]

The aqueduct to the sultan's palace was another matter. As Makhzen city property, it fell under the control of the municipal commission and thus subject to the Services Municipaux. The municipal works administration built a covered reservoir at the spring's source, cleaned and repaired the water channel, then extended the line into the *medina* to supply a new fountain in the Teben market. The work on the Aïn Reboula line increased its flow (even though some water was diverted for the residency's use), but unexpectedly decreased the flow of the Aïn Attig aqueduct, whose source was only four kilometers from that of the Aïn Reboula. In any event, neither aqueduct could provide for the anticipated increase in water demand in the future.[52]

French civil engineers presented four plans to the residency for supplying new water to Rabat: laying additional pipelines from the Aïn Attig and Aïn Reboula springs, building a new pipeline from a spring near the Chella necropolis, digging wells to tap existing underground pools, or constructing a high dam on the Bou Regreg River. Each plan had its drawbacks and each was beyond the financial capabilities of the city. Aware of this, the Services Municipaux recommended that once the residency had chosen a water plan for Rabat—and in the end it opted for a mix of improvements, new lines, and new wells—a private company finance and build the new system, selling water to the city and private users alike. Within two years the French-owned and operated Société Marocaine de Distribution d'Eau, de Gaz, et d'Électricité began supplying water to the city. The initial contract was approved by the municipal commission in May 1916.[53]

The water needs of Rabat increased as the result of the growth in its population, the necessity to supply an "important" quantity of water to the palace, and the requisites of a "garden city." In 1918 the municipality secured the right to purchase, pump, and distribute the waters of the Aïn Attig spring and the Société Marocaine de Distribution commenced additional work on the Aïn Reboula channel.[54] By year's end Aïn Reboula was providing 16,000 cubic meters of water a day to the city. As a result of drought in 1920 and 1921, Aïn Reboula's flow dropped to 4,000 cubic meters per day, which Léon Petit predicted could easily fall by another 50 percent (down to 2,000 cubic meters or 50 liters of water per inhabitant per day) with another dry year. As a minimum, Petit figured that Rabat needed to keep its water flow between 4,000 to 5,000 cubic meters a day, even though he noted that this would only provide the citizens of Rabat with half the water available in cities that were "well-supplied" with water. Given Rabat's ever-expanding requirements, he recommended that its water capacity be boosted to 7,000 cubic meters, which still would require a drastic cutback in the watering of gardens and open green spaces. Failure to do this, however, might mean the end of French Rabat. As Petit told the readers of *L'Écho du Maroc* in a frightening glimpse into the future: "In Africa a garden city without a garden is little more than a string of buildings planted in a kind of polluted and evil-smelling Sahara."[55]

The municipal commission continued to weigh its options. With Aïn Reboula at a low point, Aïn Attig less than satisfactory, and the waters of the third spring—Aïn-Sidi-Yahia-des-Zaërs—unclean and inadequate, the commission turned to the father of waters, the Bou Regreg. With the construction of a dam and reservoir to gather the water lost to the Atlantic, the Bou Regreg could wash the streets and irrigate the gardens of Rabat and even soak the farmlands of Souissi and Oulja on the river's right bank. Aïn Reboula could then easily provide the city with sufficient drinking water. Petit described the sort of dam needed to do the trick, but admitted that it would have to be sited at an elevation lower than the Rabat Plateau. As a result, a powerful battery of turbine pumps would be needed to raise the water to the level of the city and farmlands. The cost of all this was more difficult to explain than the engineering. What is more, Petit had no idea where the money would come from. But he did calculate that a user's tax could easily raise two million francs a year, enough to maintain the dam, the reservoir, and the pumps as well as to pay back any borrowed capital over a thirty-year period. Petit insisted there could be no hesitation on this issue. The citizens of Rabat had to demand the construction of a dam on the Bou Regreg for it alone could quench the city's thirst.[56]

The protectorate preferred a less expensive way to fill Rabat's water glass. In 1923 the Department of Public Works approved the purchase of more equipment to increase the flow at Aïn Reboula and Aïn-Sidi-Yahia-des-Zaërs, authorized the drilling of a new well near the Temesna gate to boost the flow along the Aïn Attig channel, and agreed to the construction of a water-treatment plant.[57] These measures prevented any water crisis. But the search for an ample and reliable water source for Rabat only ended with the building of a high dam on the Bou Regreg, inaugurated a half-century later in 1974.[58]

Rabat's demand for electricity was equally difficult to meet. In 1913 Rabat had only one tiny electric generator producing current for the residency and its adjacent offices. The following year the city initiated talks with private contractors for the citywide distribution of electric power. Not until 1916, however, were the specific terms of an electricity concession with the Société Marocaine de Distribution d'Eau, de Gaz, et d'Électricité discussed in the municipal commission. At first commission members balked at what they considered to be excessively high electric rates, threatening to end the negotiations with the company before they had started. Only after Gaston Delure, the protectorate's director of public works, explained that the Société Marocaine de Distribution had purposely kept Rabat's water rates low (leaving the company "an insignificant margin of profit") so that it would be given the electricity concession in compensation, were the talks continued. Apparently it was understood by protectorate administrators and company officials—although no one had informed the members of the municipal commission—that without a coupling of the electricity and water concessions, the Société Marocaine de Distribution would not have taken either.[59]

The bill for Rabat's electricity was the result of the high cost of borrowing money (the current interest rate for private companies was between 8 and 10 percent) and the dramatic rise in the price of raw materials, particularly metals. Nevertheless, the Société Marocaine de Distribution quoted Rabat the same price for the lighting of its city streets as it was charging Casablanca. The rates for private consumers, however, would be higher. Delure explained that electric power consumption was far greater in Casablanca than in Rabat—"Casablanca being much more important than Rabat"—and thus overhead costs and in turn electricity bills were lower.[60]

Delure portrayed the Société Marocaine de Distribution as a "responsible" company with substantial financial resources and an excellent record of service and accomplishment, all of which argued for the fact that the terms of the concession—"as advantageous as the circumstances permit"—would be fulfilled. The future was anyone's guess, but Delure predicted that once the Société Marocaine de Distribution had constructed a power station and strung power lines in the city, it would be reluctant to lose the concession. This surely gave the municipal commission some leverage in subsequent negotiations. Based on Delure's endorsement of the company the commission unanimously approved the contract. It provided for both a high- and low-tension power grid, supplying a minimum of 200 horsepower to the city.[61]

Within two years the municipal commission and the Société Marocaine de Distribution were at odds. The commission refused to approve the company's request for a change in the contract terms in part because two months previous there had been a steep hike in electric bills with little fore-warning and no explanation. Once again a protectorate bureaucrat visited the commission to speak on the company's behalf. Civil Affairs Director Guillaume de Tarde repeated what Delure had said in 1916, that the profits to the Société Marocaine de Distribution for both the electricity and water concessions came only through the rates for electricity. Given the general price rise over the past two years and the more than threefold boost in the cost of the coal (from 125 to 400 francs a ton) that fueled the company's power plant on the right bank of the Bou Regreg, de Tarde characterized the rate increase as "by no means excessive."[62]

Municipal Services Director Revilliod asked de Tarde if he would agree to arbitrate the dispute between the commission and the company, but de Tarde made it clear that the matter was already settled, that the residency had decided not to accept the commission's "advice" on the concession rider. In short, in its "purely consultative role" the commission had expressed an opinion that the residency had "taken note of," but in the end had decided to disregard. This was hardly the sort of hardball negotiating with the Société Marocaine de Distribution that Delure had earlier alluded to. Reluctant to give in without a fight, the French members of the commission reaffirmed their earlier negative vote with de Tarde still in the room.[63]

They were right to do so. By early July 1919, unwilling to risk the con-sequences of the commission's ill will, the Société Marocaine de Distribution agreed to raise prices in three stages rather than insist on a onetime increase. As a result of what they took to be a compromise, the French members of the commission quickly approved the full concession agreement, including the rider. But they warned that all future contract terms had to be worked out in advance between the commission and the company, so that never again would the city be faced with a "fait accompli."[64]

In 1919 and again in 1920 power failures in Rabat (some of which lasted for several days) called into question the technical competence of the Société Marocaine de Distribution, the terms of its concession with the city, and the ties between the company's directors and protectorate administrators. In August 1920 a delegation of electricity consumers (which included municipal commissioner Petit) demanded legal action against the directors of the Société Marocaine de Distribution as well as confiscation of its property because Rabat had gone for twenty-four days without electric power during the past three months. Secondhand equipment (including eleven-year-old boilers that had spent "several weeks" underwater in a shipwreck), incom-petent native personnel ("of almost zero professional value"), and an absence of replacement parts were held responsible. How could such a mixture spell anything but disaster? Interim Municipal Services Director Jean Courtin immediately ordered an inspection of the company's equipment and directed that a fine be levied on the company for every future power outage that lasted longer than one hour.[65]

Before the inspector's official report was made public, Rabat experienced yet another series of blackouts. Consumer patience cracked. "The incompetence of the Société Marocaine de Distribution has resulted in far too much damage to Rabat," insisted *L'Écho du Maroc*. "It has gone beyond all reasonable limits."[66] Businessmen joined in the angry protest. How could Rabat's commerce and industry survive the consequences of the company's "deplorable management," they asked, when power failures were the norm rather than the exception and when the city's interests took a backseat to those of a private company? Rabat's chamber of commerce demanded that the Société Marocaine de Distribution immediately forfeit the electricity concession. "We understand its resolve," editorialized *L'Écho du Maroc*. "For no matter what happens, we cannot be more poorly served than we are at present." According to the newspaper's sources, the concession agreement lacked all the "elementary guarantees" essential in such affairs. It was a "joke" that had lasted too long and had cost the city dearly. Yet why was the residency reluctant to act? Did it fear upsetting those "occult powers" of big business and banking with whom it always cooperated so closely? Had Lyautey forgotten that there was a "courageous and hard-working" expatriate community in Rabat—continually lured by "wonderful promises" that were "never kept"—and that this community merited more than the residency's indifference?[67]

Despite the blunt talk and the hint of official corruption, there was no action on the part of the residency. Courtin expressed the vague hope that the company's problems might be solved by the beginning of 1921, implying that nothing more could be done—unless, of course, Rabat found a fairy godmother with a magic wand.[68] At the same time Albert Petsche, the Société Marocaine de Distribution director in Rabat, assured the finance and public works committees of the municipal commission that changes in equipment and personnel were on the way.[69]

Electric service did improve the following year and, as a result, sympathy increased for the company. Petit even blamed the Prost plan for some of the company's problems. Since the garden-city concept specified the dispersal rather than the concentration of Rabat's inhabitants, 15,000 Europeans (rather than the projected 150,000) were spread over a city space of 1,000 hectares that included 40 kilometers of streets and boulevards (with another 60 on the drawing boards). For the Société Marocaine de Distribution this meant supplying 2,000 customers on a power-line net-work that was 40 kilometers long. This worked out to be one customer for every 20 meters. In other cities that were "set up fairly well" the proportion was 10 or 20 times that. This deliberate scattering of the population, Petit explained, had required increased installation, maintenance, and power-supply costs. In addition, the overextended power line and Rabat's single electric-power generator—smaller in capacity than that of "the smallest sub-prefecture of France or of *le plus ordinaire des chef-lieux de canton"*—had contributed to the power shortages and failures in 1919 and 1920.[70] All this was Petit's preface to a commission request for a protectorate subsidy of five million francs to help pay the city's electric bill. As usual, even if the residency was the author of some of Rabat's electric discontent, it refused to pick up the tab.[71]

In 1922 the Société Marocaine de Distribution was granted a fifty-year monopoly on the supply of electric power to Rabat with the proviso that, should less expensive power become available from a new thermal plant at Casablanca or from hydroelectric generators on the Oum er Rebia River, it would cease its own power production, yet continue the distribution of electricity to the city. Two years later the Casablanca plant went into operation. This alone finally reduced the costs for Rabat's electric lights.[72]

Because municipal commissioners were always sensitive to the special interests of the city—in particular to the tax burden on the European resident of Rabat—there was always genuine and sustained enthusiasm among the commission members for the construction of port facilities, the development of the land adjacent to Rabat, and the building of railroad lines to connect the hinterland with the coast. These projects would have an immediate and hopefully positive impact on the economic life of the city.

A port at Rabat was considered one of the "essential factors" of the city's development. In 1914 Eugène Bigaré, the owner of one of Rabat's two flour mills, called it "the only way of allowing commerce and industry to develop and of giving our city a prosperity to which its geographical position entitles it."[73] The "considerable delay" in its construction in 1918 brought complaints from the commission that the important economic interests already engaged were being jeopardized.[74] The prosperity of the port was linked in turn to the building of roads and railroad lines to connect the interior with the coast. Bernaudat insisted in 1915 that the projected Casablanca-Fez line was wrong-headed because it bypassed Rabat. He argued for a Casablanca-Rabat-Kénitra-Fez route that would include Rabat and also cross "more fertile country." Rabat's lobbying paid off. The long-awaited Rabat-Fez line was finally inaugurated in April 1923.[75] In 1921 the commission championed a rail line to

Oued Zem so that 500,000 tons of phosphates a year could be shipped through the port of Rabat, making an enormous contribution to the city's economy. In addition, "a great and fertile region" would be opened to colonization. In short order 500 European families could put 100,000 hectares of land to the plow and in the process extend the trade and commerce of Rabat to the countryside.[76]

According to Rabat's promoters, Rabat-Salé had always been the "natural outlet" to the sea for the commerce of the tribes of the "*petit* hinterland"— the Zemmour and Zaër confederations—as well as for the trade of the "*grand* hinterland" that extended beyond Meknès and Fez to Kasbah Tadla, Khénifra, and the upper Moulouya. With the establishment of the protectorate and the pacification of the region around Rabat-Salé, Rabat had once more taken its place—after Casablanca to be sure—as a significant import-export entrepôt and maritime center.[77] What Rabat needed to emerge as a major urban force in Morocco was the protectorate's sustained commitment to its economic development.

It was only natural to find the municipal commission arrayed against the residency whenever that resolve was in doubt or whenever the protectorate's leadership in matters economic proved faulty. During the monetary crisis of 1919 when the rise in the value of the silver peseta hassani sliced the worth of the paper French franc and brought European business to a standstill, the municipal commission demanded that the residency call on the "elements of order and achievement" in the country and "heed their suggestions." Convinced that protectorate inaction had compromised "security in general" and "French interests in particular," the commission took the lead in arguing for the suppression of the peseta hassani and its replacement by the franc as Morocco's sole legal tender.[78]

Although the Rabat commission refused to join the wave of municipal resignations that accompanied European protest across the country, its disagreement with protectorate financial policy—as well as its unhappiness with Lyautey, who was in Paris and uncharacteristically mute—were never in doubt. The European uproar, displayed through angry press commentary and a series of volatile mass gatherings, succeeded in forcing Paris to agree to "demonetize" the peseta hassani. *L'Écho du Maroc* credited the triumph to popular agitation akin to that of 1789 and insisted that Morocco would never be the same again. The furious negotiations between the "representatives of the people" and protectorate administrators under pressure did have the scent of something historic about them. France could not allow its currency to be placed in an "unfavorable position," insisted *L'Écho du Maroc*, in a country for which it had borne such heavy sacrifices and for which it had spilled its blood so generously. And Frenchmen in Morocco had seen to it that it would not be.[79]

Neither Europeans in Morocco nor Frenchmen in Rabat, however, were able to capitalize on that initial and impressive demonstration of force to rush the protectorate citadel. When Lyautey returned to Morocco, he brought a carrot: France's agreement to build the Casablanca-Rabat-Kénitra-Fez rail road, and a stick: the reminder that France was not sovereign in Morocco. Because Morocco was a protectorate, not a colony, he explained for the hundredth time, French political institutions had no place on Moroccan soil. "Our nationals can have professional organizations and a professional representation," Lyautey told the assembled members of Rabat's municipal notables, "but cannot have any political representation." He warned that protests and polemics on this matter were not only useless—"wasted ink and lost time"— but dangerous: The Metropole would act swiftly to end them.[80]

Even though Rabat's municipal commission under Lyautey was never more than a consultative body, its composition and the opinions it expressed—often with amazing forcefulness and candor—made it clear that Frenchmen, not Moroccans, ruled Rabat.[81] In many matters of city business, from the most mundane to the highly technical, French commission members (as well as top city administrators and protectorate bureaucrats) also revealed that their cultural prejudices divided the city as much as the walls and broad thoroughfares of Prost's plan. To these attitudes the Moroccan commissioners were not insensitive, countering whenever and as best they could the French initiatives that neglected, denigrated, or otherwise marginalized their participation in the life of their own city.

In arguing for an increase in the number of French representatives on the municipal commission in 1918, Henri Legard, owner of Rabat's largest brickyard, stated what most Europeans believed to be true, that only the French members of the commission had a "real understanding" of Rabat's major public works projects. While this may have been so about a myriad of technical details, there was no lack of understanding or interest on the part of the Moroccan members of the municipal commission in the sewers and streets, port facilities, and rail lines that were key components of the city plan. In fact, they resisted whatever they found unacceptable. This was the case with the proposal to demolish the El-Gza gate in 1918. For the French this portal into the *medina* was a "hindrance" to automobile traffic; for the Moroccans it was a structure of historic importance as well as a barricade to further *medina* congestion. Because of the Moroccan protest the gate survived, but it often sparked debate in the municipal commission. To soothe his compatriots Revilliod noted that the time would soon be at hand when the entire *medina* would be "left to the natives" because every European would live outside its walls. Automobile traffic would decrease and the El-Gza gate would become less and less an obstacle.[82]

Moroccan merchants and businessmen were regularly awarded city contracts for all but the most lucrative concessions and monopolies. In most instances, however, they and their business practices and business problems came under closer scrutiny than French contractors. This was surely the case in the "Labiod affair." The day after Christmas 1918 Revilliod announced to the municipal commission that the current supplier of bulk charcoal to the city, Hadj Omar Labiod, had not kept his commitments and Rabat was on the verge of running out of fuel for its homes and workshops. He recalled that more than five months earlier, when the contract for the supply of the city's charcoal had been up for renewal, the members of the municipal commission "and particularly the native members" had complained that the current price was too high (24.50 Fr. per 100 kilograms) and asked for new contract bids.[83]

Revilliod had feared that a change in contractor might not be in Rabat's best interests. The current supplier, Haïm Biton, a well-known Jewish merchant whose advertisements appeared regularly in the *Annuaire du Maroc,* had fulfilled his obligations faithfully; he had an on-hand reserve of 16,000 quintals of charcoal that would easily cover the city's winter needs. Was there enough time, Revilliod had wondered, for a new contractor to accumulate a large winter reserve? And would a new contractor be able to provide charcoal at a price appreciably below Biton's? Nevertheless, on the "strong insistence" of the Moroccan members, the municipal commission unanimously agreed to open the charcoal contract for bidding. The contract was to be for two years and it stipulated an on-hand reserve of 3,000 quintals, the average city charcoal consumption for one month.[84]

The contract was awarded to Labiod whose candidacy was "warmly supported" by all the Moroccan members of the commission, who presented the "most positive information" about him. It was as much a question of preference as price. Labiod agreed to supply charcoal to the city at 21 Fr. per 100 kilograms, a rate nearly 17 percent less than Biton had charged. On the other hand, in spite of the endorsement and the price—and in fact perhaps because of both—Revilliod confessed that from the very beginning he had misgivings about Labiod. Given the costs of labor and transportation, he worried that Labiod's selling price was too low. The contract with the city might well bankrupt him and leave Rabat without fuel. In addition, despite the insistent prodding of the municipal administration and the protectorate's service of rivers and forests (Service des Eaux and

Forêts), Labiod seemed in no hurry to set up his charcoal manufactories *(charbonnières)* in the Mamora Forest. He claimed to be having a hard time finding workers in Rabat because of the higher salaries paid in the charcoal camps around Casablanca. On other occasions, so said Revilliod, Labiod gave equally "unacceptable excuses" for his inaction.[85]

In the hopes of averting a calamity Revilliod arranged for Biton to sell Labiod 5,000 quintals of charcoal. For a time this permitted him to meet the supply requirements of his contract. As winter approached, however, Labiod's reserve dwindled. Since Revilliod believed that there was still an "insignificant effort" at charcoal production in the forest, he once again alerted Labiod to the danger. But Labiod insisted that he could meet his obligations. And the Moroccan members of the municipal commission—whom Revilliod now called "his native protectors"—backed him up.[86]

Although the municipal commission stood by Labiod, Revilliod knew that the contractor was at the end of his rope. By December his charcoal reserve was exhausted and it was apparent that he could not restock. As a precaution, Revilliod asked several other charcoal merchants to be prepared to aid the city in case of a fuel crisis. Biton alone could promise to provide—albeit "in limited quantities"—the charcoal that the city required.[87]

In a showdown meeting on 26 December, Revilliod asked Municipal Services Director Gabriel Communaux of Salé, Garde Général Pierre Roy of the service of rivers and forests, and Labiod himself to testify before the municipal commission. Communaux revealed that Labiod had won the charcoal contract for Salé with a low bid of 19.50 Fr. per 100 kilograms, but he had yet to make a single delivery. As a result, Salé's needs had been handled on an erratic basis by a combination of Moroccan and European suppliers. Roy expressed no surprise at the situation because there had never been enough workers in the forest at any one time for Labiod to mount a successful charcoal operation. The "rare workers" who had shown up complained bitterly about the low salaries Labiod was paying them and soon deserted the camps. At the end of December when there should have been thirty-five to forty *charbonnières* in the Mamora, there were barely ten. Most of the 30,000 cubic meters of wood (which would have produced 20 to 25,000 quintals of charcoal) that the service of rivers and forests had cut for Labiod remained untouched. Roy concluded that Labiod was more interested in the profits on the charcoal he could purchase for resale to the city than in the manufacture of the charcoal itself.[88]

Labiod could not explain in any convincing manner why he had failed to live up to the terms of the contract. He put part of the blame on his workers, but Roy asserted that there had been too few of them to make much of a difference at all. Labiod said that he had sent 1,000 sacks of charcoal to Casablanca to meet a shortage there and this had cut into his reserve for Rabat. But Revilliod reminded the municipal commission that this was some of the charcoal supplied by Biton to Labiod at Revilliod's request. As Casablanca's stockpile of charcoal dwindled, Biton, who was one of Casablanca's contractors, had been forced to buy back from Labiod what he needed. The salient point was that Labiod had sold Rabat's reserve and profited from it.[89]

On Revilliod's recommendation the municipal commission broke its contract with Labiod (who forfeited his security deposit of 5,000 francs) and approved the purchase of as much charcoal as Biton could provide at 23.50 Fr. per 100 kilograms. These were emergency measures to deal with the present, but Revilliod made it clear that he wanted the commission's guidance on how to proceed in the future. He recalled that the open-marketplace charcoal trade of an earlier time had failed to provide the city with sufficient winter fuel. This was why the municipal commission had decided to use a contract system based on competitive bidding. As the Labiod experience proved, however, there was still no guarantee that Rabat would be provided with the charcoal it needed.[90]

Despite the disappointment with Labiod, Revilliod recommended sticking with a competitive-bid system because the previous year with Biton had been quite successful. He advised the municipal commission to require an even higher security deposit and to make periodic inspections of the *charbonnières* to ensure that enough workers were on the job and that a sufficient quantity of charcoal was being produced. Should the contractor fail to live up to its terms, the contract would terminate immediately.[91]

In his rush to condemn Labiod, Revilliod overlooked the structural problem. It was in fact true that the salaries of charcoal workers in Rabat and Salé were so low that workers were leaving the forests to seek other jobs. (To be sure, Labiod had made matters worse.) For this very reason in October 1919 Haïm Biton also became "clearly incapable" of fulfilling his contract with the city. To reverse this situation and to ensure the cities' winter provisioning required boosting the wholesale price for charcoal from 23.50 Fr. to 26 Fr. per 100 kilograms. Revilliod's successor, Léopold Bénazet, engineered precisely such a reform that had the great virtue of increasing the pay of the charcoal workers while leaving the retail price of charcoal unchanged.[92]

Like the discussions on public works, where Frenchmen dismissed Moroccan competence in technical matters, or the "Labiod affair," which passed a French verdict on the methods and mores of Moroccan merchants (and even on the judgment of the Moroccan members of the municipal commission), the names of Rabat's city streets also reflected French sentiments (or the lack of them) toward things Moroccan. In 1917 the municipal commission's subcommittee on street names suggested that the Route Razzia be renamed the Rue Van-Vollenhoven in honor of Jacques Van Vollenhoven, "one of the noblest colonists" of the Rabat region, who had been killed at the battle of Skourra, on 8 July 1917. (He was also the brother of the governor-general of French West Africa.) Only after the Moroccan members of the commission protested the change, reminding their French colleagues that Razzia had been a Muslim notable who had gifted extensive property to the Ministry of Religious Property, was the plan scrapped. Van Vollenhoven's name was saved for a street in the "new city."[93] In 1923 L'Écho du Maroc wanted the most important thoroughfare in Rabat, the Avenue Dar-El-Makhzen, rebaptized the Avenue du Maréchal-Lyautey. Municipal Services Director Truau was reluctant to make that change and suggested instead that the Place de la Gare, which intersected the Avenue Dar-El-Makhzen and which Lyautey himself had laid out, could at some later date become the Place du Maréchal-Lyautey. Truau's concern was not only to respect the historic Arab nomenclature, but to honor Lyautey's wish to have nothing named for him until after he had left Morocco.[94]

Of the forty-seven street names approved by the municipal commission in April 1924 thirty celebrated France and Frenchmen. The list included French cities (Rue de Marseille, de Nancy, de Rouen), soldiers (Square Poeymirau, Rue du Général-Brulard), diplomats and civil servants (Avenue de Saint-Aulaire, Rue Saint-René-Taillandier), one Rabat municipal commissioner (Quai Léon-Petit), and even the French luxury hotel opened the year before in Marrakesh (Rue de la Mamounia). The remaining seventeen streets paid homage to ten of Morocco's cities (Rue de Casablanca, de Sefrou, de Salé), four of Morocco's ruling dynasties (Rue des Almohades, des Mérinides, des Saadiens, and des Alaouites), the founder of the city of Rabat (Rue Yacoub-el-Mansour), and the first Arab dynast to rule in Morocco (Rue Moulay-Idriss).[95] When it became apparent that two streets had been overlooked in the collective baptism, Truau added the names of two former pashas of Rabat (Rue Seddik-Bargach and Rue de Bouznika).[96] But the balance was always tipped in the French favor. In fact, the municipal commission did not even wait for "illustrious" Frenchmen to die before honoring them. Breaking with the supposed "injustice" of this custom, in 1925 Truau nominated Pierre de Sorbier de Pougnadoresse, the protectorate's retiring secretary-general, and Louis Gentil, the geographer and explorer of Morocco, for commemoration by street sign. This would express Rabat's gratitude in their lifetime to those whose "determination, talent, and activity" had been used for the "greater good" of the country or the city, something that was not done for any Moroccan. Finally, while fighting still continued on the northern front during the 1925-26 Rif war, Truau recommended that a street be named the Rue de l'Ouergha as a small reminder of the thanks owed to those who were battling "for greater France." Somewhere in the patriotic fervor of the moment the sultan, his government, and his people had gotten lost.[97]

Almost everywhere in the Rabat that Lyautey remade and Frenchmen ruled, Moroccans lost prestige, influence, and authority as well as land and money. Ultimately they "disappeared" from the municipal commission, yielding the field to protectorate administrators, who effectively controlled all the operations of city government, and French commissioners, who even though they often engaged Lyautey's bureaucrats in tugs-of-war on all manner of things, rarely saw anything from a Moroccan viewpoint. To be sure, Lyautey was adept at using Moroccan sovereignty as a shield for his own authority, reminding colonial Frenchmen of the limits of their power and denouncing the displays of municipal bad temper (or worse, municipal revolt) as the expression of a narrow *"arrondissement* spirit."[98] In this way, he may have prevented the total eclipse of an official Moroccan municipal presence. But the Lyautey vision of one Rabat living two different but interwoven lives, a separate yet equal expression of a Franco-Moroccan partnership, never became a reality.

CHAPTER 7

In Search of Indirect Rule in Casablanca
■ ■ ■ ■

iven the revolution made by Frenchmen in Rabat, it should come as no surprise that indirect rule never became Morocco's truth. Finding the "right" Moroccans to make it work—Moroccans willing to commit themselves to the French for whatever mix of personal, political, economic, social, even patriotic reasons—was never a simple task. The "abdication" of Sultan Abd el-Hafid had made this clear from the start. French expectations of, and demands on, native leaders added to the difficulty of ruling indirectly. Moreover, Frenchmen refused to play by their own rules, making as well as unmaking native leaders rather than merely supervising an established native elite as the rule book required. As a result, the search for indirect rule, despite some noteworthy efforts to seek it out, was ultimately unsuccessful.

Finding the right man in Casablanca, the protectorate's major port and leading commercial center, was complicated by the fact that the city lacked a Muslim aristocracy or bourgeoisie deemed worthy or capable of directing public affairs or managing Franco-Moroccan relations. In the sultan's words Casablanca was a "Bedouin city" without the human or material fabric of Islamic culture and tradition that marked Makhzen cities such as Fez and Meknès, Rabat and Marrakesh.[1] To the sultan the talent pool in Casablanca was very shallow. At the same time Casablanca's potential as an economic powerhouse had attracted new men and new money to the city, transforming a tranquil seaport into a bustling "Chicago on the Atlantic" in a short period of time.[2] When Paul Deschanel, president of France's Chamber of Deputies, first saw Casablanca in 1914, he compared it to the boomtowns that he had visited on a tour of the American West, produced by a kind of "spontaneous explosion." This new Casablanca—that Lyautey hoped would soon be a "prestigious witness to French energy and initiative"—demanded a Moroccan administration that could cope with these profound changes and guide the city toward its Franco-Moroccan destiny.[3]

French concern with Casablanca's urban administration predated the protectorate. In August 1910 the sultan named Si Mohammed Ben Mohamed Ben Guebbas, then city governor of Tangier and the son of the sultan's minister of war, to the post of city governor *(caïd)* of Casablanca. The French minister at Tangier, Eugène Regnault, assured General Charles Moinier, commander of the French troops at Casablanca, that the nomination was "completely satisfactory from the political point of view." Although Ben Guebbas was "as yet untested," Regnault insisted that he had "every reason to believe that the new pasha, who is inspired by the very best intentions, will soon take to administrative matters. In your dealings with this sharifian official, I would be grateful," the diplomat gently instructed, "if you would take into consideration the services rendered to us by his father which are sufficient to justify your special goodwill with regard to his son."[4]

Ben Guebbas lasted less than three months. He slipped out of Casablanca on a boat to Tangier at the beginning of November, leaving Moinier a letter in which he said he was just going to visit his father. By month's end Moinier realized that the *caïd* would never return. Moinier speculated that Ben Guebbas had not found what he was looking for in Casablanca. In the first place his expenses were more than his salary would allow and, coupled with the "rigorous" French supervision of any other sources of income, he found himself with insufficient funds to live a *caïd's* life. Secondly, he wrongly assumed that he would be the most important Makhzen administrator in the city. His competitor was the sultan's uncle, Sidi El Hadj Mohammed el-Omrani, the sultan's "direct representative" *(khalifa)* at Casablanca and the principal go-between with the French military authorities. The functions of *caïd* and *khalifa* overlapped in a somewhat ragged fashion, particularly in the important matter of the proper intermediary in contacts between foreign consulates and local *caïds*. The confusion, as Moinier pointed out to the French chargé d'affaires at Tangier, extended to the matter of nomenclature. Although Ben Guebbas acted the part of a pasha of Casablanca and was referred to as such by Moroccans and Europeans alike, by the sultan's edict *(dahir)* he had been named *caïd*. "Pasha" was the title usually reserved for the sultan's *khalifa* in port cities and, therefore, it was only el-Omrani's.[5]

Ben Guebbas wanted to be both *caïd* and *khalifa*, a pasha of undisputed standing and authority. To this aim the French had no real objection since Ben Guebbas handled himself "very correctly" at Casablanca and there

were obvious advantages to eliminating any political infighting or administrative tangle at the peak of the native hierarchy. Clear lines of power and
responsibility would compensate for any "regret" the French might have at
el-Omrani's departure even though he would be missed, for he had given
completely of his experience, intelligence, and "urbanity."[6]

Nothing came of Ben Guebbas's ambition, however, and in the end it was
he who left Casablanca, not el-Omrani, who continued to tighten his connections with the French. In January 1912 el-Omrani received the officer's cross
of the Legion of Honor for his leadership of a military contingent at the time
of the "rescue" of Fez, proof positive of France's high regard.[7] And when el-
Omrani died, his nephew, Moulay Idriss el-Omrani, became pasha of the city.[8]

Unfortunately, the nephew was not at all like the uncle. Colonel Antoine
Targe, commander of the Casablanca subdivision with ultimate authority
over both civil and military services in Casablanca and Settat, described him
as a personage of little consequence, "without style," lazy, and a miser to
boot. He had none of the "indispensable" personal qualities requisite for the
chief native administrator of the city, and because his avarice knew no
bounds, he had become a political liability.[9] In specific, the pasha had
become obsessed with inheriting all of what he imagined to be the "colos-
sal fortune" of his uncle. The executor of the estate was Si Hamadi, the late
pasha's secretary, who, according to the stipulations of Koranic law, managed
the estate until a final settlement could be made. Convinced that Si Hamadi
was stealing whatever he could of his uncle's fortune, Moulay Idriss impris-
oned him in the Dar El Makhzen for several months to force him to admit
his crime and, more important, to give up any rights to the inheritance. This
violated Koranic law and trampled justice. During the French investigation
into the matter, the pasha candidly acknowledged that Si Hamadi had been
"kept under surveillance in the Dar El Makhzen without the freedom to
leave the cell where he was being detained." Both the detention and treat-
ment of Si Hamadi had been "arbitrary and illegal." Knowingly and with mal-
ice, Moulay Idriss had abused his authority as a Makhzen official.[10]

Had the pasha been a leader of uncontested merit and recognized
authority, had he rendered unique services to the Makhzen or to France in
years gone by, he might have survived the inquiry with only a verbal reprimand or disciplinary note in his personnel file. This was not the case. Moulay
Idriss el-Omrani was "notoriously incompetent" as pasha, failing to keep the
French informed on native opinion "often because of inability, more often
because of inertia or ill will." His apathy and genuine distaste for administrative responsibilities—as opposed to his appetite for the authority, prestige,
and opportunities of his office—had caused the French to lose touch with the

native population of the city. During moments of uncertainty at the start of the European war, the pasha had been "no use at all."[11] In short, the Si Hamadi affair was only the latest in a string of disappointments that argued for Moulay Idriss's removal. On 6 December 1914 the sultan signed the edict revoking the pasha's appointment.

Among the French authorities in Casablanca the Si Hamadi affair also had an unsettling impact. When Captain Gaston Cottenest, head of the military intelligence service of the Région de la Chaouïa and a friend and confidant of the late Sidi Mohammed, had tried to arbitrate the dispute, the pasha accused him of prejudice in the case and, worse, acting in a dishonest manner. Behind the pasha, there seemed to be Frenchmen at work: Alfred Collieaux, the municipal services director of Casablanca; Joseph Court, Collieaux's assistant; and Georges Klépper, head of the Contrôle Civil in Casablanca. All three had sided with the pasha against Si Hamadi and, although it was never proven, had probably advised the pasha to protest Captain Cottenest's intervention. This incident, coupled with the Services Municipaux's failure to restrain the pasha from taking the law into his own hands and reluctance to keep the officers of the Casablanca subdivision informed, underscored civil-military rivalries and policy disagreements.[12]

The heart of the matter was native affairs. Collieaux left no doubt about his disapproval of the previous military administration of the city that he characterized as much too heavy-handed and far too tightly controlled. He championed an opposite model, a native administration with as little French involvement as possible and in which the pasha's authority would be the "keystone." Obviously the Si Hamadi affair threatened to compromise Collieaux's goal by unmasking the abuses of unsupervised native authority. Still, in defense of his actions Pasha Moulay Idriss el-Omrani later claimed he had the "tacit approval" of the municipal authorities in Casablanca—and unfortunately he probably did.[13]

Writing to Lyautey on the situation in Casablanca, Targe argued that Collieaux's policies were wrongheaded and detrimental to French influence in Morocco. Whether inexperienced or blindly self-confident, Collieaux was pushing Casablanca toward a system of "native administration in which the protectorate formula is unskillfully applied and which renders nonexistent the contacts of the [military] supervisory authorities with the Muslim population." Furthermore, Collieaux was ignoring the needs and aspirations of the European city. "He behaves like a mayor of Paris who sees no farther than the Ile Saint-Louis." Targe, who for a short time had himself headed Casablanca's municipal administration, recommended firing Collieaux (ironically he had pushed for Collieaux's appointment in the first place) and placing the city in the hands of someone who had the confidence of both businessmen and the native population, admittedly a "rare bird." "But, in any case, even the return of a soldier to the city administration would be a positive step from my point of view." Most important, he thought it "indispensable" that the subdivision's military intelligence service, which Cottenest headed, alone be charged with formulating Casablanca's native policy and with supervising the native city administration and the system of native justice.[14]

In the end, Collieaux remained in Casablanca, but Lyautey, who valued Targe's assessment, made it clear that the civilian municipal authorities had acted incorrectly and perhaps even dangerously by failing to inform the subdivision of the Si Hamadi affair. The pasha was not a mere local official, but "a political personality whose actions must be supervised by those authorities responsible for the security of the [Chaouïa] territory." It was up to the subdivision's military intelligence service, the *bureau de renseignements,* to centralize information and establish a uniform native policy for the entire Chaouïa. "As a result, in the future all the contacts of the municipal authorities with the pasha and other political personalities will be handled according to the orders from the commander of the subdivision, and each contact will be the subject of a report sent to him."[15] The chain of command was thus carefully reforged, leaving Collieaux less freedom of movement with the native political elite. The lone human casualty of the Si Hamadi affair was Pasha Moulay Idriss el-Omrani, not only the victim of his own greed, but of his inability to measure up to French expectations.

In addition to sacking the pasha, the French moved against the brothers Ben Kirane, who had made Casablanca a corrupt family fief by holding and exploiting the principal posts in the city administration. The oldest of the clan, Si Larbi, was the collector of market and gate taxes *(amin el-moustafad);* Si El Hadj Abdelkrim was the market supervisor *(mohtaseb);* Si Ahmed was the pasha's representative and second in command *(khalifa);* and Si El Fathi was the head of customs and finances *(amin el-diouana).* Four other Ben Kiranes worked at private businesses which profited directly from the public functions of their well-placed brothers.[16]

To listen to the French the vices of the Ben Kiranes were right out of the tales of *The Arabian Nights.* Testimony before the Conseil de Guerre at Casablanca, taken to track German business activity in Morocco after the outbreak of European hostilities, unexpectedly revealed that half of the profits from the gate taxes were being shared by Larbi, Abdelkrim, Ahmed, and three other Ben Kirane siblings. The gate tax concessionaire, German businessman Henri Tönnies, split his profits with Abderrahman Ben Kirane, who was the front man for his brothers. The most seriously compromised in the affair was Larbi, whose job it was to lease out the gate tax concession; apparently he sold it with one hand and purchased it with the other. French authorities insisted that this gate tax scam was only the tip of the iceberg.[17]

Because the Ben Kiranes were Fassis, their stranglehold on Casablanca was humiliating as well as costly. It did not square with the French notion of the "honest administration of the affairs of the native city," nor with French aspirations for Casablanca. Under the Ben Kiranes Casablanca was an orange to be paid for and squeezed. It was depressing as well to the local Casablancan bourgeoisie, who had always been pushed aside by the Makhzen in favor of outsiders from Fez and other cities with a Makhzen pedigree. "This hold on the most visible native administrative posts in Casablanca by a family of Fassis seems unacceptable," wrote Targe to Lyautey. "It presents serious inconveniences as well, fostering among the notables who were born and raised in this city, a real and a priori legitimate discontent."[18] The fate of the Ben Kiranes was decided. Only the timing of their ouster remained to be set.

At Casablanca the immediate need was for a pasha of "exceptional energy" and "unmatched prestige" among both the native and European populations.[19] The leading candidate was a former minister of Sultan Abd el-Aziz, Si El Hadj Ben Abdelkrim Omar Tazi. Targe reported to Lyautey that he was "rich, influential, intelligent, [and] known and appreciated by Europeans."[20] Indeed, as pasha, Tazi would come close to the French beau ideal.

Omar Tazi was in his late forties in 1914. Born in Fez, he had had no formal education beyond rudimentary religious instruction at a Koranic school. That had not prevented him from becoming minister of finance, then chamberlain, to the sultan. He was in fact an "intimate adviser" to Abd el-Aziz and more than that, a "real Grand Vizir" without the title, who often had the preponderant voice in the meetings of the sultan's ministers.[21] Tazi had been "useful" to the French "on several occasions," notably with regard to el-Hiba, the rebel sultan of the south, whom he had tried but failed to negotiate into submission. A partisan of Abd el-Aziz to the bitter end, he had rallied late to el-Aziz's rival and successor, Abd el-Hafid, which is why after 1908 he remained (or had been put) on the sidelines of Makhzen politics. "Very much neglected and almost kept on the outside until now," a French intelligence report explained, Tazi was once again acceptable—*ministrable* in the French political vocabulary—to the Makhzen under Sultan Moulay Youssef.[22]

During his years in the political wilderness, Tazi had made a considerable fortune in business and real estate in Casablanca. Because of his name and money, he was recognized as a man of influence and authority in the city. And the guess was that Tazi, a Casablancan of both the head and the heart, would put all his energy into the job as pasha and use his contacts to advance the French cause.[23] As Daniel Rivet has pointed out, Tazi was a "good prototype" of the Moroccan *grand négociant,* resigned to French tutelage and now willing to help France reinvigorate Morocco.[24]

With suitable pomp Tazi was invested as pasha on 7 December 1914, the imperial *dahir* read in the mosques before the assembled notables "according to the ancient custom," while a twenty-one gun salute boomed in the city. As a condition of his appointment, Tazi agreed to cease dealing directly with any of his businesses and to manage his personal wealth through a proxy.[25] In this way some of the indiscretions of the Ben Kiranes might be avoided. On the other hand it was among the Casablanca merchant class (and especially among the businessmen from Fez) that Tazi's appointment was greeted with greatest enthusiasm because of the hope for material gain. Others in the native population remained "indifferent" to the change in pasha. Although recognizing that the former pasha was an "ignoramus," who cared little about city government and less about the administration of justice, they were convinced that with or without Tazi real power rested "completely in the hands of the French authorities."[26]

Lyautey was delighted with Tazi. "You know," he wrote to Collieaux, "that the nomination to the government of Casablanca of a personage of the importance of El Hadj Omar has had the effect of increasing the prestige of all the functions of government which the lackluster personality of [Moulay Idriss] el-Omrani had diminished." He quickly cautioned: "This does not mean, however, that supervision—especially in the area of native penal matters—should not continue to be exercised in a discreet, but effective fashion."[27] One of the predictable consequences of the Si Hamadi affair had been Lyautey's insistence that the Casablanca municipal authorities closely oversee the pasha's management of city affairs and especially the dispensing of justice.

Tazi's judicial style was to handle the most important legal cases himself and leave the rest to his two *khalifas.* To French consternation he initially favored Ahmed Ben Kirane in whom he seemed to place "full confidence."[28] It was, therefore, imperative that the "political success" of having placed a former vizir at the head of the city of Casablanca be followed up by the purge of the Ben Kiranes. Ahmed, characterized by Targe as the "old-Makhzen type of bureaucrat, insignificant and greedy," was replaced as *khalifa* by Si Abdelkrim Ould Bou Azza Ben Msik, a wealthy Casablanca notable of public-spirited generosity and irreproachable morality, held in esteem by Europeans and Moroccans alike. Ben Msik was a longtime French protégé who, despite lucrative competing offers (mainly German) preferred to stay with France. His nomination would have "happy consequences," predicted

Targe, and be welcomed by all Casablancans who would see in this act "our very real concern not to keep them outside the administration of their city any longer."[29] Si Abdelkrim Ben Ahmed el-Heddaoui replaced Larbi Ben Kirane as market and gate tax collector. Heddaoui was a knowledgeable and competent scholar-administrator who had studied at Fez, and since 1898 had been charged with the management of "religious properties" at Casablanca. "Among the native population, he enjoys a moral influence of the highest order as a result of his education and his integrity." And his relations with the French authorities had always been "excellent."[30]

The solitary holdover from Moulay Idriss el-Omrani's administration was the second *khalifa,* Moulay Ahmed Ben Mansour, an "old soldier" from the former Franco-Moroccan port police at Rabat, mandated by the 1906 Act of Algeciras. Ben Mansour lacked the finesse and "intellectual breadth" to be an able counsellor to the pasha, and, in fact, was little appreciated by Tazi. But, as Targe explained to Lyautey, "his military past, his former services, and his qualities of energy, of loyalty, and of discipline make him a very precious agent whom we could call on should the need arise."[31]

Tazi's tenure as pasha lasted almost four years (until September 1918) and was very successful. The pasha presided over the wartime years of Casablanca's mushroom growth and development, handling municipal affairs "intelligently and with great tact," and managed to keep the respect of both the native and European populations; not easy since one of his major responsibilities was to sort out an increasing number of "delicate matters" involving Europeans. According to French reports, Tazi was "very much in his element" as pasha and carried out his duties with "the greatest distinction . . . devoting himself wholeheartedly to the development of the French cause and the economic progress of the city." In short, he favored the French influx of men and money, which required a native leadership that encouraged cooperation and inspired confidence.[32]

Tazi realized the importance of his accomplishment at Casablanca and that his post was potentially more powerful and profitable than that of any minister to the sultan. Still, it remained less prestigious. All the while at Casablanca he angled for appointment to Rabat, ever troubled by thoughts of his Makhzen rivals whom he knew would try to block his advance and subject to bouts of depression about his own career and upward prospects. In 1917 when Mohammed el-Mokri was named the sultan's *grand vizir,* Tazi was unable to conceal his "deep disappointment" for he had set his cap for this post. A year later, amid rumors that el-Mokri's son would be named pasha of Casablanca and Mokri's "close friend," Larbi Ben Kirane, would return in vindicated triumph to Casablanca as *khalifa,* Tazi accepted appointment as minister of state property. But not before he had secured his brother's selection as pasha through Lyautey's direct intervention with the sultan. This effectively checked any el-Mokri move on Casablanca (but only after a week of furious negotiating) and preserved Tazi's influence in the city.[33]

The sole blemish on Tazi's service record was the notation that he had had "some difficulties with the chief judge of the Koranic court [cadi]."[34] This was a gentle understatement. The feud between the pasha and the *cadi* of Casablanca, Si Ahmed Ben el-Mahmoun el-Belghiti, had at its origin the different political loyalties of the two men. It became a quarrel over rank, precedence, and authority in Casablanca, which seriously affected both French policy and plans for native government.

As a representative of Sultan Abd el-Aziz, Tazi had been sent to Mogador in 1908 to raise an army to fight against the pretender, Abd el-Hafid. Cadi of Mogador and a Hafidist, el-Belghiti had managed to disguise his true allegiance from Tazi. When he judged the moment ripe, however, he raised the pretender's banner and rallied Mogador's citizens and even Tazi's soldiers to the cause. Forced to take refuge in the French consulate, Tazi barely escaped capture by his own troops. Deceived and humiliated, he never forgot nor forgave.[35]

In 1914 el-Belghiti was named a member of the Conseil Supérieur d'Ouléma at Rabat, the highest religious appeals court in the French-reformed Muslim legal system. By background and talent he was suited for the post. Originally from Fez, el-Belghiti was well educated (he was in the first rank of the doctors of religious law, *alem de première classe*) and of good character. Among the French he was known as one of the "best reputed jurisconsuls," although he could be abrupt and "a bit violent" toward those who came before his tribunal. Independent-minded, at times unyielding, and of rebellious spirit, el-Belghiti promised to be a handful for both Tazi and the French when he was named *cadi* of Casablanca in December 1914.[36]

Despite the facade of courtesy and politeness, neither Tazi nor el-Belghiti could ever trust one another. Tazi had "protested strongly" to the minister of justice when he learned that his old adversary was to be named *cadi* of Casablanca. Unable to block the appointment, he attempted a rapprochement, and even offered the *cadi* (who was apparently often short of cash) gifts of money. In this the *cadi* saw only a snare. "'To be sure, Tazi was discreet,' he told a confidant, 'but didn't he inform against his friend [Si el-Mehdi] el-Araki, by producing the register which listed the sums of money he had given him? This man merits no confidence.'" For his part "quite offended" at el-Belghiti's refusal of the money, Tazi determined to rid himself of the *cadi,* which, notwithstanding an appeal to the *grand vizir,* he could not do.[37]

The Tazi-el-Belghiti feud, which continually showed up on new ground, defined the contours of Casablanca's native administration. In January 1915 Tazi wrote to Targe of the "difficulty" he was having with el-Belghiti. It was "customary," Tazi maintained, that the preparation and signing of commercial acts have the pasha's "authorization." Yet he had been presented documents in a recent litigation that did not carry his stamp. Questioning their genuineness, he asked el-Belghiti to let him see his commercial register so that he could verify if the documents had been listed or not—and, if so, in what manner. Despite Tazi's "care" to explain what he was after and why, el-Belghiti "categorically refused" to send the register.

"I had always thought," Tazi reasoned on paper, "that the pasha was the highest Makhzen administrator of the city and that his directives were to be followed by all other Makhzen administrators in Casablanca, especially when it concerned matters under his direct authority." El-Belghiti was apparently unwilling to accept a request from a higher-placed administrator. Rather than permit the "disagreement" to become a "struggle" between the two, Tazi asked for instructions. Was el-Belghiti to follow the pasha's orders or was he "absolutely independent"? If the first were so, concluded Tazi, "it would probably be necessary to issue him a disciplinary note for his attitude toward me"; if the second, "I would know where I stand in my administrative dealings with him."[38]

Targe asked Collieaux to remind el-Belghiti that his "categorical refusal" of the pasha's request could cause a "tension prejudicial to the goal we seek, which is the normal functioning of administrative affairs." The pasha was, after all, the "first representative of the Makhzen" and all sharifian administrators had to recognize his "preponderant role" by demonstrating "the most complete subordination" on all matters of administration. It was Collieaux's duty, Targe underscored, to work to make the native chain of command operate harmoniously. At the same time he called on Lyautey to make a "decision of principle," defining to what degree and in what form sharifian officials should be subordinated to the pasha. The question was of "capital importance," he believed, "especially as we work to enhance and reaffirm the prestige of the Makhzen and its direct representatives." Left to himself to decide, Targe made it clear he would permit Pasha Tazi "a clear preponderance" over all other Makhzen administrators in the handling of city matters.[39]

Collieaux reported that the custom of having the pasha authorize the preparation and signing of commercial acts had begun with a former pasha of Casablanca, the uncle of Sultan Abd el-Aziz, who had been given this benefit of office (since the pasha's cachet was never given free of charge) as a way of increasing his income. There was nothing in the texts of the *dahirs* that made it legal. Beyond this vague right of authorization, which remained something to be negotiated between pasha and *cadi*, it was impossible for the pasha to go.

> The pasha's pretension to verify for himself the validity or authenticity of the documents that have been submitted to him based on the records or registers in the *cadi's* possession, does not seem permissible. To the religious magistrate alone belongs the responsibility for handling these investigations.

Despite Collieaux's previous support of Pasha Moulay Idriss el-Omrani, he now appeared to be more sensitive than Targe to the delicate balance that had to be maintained between the need to strengthen the prestige and pre-eminence of sharifian authority, represented by the pasha, and the concern to safeguard the independence that tradition assigned to Koranic law, represented by the *cadi*. As Collieaux saw it, although the pasha was at the top of the sharifian hierarchy, he had no right to interfere, no *droit d'immixtion directe* in the duties of his subordinates, who were carrying out their own statutory responsibilities. "Observing this principle of non-intervention must be rigorously maintained in everything that touches Koranic law which is separate from the secular authority in all Muslim countries."[40]

These were Lyautey's views as well. Although the pasha was "the highest expression of sharifian authority" in Casablanca, this was only a question of "precedence." In their respective spheres the pasha and the *cadi* "have always been and remain independent of each other." Thus, "the pasha has no right to exercise any supervision over the acts of the *cadi*." Nevertheless, once asked for the registers, el-Belghiti should have turned them over to Tazi, and then immediately alerted the French supervisors. Of course, it would have been "preferable" for Tazi to have requested only the information he needed, not the registers themselves.

> For El Hadj Omar is too well aware of the traditions of the Makhzen and of the independence of the *cadis* vis-à-vis the administrative authorities—something which has always been recognized—not to know that this was one thing he should not touch. It is in our greatest interest to prevent any injury to the independence of the administrative power and the judicial power and to avoid any precedents in this respect.

At the same time the sharing of necessary information between "two high administrators" was vital to good government "as long as this does not lead to meddling in each other's responsibilities."[41]

Still, Collieaux had a rather broad conception of Tazi's independent role as pasha. Tazi was like a prefect in France who, although he did not supervise his subordinates directly, exercised in the name of the government a "general oversight" on the entire administrative apparatus, acting as both coordinator and arbiter among its various offices. In addition, Tazi had the ability to be a "mentor" to those in his service because of the "moral influence" inherent in his high position, his own background and experience, and—should he wish to bring them to bear—his impartiality and expertise in dealing with people. Without doubt Tazi was capable of increasing "sharifian prestige" at Casablanca. He demonstrated great activity and personal initiative and yet was responsive to suggestions from the control officers who tried to be his "discreet guide," his "collaborateur écouté." This "high personality," concluded Collieaux, "must be more than a hand which puts the Islamic stamp of approval on our actions: I believe that no measure ought to be taken without first getting his advice."[42]

Here, too, Collieaux and Lyautey were in agreement. Both believed in native city government, but both counted for its ultimate success on the ability of French officials to handle the participants. Collieaux knew, for example, that he could negotiate a "truce" between the pasha and the *cadi,* but probably no more than that. And in the end, the smoldering feud between the two might even be preferable to "a too-perfect understanding" between the "former merchant prince" (*gros tajer*) and the magistrate. "A pasha of Tazi's intelligence and command is even less easy to handle than one reputed for his shrewdness in business dealings." With Tazi, according to Collieaux, the key to good government was his ambition for higher office. More than anything else, this would keep him on the straight and narrow.[43]

The Tazi-el-Belghiti feud lasted throughout the tenure of both men at Casablanca. El-Belghiti's personality was undoubtedly a factor in the continued dispute, for he had difficulties with the supervisory officers, with native petitioners, and with even the saintliest of his colleagues, Abdelkrim Ben Msik, whose politeness was legendary: On his deathbed he was still offering mint tea to his doctors. All complained of the *cadi*'s lack of courtesy and some reported his insulting language.[44] The pasha was no exception. He had gone to see el-Belghiti about a grievance in an inheritance case and was greeted with "unbecoming and rude expressions" that got worse as the conversation went on, "words that the ear refused to hear and which the mouth of any man proud of his name should refuse to speak."[45] This episode caused the penultimate break between the two men. "Worn out and disgusted" by the incident and from all the trouble el-Belghiti had caused him,

Tazi begged the sultan to fire him. Instead, the sultan dispatched the *grand vizir* to Casablanca to try for a reconciliation.[46]

El-Belghiti bedeviled the French as much as he did the pasha. Collieaux believed that the *cadi*'s disagreeable nature and outright "animosity" toward many protectorate bureaucrats were rooted in his resentment over the "discreet and consistent supervision" of French officials.[47] El-Belghiti simply refused to have his fierce independence curbed. On the other hand, Colonel Jean Calmel, Targe's successor as military commander of the Casablanca subdivision, saw the "eminent jurist" as a retrograde figure of the past, closed to every new idea, and prisoner of the "appetites and reproachable habits of the magistrates of old Morocco." This made him a liability in a post that required close cooperation with the French, especially on sensitive matters such as property registration.[48] "Since he has been *cadi* in Casablanca, Moulay Ahmed el-Belghiti has never collaborated sincerely with the supervisory authorities in spite of all that has been done to guide and direct him, in a word to give him confidence." His "hostile attitude to our cause is notoriously well known."[49] In 1915 Calmel asked Lyautey to have el-Belghiti replaced, but an internal investigation found nothing to justify his removal or to warrant even a disciplinary note from the sultan.[50] Calmel renewed the request three years later, seconding Tazi's plea to the sultan, since by then the problem was not only the *cadi*'s attitude, but a question of native policy. "His rupture with the pasha is well known to everyone; it has even been displayed publicly. Under these conditions I consider that his retention, even temporarily, would greatly compromise the principle of authority."[51] El-Belghiti was forced to resign. At the sultan's insistence, however, his departure was postponed until April 1919, ten months after Calmel's request and eight months after Tazi had left Casablanca for a higher post in Rabat. When el-Belghiti finally left for retirement in Fez, it appeared to be of his own free will; his reputation, pride, and independence remained intact.[52]

Omar Tazi's political masterstroke was securing the appointment of his brother to succeed him as pasha of Casablanca.[53] It gave him one foot in Rabat and another in Casablanca and perhaps hinted at the formation of a municipal dynasty to rival the Bargachs. It also left no doubt who had won the long tug-of-war with el-Belghiti. Managing that victory, however, proved more difficult than winning it.

For twelve years Abdellatif Tazi had lived modestly at Mazagan as manager of Tazi family property and investments in the Doukkala. At first he was not inclined to accept a major public office. His personal fortune was small and he was financially dependent upon his brothers' generosity and the stipend he received as the city's chief customs officer, a post he had held for six years. His reputation at Mazagan was as a quiet man of faith, hospitality, and charity. Although Abdellatif did not seem to be cut from pasha's cloth, both his brother and the French found much to admire. He was intelligent, conscientious, and talented. Moreover, he was a Tazi, which, given El Hadj Omar's record of success, was a mark in his favor. Abdellatif himself worried most about the expenses of office, and only after his brother promised him a monthly allowance of 3,000 pesetas hassani if he took the job, was he willing to say yes.[54]

Abdellatif's concern over money was not inappropriate, given the expenses of office. A monthly salary of 1,500 pesetas hassani had been satisfactory for his brother, who had an immense personal fortune to fall back on, but the 1,400 pesetas Abdellatif was offered was inadequate.[55] After four months as pasha, he requested an increase, not only because of his expenses, but because the pashas of Rabat and other municipalities were being paid more than he was. "In every respect," he argued, "the position of pasha of Casablanca is superior to that of those of my colleagues from other cities."[56] This was pride mixed with need. Calmel endorsed the request, calling the pasha's salary "frankly insufficient." "I would even go so far as to say that it should be doubled."[57] There was no salary adjustment, however, and Tazi's finances became more desperate. The worst of it was that El Hadj Omar had not made good on his monthly financial pledge. The French supervisory officer closest to the pasha warned Calmel that there was no way Abdellatif could run an "honest administration" on 1,400 pesetas a month and that the control authorities would have to "close their eyes to the irregularities (sources of profit) which will take place, if they are not too shocking." There were only two legal remedies, he added, to help the pasha out: increasing his pay or granting him authority over the territory of a tribe.[58] Neither was approved.

From the pasha's real financial distress began a series of petty abuses that increased over the next two years. They spread to the pasha's official entourage—the khalifas, cadis, and notaries (adels)—and to the small group of Fassi families in Casablanca who were associates, allies, or friends of the Tazis.[59] Remembering the Ben Kiranes was unavoidable. Following an investigation in 1921 into the handling of the funds of Casablanca's native welfare society (Caisse de la Société de Bienfaisance Indigène de Casablanca), the pasha was confronted with the "grave facts" of his personal negligence and financial mismanagement and pressed to resign.[60] The magnitude of the problem was reflected in an additional penalty: The former pasha was directed by the grand vizir to return 100,000 francs to the Caisse.[61] Through it all, Omar Tazi, the architect of his brother's appointment, remained strangely silent.

After the pasha's resignation, Lyautey ordered a shake-up at Casablanca because of "the imperious necessity to clean up the native administration." He wanted a "complete review" of the pasha's staff, "eliminating those individuals who revolved around the ex-pasha and whose activities were open to criticism," and an investigation as well of the staff of the *cadi* "whose connivance with the ex-pasha unfortunately is not in doubt." He added the prudent note: "But the happy effects that we are justified in expecting from this reorganization and purge can only be realized if there is a constant and serious supervision of the pasha and his collaborators. . . ."[62]

The investigation and the resulting punishments were disheartening. All the top offenders had come well recommended. Khalifa Si Mohammed Ben Bouazza Ben el-Hejjamia, a Casablanca importer and property owner (and a French commercial agent for some time) had been the choice of Pasha Omar Tazi to replace the goodly Abdelkrim Ben Msik.[63] Calmel supported the nomination with the statement that "local opinion is always flattered to see a hometown boy *(un enfant du pays)* given a Makhzen post; in addition, these administrators are more interested in local matters and are less open to the temptations of corruption."[64] Indeed, Ben Bouazza's appointment had had "the best effect" on the native population of Casablanca and until the investigation and his dismissal, he seemed to be handling the duties of his office—his specialty was commercial affairs—quite well.[65]

Cadi Si Mohamed Ben Taieb el-Bedraoui had followed the tempestuous and unlamented el-Belghiti in office. A religious scholar *(fqih)* and, like el-Belghiti, a member of the Conseil Supérieur d'Ouléma and a Fassi, el-Bedraoui had been appointed by the sultan in April 1919. He had been nominated by Pasha Abdellatif Tazi with Lyautey's blessing. "He hails from Fez," Lyautey wrote, "where he is counted among the most reputed jurisconsuls. His personal situation and his rank, in addition to his learning, mark him for an important position. His moral integrity is considered irreproachable in the native community."[66] Like Ben Bouazza, el-Bedraoui was relieved of his post.[67]

The third personality of consequence compromised in the corruption at Casablanca was Si Boubeker Bou Chentoufi Es Slaoui, *cadi* of Casablanca-Banlieue. Chentoufi was an excellent Muslim jurist and administrator. Born at Salé, he had studied at the Karaouiyne University and held the rank of *alem de première classe*. He was known and well connected in the Makhzen administration for he had served as first secretary to the minister of state property at Rabat, as assessor of state property at Safi, and as intendant of the imperial palace at Marrakesh.[68] Before coming to Casablanca he had been *cadi* of Oujda where, according to Délégué à la Résidence Générale

Urbain Blanc, he had made a very good impression. It was his ability and willingness to adopt French administrative methods that won him praise: "His duties as first secretary at the Ministry of State Property introduced him to our methods and our administrative procedures and made of him an excellent native administrator."[69] Chentoufi escaped with only a reprimand from the sultan for "serious failings in his service."[70]

Amidst the debris of the native administration, Lyautey asked Contrôleur Civil Joseph Charrier, a specialist in Casablanca's native family affairs, to investigate and report back on potential candidates for pasha. "If it is possible, in fact, to find good elements *(de bons éléments)* among the local native families, I think that it is preferable to appeal for their cooperation rather than to seek an outside candidate."[71] Within the week Charrier had come up with two names: Si Mohammed Ben Kacem, nephew and former *khalifa* to Caïd Si Ahmed Ben Larbi des Médiouna when the *caïd* had himself been pasha of Casablanca, and Si el-Aida Ben Moham el-Harrizi, a Casablanca merchant and wealthy landowner. Neither man, however, wanted the job. And Ben Kacem volunteered that "no Casablancan worth his salt *(digne d'être pris au sérieux)* would allow himself to be a candidate for the post of pasha."[72] The financial difficulties of Pasha Abdellatif Tazi and the circumstances of his fall provided a troubling tale for any would-be successor. There were social politics as well. Tazi's ouster was a blow to the Tazi family and to a number of Fassis of Casablanca. They were sure to be hostile to any new pasha outside their circle. No clear-thinking Casablancan wanted such odds or enemies.

Nevertheless, Charrier hesitated to suggest a Fassi. He knew all the prominent Fassi families in Casablanca: the Ben Djellouns, Yacoubis, Kairouanis, Ben Kiranes, Filalis, Bennis, and Tahiris, many of whom had held official positions and had been removed for "well known reasons." His guess was that any Fassi would cause the same kinds of difficulties as Pasha Tazi had.

> The situation is quite clear: no serious candidate is possible among the Casablancans [and there are] definite risks with the Fassis and other strangers to the city who might be better qualified, but who come with unlimited ambitions and appetites.[73]

The absence of candidates opened the way for a dark horse, Moulay Ahmed Ben Mansour, Casablanca's second *khalifa,* who had been serving as interim pasha since Abdellatif Tazi's resignation. Ben Mansour was remarkable for his powers of survival. Since 1913 he had been second *khalifa* in charge of penal cases; he had outlasted three pashas and four first *khalifas*. Yet he was usually overlooked as a candidate for higher office, probably because his service reports described him in rather pedestrian terms. He was a "good soul," a *bon esprit* who handled his job well, but without "brilliance." He was "very devoted" to France because "he owes us his situation" and was "in the right spot doing what he does."[74] Taken together, this meant that he had limited ability. As a result, being interim pasha was not a stepping-stone to the job itself.

Surprisingly, Ben Mansour wanted to be pasha. In a letter to Charrier, he insisted that he had both the talent and the record to justify a promotion. He pointed out that he had been one of the first Moroccan leaders to recognize the benefits of France to a Morocco "in anarchy." From the very beginning he had placed himself squarely and loyally on the side of cooperation with France. In truth, his career, which he recounted in spare prose, was one of fidelity and achievement.[75]

Well before the protectorate, Ben Mansour had had a string of French connections, first as secretary to the Moroccan minister of foreign affairs (1895-1897), then as secretary to the minister of war (1897-1900), and subsequently as liaison officer to the English and French military missions in Morocco (1900-1903). In 1907, after having led sharifian forces between Fez and Tangier, he raised, then commanded, the Franco-Moroccan police force *(tabor)* of Rabat. When the city of Salé, across the river from Rabat, refused to admit the *tabor* and tottered on the brink of revolt, he attacked and occupied the city, bringing it and all the tribes surrounding Rabat, Salé, and Kénitra to heel.[76]

Four years later (in 1911) when Sultan Abd el-Hafid was besieged in Fez by rebel tribesmen, Ben Mansour proved the invaluable guide to General Moinier's slow-moving relief column from Casablanca. At the head of his own troops, Ben Mansour met Moinier and shepherded him via Rabat and Kénitra to Fez. He was responsible for quartering the French in Rabat, arranging for the river crossing from Rabat to Salé, and protecting their endless supply convoys. Once at Fez, his troops joined the French in combat action against the rebel tribes, particularly in Zaër and Zemmour territory.[77]

In compensation for all this, Colonels Maurice Pellé and Albert Niessel recommended Ben Mansour for a Makhzen office. As Ben Mansour remembered it, Henri Gaillard, the French consul at Fez, had reacted "very favorably," emphasizing that in the "new Makhzen" there would be a place for him. Within the month Ben Mansour was told he would be named *khalifa* to the pasha of Casablanca. But Gaillard promised that in a short time he would be appointed to an even "higher post."[78] After nine years as *khalifa* at Casablanca, Ben Mansour was still waiting.

In addition to the promise unfulfilled, Ben Mansour reminded Charrier that as *khalifa* he had "rendered loyal services to the Makhzen and to the French cause." He was one of the links between the French administration and the native elite of Casablanca on many matters of consequence, particularly the touchy issue of Franco-Muslim education, a key element in French native affairs policy. "I was charged . . ." he pointed out, "with the necessary propaganda on behalf of the Franco-Arab schools and with each demonstration of support whenever it was necessary to call on the native population. . . ." "My past speaks for my sentiments," he concluded somewhat dramatically, "and I only desire one thing, that it be completely understood, so that it in turn can speak for my future."[79]

Charrier was swayed by Ben Mansour's statement, for he recommended him to Lyautey in positive terms and without reservation. Ben Mansour, said Charrier, had "never ceased collaborating with the most total sincerity and the most complete loyalty with the French authorities." Although not a man of great wealth or intelligence, Ben Mansour was considered by all to be a hardworking, just, and honest *khalifa*. He deserved "to be compensated now for his previous services and placed in a position to give us the full measure of his good will and his long experience of administrative affairs."[80]

In a more detailed endorsement, Charrier explained how Ben Mansour fit in with the general needs of French policy and the special requirements of urban administration at Casablanca. His energy, constancy, and devotion to the French effort were beyond doubt. His honesty and personal integrity were common knowledge. All of whom Charrier had asked about corruption in the pasha's entourage had answered: "Moulay Ahmed has remained outside of all this dishonesty. He is a man who follows the straight and narrow." Alone of all the Makhzen city administrators, he had not enriched himself and, Charrier underscored, *"he still pays his own rent."*[81] Given the troubles of the past, Ben Mansour seemed the right man for the job.

Charrier recalled that Casablanca was no ordinary Makhzen city. There was no old Muslim aristocracy or bourgeoisie. Here the notables among the native population were "solid folk" *(braves gens):* property owners, landowners, or merchants without much education and little interest in political intrigue. They wanted their persons and property respected and to go about their business in peace. According to Charrier, Casablanca's leadership problems were not the fault of its elite, but of a set of ambitious, often brilliant administrators bent on advancing their Makhzen careers through the accumulation of "scandalous fortunes." "We can and in my opinion we must put an end to these practices which have been condemned by past experience and to which the entire population is opposed." His answer was "an honest man" who knew his job and the territory, generously supplied with money to handle his legitimate expenses, resolutely denied the extravagances of high office, and faithfully seconded by two "carefully chosen" *khalifas*. Such a setup, supervised "without weakness," would solve Casablanca's problems once and for all. The honest man, so said Charrier playing the part of Diogenes, was Ben Mansour.[82]

Lyautey approved Charrier's selection, convinced that the choice of Ben Mansour would be acceptable to the "large majority" of Casablanca's native population and in conformity with the interests of "our policy." In Ben Mansour France had a "sure, disinterested, and devoted collaborator." He was, as well, a faithful servant of the Makhzen. Lyautey instructed Counsellor to the Sharifian Government Raoul Marc, the liaison officer to the sultan, to bring the matter to His Majesty's attention at once, since it was important to have a successor to Tazi as quickly as possible. "I would therefore attach some value to having Moulay Ben Mansour named without delay and I leave it to your care and to your authority with the Makhzen to secure it. . . ."[83] Marc, whose own reputation as a fixer was on the line, had the sultan's signature on the *dahir* of appointment four days later.[84]

The purge of the Casablanca administration was over by the end of May. Order was being restored to the Dar El Makhzen "little by little," Charrier reported, and a "prompt and complete reorganization" was under way.[85] The new team was in place by September. Pasha Ben Mansour was assisted by first *khalifa* Si Hadj Djilali Ben Guendaoui, a member of a Casablanca family originally from the Sous. He belonged to the Casablanca municipal commission and owned several buildings in the city. Judged "devoted, sure, and loyal," he was "well considered and very influential" among the native population. Guendaoui "would make a very good *khalifa*," Charrier had noted in April 1921, and his name topped the list of three Charrier submitted to Lyautey.[86] Guendaoui was a good bet. At year's end Charrier noted that Guendaoui lived a quiet life, was somewhat unpolished, and not very well educated, but he was "animated by good intentions and totally foreign to intrigues."[87] These were qualities that counted.

For the post of second *khalifa* the French authorities first submitted the name of Si Ahmed Ben Sayah el-Abdellaoui, an Algerian who had lived in Fez for the previous twenty years. He belonged to the Tijaniya brotherhood and during the Great War had been sent to Mauretania by the residency to keep the members of that religious fraternity calm in the face of German anti-French propaganda. Successful in this mission, he was counted as a friend of France. In addition, he had always had "an excellent attitude toward the protectorate authorities" and was "very well thought of among the native population."[88]

The *grand vizir* objected to Ben Sayah, however, saying that it was better to name a Casablancan (as undoubtedly the French had been telling him) rather than an outsider. Whether this was the real reason for his opposition or a simple ruse was impossible to know. The *grand vizir* suggested Abdelkrim Ben Kirane for the job, but he was clearly unacceptable to the French. Contrôleur en Chef of the Région Civile de la Chaouïa Alexandre Laurent, who headed the Contrôle Civil at Casablanca, reminded Urbain Blanc that Ben Kirane had been revoked as market inspector of Casablanca in 1915 for embezzlement. Since then, his attitude toward the authorities had been "correct," but reserved and "not without a touch of bitterness." His influence in the city nevertheless was "uncontestable" because of the size of his personal fortune and the importance accorded his family. In addition, the *grand vizir* favored the Ben Kiranes and since their fall had been waiting for the right opportunity to return them to the Casablanca administration.[89]

To block Ben Kirane and to avoid insisting on the Makhzen's approval of Ben Sayah, the French proposed Sidi Ali Bel Hadj Ahmed el-Kairouani. El-Kairouani was a well-off merchant of "excellent conduct" and "good reputation" from a Casablanca family "unanimously well thought of and respected" in the city. He had been asked once before to be a *khalifa* candidate, but had refused, presumably unwilling to risk the social and economic pitfalls. Now he was ready to give the task a try. Were he named, he pledged to turn over the direction of his business to his father.[90] The appointment was made on 3 September 1921.

The city was now in the hands of men of some talent and ability (although only the pasha had experience in government), of unquestioned loyalty to France and the protectorate regime, of integrity and personal honesty. All of them were Casablancans, representatives of an urban commercial class that identified with the past and the future of the city. Unfortunately, the team barely lasted to the end of the year. El-Kairouani resigned after five months because the workload was too heavy and his father too old, his brothers too young, to manage the family enterprise. His leave-taking was a disappointment. "He handled a heavy task for which he was little prepared quite conscientiously," wrote Laurent, "and I regret to see him depart the Dar El Makhzen."[91] Guendaoui resigned three months later (in April 1922) because of failing health. He, too, was a loss. He had conducted himself "perfectly" in a tough and delicate job situation that was completely new to him. He had helped end the "leadership crisis" that now was creeping back again. From beginning to end he had been frank, loyal, and up to the mark.[92] Both departures, although voluntary, honorable, and regretted, were surely connected to the sorry fate of Pasha Ben Mansour.

Despite Charrier's endorsement and Lyautey's optimism, Ben Mansour had not been the right man for the job. His appointment had been opposed by the Fassis in what Charrier delicately termed "local attempts at obstruction."[93] In addition, Commissaire du Gouvernement Antoine Bertrand, who had worked with Ben Mansour on a day-to-day basis for some time, had argued that he was not the clay from which pashas were formed.[94] Even though the Fassis were not listened to and Bertrand himself was packed off to Mazagan, Ben Mansour wilted under the adverse comment. As the Fassi chorus continued, it discouraged both Ben Mansour and his close collaborators. When Khalifa el-Kairouani resigned in January 1922, Laurent confessed that because of "all those who were working to hinder the pasha," he couldn't find a replacement: "No really serious candidate will run the risk under these circumstances of offering him his collaboration."[95] Then, when an uncomfortable situation developed between Ben Mansour and Bertrand's successor, Jean Peyrou, the pasha's confidence snapped. He asked for another post and in March 1922 he was named pasha of Oujda.

As pieced together in a French investigative report, the Ben Mansour-Peyrou *mésalliance* was a classic case of mismatched personalities, unfortunate circumstances, and mistakes on both sides. Despite his good will and experience, Ben Mansour was strangely puzzled by the steady barrage of criticism—the lot of every pasha at Casablanca—that came his way. It began to affect his personality, making him agitated and suspicious. Soon the routine incidents of urban administration took on tragic dimensions. When reproached in the Casablanca press for reintroducing criminal punishments that had been abolished at French insistence because of their brutality, for example, he wrongly assumed that he had lost the ear of the residency, and fell into a "nervous depression."[96]

What Ben Mansour needed, so the report writer diagnosed, was a firm tutor and sage adviser. Peyrou had started out that way but "weak of character although knowledgeable in his job," he became frightened at seeing the pasha "attacked, criticized, and distraught." He abruptly distanced himself from Ben Mansour to escape responsibility for what he took to be a deteriorating situation. This only made matters worse. Unable to explain Peyrou's sudden reserve and deprived of his counsel, Ben Mansour was further distressed. All this moved from the private to the public at the Dar El Makhzen where both Europeans and Moroccans witnessed "the real uneasiness" between the two men, interpreting it correctly as a broken relationship, and more, a sign of the pasha's loss of control and influence.[97]

The split between "the first Muslim magistrate of the city" and the *commissaire du gouvernement* placed at his side" was judged incapable of resolution. Neither man had been up to his task. Each had defects in character and ability. Ben Mansour needed to be supervised by an administrator who was "able *(avisé)* and mature in his understanding of men and most especially of the native population." This was not Peyrou. "Fearful and weak," Peyrou might have done better with a pasha "de grand style," but clearly he had failed with Ben Mansour. Too late he realized this himself. He admitted that he had foreseen "difficulties that he had not the stature to handle" and that he had abdicated his role as instructor and guide. As for Ben Mansour, he was no Omar Tazi. For that he was not to blame. "He only gave us what we had a right to expect. He was an excellent *khalifa* who was unable to move higher up."[98]

The evenhanded report ignored the serious consequences of the Ben Mansour-Peyrou relationship to the leadership situation of the city. Less than a year after Charrier's recommendations had become policy, all was in shambles. Casablanca had no pasha, no *khalifas,* and no immediate prospects. Some of this was surely Charrier's fault. He had plumped for Ben Mansour without taking French service reports, the objections of the *commissaire du gouvernement,* and Fassi opposition seriously. In fact, he never mentioned any of this in writing to Lyautey until after the pasha's appointment.[99] This was particularly distressing because Charrier, as his reports demonstrated, was no novice in native affairs. He had over a decade of experience in Algeria and Morocco, including a stint as municipal services director in Salé, no easy berth. Moreover, Lyautey both valued Charrier's administrative talent and depended on his "consummate understanding of the native social and cultural setting *(milieux indigènes)."*[100]

Once installed, Ben Mansour and his team deserved the special attention that Charrier had promised, namely supervision "without weakness." In Ben Mansour's case it was especially important. There was honest concern about his "vieux Makhzen" methods. Restoration of archaic brutal punishments could not be tolerated, especially at Casablanca.[101] In addition, the pasha had packed his tribunal with unpaid assistants (one interpreter, three scribes, and forty attendants), who solicited tips and bribes for services or favors rendered.[102] This was "incompatible" with the most elementary French administrative procedures. Every situation had its exceptions, but Counsellor to the Sharifian Government Marc thought this went out of bounds: "I have good reason to believe in fact that there exists no grounds to justify an indulgence for the pasha of Casablanca of the sort that is routinely approved for the tribal *caids."*[103] Peyrou was criticized for allowing the punishments and told to tell the pasha that he would have to rid himself of the new appointees. That might well have gone beyond his abilities. But how could Peyrou—a new man in Casablanca—have been permitted to unmake policy by his "weak" personality? After all, Charrier's prime responsibility, made very clear by Laurent in July 1921, was to oversee the native administration in Casablanca, which, given the nature of things and the chain of command, meant supervising the supervisors.[104]

During Ben Mansour's brief tenure, Casablanca was further upset by difficulties with Cadi Mohamed Ben Allalech Chraïbi, the replacement for the revoked Mohamed Ben Taieb el-Bedraoui. Chraïbi came from a family of scholars from Fez where he had taught law at the Karaouiyne University for twenty years. He had moved from Fez to Rabat as a secretary in the Ministry of Justice and religious judge in the Koranic appeals court.[105] His background, education, and experience meant that he came with excellent recommendations to Casablanca. Nevertheless, all did not go well.

Commissaire du Gouvernement Gabriel Beaujolin, responsible for supervising the *cadi,* remembered that Chraïbi had a "marked aversion" to coming to his office, which he put down as Chraïbi's "exaggerated sense of his own importance" and "haughty arrogance bordering on impoliteness." This was a problem because Chraïbi was unfamiliar with French procedures and ignorant of the "particularly complex and difficult situation" at Casablanca. He seemed to prefer not to know and this led to a series of unhappy incidents.[106]

A dispute over the legality of a marriage between an Algerian woman and a Moroccan man led to an impasse between Chraïbi and Beaujolin. Since the woman was a French subject, the couple had been married under French law. Chraïbi declared the union illegal and threatened to jail them both, unless they married according to the Muslim rite. To boost his side of the argument Chraïbi appealed directly to Charrier, bypassing Beaujolin. When Beaujolin learned of this, he reminded Chraïbi that he, Beaujolin, was the obligatory "intermediary" in such affairs. Chraïbi explained that since Beaujolin had not supported him in a previous matter, he thought it "useless" to go to him, and instead went straight to Charrier. The *cadi* added that he intended to complain to Rabat that Beaujolin was meddling in things having to do with the Koranic law and until that situation was resolved, he would not meet with him again.[107]

Beaujolin was stunned. He asked Laurent to make the *cadi* apologize and in so doing bring him "to a better understanding of the role of his supervisor."[108] To the Counsellor to the Sharifian Government Beaujolin added that Chraïbi ought to be "severely taken to task" by the Makhzen and told "in no uncertain terms" that the *commissaire du gouvernement* had "the right to send for him and to demand explanations from him" and that he was the "necessary intermediary between him and the higher authorities." "It would also be worthwhile," Beaujolin concluded, "to make him understand that the present conditions of this city are far different from those under the former Makhzen and that with too much inflexibility and too great a tendency to be coercive, he will quickly make his situation impossible."[109]

Charrier's assessment was similar to Beaujolin's. Because of Chraïbi's personality and ignorance of Casablanca, the *cadi* had no idea of the risks he was running, of the troubles that lay ahead. "He may be an excellent jurist," Charrier admitted,

> he is certainly very intelligent and very distinguished, but he is blinded by an incommensurable pride. Believing that he is doubly "taboo," first because he is a *sharif* (he pretends to be), then, because he is a *cadi*, he rebels at the thought that his administrative actions must be submitted to the approval of the Contrôle. . . . I have tried to make him understand that good results can only come about through loyal collaboration, that no one seeks to diminish the Koranic law in the person of the *cadi*, that to the contrary all our efforts have sought to affirm his moral authority and to increase his prestige.

Charrier had no luck.

> [W]e must let the *cadi* know right away that his pretensions are insupportable and that they will not be tolerated much longer. . . . He seems to want to ignore the most elementary rules of good manners as well as the instructions from higher-ups which are as applicable to him as to the other magistrates and bureaucrats. . . . If we don't cauterize this wound vigorously at the start, we risk greater difficulties in the future.[110]

The cauterizing iron must have worked. Within five months Charrier noted that the "few difficulties" Chraïbi had had at the beginning of his tenure had been resolved. "His attitude is now excellent." He added that Chraïbi was a "good magistrate"—"un magistrat de grande valeur"—precisely in the right spot at Casablanca.[111] Described a year later by Contrôleur Civil Michel Pozzo de Borgo, Chraïbi was "quite up to the task" at Casablanca, a "very hard worker, very much in control of himself, and very honest." He was slow with his decisions because of an "excess of prudence" and seemed at times to be a "slave to the law texts." But Pozzo pronounced the highest accolade: Chraïbi "seems capable of fulfilling the functions of *cadi* in the most delicate post that there is in Morocco."[112]

The transformation was complete. Chraïbi the arrogant and rebellious had been fitted into the protectorate system. Yet he retained his pride and his combativeness, even if he surrendered some of his independence. He was still on the job when Lyautey left Morocco two years and nine months later, and had proven on at least one memorable occasion—a rough-and-tumble territorial dispute with Boubeker Bou Chentoufi, the *cadi* of Casablanca-Banlieue—that he was as feisty as ever.[113]

In Casablanca the search continued for a new pasha and his *khalifas*. The interregnum was short-lived. Si Mohammed Ben Abdelouahad, the president of the Haut Tribunal Chérifien (the secular appeals court for Muslims) and the sultan's candidate, was appointed the fourth pasha of the city in five years.[114] And he immediately suggested two candidates for *khalifa*: Mohammed Ben Abdallah el-Marrekechi, secretary in the Ministry of Education, "because of the confidence he inspires in us as well as because of his qualifications to handle this responsibility" and Abderrahmane Ben Lahssen Ben Bouazza el-Beidaoui, a member of the Casablanca municipal commission.[115] Ben Abdallah was unknown in Casablanca, but Ben Bouazza, on the other hand, was "well known" in the city. He had been one of the three candidates suggested by Charrier in April 1921 to replace Khalifa Mohammed Ben Bouazza Ben el-Hejjamia. At that time Laurent had endorsed Ben Bouazza, but with some reservation. He worried if his "rather close connections" with the pasha of Marrakesh and Caïd el-Ayadi of the Rehamna would prove the *khalifa*'s undoing. Now he dismissed this concern: "These relationships, having come to an end, nothing any longer blocks the appointment of Si Abderrahmane. . . ."[116]

Ben Abdallah refused the job offer. Ben Bouazza accepted, and was named first *khalifa* in early May 1922. He belonged to a "very good" Casablanca family and owned enough property in the city to allow him a comfortable life. Influential and considered a wise and honest man, Ben Bouazza was by nature "very cold" and remained somewhat distant from other Muslims of his social rank, which meant he had few friends to sing his praises, but also few enemies to work behind his back. The French gave him high marks for fidelity and hard work. Seven years on the municipal commission, three years on the city tax board (the Commission de la Taxe Urbaine), one year on the board of directors of the 1916 Casablanca Exposition; Ben Bouazza had put in his time. In addition, he was one of the oldest French protégés. As *khalifa*, he was faced with intense on-the-job training and considerable homework. But, proud of his Makhzen position, he worked even harder.[117] When he resigned in October 1924 because of poor health, Laurent nominated him for the rank of chevalier in the Order of the

Ouissam Alaouite Chérifien for his "good and loyal services." His tenure had been "excellent." He had had "all the makings of a first-rate *khalifa*."[118]

Having been turned down by one *khalifa* candidate, Pasha Abdelouahad looked to Fez for a second and found him in El-Ghali Ben Larbi el-Mernissi, someone who was "capable of fulfilling the responsibilities of the position and willing to accept it."[119] El-Mernissi was unknown to Laurent, but the bits and pieces he picked up at Casablanca were favorable: "he is rich, from a good family, and interested in entering the Makhzen."[120] Secretary-General Pierre de Sorbier de Pougnadoresse supplied the rest of the relevant biographical data. El-Mernissi had never held an administrative post, but was a learned and intelligent man "quite capable of handling the post of second *khalifa* in an honorable way."

> Easy to get along with, distinguished, maintaining good relations with French administrators and diverse Europeans, he fulfills . . . the necessary requirements to hold a Makhzen position at Casablanca. It is these qualities which mark him for this post in preference to other Fassi candidates who perhaps would have been better qualified from the point of view of administrative competence, but who do not have, as he does, the experience of dealing with Europeans.

El-Mernissi was reputed to be "completely" honest, but somewhat of a spendthrift and not quite as rich as the Casablanca gossip had it. He would be "supported and helped" financially by his brother, Si M'Hamed el-Mernissi, who had a "solid" fortune and impressive protectorate credentials. M'Hamed was a member of the Conseil d'Administration de l'Office des Phosphates and the Chambre Indigène de Commerce et d'Agriculture de Fès, and a chevalier of the Legion of Honor to boot.[121] Apparently memories of the brothers Tazi, where such an arrangement had proven fatal, had been forgotten.

Approved by the Makhzen, el-Mernissi was installed in July 1922. The new *khalifa* did not disappoint the French, for he was "very zealous, a very hard worker, and active." After six months on the job, Pozzo de Borgo judged him "capable of doing better and better."[122] But his working relationship with the pasha, which had begun so harmoniously, deteriorated over time.

The pasha's complaints against the *khalifa* began in April 1924. They ranged from charges of personal misconduct and malfeasance in office to promoting discord among courthouse officials and plaintiffs. Assigned to investigate the case of a young prostitute accused of stealing, el-Mernissi had the woman taken to his house where she remained under lock and key for three days. Only after an outraged pasha inquired into the matter did el-Mernissi return the woman to prison.[123]

El-Mernissi was also at odds with the pasha's officers who collected fines and taxes (moqqadems). He claimed that they were lazy and, as a result, the recovery of funds was delayed. Pozzo de Borgo agreed with el-Mernissi and told the pasha that changes would have to be made on his staff. The pasha saw things differently. He told Laurent that el-Mernissi deliberately sought "to provoke trouble" with the moqqadems. He "set traps" for them "in complicity with his friend"—Pozzo de Borgo—in order to achieve his secret goal of stripping them of their tax-collecting function. "It also appears quite clear that my second khalifa is seeking with the help of his friends to sow discord and to promote disorder in the Dar El Makhzen."[124] Here Pasha Abdelouahad referred to a small group in the Fassi population of Casablanca, who had taken the khalifa's side in the feud and were exploiting it to their own advantage.[125]

The pasha used the same words the next day to describe el-Mernissi's involvement in a dispute between a tailor and a butcher that seemed to have been settled amicably, then broke out once more. "His objective, by Heaven, is to promote disorder, sow discord and provoke hatred among the plaintiffs." "I am only keeping you abreast of these facts," the pasha insisted, "because I am compelled to do so by the conduct of my khalifa and his malevolent actions toward me."[126]

The question of the moqqadems involved authority and money. The khalifa's retainers (mokazenis) had handled fines and taxes until Pasha Abdelouahad brought his moqqadems into the courthouse. The change surely provoked the khalifa's ire. Although el-Mernissi convinced the contrôleur to side with him, he lost the tug-of-war. He asked to leave Casablanca and in October 1924 he was named caïd of the Hamyan-Lemta in the Région de Fès.[127]

For the French the hunt for the "right" men for Casablanca was unending and thus the search for indirect rule never finished. The requisite qualities of talent, character, and loyalty were rarely present in Moroccan leaders in the correct proportions to satisfy them. There was a constant struggle with "certain peculiarities" of the native character: the "atavistic inclination toward domination (la prépotence), plunder, and the despotic (l'arbitraire)," which the French considered "odious faults."[128] Talent and loyalty were easier to identify and test, but even here there was never universal agreement. With rare exceptions and despite the eagerness of some Moroccan leaders to cooperate with them, no native administrator measured up to the French standard. The unhappy parade of Moroccan bureaucrats at Casablanca attested to that fact.

What could Frenchmen expect? Just as they transformed Casablanca, they intended to transform Casablancans, yet with only slight regard for the ways of thinking and doing that marked Moroccans as people of another culture. This lack of understanding was bound to produce disappointment and frustration, stubbornness and anger on both sides. Lyautey insisted that respect for the attitudes, customs, and traditions of native society was the cornerstone of indirect rule. Yet the French "revolution" he presided over in Casablanca was no respecter of persons or their beliefs.

Making indirect rule more difficult at Casablanca was the mix of French civil-military administration with its overlapping lines of responsibility and authority. This undoubtedly put Colonel Antoine Targe and Municipal Services Director Alfred Collieaux at odds in 1914. Targe was concerned above all with military security and convinced of the superior judgment and expertise of his army intelligence officers, whereas Collieaux moved with greater ease and confidence among the native elite and depended for advice on his own civil staff of municipal administrators. This produced at least two notions of indirect rule and real disagreement at the top on matters of "native policy." Despite Lyautey's oft-repeated conviction that what mattered most overseas was not whether one was a soldier or a civilian but whether one was a "colonial," this did not square with the realities in Casablanca.

Moreover, the Contrôle Civil also demanded to be heard. As Joseph Charrier and Alexandre Laurent demonstrated in Casablanca, the contrôleurs civils had an important, often decisive say in the selection of the city's pashas, khalifas, and cadis. Their recommendations took precedence over Makhzen suggestions, even though the sultan, the grand vizir, and (in the case of lesser bureaucrats) the pasha were consulted. This could have both positive and negative consequences. But although Lyautey worried on paper in 1916 that the contrôleurs were becoming "sharifian administrators" and not governing indirectly but directly in the name of the sultan and France, this was precisely where the method of indirect rule had ended up.[129]

CHAPTER 8

The Pashas of Settat, the *Caïds* of the Chaouïa
■ ■ ■ ■

A mong Morocco's tribes Lyautey's indirect rule differed little in theory or in practice from its employ in the cities. As at Casablanca, Frenchmen disagreed on the precise nature of the relationship with their rural "partners" and the extent of their powers of intervention in the life of the Moroccan countryside. But everywhere they had wide authority over the pashas and *caïds* of the tribes and most often they used it to further Lyautey's great ambition for colonial rule: political betterment, economic development, and social improvement. This commitment to change is even clearer in the testimony of the military officers and the *contrôleurs civils* from the Chaouïa than in the reports from Casablanca. To be sure, these goals and the paths toward them were established by Frenchmen, not Moroccans, and thus resentment and resistance were inevitable. This was the fate of any enterprise, no matter how culturally sensitive it proclaimed itself to be, where decision-making remained essentially a one-sided and very directed affair.

After the Chaouïa exploded in armed resistance to the landing of the French expeditionary force at Casablanca in 1907, Paris authorized French troops to occupy Settat, seventy kilometers south of the city, and as much of the Chaouïa hinterland as necessary to protect the military beachhead from sudden attack. This occupation, completed in 1908, began the French "partnership" with the pashas of Settat and the *caïds* of the Chaouïa whose right to rule had been severely challenged by rebellious tribesmen (in 1902-03) and soundly shaken by the civil war between the two sultans (in 1907-08).[1] French intervention put an end to these trials for the Makhzen's governors, but then imposed its own tests and burdens that in the end made them little more than creatures of France.

Among the notables of the Chaouïa, the most arresting figure was Tounsi Ben el-Bahloul, *caïd* of the Oulad Bou Ziri, a Berber tribe located to the south and west of Settat on land that today is crossed by the main road from Casablanca to Marrakesh. For the French to whom Tounsi was attached with "the most certain devotion" he incarnated "the perfect native leader" and they quickly invested him "with a sort of scepter."[2] Tounsi was of the Oulad Affif fraction of the Oulad Bou Ziri, and his family had provided *caïds* for the Oulad Bou Ziri for four generations. *Khalifa* to his father, Caïd Bahloul Ben Selham, Tounsi succeeded him as *caïd* in 1902, but in name only. At the time of his father's death Tounsi was on campaign fighting for the sultan against the pretender at Taza. Before he could return home and claim his inheritance, he became embroiled in a dispute with the sultan over the terms of the legacy that lasted for years and ultimately landed him in a Fez jail. Released in 1908 to join French army operations in the Chaouïa against the Hafid rising, Tounsi won the praise of French commanders for the information he supplied on the enemy and for his expertise in guiding French pursuit columns. Major Charles Huot, who later headed the French intelligence service in Morocco, admitted that Tounsi had been a "precious" informant who had served "loyally and with much good will." "He has earned the right to our favor *(bienveillance)* and our protection."[3] When the French took Settat, Tounsi exacted what he held to be rightfully his—a *caïdat* of 900 tents, about one-third of all the tents of the Oulad Bou Ziri.[4]

In March 1910 Chef de Bataillon Pierre Forey, whose responsibility it was to oversee the *caïds* at Settat, protested that Messaoud Ould Tounza, *caïd* over the remaining two-thirds of the tents of the Oulad Bou Ziri, was either in cahoots with a local band of thieves or powerless to stop them. In addition, Messaoud had been the object of "incessant complaints" from those under his authority and had received "severe reprimands" from French officers. Some months before he had been fined for "irregular tax levies" in his tribe. "Long ago," Forey insisted,

> I would have requested the dismissal of this *caïd*, who seems absolutely unsubmissive to our administrative procedures, and proposed the consolidation of the entire Oulad Bou Ziri under the sole authority of Caïd Tounsi Ould Bahloul, had I not feared the rejection of this plan and the Makhzen's appointment of a new *caïd* clearly hostile to our influence.[5]

What he suggested instead was a fine of 200 francs for Caïd Messaoud. His "plan," however, showed a growing confidence in Tounsi as a leader and as a partisan of France.

The French service reports on Tounsi bore this out. A 1911 note described him as an "excellent *caïd,* very favorable to French ideas, devoted, active, [and] energetic." For 1912 the report claimed Tounsi to be a "very good leader, intelligent and vigorous. Will be excellent when trained *(rompu)* in our methods of command." That same year Tounsi led a group of "Chaouïa partisans" as part of the Mangin column against Marrakesh and again received high commendation from the French officers in charge of the operation. In 1913 the assessment of Tounsi was equally positive: "Can make an excellent *caïd.* From the first he made himself available to the French authorities. Has actively served our political action."[6]

When Lyautey restructured the Settat command at the end of 1912, it was no surprise that Tounsi was rewarded. Caïd Messaoud was finally removed and the 1,977 tents of the Bou Ziri under his authority were split three ways among Caïd Ali Ben El Hadj el-Maâti of the Mzamza, Caïd Ben Chaboun Ben Mohamed of the Oulad Sidi Ben Daoud, and Tounsi. Tounsi's *caïdat*—still the smallest in the Settat area—was increased by 668 tents, not the inflated command that Forey had once envisioned, but a significant compensation.[7]

Over the years Tounsi continued to impress. Captain Jules Maitrat was certain of his intelligence, energy, loyalty, ability, and keen interest in the "things of progress." He "uses our farm implements, machinery, [and] automobiles," Maitrat noted with pride. He ventured that Tounsi had "all the qualities to make an excellent native leader, capable of adapting to our methods of command." In 1915 Maitrat judged that Tounsi was "assimilating very well" to the French administrative system, and in his 1916 report he announced that Tounsi understood and applied "to the best of his ability" those administrative procedures explained to him. He was respectful of all the orders given him, even though sometimes, "like all the native chiefs," he tried to elude the supervision of the French authorities. His faithfulness to the protectorate government and to the Makhzen, however, was never in question. Maitrat concluded that Tounsi was able "to command a tribe more important than the Oulad Bou Ziri," in fact quite capable of exercising a large command "with distinction." In Maitrat's view Tounsi had passed his apprenticeship with flying colors. He had now "perfectly assimilated" the administrative practices of the protectorate.[8]

The only doubt about Tounsi, first mentioned by Maitrat in 1914, was his "suspicious nature" and "a pride that was easily wounded." This made him rather "delicate to handle." He was "proud and clever," according to Maitrat's successor, and ambitious as well. Tounsi definitely aspired to a more important role in the protectorate and often compared himself to the *grands caïds* of the south whom in his own way he tried to imitate. Whatever

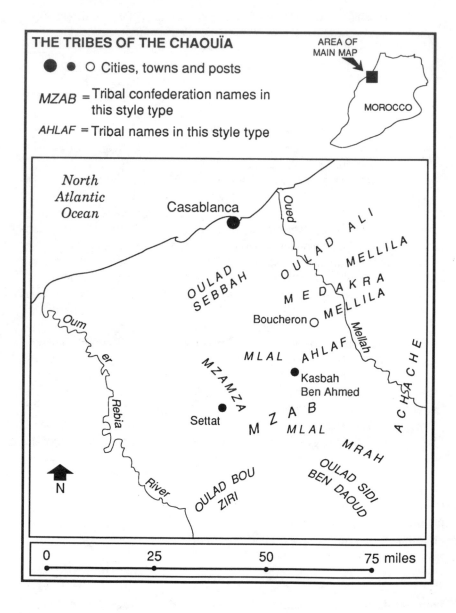

THE TRIBES OF THE CHAOUÏA

AREA OF MAIN MAP

● ● ○ Cities, towns and posts

MZAB = Tribal confederation names in this style type

AHLAF = Tribal names in this style type

MOROCCO

North Atlantic Ocean

Casablanca

Oued

OULAD ALI

MELLILA

OULAD SEBBAH

MEDAKRA

Boucheron ○ MELLILA

Mellah

MLAL AHLAF

ACHACHE

MZAMZA

Kasbah Ben Ahmed

Settat

MZAB

MLAL

MRAH

Oum er Rebia River

OULAD BOU ZIRI

OULAD SIDI BEN DAOUD

N

0   25   50   75 miles

Tounsi's dreams, Chef de Bataillon François Rey judged that before he could be promoted to a more important command "in the still distant future," he would have to demonstrate, even more than he had already, "his devotion to France."[9]

Pride and ambition combined to produce in Tounsi the genuine feeling that he had earned more authority and independence. In May 1918 when the *caïd* of the Oulad Sidi Ben Daoud was revoked, Tounsi wrote directly to General Jean Calmel, military commander of the Casablanca region, to ask that the tents of the Oulad Bou Ziri placed in that *caïdat* in 1912 now be put under his command. He reminded Calmel that he currently commanded only half of the Bou Ziri, his "tribe of origin," and that this step toward reunification was long overdue. He recalled the completeness of his fidelity: "You will be compensating a man who has worked with you from the very depths of his soul."[10]

Unfortunately, this was an "inopportune" time for a tribal reshuffling. A *caïd* had already been appointed for the Oulad Sidi Ben Daoud and stripping him of a part of his new command was impossible. Calmel wrote to Tounsi that the matter was closed. The Makhzen had made its decision and the appointment of the new *caïd*, Si Mohammed Ben El Hadj Salah, had been announced. It was a short, almost discourteous note that took little account of Tounsi's feelings.[11]

If not with fields of tents, Tounsi was compensated with the medals and decorations of France and the sharifian empire: Chevalier of the Legion of Honor (1915), Officier, then Commandeur of the Ouissam Alaouite Chérifien (1916, 1922), the Médaille Commemorative du Maroc, and Chevalier of the Nicham Iftikhar de Tunis.[12] With these honors and the service they recognized came secure wealth. In 1916 Tounsi's annual income was estimated at 14,380 pesetas hassani, based on the return from tribal taxes and market fees, and his personal fortune calculated at 120,000 French francs.[13]

Pierre Coudert, Rey's successor, fully appreciated Tounsi's ambition, intellect, and openness to "modern ideas." Tounsi was "quite above the majority of the other *caïds* of the Contrôle in intelligence, competence, and an understanding which perfectly comprehends the modern mentality. He sees the world in a dynamic form and that is the highest compliment that anyone can pay a Muslim." As a tribal leader, Tounsi was stern, powerful, and had the tendency to abuse his authority. But kept "on his toes" and supervised tactfully yet without weakness, he would always be "a useful and devoted deputy," providing the French "precious assistance."[14]

Tounsi was not without fault. "He is neither more nor less honest than the other *caïds*," went one report, "but thanks to much tact and savoir faire, he avoids incrimination."[15] This was not always the case. In June 1920 Tounsi was fined 1,000 francs for paying workers to harvest his crops, then forcing them to return the money to him.[16] And the following year he received a letter of reprimand from the regional commander for "careless-ness" in his service.[17] Still, the decorations outweighed the discipline. Coudert believed that Tounsi was an excellent native leader, who in 1923 was now ready for the greater command that he had waited for so long and with such impatience.[18]

Tounsi fit in with Coudert's notions about the changes in Moroccan society he saw taking place and the new native leadership they required. According to Coudert, the days of the unlettered rural *caïd* and the small *caïdat* were numbered. Morocco was evolving and "very rapidly" in the "rich zones" of commerce and agriculture around important market centers such as Settat. "The administrative life is intensifying at the same pace as the economic life and the old cadres of the native bureaucracy are becoming inadequate."[19] In the past an old guard had kept order, collected taxes, and handled the day-to-day administration of the tribes. This was accomplished less because of intelligence and hard work than because these leaders were wealthy "men of the region" *(hommes du terroir)*, enjoying great social prestige and exercising considerable political power. A knowledge of the land and its people and an indisputable authority over both produced a patriarchal leadership that got things done. In the assessment and collection of taxes and in routine tribal management, they were indispensable to the French and rendered them "appreciable services."[20]

Loftier matters, however, were beyond their reach. Not one among the *caïds* of Settat was capable of understanding government policy, be it shar-ifian or protectorate, that was explained in terms of the general interest. Too close to those whom they governed, they remained influenced by them to an unfortunate degree, becoming defenders of the particular, the local, and the tribal. Government policy was something to be resisted, not promoted. But it was here, especially with the protectorate's colonization plans, that the supervisory officers most needed the support of native leaders of "great authority" and of "understanding adapted to the demands of the evolution which is taking place in this country."[21]

No one with the exception of Tounsi possessed sufficient breadth of intelligence and understanding to be able to act as a real local delegate of the Makhzen with all the political responsibilities and obligations that this required. In fact, at Settat both the native and European population, surrounded by a scattering of unimportant *caïds* ("la poussière des caïds"), keenly felt the absence of a single Makhzen political leader. Unity—such as it was—was only achieved through the presence of a representative of the protectorate regime, the *contrôleur civil.*[22]

With the law it was the same. No *caïd* at Settat had shown a true aptitude for the job of examining magistrate in those criminal matters within the competence of the Haut Tribunal Chérifien, the secular court of appeals for Muslims. Not one had sufficient knowledge to follow the proper procedures in important civil or penal affairs submitted to their judgment. To be sure, the *caïds* were "excellent" in handling affairs of small importance where a quick oral procedure in the patriarchal style and with a certain margin of arbitrariness was in order. But the written procedure with the "baggage of culture" and the effort at concentration and study that it required was closed to them.[23]

Issues of government policy and justice—precisely where the *caïds* were inferior—were growing day by day in significance and complexity. Because of the inadequacy of the *caïds,* the tasks of the *contrôleurs civils* were on the increase. Forced to substitute for the *caïds* while "at the same time preserving the forms imposed by the protectorate system," the *contrôleurs* were sinking under the weight of detail work, permanently distracted from their duty to direct, galvanize, and supervise.[24] Overburdened by the tasks of direct rule, Coudert clamored for the indirect rule of the protectorate ideal.

"The time is near," Coudert predicted, "when new men will be required." Alongside each *chef d'annexe* there needed to be a native administrator of energy and talent, "a sort of super-*caïd" (sur-caïd),* who, as a result of his intellect and education, his social rank, and his administrative and political abilities, was capable of assuming authority over the small rural *caïdats* and of representing the Makhzen with dignity in the *circonscription d'annexe,* which to Coudert was "without doubt the administrative and political life cell of the heterogeneous groups which constitute the population of this country."[25]

Coudert recognized that any change in the native structure of command was a potential "source of trouble, sometimes of upheaval in native society" and so had to be made "very prudently" and only as the opportunities presented themselves, never through a "brusque reform." Still, he kept a blueprint close at hand. For Greater Settat (Settat-Banlieue) Coudert envisioned two commands: the city of Settat plus the Mzamza tribe that surrounded the city and the united tribes of the Oulad Sidi Ben Daoud and Oulad Bou Ziri.[26]

The first was already in place under the control of Pasha and Caïd Boubeker Ben El Hadj el-Maâti. Coudert hoped, however, that after Boubeker's death the Makhzen would designate a successor chosen from among the notables who was "a bit modern, of a social rank superior to that of our rural *caïds (caïds de campagne),* [and] worthy at last to represent governmental authority in a city whose rapid development is assured from this moment on." Coudert insisted that the double job of pasha and *caïd* was an economic necessity. No pasha of Settat could live "suitably" on the monthly allocation of 1,500 francs from the department of sharifian affairs, something being proven in the case of the pashas of Casablanca. As *caïd* of the Mzamza, the pasha would have an annual income of between 50,000 and 60,000 francs that would permit him "to maintain a social rank worthy of his functions."[27]

The second command was tailor-made for Tounsi whom Coudert characterized as "a striking personality" *(une personnalité marquante)* of great ambition and ability. It was larger than the unified Oulad Bou Ziri *caïdat* that Tounsi had wanted since 1918, although it was not the combined fief over three tribes and the city of Settat that Tounsi now aspired to. Coudert believed that Tounsi's dream command was far too grand. It was too extensive for his abilities and it would establish an unfortunate precedent in the Chaouïa, a region that had not known the "feudalism" of the High Atlas.[28] Not even Coudert wanted to handle that political and social engineering. The united command of the Oulad Sidi Ben Daoud and Oulad Bou Ziri was something else. It would better employ Tounsi's talents and be a step in an organizational direction that Coudert believed to be the road to the future.

In the end Coudert's proposal was rejected by higher-ups. Contrôleur Civil Alexandre Laurent, Chef de la Région Civile de la Chaouïa, told Lyautey that he did not share Coudert's enthusiasm for the change nor did he understand how Coudert's idea of a *sur-caïd* squared with his fear of creating a feudal fief in the Chaouïa. The new project for a native command seemed to him "a dangerous utopia" fraught with all kinds of "dangerous political repercussions."[29] And Tounsi's unexpected death in December 1923 deprived Coudert of the man most likely to succeed as *sur-caïd*.[30]

Tounsi's longtime rival and competitor for French favor in the Chaouïa was the pasha of Settat and *caïd* of the Mzamza, Si Boubeker Ben El Hadj el-Maâti. For five years (1909-1914) Boubeker had served as *khalifa* to his older brother, Ali. When Ali was dismissed as *caïd* in 1914 and compelled to reside at Mazagan, Boubeker succeeded him. This promotion at age thirty-eight was an expected reward and the regular method of keeping all in the family. Boubeker came from a line of *caïds*. His grandfather, Abdelkebir Ben Madani had been *caïd* of the Oulad Bou Rezq and Chtouka from 1854 to 1877 and his father, El Hadj el-Maâti, a supporter of Sultan Abd el-Aziz and an instant partisan of the French, had been *caïd* of the Mzamza from 1877 to 1908.[31]

From the first, Boubeker was credited with a "zeal and devotion" that merited recompense. His conscientious and rapid census of crops and livestock for the 1914 tax, the *tertib,* earned him a quick reputation as an "excellent *caïd*" and "a most precious assistant."[32] Maitrat marked him as someone to watch "with the greatest interest." A modest, unassuming exterior— "d'aspect un peu lourd"—concealed a hardworking and dedicated man with "a great fund of talent, intelligence and good sense," a "knowledgeable administrator," capable of contributing to the economic development of Settat. Boubeker was well thought of by both the native and the European populations and "very open" to the directives of the Makhzen and the protectorate authorities. "He has given the most entire satisfaction," noted Maitrat, "since his assumption of command in February 1914."[33]

A physical disability prevented Boubeker from riding horseback, which limited his contact with the rural population of the Mzamza and forced him to turn over the day-to-day administration of the *caïdat* to his *khalifa* and brother, Bouchaïb. In tribal matters, then, he was never completely in the saddle and the French lamented his lack of initiative and command. His high standing among the rural *caïds* was not owed to his own activity—he had never participated in the political life of the region nor was he a man of considerable wealth—but credited to his family.[34] This was a less than satisfactory situation and Coudert once mused that sometime Boubeker ought to be unburdened of his *caïdal* duties that he was not able to handle with any ease or great success.[35]

On the other hand, Boubeker was consistently rated an excellent native leader, an honest man—"something that is rare in a *caïd*"—a very good pasha of Settat, and a loyal partner of the French.[36] "Caïd Boubeker is a compliant *caïd*," reported Coudert, "who has pro-French sentiments and who better than anyone else responds to my political action directed at the acquisition of land in the countryside *(bled collectif)* for colonization. With his help I have been able to obtain 3,600 hectares in the Moualin El Oued, 800 in the Rhenan for woodlands, 300 in the Araër."[37] As far as Coudert was concerned, Boubeker was "one of the best *caïds*" in the Chaouïa, judged in terms of what he did to aid the French effort.[38] On this score there could be no greater contrast with Tounsi, who, although more intelligent and a better administrator, always put his own interests first. "In truth," Coudert explained when he once suspected Tounsi of bad-mouthing Boubeker,

> [Tounsi] follows his own course and thinks of one thing alone: How to increase his command, which means intriguing whenever necessary against his fellow *caïds* and trying to win the support of top administrators (French as well as sharifian) to whom his methods with all their devious twists and turns are unknown.[39]

Boubeker's death in October 1926, three years after Tounsi's, allowed Coudert to argue again for changes in the Mzamza command. Now as then the goal was to raise the importance of the command by putting it in the hands of an intelligent, talented, well-connected, and hardworking political leader. Coudert specified a "new man," chosen from among the Makhzen notables, who had a record of sharifian and protectorate service and who was "educated and able to direct the city's tribunal of justice," which was becoming more and more crowded. Named pasha of Settat and *caïd* of the Mzamza, he would draw on tribal revenues from the agriculture and livestock tax *(tertib)* and the market taxes, which, added to his stipend as pasha, would permit him a lifestyle equal to the importance of his office.[40]

The human obstacles to the plan were *khalifas* Si Bouchaïb Ben El Hadj el-Maâti and Abdelmejid Ben El Hadj el-Maâti, brothers to the late *caïd*. To exclude Bouchaïb from the succession would ignore his long years of "valuable service" and unsettle the Mzamza who had an attachment to the families of their former *caïds* as well as a preference to be administered by their own.[41] Yet despite Bouchaïb's many good qualities, he was without "sufficient stature" to handle the dual task of *caïd* and pasha. And Abdelmejid had not the proper *caïdal* temperament. He was known as a "hotblood" who had trouble with the large Jewish community in Settat. He lacked "levelheadedness, balance, and self-control, indispensable for a good native leader."[42]

As a compromise, Coudert proposed to keep Bouchaïb and Abdelmejid in their current posts. This would reduce the unpopularity of change at the top by providing continuity at the *khalifal* level. In addition, it would honor and reward the past accomplishments of the el-Maâti. To ensure Bouchaïb's compensation—often a difficulty when the *caïd* and *khalifa* were not blood relations and sometimes even when they were—Coudert specified that one-third of the monies from the *tertib* (all of which had usually gone to the *caïd)* should be paid to the first *khalifa*. This would prevent Bouchaïb's impoverishment and reduce any temptation he might have to exploit his own tribesmen. For Abdelmejid Coudert advanced something similar. If he proved satisfactory to the new pasha as second *khalifa,* then he might be appointed market inspector *(mohtaseb)* as well, thereby giving him a secure and adequate income.[43]

This time Coudert's proposals were endorsed by Laurent and approved by Resident General Théodore Steeg. In January 1927, Si Mohammed Ben Mohamed Ben Guebbas, the scion of one of Morocco's most prominent families (who in 1914 had dreamt of being the "real" pasha of Casablanca), became the pasha of Settat and the *caïd* of the Mzamza.[44]

After the deaths of Tounsi el-Bahloul and Boubeker el-Maâti and the investiture of Ben Guebbas, it was of considerable political interest to the

French that a protectorate "scepter" be placed in other, equally worthy local hands. For this distinction Coudert recommended Lahcen Ben Larbi Ben Cherki el-Hamdaoui el-Mzabi, *caïd* of the Mlal, a tribe of the Mzab confederation situated east of Settat and centered on Kasbah Ben Ahmed. Half a generation younger than Tounsi and Boubeker, Lahcen was a logical choice "first of all because of his past merits, then because of the qualities he is currently displaying in his functions as tribal leader, and third because of his attitude toward the protector government."[45]

From the very first days of the French occupation in Morocco, Lahcen had made himself known. His youth, bravery, and devotion attracted the attention of the French officers attached to the sultan's army in the Haouz in 1908 who recommended him for the rank of officer of the Nicham Iftikhar. Two years later he earned French gratitude for his "brilliant leadership" in "particularly difficult circumstances" of a column in the Tadla. As *caïd* of the Mlal from 1911, Lahcen demonstrated his nonmartial side by adapting the tribe to the new conditions of a peacetime existence. "By nature loyal and frank, possessed of an open and practical mind, a friend of the new and of progress—not by discipline and flattery, but by conviction—Caïd Lahcen continues, as tribal chieftain, to serve the French cause in Morocco with devotion. . . ." In addition, a "fils de grande tente," Lahcen owed to his ascendance a prestige and authority that extended beyond the region. This served his political interests and, in turn, those of France, "since his loyalty to us is firm."[46]

Laurent seconded Coudert's support for Lahcen and the proposal that the *caïd* be made a chevalier of the Legion of Honor as a visible sign of French esteem. He described Lahcen as "energetic, active, intelligent, and very devoted to France," quite capable of following in his family tradition to become "an important *caïd* in the Chaouïa." Laurent recalled that Lahcen had served three years as *khalifa*, first to his father, Caïd Si Larbi Ben Cherki, then to his father's successor, Caïd Moulay Abdesselam Ben el-Mekki. In 1911 he became *caïd* of the Mlal, a post that he held for the next fourteen years. During that time, Laurent emphasized, Lahcen had become "assimilated" to "our modern work methods." "He has the desire to do well and his collaboration is precious."[47]

Lahcen was a second-generation partisan of France. The reputation and accomplishments of his father had much to do with his own standing with the French and their persistent loyalty to him. At critical moments of French exasperation—and in truth the "making" of this *caïd* had taken fifteen years—it was the memory of his father that pulled him through. Lahcen's father, Si Larbi Ben Cherki, was born in 1859 among the Hamdaoua fraction of the Mlal. At age thirty-eight he was *caïd* of the Mzab confederation (comprised of four tribes: the Mlal, the Beni Brahim, the Oulad Mrah, and the Oulad Chebana) and the Achache.[48] He volunteered himself to the French in February 1908 and by July he was being characterized as "very sharp, remarkably intelligent, and very open-minded." In part this was because he was both willing and able to render "the greatest services" to the French. During their march into Mzab and Achache territory, Larbi put his "perfect knowledge" of the region and its peoples at their disposal "with complete devotion." And after the French establishment of a post at Kasbah Ben Ahmed, he continued with "the same zealousness" to induce the tribes of the area to accept the French occupation.[49]

Larbi "quickly understood" what "powerful support" the French could provide to reestablish his own authority among the Mzab, which the turbulent events of 1907-08 had caused him to lose to the Hafidists. And he understood how important the French could be to consolidate his influence over the Achache that had up to then been "more nominal than effective." Correct, competent, and appealing, Larbi was a diplomat and politician rather than a military leader. He was able to grasp the realities of the moment and act accordingly. The French knew that it was in his interest to serve them and that he would certainly do it "with zeal and dedication." "His great influence in the region [and] his sharp intelligence put him in a position to be most useful to us."[50]

It was up to Larbi to make sure that what he did for the French was matched by things done for him, for he had "completely compromised himself with his fellow Muslims." "He has not hesitated to place himself totally on our side," went a French report, "and he realizes full well that we will be ever grateful for his complete devotion."[51] In the political reckoning after the conquest of the Chaouïa, Larbi was restored to full authority over the Mzab and Achache. To inaugurate his "new regime" he even celebrated à la française with cigarettes, red wine, and champagne, perhaps not quite the sort of progress, however, that France had intended.[52]

Larbi died in July 1909 and thus was a French collaborator in the Chaouïa for less than eighteen months. Nevertheless, he left an indelible impression. Whenever Lahcen was mentioned, Larbi was invoked, made heroic by the accolade, "the companion of General d'Amade," and by the fact that he had died just before he was to receive the cross of the Legion of Honor, the first of Morocco's tribal leaders to be so honored.[53]

Since Larbi's sons were either too young (Lahcen was eighteen in 1909) or incompetent, there could not be a quick family succession to the leadership of the Mzab and the Achache. This posed a problem. Chef de Bataillon Jules Mouveaux, who commanded French troops among the Achache, predicted "rather serious consequences" as a result of the open competition among the many candidates for *caïd*. Since there was no clear front-runner, he wondered if it might not be wise to split Larbi's "grand caïdat" into five smaller ones or even two middle-sized groupings. This would have the advantage of satisfying several ambitions at the same time, but the disadvantage of opening more positions to the play of Makhzen politics. Mouveaux also worried that the Makhzen might try to impose its own candidate on the Achache, as it had attempted unsuccessfully to do with the nomination of Mohammed Ben Bou Abid, the well-known adversary of Caïd Larbi, in July 1908.[54]

Given the uncertainties, Mouveaux finally recommended keeping the Mzab-Achache command intact and appointing Moulay Abdesselam Ben el-Mekki as *caïd*.

> Age fifty-one [and] possessing a real influence in all the Mzab tribes, he is better able than anyone else to impose his authority on the native personalities of the region. I realize that his control will be more difficult to impose over the Achache, but I know him well enough to avow that he will rise to the task before him. Serious, thoughtful, energetic, [and] completely devoted to the French cause, he will make it a point of honor to promote our views and to maintain the peace and quiet which for the past year has remained unbroken throughout the region.[55]

No one counted on the antics of Lahcen and his older brother, Mohammed. Two days after their father's death, they requested permission to go to Casablanca to speak with General Moinier about the leadership question. They wanted the tribal command to go to someone in their family—even though it was not entirely clear to whom—because of the past services of their father. Although it was known that Caïd Larbi preferred Lahcen over anyone else as his successor, Mouveaux guessed that the brothers had composed their differences and would present Mohammed for the *caïdat* with Lahcen as his *khalifa*. But he called their scheme "unacceptable" and refused permission for the trip.[56]

Moinier had turned over the duties of *caïd* to Moulay Abdesselam, then asked the chargé d'affaires at Tangier to do all he could to have the sultan finalize the appointment. In selecting Moulay Abdesselam, Moinier said that his overriding concern was "the maintenance of order and good government."

> There would be serious disadvantages to putting a command as delicate and as important as that of the Mzab and Achache tribes,

which are situated in a relatively isolated region of the Chaouïa and in contact with outside populations where there is never peace and quiet, into the hands of native leaders who have yet to prove their ability and devotion.

Nevertheless, Moinier was willing to consider the return of the *caïdat* to the family of Caïd Larbi after Moulay Abdesselam's tenure. It was only Lahcen's youth—and here Moinier himself excluded Mohammed from the succession—that prevented his appointment.[57]

To make French intentions clear and to placate all parties (except perhaps Mohammed) Mouveaux counseled naming Lahcen *khalifa* to Moulay Abdesselam. The return of the *caïdat* to the family of Caïd Larbi and to the son "most capable" of succeeding him would then be only a matter of time.[58] But in the midst of the discussions at Ben Ahmed, Lahcen left for Casablanca on his own to urge Moinier "to name him *caïd*." It was an act of defiance that got him nowhere. Moinier refused to see him and after Lahcen returned home Mouveaux lectured him on the "foolishness of his ways," which apparently had included Lahcen's threat to "turn German" were he passed over for *caïd*. Mouveaux, who took none of this too seriously, pledged to watch the sons of Caïd Larbi "more closely," to subject them and their entourage to "a tighter surveillance."[59]

When all was said and done, Lahcen was named *khalifa* to Moulay Abdesselam, but only for the Mlal fraction of the Mzab. Two years later in 1911 he was named *caïd* of the Mlal, in part because of his superior conduct with the Tadla column.[60] The promotion was premature. Lahcen tended to put his personal interests first, those of the tribe second. This may only have been partly his fault. The regional commander admitted that Lahcen had been "indulged" by French officers who had been much too lenient with him because of his tender age.[61] In any event, Captain Ferdinand Lapasset repeated what Mouveaux had first pointed out, that Lahcen required guidance and had to be watched carefully. He could only succeed as a *caïd* if he were "firmly directed."[62]

Lahcen was worth the effort because he remained "very devoted" to the French cause, feeling rightly or wrongly that without French support "he would be nothing." These sentiments merited encouragement. Over time he did improve as a tribal leader. Lapasset reported in mid-1912 that once "taken very firmly in hand," Lahcen was rendering "good service" and would give "even better" when he felt himself "really guided and supported." At the end of 1913, Lieutenant Pierre Jacquet, Lapasset's successor as bureau chief at Ben Ahmed, observed that Lahcen led his tribe "with authority," exe-

cuted orders "with punctuality," and followed the advice of the bureau officers "with eagerness." He had all the makings of an "excellent *caïd,*" precisely what he will become, predicted Jacquet, "if he is counseled and
backed up." Lahcen's only desire seemed to be to "do well."[63]

In 1914 Moulay Abdesselam was dismissed as *caïd* of the Mzab and sent
to Marrakesh under house arrest. In the command shake-up that followed,
the "important fraction" of the Djemouha was attached to Lahcen's *caïdat.*
If not the once-promised command of the Mzab and Achache, it was another
indication of French confidence and future hopes for Lahcen. He has "all the
qualities of an excellent *caïd,*" wrote Captain Maitrat, the *contrôleur en chef*
at Settat who had also targeted Tounsi as a comer, and would do "quite well
if directed with intelligence and firmness." Maitrat did not hide the fact that
Lahcen still gave cause for some concern. He was "unsteady" and had a
weakness for the frivolous ("tendances à faire la fête"), which, however
explained away, were not praiseworthy attributes.[64]

In March 1916 Captain Alfred de Féraudy was appointed bureau chief at
Ben Ahmed. His first report on Lahcen was a devastating critique of the *caïd's*
character and leadership record and concluded with a call for his removal
and exile. "Since my arrival at Ben Ahmed, not a day has gone by when I
have not been besieged with complaints—almost all well-founded—against
Lahcen whose manner of service as well as personal conduct have become
intolerable." Capricious and tyrannical, Lahcen had committed the worst
abuses—selling offices, extorting money, and imposing burdensome taxes
on his tribesmen—to satisfy his private vices and pay for his prodigal life.
The most recent outrage had occurred in mid-April. Lahcen claimed that
thieves had broken into his tent and made off with 35,000 francs. De
Féraudy's investigation into the matter, however, revealed that the burglary
had been "staged" in order to fool his creditors. "Abhorred by those he governs, whom he scandalizes by his drunkenness and constant debauches,
[and] driven to shameful expedients by his excessive expenses, he should
no longer be maintained in this post. . . ."[65]

With regret Maitrat endorsed de Féraudy's recommendation. He recalled
that Lahcen had inherited "a preponderant situation" in the region. Without
great effort he could have held on to the esteem, affection, and respect everyone had felt toward his father. To be sure, as a young man Lahcen had
strayed from the straight and narrow, but Captains Jacquet and Pierre Sajous
had helped him make amends. Their successor as bureau chief at Ben
Ahmed, Captain Eugène Bertrand, had had less success and in truth often
turned a blind eye to Lahcen's penchant for drink and good times. In addition, Lahcen's expensive tastes had seriously jeopardized his own financial

situation and that of his relatives, all bound together in Caïd Larbi's inheritance that Lahcen was supposed to manage. In view of the personalities, the interests, and the sum of money involved, the staged theft (the *simulation du vol*), was of great importance.[66] It was in fact the last straw.

Maitrat concluded that Lahcen could "no longer be tolerated" at the head of a tribe. "His peers scorn him because of his excesses [and] those he governs have lost their esteem or respect for him because of his extortions and abuses of power. He has misled the French authorities many times during the course of investigations. We can put no confidence in him." Despite such a harsh and unequivocal judgment, Maitrat still hoped that at some future date Lahcen, made "wise and mature by these setbacks," might yet be of use.[67]

That hope shaped the final settlement with Lahcen. De Féraudy had proposed splitting Lahcen's command in two, placing the Djemouha under the authority of Caïd M'Hamed Ben El Hadj of the Menia and the Mlal under the control of El Hadj Taghi Ben Cherki, Lahcen's uncle and the tribe's *khalifa*. This solution would protect the social rank of the family of Caïd Larbi that the French authorities wished to do at all costs. El Hadj Taghi was "in the prime of life—active, intelligent, energetic, and educated." He had "appetites" as well, but Maitrat believed that "the fate reserved for his nephew will serve as an example and in all probability will cause him to moderate them."[68] In the end, although Lahcen was sent to Mogador in disgrace, he was permitted to keep his title as *caïd* and his command was not partitioned. His uncle, who remained *khalifa* of the Mlal and Djemouha, was charged with the governance of the *caïdat* in Lahcen's absence. This was a regency solution that held out the possibility of Lahcen's return, precisely how General Calmel, the military commander at Casablanca, explained it to Lyautey.[69] Even de Féraudy's year-end report acknowledged somewhat surprisingly that Lahcen was yet "capable of becoming a good native leader, if he straightened himself out."[70] It may also have been an admission that good men were hard to find. "The Mzab," de Féraudy put it bluntly, "is poor in men of any value."[71]

The regency frustrated the ambitions of those in Lahcen's family and in the tribe who wanted to become *caïd*, but in other ways it made the French task more difficult. With a *caïd* in nothing but name Calmel feared that the Mlal would explode in family quarrels and litigation over inheritances. Inevitably his administrators would be drawn in. He warned his men "to steer clear" of all of this, especially the long-smoldering dispute over the legacies of former *caïds* Mohammed Ben Ahmed (*caïd* of the Mzab and Achache from 1882 to 1897) and Cherki, both of which had been awarded to Caïd

Larbi by the Makhzen, "as a result of a decision by the sovereign authority." French supervisory officers had no reason to examine "either the virtue or the legality" of this decision, which had been made prior to the establishment of the protectorate. If the interested parties had complaints, they should be told to follow the normal legal channel, namely the route of Koranic law. The *contrôleurs* should "in no way" intervene in this process except to ensure that all the legal forms were observed, that the *cadi* rendered his judgment in a reasonable amount of time, and that the litigants were aware of their right of appeal.[72] Calmel wanted no repetition of the tangled Si Hamadi affair at Casablanca that had ensnared French civil and military administrators and ultimately pitted them against one another.

Sixteen months after Lahcen's exile, Lyautey inquired of Calmel if the moment had not come to restore the *caïd* to his command, "to grant him our confidence once again."[73] Opinion was divided. De Féraudy was unimpressed with Lahcen's progress. What he had heard about the *caïd* at Mogador was "not favorable."[74] And, Octave Peyssonnel, de Féraudy's successor at Ben Ahmed, was flatly opposed to Lahcen's return. He reported that Lahcen had left the Mlal and Djemouha with bitter memories and that his return would cause "a real malaise" among the native population. Moreover, should he return, Lahcen would be faced with a legal battle with the heirs of Ben Ahmed, grown bold and vocal in his absence. "As for me," Peyssonnel concluded,

> I think there is every reason to fear that in taking back his command, Caïd Lahcen's first concern—as much the result of his lavish lifestyle as of his unpaid debts—will be to exploit those under his authority and to put pressure on the judges of Koranic law to secure legal decisions favorable to himself. In such circumstances is it in our interest to restore a debtor *caïd*, detested by at least three-fourths of those under his rule, little loved by his family, and uncongenial to his colleagues?[75]

On the other hand, Captain Émile Riottot, Peyssonnel's direct superior, downplayed the negative consequences of Lahcen's return. He pointed out that Lahcen's past behavior had been tolerated by previous administrators and that this had actually encouraged his "weakness of character." His debts were a result of "mistaken conduct," Riottot explained, which "we permitted to get worse." "Thus we are morally a bit responsible for the maladjustment and the past mistakes of this young *caïd*." Riottot advised restoring Lahcen to his command, but with "meticulous supervision" *(un contrôle très minutieux)* and scrupulous attention to his administrative education.[76]

Calmel sided with Riottot. He told Lyautey that there was in fact "a serious malaise" in the Mzab produced by the constant change in native leadership. Two important families had shared the command in this region in the past: Lahcen's in the north among the Mlal and Abdesselam's in the south amidst the Mrah. At the present time while Lahcen was in exile at Mogador and Abdesselam at Marrakesh, the tribes were divided among leaders "of little stature."

> To return more or less to the former state of things, moving carefully and cautiously as circumstances dictate, seems to me the direction to follow in our native policy in this region, if we wish to restore calm here. . . . We are still too close to the conquest and it is not in our interest to forget the services rendered by those who were the first to rally to our cause.

In sum, Calmel wanted Lahcen returned to his command. But he did stipulate two conditions before this could happen: Lahcen's debts—estimated at more than 100,000 francs—had to be paid off and his father's inheritance had to be settled.[77]

Lyautey accepted Calmel's recommendation. Three months later Calmel reported that Lahcen had met the conditions for his reinstatement. He had sold some of his property to pay off his creditors and had reached a "friendly settlement" with the heirs of Caïd Ben Ahmed, ending the inheritance litigation. Calmel set up one final hurdle. He insisted upon screening Lahcen's choice for *khalifa*.[78] Here, too, Lahcen acquiesced. As a result, in March 1918 Lyautey restored Lahcen to his command. Hadj Cherki Ben El Hadj Driss el-Taghi, Lahcen's brother-in-law and his proxy during the Mogador exile, was named *khalifa*.[79] To make Lahcen's return more than a single act of grace, former *caïd* Moulay Abdesselam was also permitted to come home from his exile in Marrakesh.[80]

Back at Ben Ahmed Lahcen received stern counsel from the French supervisory officers. He was expected to live an exemplary life in order to win back all the affection, sympathy, and influence he had lost. For two years, however, there was no sign of any metamorphosis. Feared and resented by those he ruled, Lahcen seemed to be the impulsive authoritarian of old, lacking skill, evenhandedness, or understanding. Bristling with self-importance, he resisted supervision, preferring the "bad advice" of his sidekicks to the suggestions of French officials.[81] Drinking and excessive spending—*la vie large*—remained his vices and he appeared "little disposed" to give up a life of pleasure for a life of duty.[82] Despite all the promises and

potential, Chef de l'Annexe René Croix-Marie feared that Lahcen was incapable of reform. If all Croix-Marie said was true, Coudert concluded with
regret, "nothing will work with him."[83]

A change occurred sometime in 1920. Croix-Marie reported that Lahcen
seemed to have abandonned his "intemperate ways." He had been a satisfactory leader throughout the entire year, demonstrating "zeal and activity in
the governance of his tribe."[84] In 1921 Croix-Marie commented favorably on
Lahcen's intelligence and "good will." During the course of the year, Lahcen
had steered clear of all trouble. In sum, he had been a "good *caïd*."[85] Coudert
was apparently convinced. He returned to the assessments of days past.
Lahcen once again became "a *caïd* of stature, the scion of a noble family, a
leader who could have his command expanded."[86] In 1922 the progress continued. Lahcen was "rather liked" by those under his rule and seemed to have
a firm hold on the influence of his father.[87] Yet there were nagging reminders
of the past. Coudert noted that Lahcen still had the "unfortunate tendency"
to exploit those under his authority in order to meet his large expenses; during the year he had been fined 1,000 francs as a disciplinary measure.[88]

Nevertheless with Lahcen the positive always eclipsed the negative. This
was clearly evident in July 1925 when, at a moment of serious French
reverses in the Rif war, Lahcen asked for and was given the command of the
1ère Mehalla des Chaouïa, a unit of the sultan's army on the northern front.
It was not surprising, then, that at war's end and on the recommendation
of both Coudert and Laurent, Lahcen would finally be invested with the protectorate's "scepter."[89]

Unlike Tounsi el-Bahloul, Boubeker el-Maâti, and Lahcen el-Mzabi,
Abdelqader Ben El Hadj el-Maâti Ould Fardjia was a native leader made
important solely by the French. A notable of the Medakra tribe, he opposed
the French invasion. But he rallied to them once they established a military post at Boucheron at the end of March 1908. His "frank and energetic"
cooperation was a dramatic and dangerous reversal, earning him the
hatred of those who continued to resist; he was attacked and wounded
"very seriously" by his former *compagnons de guerre* at the beginning
of April.[90]

As a reward for his loyalty, the French military authorities picked
Abdelqader to be *caïd* of the Oulad Sebbah fraction of the Medakra. This was
a significant advance. Although his family was "honorably known" among
the Medakra and several members had led groups of the Oulad Amor fraction in fights with neighboring tribes, neither he nor his kin had ever had any
connections with the Makhzen. The French designation was an opportunity
for Abdelqader and he took it.[91]

Abdelqader was judged to be a leader of "great intelligence, strength, and tact." Thoughtful and prudent, he maintained an "impartial attitude" in the "very delicate conflicts" that arose from time to time between his tribesmen and Europeans, "deftly" avoiding the "traditional troubles" with foreign protégés. He never forgot that he had been chosen by the French. "Deferential without being servile, he seems to be seriously won over to our cause." His future was bright. He was "perfectly able at the opportune moment to exercise a larger command than that which he presently controls."[92]

Proud of his rank, power, and position, Abdelqader pursued his own ends. He consciously pushed his family members forward, such as his nephew, Bouchaïb, and worked to eliminate potential rivals, such as Ali Ben el-Arbi, sheik of the Oulad Zidan, whom he detested. He harbored grudges, but was patient, biding his time until the right moment came for revenge. He enjoyed exercising power so much that without surveillance it was feared he would abuse it. And he was not always frank, telling the French only what he thought they wanted to hear. None of this compromised his usefulness as an "excellent deputy," unspoiled by "Makhzen traditions." But he was to be kept "well in hand," even by judiciously supporting his enemies, who might act as "counterweights" to his influence.[93]

After the dismissal of the *caïd* of the Oulad Ali in 1913, Abdelqader's command was expanded to a joint command of the Oulad Sebbah and Oulad Ali. Among the French, his reputation in the region continued to rise. He accepted the advice of the supervisory officers and executed the orders he was given "with zeal." Extremely capable, he had caught on "without difficulty" to the methods of the protectorate and used them. "This *chef indigène,* who was a brilliant wartime leader," noted Contrôleur Civil Georges Rousseau in 1915, "is at present a good peacetime *caïd,* quite above the ordinary." "Seriously favorable to our cause, he knows how to behave in a deferential and subordinate manner with the supervising authorities without being obsequious, yet all the while he retains a certain independence of character and expression which makes him even more valuable." Without a doubt, he was "from every point of view by far the most competent native leader in the entire Medakra and even in all the circumscription of Boulhaut-Boucheron. He is capable of commanding all of the tribes of the Medakra together under a single *caïdat.*"[94]

Rousseau's successor at Boucheron saw another side of Abdelqader. According to Louis Contard, although Abdelqader was "very intelligent" and "energetic," he was only a "good *caïd*" when he was being watched. Left to himself, he abused his authority by oppressing those under his rule and satisfying his personal grudges. "Vain," "malicious," "hateful," and "vindictive" were the adjectives that Contard used to define the character of the *caïd*. Moreover, Abdelqader was an intriguer and a politician, who meddled in things that ought not to concern him and had even schemed in Casablanca to get the post of *caïd* of the Mellila. Finally, Contard questioned Abdelqader's loyalty to France. "He follows our advice only because it is politic to do so and so that he will not stand out from the other native leaders who accept our counsel willingly." Perhaps most unsettling of all, Contard believed that Abdelqader was "linked to all those who, whether near or far, have complained of our intervention in Morocco." In brief, he was "too intelligent and too clever," requiring surveillance all the time "without any letup."[95]

The duplicity that Contard sensed ("he slips through our hands like an eel" was one of Contard's descriptive phrases) was bound to put the *contrôleur* and the *caïd* at odds.[96] This is precisely what happened. Although from the beginning Abdelqader accepted Contard's authority "with difficulty," things got worse in 1917.[97] The *caïd* became openly hostile to Contard, forcing Chef du Contrôle Civil de Chaouïa-Nord Louis Bergé to threaten Abdelqadar with dismissal "pure and simple," if there was no improvement in their relationship.[98]

Three months later Contard reported that it was "absolutely impossible" for him to have any confidence at all in Abdelqader and he recommended his removal as *caïd*. He urged that all the tribes of the Medakra, including the Oulad Ali, be turned over to Caïd Mohamed Ben Larbi of the Ahlaf and Mellila, whose "honest and obedient nature" would put everything to rights. If the Oulad Sebbah and Oulad Ali were to remain a separate command, he suggested Mohamed Ben Seghir, "an influential and well-off notable of the Mezaraa (Oulad Sebbah)," or Ali Ben el-Arbi, "a very influential notable of the Oulad Zidan (Oulad Sebbah)," as the new *caïd*. El-Arbi was more intelligent than Ben Seghir, Contard noted, but also vindictive and his "great shrewdness" would make him "difficult to handle."[99]

In the end, Contard was transferred; Abdelqader stayed in place. This did not mean, however, that Abdelqader had won the tug-of-war. Contard's successor at Boucheron, Paul Metour, confirmed all of Contard's censures: Abdelqader was "unreliable, an intriguer, a politician, and vindictive." "Neither his manner of service, nor his family or personal relations, nor his education indicates that he should be designated to hold a post other than that which he currently occupies."[100] Abdelqader's upward advance was permanently stalled.

This remained the judgment on Abdelqader: a man of promise whose ambitions and methods made the French doubt his ability and sincerity. There was no question that he had rendered "real services," but his "partisan nature" and "exactions" had caused real troubles.[101] In 1920 the majority of the Oulad Ali went into open opposition against him, led by its former *caïd,* El Hadj Larbi Ould Medkouria, whom Abdelqader had replaced seven years before. The rebellion was put down and Medkouria spent six months in a Casablanca prison.[102] But the disturbance proved the point. Abdelqader was not the leader that he claimed to be. Years later Medkouria still had an influence among the Oulad Ali that worried the French because it showed how ineffective Abdelqader had been even with French support.[103]

In Settat and the Chaouïa the terms of the protectorate "partnership"—as, in fact, the terms of the Treaty of Fez—were dictated to the Moroccans by the French. Not surprisingly, indirect rule only worked with partners whom the French selected or approved, then guided, trained, and supervised according to their own ideas, values, and methods. In some cases, these native leaders were part of a governing elite that had commanded before the days of the French; in some cases they were not. In every instance, however, their position rested largely on France's continuing favor that made them agents of French action rather than independent actors in their own right.

Some Moroccan leaders were eager collaborators, committing themselves to the French for the rewards that they could offer. But few fully measured up to French expectations. According to French service reports, they were mired in the Makhzen past and had neither the ability, education, or inclination to become governors in the French manner. As with the pashas, *khalifas,* and *cadis* of Casablanca, the litany of French complaints ranged from recalcitrance to overzealousness, from incompetence to dishonesty. Even so, French judgments rarely tallied, reflecting the diversity of opinion among individual bureau chiefs whose tour of duty at any given post was seldom longer than two years. As much by circumstance as by design, the pashas of Settat and the *caïds* of the Chaouïa ended up as the somewhat hapless intermediaries between the protectorate authorities and the Moroccan population. Lyautey's method had left them somewhat uncomfortably situated between the directives of one culture and the commands of another.

CHAPTER 9

Rebellion in the Rif

■ ■ ■ ■

I n July 1921 a Spanish army was defeated at Anoual, near Melilla, by a coalition of Moroccan tribes from the Rif mountains. This military disaster, perhaps the worst colonial setback suffered by a European nation since the Italians were routed by the Abyssinians at Adowa and far more devastating than the French defeat at El Herri, seemed for a time to bother the French not at all.[1] Part of this was owed to Lyautey. Although he was more alert than most to the "national character" of what was happening in the Rif and to the indisputable leadership qualities of the obscure tribal notable, Mohammed Ben Abd el-Krim el-Khettabi, Lyautey believed that the Spanish had brought this calamity on themselves, proving what he had known all along, that they had no method to match his. According to Lyautey, it was Spanish failure that had created Riffi success. He remained sure that regardless of what Abd el-Krim did in the north, he held all the cards he needed to keep the protectorate secure in the south.[2]

French intelligence reports reinforced Lyautey's serenity. The *contrôleur civil* at Mechra Bel Ksiri near the Spanish zone insisted that the military events in the Rif had made "no impression" on the native population, which seemed only interested in matters closer to home, in particular French military operations near Ouezzane and the local changes in the native command initiated by the French. The situation was the same at Petitjean. At El Ksar el Kébir in the Spanish zone, however, the talk was that France would profit from the Spanish collapse to extend its own influence in the Rif. Anticipating such a move, El Ksar's pasha, notoriously unfriendly to France, had begun a slow rapprochement with French military authorities; and some members of the city's Jewish community, fearful that a sudden Spanish disintegration could expose them to the untender mercies of victorious tribesmen before the French could arrive, had already sought refuge in the French zone.[3]

The monthly reports of the department of native affairs (Direction des Affaires Indigènes et du Service des Renseignements) proclaimed the protectorate's overall political health to be excellent. Aware of the "events" in the Spanish zone, the majority of the native population showed no desire "to free itself from a tutelage of which it recognized the happy results," even if Abd el-Krim's "new idea"—the notion of an independent Rif state—had captured the imagination of some of the urban intellectuals. Following the Lyautey line, the intelligence service explained the "tribal revolt" as the result of a long-standing and widespread discontent with Spain's "arbitrary procedures" in matters of colonization as well as a "false conception" of native policy. This was why the "rebellion" was exclusively anti-Spanish in nature and why it would be especially difficult for Spain to restore the political and military status quo ante. Paradoxically, the report noted, the Rif tribes had used some of Lyautey against Spain. From the beginning they had employed the "spot of oil" technique to spread the dissidence from the spine of the Rif to the bone of the Djebala in the northwest.[4]

Although it was reassuring to conclude that Anoual and its aftermath were having little impact on the Moroccan population in the south, the Rif presented Lyautey with a serious problem. "What we must realize," came the assessment from the Région de Taza, "is that the tribes freed from Spanish domination—and in the main armed—constitute a threat that could be turned against us from one moment to the next." Also, the Spanish defeat meant something quite different to the as yet unsubmitted tribes along the northern tier of the French zone. The fresh opportunity for pillage, the swelling ambition of tribal leaders, the expansive force of new ideas all encouraged resistance to French pacification. Moreover, the "struggle for independence" twist that Abd el-Krim gave to his fight against the Spanish unnerved Lyautey. In addition to stimulating the Moroccan national memory it opened the door to external great power influences (particularly English and German) that France had been trying to shut out since the end of the Great War. Thus, despite Abd el-Krim's insistence that he had no hostile intentions toward France—statements expressing his more than justified concern over an immediate French intervention—what he did compromised the protectorate's security in more ways than one.[5]

Prudence dictated serious attention to the "grave events" that were taking place in the Spanish zone and to the "true nature" of Abd el-Krim's movement, which, as time passed, became the chief topic of conversation among educated Moroccans of the cities. Frenchmen pushed the notion that

Abd el-Krim was a rebel to both protectorate and sharifian authority and, as such, a twin terror. But to most Moroccans he appeared as yet another in a line of tribal resisters to Europe's push and to some an avenging holy warrior bent on ousting the infidels and their accomplices. This fit him squarely into Moroccan historical patterns. To a youthful Muslim audience, aware of the postwar changes in the Middle East, Abd el-Krim may have seemed something more, a modernizing nationalist whose "adventure" against Spain now opened new possibilities and new hopes for the world of Islam.[6]

While all of this sensitized Lyautey to the dangers of Abd el-Krim's rebellion, none of it convinced him to come to Spain's aid. He remained cold to the Spanish predicament, fixed on the thought that the reestablishment of Spain's control in the north would bring a reprise of the unfriendly colonial encounters that had always marked Franco-Spanish relations in Morocco. And he was angered that amidst its own military collapse Spain had continued to pay agitators within the French zone to stir up trouble in an effort to force France to shoulder a part of the Rif burden that Spain was bearing alone.[7] At the same time Lyautey was not above dealing with Abd el-Krim, allowing the Riffians to purchase supplies at French-controlled markets along the Ouergha and Moulouya Rivers and engaging Abd el-Krim's representatives in quiet conversations on any number of political and military matters. The purpose in all of this, however, as systematically anti-Spanish as it may have appeared to Madrid and Tetouan, was probably, as Daniel Rivet has concluded, to avoid any French military involvement in the north while the Middle Atlas still defied pacification.[8]

The Spanish road back to Anoual was tortoise-like and without a hint of any major changes in military strategy or political thinking. Lyautey credited the slow Spanish success to rivalries within the Abd el-Krim camp and payoffs to tribal leaders.[9] The halt of the Spanish advance in January 1922, albeit owing to bad weather, served to boost Abd el-Krim's reputation. According to French reports, he was putting this new prestige to work, like every European state builder of the past, to organize his "country." Having consolidated his authority over the Ghomara tribes along the coast toward Tetouan, he extended his reach south and west to the Beni Ahmed, who were supplying fighting men to aid the Khmès against Spanish attacks north of Chechaouen. He also prepared to move among the tribes on the right bank of the Ouergha—by treaty inside the French zone, but as yet outside of French control—to provide a steady flow of men and supplies to the Rif. Any step in this direction would immediately alter the military and political situation in a way "unfavorable" to the French, creating "serious complications"

on their northern front, still classified as "passive" in Lyautey's overall pacification plan. Distracted by Spanish troop movements closer to the Rif heartland where by November 1922 the Spanish army had finally reached the
Anoual line, Abd el-Krim failed to bring the border tribes under his control.
But it was not for lack of trying. The fear of a sudden appearance of large
concentrations of well-armed troops along the zonal boundary kept Lyautey
a vigilant observer of all Rif activities.[10]

Abd el-Krim's proclamation of an "independent republic of the Rif"—a
step backward to the historic Rif before the Spanish occupation, a step forward to the transformation of the collection of Rif tribes into a fledgling
Islamic state with a government and a flag—defiantly rejected any compromise with Spain, ensuring that the fighting throughout the north would
continue. It also challenged the entire protectorate setup, for according to the
Treaty of Fez, all Morocco was under French protection even if the mountainous northeast (what the French called the zone d'influence espagnole) had
subsequently been turned over to Spain. Still, Lyautey seemed less concerned with Abd el-Krim than with Spain. The Spanish recruitment of
Moulay Ahmed el-Raissouli and Abd el-Malek, two longtime adversaries of
France, to help them against Abd el-Krim infuriated him. Once on the
Spanish payroll, they predictably challenged French influence among the
Beni Zeroual and Marnissa tribes, causing Lyautey to complain that Spain
had now replaced Germany as the great European opponent of the French
protectorate in Morocco.[11]

Abd el-Krim's continued military progress against Spain, including his
decisive triumph over those native leaders paid from the Spanish wallet,
made him the unrivalled "champion of Rif independence." By April 1923 the
French acknowledged that his prestige had never been so great, his authority never so extensive. Only the Beni Zeroual—conscious of their own
strength, jealous of their own autonomy—seemed resolved to resist his
sway. However, with little else to hold Abd el-Krim in check along most of
the zonal frontier, he was destined to become "a certain danger" to France.[12]

Throughout the summer of 1923 the events of the Spanish zone magnetized the unsubmitted border tribes along the northern front of the Région
de Fez. They welcomed Abd el-Krim's emissaries with enthusiasm, listened
wide-eyed to the accounts of his victories, professed sympathy for his cause,
and pledged to work for his ultimate triumph. To shield the tribes under
French control from some of this excitement Colonel Paul Colombat's mobile
group at Ouezzane roved near the zonal frontier, countering Abd el-Krim's
stories with a close-up demonstration of French military power. Not surprisingly Colombat's tour provoked "a certain uneasiness" among the Beni

Zeroual that even Sharif Si Abderrahmane Derkaoui, the assertive leader of a religious brotherhood and a dependable French agent, could not quell. "In light of these events," French intelligence acknowledged matter-of-factly, "it is becoming more and more apparent that the *sharif*'s temporal influence is not up to the level of his spiritual power."[13] In truth, measured by Abd el-Krim, everyone else was of lesser stature.

In addition to Colombat's show of force, Lyautey stepped up the political activity of those Moroccan leaders in the pay of the French. This was intended to strengthen the "Makhzen party" among the tribes in the French zone that were still not under French control. Usually the prelude to a military advance, this was only a response to Abd el-Krim's own politicking, which was eroding French "rights" and prestige. Although the northern front remained calm, Abd el-Krim's influence was seeping southward. At Fez a Moroccan Homer had begun to sing of the "lions of the Rif" and the "Moroccan patriotism" that fired their courage.[14]

In September 1923 General Miguel Primo de Rivera, the captain general of Catalonia and a popular senior army officer, took control of the government of Spain in a bloodless coup d'état. Known for his blunt condemnations of Spain's Moroccan policy—on one occasion he suggested swapping Morocco for Gibraltar, on another he denounced Morocco as a "strategic weakness"—Primo hedged on his "abandonist" sentiments to enlist the support of the pro-Morocco *africanistas* in the Spanish army.[15] During the first hundred days of his peninsular dictatorship, he deliberately followed a wait-and-see policy in Morocco while reducing troop strength, introducing army reforms, and quietly seeking a negotiated peace. The peace feelers turned out to be a serious mistake. They signaled Spanish weakness to Abd el-Krim, fast becoming a "world historical figure" (according to a French observer, a real "Vercingetorix of the Rif") who brushed aside all thought of compromise.[16] Soon pummelled by Rif attacks in both the east and the west, Primo declared for the "semi-abandonment" of the Spanish zone at midyear 1924 in the most unfavorable of political and military circumstances. The disciplined retreat to more secure lines, painfully carried out during the next six months, was a victory for Primo's pragmatism and common sense, but a setback for Spain. It left Abd el-Krim undefeated and in full possession of the field of battle.[17]

The Spanish withdrawal had serious consequences for France. As Lyautey had warned Paris in February 1924, nothing would be more "unfavorable" for the protectorate than the establishment along the Mediterranean coast and so close to Fez of "an autonomous Muslim entity [*un groupement musulman autonome*], organized and modernized, [and] supported by numerous and warlike populations exalted by their constant successes against the Spanish. . . ." Such an entity would become the "natural center of attraction" not only for dissidents and malcontents but for all those in the Moroccan population, particularly the young, for whom recent events in Europe and the Middle East have "singularly broadened their horizons and raised multiple and xenophobic aspirations."[18] Spain's humiliating exit turned Lyautey's fears into realities.

Abd el-Krim's war making dictated a constant search for new resources. Among the unsubmitted tribes of the French zone, Abd el-Krim had only mixed success in naming *caïds,* collecting taxes, recruiting soldiers, and requisitioning supplies. In fact, his demands and strong-arm tactics, his "brutalities and exactions" often undermined his popularity, causing "sharp discontent" and some armed resistance.[19] The Beni Zeroual were a case in point. Pressed by the Riffians, the confederation's leaders nonetheless refused to send any contingents to join Abd el-Krim and committed themselves to defending their territorial boundaries by force. Although somewhat shaky in their initial resolve, the Beni Zeroual defeated a Riffi group at Tazouguert in mid-April 1924 (which caused the death of Ahmidou Tazi, a dissident Beni Zeroual leader), then engaged in a series of "violent contests" along the Ouergha River. This forced the quick Riffi evacuation of Beni Zeroual territory. A reprise of the attacks by Riffi *harkas* near the end of the month and at the beginning of May, which brought the neighboring Beni Ahmed and Beni Mestara into the fray, still failed to break Beni Zeroual confidence. With French encouragement, which included money and the promise of military support, the Beni Zeroual took the offensive in the east against the Mezraoua and the Beni Melloul (the sole dissenting Beni Zeroual fraction), in the southeast against the Jaïa, and in the north against the Beni Ahmed, all of whom had made common cause with Abd el-Krim. By mid-May the Mezraoua and Jaïa had switched sides to join the Beni Zeroual; and the Beni Ahmed was split down the middle.[20]

Taking advantage of this reverse to Abd el-Krim, 12,000 French troops from Aïn Aïcha crossed the Ouergha River on 27 May to occupy its right bank. Without a shot being fired the French advanced among the Mezziat, the Ghioua, and the Senhaja de Mosbah (all located southeast of the Beni Zeroual), establishing a new military front and bringing 25,000 additional tribesmen "under the sultan's authority and France's influence."[21] This giant step into the "dense" and "dangerous" riverbank tribes had always been part of French plans, for these groups bordered the lands of the Hayaïna confederation, which provided only a "thin shield" for road and rail communications from Fez to Taza and from Morocco to Algeria. But it had taken Lyautey a long time to make his move against these "anarchic and bellicose" mountain peoples who were now in close contact with the Riffians. Finally the "latent danger" to Fez was to be eliminated and these populations "disciplined."[22]

Taken by surprise, Abd el-Krim called for a holy war against the French and began supplying the border tribes with guns and money. On 6 and 8 June Riffi *harkas* attacked French troups near Bou Adel; on both occasions the Riffians withdrew with heavy losses. These two encounters increased French prestige throughout the Rif, strengthened French influence with the Beni Zeroual, and speeded the French occupation of the Mezraoua and the Jaïa. At the same time Abd el-Krim had not hesitated to attack the French nor those tribes that had submitted to them. This was something new. From now on France had to be prepared to meet Abd el-Krim in battle anywhere along the entire northern front.[23]

Together with Beni Zeroual resistance, the French move north of the Ouergha effectively cut Abd el-Krim off from needed foodstuffs in a year when the harvest was "almost nil" in the Rif. Since the French now possessed the region's "best storehouses," the Riffians had either to negotiate with them or to attack them.[24] The French advance was a prod, not a declaration of war. Lyautey simply wanted to force an end to the threat from the Rif. Unwilling to stand idly by while Abd el-Krim nibbled at the tribes north of the Ouergha (and France's treaty rights), Lyautey was still open to a peaceful composition of differences. He still had no desire to enter the war and surely no interest in pulling Spain's chestnuts from the fire. Nevertheless, the war in the Rif took on a triangular shape.

The Spanish halt in offensive operations in July freed Riffi groups to harass French posts north of the Ouergha and, much more serious, to cross the Ouergha and raid the Hayaïna confederation. This was something that the French advance in the north had been calculated to avoid. Colonel Colombat routed a 2,000-man Riffi *harka* with little difficulty in July, but the Riffians gave no sign of giving up nor of disappearing into the mountains. They remained as close as they dared to the French line of defense, monitoring the activities of the posts and intensifying their propaganda among the tribes on both sides of the French line. With regret General Aldebert de Chambrun, the commander of the Région de Fez, conceded that the "deliberately anti-French" military activity of the Riffians was taking its toll and had begun to affect "in an important way" the political situation of French Morocco.[25]

In order to bolster the entire northern front from Ouezzane to the Moulouya the French pressed the Beni Zeroual to accept their "support" against Riffi aggression (this meant the military occupation of their territory), which the French hoped they would agree to "without too much reluctance."

Confederation fractions under Sharif Derkaoui's sway "sincerely" wanted "the inauguration of a Makhzen regime," whereas the others—in particular the Beni M'Ka, Beni Brahim, and Beni Melloul—tottered between hesitation and outright hostility, preferring their independence to slipping under the thumb of the French.[26]

In early September French troops crossed the Ouergha a second time, occupying the Beni Ouriaguel (unrelated to the Rif tribe of the same name) and the Ouled Kacem of the Beni Zeroual. Although this was only a partial occupation of Beni Zeroual land and some shots had been fired at the French in anger, the move was judged a success. It was timed to take advantage of Abd el-Krim's increasing involvement on the Spanish front—where the Riffians were tightening the noose around Chechaouen—as well as to benefit from Sharif Derkaoui's high standing in the confederation. Now the French braced themselves for the Rif reaction, placing money, men, and machines on a "perpetual alert." It was up to Abd el-Krim, however, whose pride and ambition had received "the most dangerous and strongest of stimulants" as a result of the Spanish withdrawal, to make the next move.[27]

With military and political action Abd el-Krim attracted the attention of the Moroccan population throughout the French zone. The Riffians fortified their side of the new military front and improved it with roads, bridges, and telegraph lines, acting every inch the successors of the Spanish. They meddled in the affairs of all the tribes along both sides of the zonal boundary, challenging France's influence and occupation rights at will. And everywhere they displayed the republic's sign of sovereignty, a red flag emblazoned with a blue star and crescent. Abd el-Krim recognized the importance of behaving like a viable state in order to attract the political support at home and abroad to become one. In an interview with an American journalist in October 1924, he hinted that real independence could only come about through the backing of England, for France would never allow a Moroccan state "immune from the authority of the sultan" to exist side by side the protectorate for very long.[28] Even with England's help it would not be easy. Two months later Lyautey again advised Paris that any independent, modernized Muslim state positioned on the Mediterranean between Morocco and Algeria—and especially if it benefitted from outside support—would represent "a very serious danger" to French interests.[29]

Lyautey continued to recommend a military course that steered clear of any involvement in the Rif or the Spanish zone and a political course that followed the one he had taken with the Beni Zeroual, namely intense political action on the tribes of the Ouergha Valley, followed up, wherever possible, by the occupation of their territory.[30] In retrospect these plans lacked boldness, perhaps reflecting Lyautey's own discomfort with a situation that had gotten out of hand. His reluctance to consider the Rif "revolt" a French problem or to cooperate with Spain in any way had helped ensure the Spanish collapse and the Rif triumph. Over and over again he lectured to Paris that any collaboration with Spain would interfere with his own efforts to "neutralize" the Rif and alienate the entire Moroccan population as well, for he insisted that "all Muslims without exception" had an "unalterable antipathy" for Spain.[31] Yet Lyautey failed to neutralize the Rif militarily or to negotiate its political fate in a way beneficial to France. This lack of military-political "method" proved to be a fatal combination.

Despite the French posture of defense, Abd el-Krim considered all French activity to be directed against him. He could not fail to see things otherwise. While he negotiated with the notables of the eastern tribal fractions of the Beni Zeroual, the French bucked up Sharif Derkaoui with assurances of support.[32] To end this tiresome tug-of-war Abd el-Krim finally attacked the Beni Zeroual in the second week of April. In a series of quick military advances he swept up the Beni M'Ka and the Beni Melloul, then overwhelmed the hesitant Beni Brahim, and finally subdued the resistant Beni Bou Bane and Ouled Kacem, whose villages were put to the torch. The takeover happened so fast that the French suspected the tribesmen had not resisted with much enthusiasm. Even Sharif Derkaoui, forced to seek refuge behind French lines, narrowly avoided capture.[33]

De Chambrun immediately reinforced French defenses on the left bank of the Ouergha by forming mobile groups at Fès el Bali, Aïn Aïcha, and Souk el Arba de Tissa. At the same time Lyautey urgently requested more troops from Algeria to prevent a "breakthrough" anywhere along the French front—which would have had "a disastrous impact" on French Morocco—and to enable him to "respond vigorously" to any aggression. He repeated to Paris that his priorities were to shield the submitted tribes south of the Ouergha, to protect French communications between Fez and Taza, and to prevent "any serious political repercussion" throughout the rest of Morocco.[34]

Among the Beni Zeroual the Riffians appointed *caïds,* imposed tribute, meted out punishment, took hostages, and, most important of all, established a workforce to construct military shelters and trenches. Forced or freely given, obedience to Abd el-Krim seemed complete. Through prestige and pressure, the "terror of the Rif" soon made allies of adversaries all along the right bank of the Ouergha. By 23 April the Jaïa and Beni Ouriaguel tribes had defected to the Riffians, leaving those French posts that had been sited among them, such as Bab Cheraga, Taleghza, Aoudour, Dar Remich, Bibane, and Mghala, in enemy territory. The Senhaja de Mosbah and Ghioua held out until 26 April, then capitulated to the Riffians; in the next three days the Mezziat and Mezraoua followed suit.[35] Lyautey complained that such was the power of Abd el-Krim that even large left-bank confederations, like the Hayaïna and Cheraga, which had been solidly on the French side for ten years, were shaky.[36]

Lyautey described the situation as certainly the most serious that he had to face since 1914. Yet he maintained that what was happening coincided precisely with the fears that he had been expressing regularly in his reports to Paris since mid-December. In accord with government policy he insisted that he had avoided any offense to the Rif. It was Abd el-Krim who had struck first and then "with a violence and suddenness" that Lyautey believed could only be explained by a headiness from his victories against Spain (or, perhaps, the conclusion of secret and successful peace negotiations with the Spanish).[37] In any event, Lyautey requested immediate military reinforcements to increase his troop strength from forty to fifty-eight battalions. Given the unsettling circumstances caused by the Riffi "invasion," especially the prospect of continued tribal defections—the "unfastening" of the tribes one by one, as he put it—and Abd el-Krim's apparent intention to strike at Fez, Lyautey declared that without additional troops he ran the risk of "losing Morocco." He explained that although the entire Moroccan population, including the notables, remained "very honestly" on the French side and were "in no way inclined to revolt," things could change if France failed to back them up with sufficient force.[38]

Understandably, Moroccans in the southern zone were "powerfully impressed" by the repeated successes of the Riffians and soon expected Abd el-Krim to send his forces directly against French troops south of the Ouergha. Already Riffi bands had begun making "daring raids" on the outskirts of Souk el Arba de Tissa, forty kilometers northeast of Fez. This violation of French Morocco sounded the beginning of a struggle that the protectorate's *Bulletin mensuel* predicted would be hard fought, for any retreat on Abd el-Krim's part, once he had crossed the Moroccan Rubicon, would fatally wound his authority. "We must therefore expect him to engage all his resources and fight us until they are exhausted." Protectorate analysts also believed that securing the rich Ouergha valley was merely Abd el-Krim's first step. As the "true" champion of Islam, his real objective was Fez, Morocco's "holy city," where pretenders were transformed into sultans overnight. Beyond Fez, he would try to pull all Morocco from France's grip and then proceed to the "conquest" of Algeria and Tunisia.[39]

Whatever Abd el-Krim's ultimate ambitions, Lyautey insisted that his own aim was to build up a force large enough to inflict "a decisive blow" against the Riffi "aggressors," chasing them from the French zone once and for all. He still wanted no part of the Rif, which he called a "hornet's nest" and which he feared might involve France in a "prolonged war," and nothing at all to do with Spanish land in the north. *To be sure, there is no question of going into the Rif nor of nibbling away at the territory of the Spanish zone.*" Lyautey desired only to take back what belonged to France—the lands invaded by Abd el-Krim—and to protect "our zone" from the "professional pillagers" of the north, ever attracted by the rich territory south of the Ouergha. He trusted that force would suffice "to eliminate the evil," but it was necessary to use that force as soon as possible.[40]

Lyautey acknowledged that the events of April had resulted from a lack of military preparedness. "The events which have just taken place on the northern front have demonstrated that the present system of organization worked as a political cover for the tribes of our zone, but did not assure the military cover of our front against an outside attack by organized units."[41] He was loath to say more, but this alone admitted the defects of his method of conquest and rule. The Riffi advance often came with the support of the local populations, showing that French economic and political pacification among the tribes (including indirect rule through the sultan and his Makhzen) mattered little when there was an alternative. This did not mean that the tribes of the French zone were ready to rally to a Rif republic or some larger Moroccan national state headed by Abd el-Krim. But it did indicate their desire to recapture their independence—despite the peace, progress, and prosperity offered by the French—and thus the fragility of Lyautey's hold over them.

The tardy French military response began on 27 April with the march of Colonel Charles Noguès's mobile group from Aïn Aïcha along the left bank of the Ouergha to Kelaa des Sless. En route Noguès rescued the post of Bou Toumeur and freed a battalion of Algerian infantrymen who had been pinned down and subjected to punishing fire (seventeen killed, forty-six wounded) north of Djebel Messaoud. At Kelaa des Sless Colonel Colombat took command of the French force and marched west to Fès el Bali, clearing the left bank of Riffians as he went. He then crossed the Ouergha and delivered the garrison at Tafrant among the Ouled Kacem. With three mobile groups under his command, General de Chambrun believed that he could protect all the threatened posts in Beni Zeroual territory, block the most important road to Fez, and maintain a military liaison with Ouezzane farther west. At the same time Aïn Aïcha and Souk el Arba de Tissa, which stood along a second route to Fez, were temporarily exposed. De Chambrun counted on the last of Lyautey's reserves as well as the troops on their way from Algeria—all ultimately under the command of Colonel Henri Freydenberg, military commander of the Région de Meknès—to plug this gap. For the time being de Chambrun had prevented a "formidable rush" on Fez. But until Lyautey was strong enough to threaten or inflict a "serious defeat" on Abd el-Krim, the danger to Fez remained a real one.[42]

To account for his embarrassing military predicament, Lyautey explained to Paris that modern weapons in the possession of the Riffians, many taken from the Spanish in the previous three years of fighting, had considerably reduced the French advantage. "This is the first time since 1907 that we have come up against artillery in the hands of the native population and have had one of our fortifications taken."[43] He renewed his call for reinforcements and requested in addition "shells and bombs of mustard-gas"—morally outlawed since the Great War—in order to interdict certain zones or vital points to the enemy.[44] He justified this extraordinary request because he was faced with something that "no other colonial power has ever confronted in Islamic Africa": the formidable alliance of "atavistic xenophobia" and religious fanaticism with modern European weapons and military practice.[45]

Silent on the matter of poison gas, Paris committed itself to repel the Riffi invasion with "the utmost energy." "Any other policy," explained Prime Minister and Minister of War Paul Painlevé, "would be disastrous for our prestige in Morocco and throughout North Africa."[46] At the same time Painlevé sent a personal envoy to Madrid to begin talks with Spain on concerted action against the Rif, abruptly ending Lyautey's policy of splendid isolation.[47] The word was that Lyautey had lost his touch.

At the end of May after a month of "ceaseless combat" de Chambrun reported 1,400 soldiers killed, wounded, and missing and 4 fortifications (of the 40 constructed in 1924) in enemy hands. Although he calculated enemy losses at almost four times those of his own, this was a stunning blow and an incredible setback to French confidence and prestige.[48] Despite de Chambrun's best efforts—and Lyautey acknowledged the hardships of a campaign hampered by rain, by communications difficulties, and by "greatly reduced" troop strength—the struggle demanded a change at the top.[49] Lyautey named General Albert Daugan, the commander of the Région de Marrakech, to head up a newly created "commandement général du front nord," which stretched from Ouezzane in the west to Kifane north of Taza in the east. In 1918 Daugan had led the famous Moroccan Division to a string of victories on the western front in France; he had a reputation as a tough, no-nonsense leader.[50] The change in command and the expanded front signalled a new appreciation of the conflict. The Ministry of War in Paris predicted that France might be faced with "a war of some length" in the Rif,

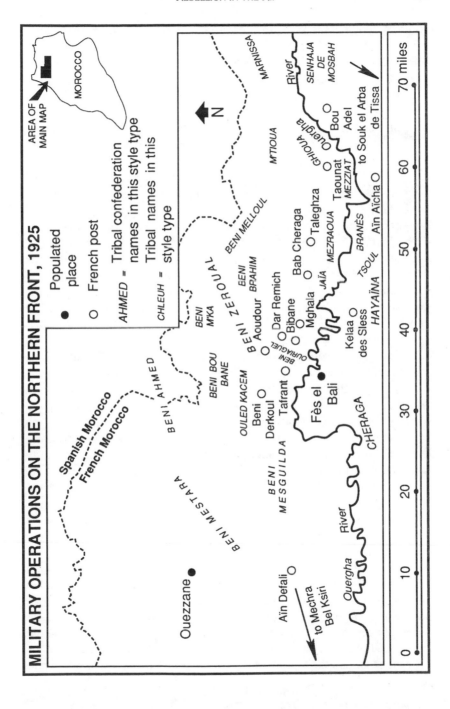

MILITARY OPERATIONS ON THE NORTHERN FRONT, 1925

requiring "painful sacrifices in men and money" and ending only after France had been able to deal its adversary "a severe lesson," making him "fully cognizant" of his military inferiority.[51] The rebellion against Spain had now become a war against France.

In an effort to stabilize the front Daugan wisely abandoned the isolated posts, whose heroic defense had been so costly and exhausting, in order to establish three strong points—Bibane and Tafrant in the west and Taounat in the east—elements of a curtain wall behind which his troops might maneuver in relative security. Even so, Bibane, the largest French fortification in Beni Zeroual territory, collapsed on 5 June and ten days later Beni Derkoul fell, triggering the defection of the entire Beni Mesguilda tribe. Riffi strikes farther west even menaced Ouezzane, forcing the evacuation of some of the civilian population of the city, and threatened the French farms of the Gharb.[52] The toughness and savagery of Riffi fighting as well as the real fear that France might not be able to "redress" the situation because of a lack of artillery and the inexperience of its "young troops" prompted Lyautey again to argue to Paris that it ought to have no scruples about authorizing the use of toxic weapons. French lives were at stake and so in truth was all French Morocco.[53]

Underscoring the seriousness of the military situation, Painlevé visited Morocco in June, irritating Lyautey and further undercutting his authority. As a trumpet for French policy, however, he sounded loud and clear. Painlevé explained the fight on the northern front as a contest between civilization and "barbarism." France's sole purpose, he informed his countrymen and world opinion, was to contain this "savage and barbaric invasion" from the Rif. France would use whatever force was necessary—although Paris stuck by its refusal to permit the use of gas—to repel these rebel hordes and to restore peace to the protectorate.[54] The Moroccan question, Painlevé insisted, was a "national issue" that engaged the future of North Africa and perhaps all of France's colonial empire as well. Not to defend Morocco would be to abandon everything. "It would be the end of our colonial empire, the end of our economic independence—impossible without colonies—the end of the prestige and influence of France in the world."[55]

As Painlevé knew, this was more than a colonial war in a dark corner of Africa. Abd el-Krim had forged a modern army, capable of defeating Spain and taking on France, and a state, eager to join the "family of nations." In many ways, confessed the French Ministry of War, he personified the aspirations of every Muslim nation that had fallen under European domination and wanted to recover its independence. As a result, the sounds of the Rif war echoed around the Muslim world from North Africa to India with a particular resonance in the Arab Middle East.[56] At the same time anti-imperialist (and anti-French) sentiment in Europe and America was drawn to the David and Goliath struggle of the "Rif republic," which bravely insisted on its right of self-determination and boldly invoked the protection of the League of Nations. In France the political division of opinion over the Rif war helped to fracture the governing Cartel des Gauches coalition and gave the Communists—tagged "abd el-criminals" by the colonial lobby—a stick with which to beat the government.[57] Domestic and foreign politics aside, what surprised Frenchmen and empire watchers worldwide was the sudden collapse of a colonial enterprise billed as the highest form of French imperialism. In this sense, Painlevé was correct: A French defeat in Morocco might be a defeat for France all across the globe.

Daugan's feverish attempts to organize a defense in depth were matched by French diplomatic efforts to secure Spanish cooperation for a negotiated end to the war. But, according to Lyautey, what was needed most was a confidence-raising military offensive to stave off the "breaking up of the tribes" and prevent a further erosion of faith in French arms. "In truth," he told Painlevé,

> the Muslim, the Moroccan understands and respects only force and by witnessing the initial and incontestable superiority of Abd el-Krim—his continued progress, the fall of our posts, the tribal dissidence—and by observing that up until now we have not responded effectively, he will soon be persuaded of our powerlessness and our weakness, if this has not already happened, and the situation will be completely compromised.

Since an offensive was the "*absolute condition* of a redressment of the situation," but as yet impossible along the northern front, Lyautey suggested a Franco-Spanish landing at Alhucemas Bay (with English participation "if possible") to assault Abd el-Krim's capital at Ajdir.[58] This dramatic turnabout in Lyautey's attitude—that in Morocco force counted for all—battered both his theory and practice of colonial conquest and rule. This and his newfound desire for cooperation with Spain (and England!) were yet further indications of the desperateness of the military situation.

On 2 July a Riffi attack north of Taza caused the defection of the Tsoul, Branès, and Riata tribes. This was the first time since the beginning of Riffi operations in mid-April that tribes safely tucked behind French lines and considered firmly under French control had decided that this was "the favorable moment to regain their independence." The political situation "seriously modified" the military situation, for French troops now found themselves submerged in the "complete collapse" of a war zone. General Albert Cambay believed the situation so perilous, the danger of encirclement and massacre so real that he recommended the withdrawal of all French troops in the Taza sector to the east toward the Moulouya in order to regroup and defend the road to Algeria.[59] Witnessing the rout north of Taza, Cambay, too, concluded bitterly that force and force alone ensured colonial control. Everything else was secondary.[60]

Despite Cambay's desperate advice, Lyautey refused to permit a maneuver that would have had the "serious inconvenience" of depriving him of a quarter of the forces he needed to shield Fez, whose security from both the military and political standpoint remained his "essential objective." Instead, recognizing that the overall situation was indeed "serious, very serious," he called for "indispensable" reinforcements—at a minimum three Malagasy battalions and the six Moroccan battalions with the Army of the Rhine—which would enable him to act quickly and with sufficient strength.[61]

Within twenty-four hours Lyautey reported better news. French forces had engaged and dispersed Riffi *harkas* at Bab Taza and northeast of Kifane, starting a change of heart among the Tsoul, who now seemed to be on the verge of returning to the French side, and even producing "a slight détente" with the Branès. Although this gave Lyautey more time than he thought he had, the situation along the northern front was still "very fragile" and upsetting. Riffi attacks might occur again at any point along the front, throwing the submitted tribes into great disarray quite like the "veritable panic" among the Hayaïna and Cheraga ("one of those contagious waves of fear that I saw twice in 1912 and again in 1919") that had brought a flood of terrified refugees into Fez during the first days of July. Still, Lyautey counted on calm, sangfroid, and especially "an irresistible tenacity" to carry him through the crisis to its resolution and French Morocco's ultimate "recovery." This "moral factor," he insisted, was the basis for everything else, at least until more reinforcements arrived.[62]

Paris was less sanguine. On 6 July General Stanislas Naulin, commander of the 30th Corps of the Army of the Rhine at Wiesbaden, was named *commandant supérieur des troupes du Maroc* and charged with the preparation, conduct, and execution of all military operations. Lyautey was reduced to providing Naulin with only "general instructions" on the overall direction of operations.[63] Although Lyautey insisted that now he could concentrate on things political, diplomatic, and administrative—and he had in fact asked Paris in June to send a senior military officer to assist him—it was clear that Morocco would be "saved" by hands other than his.[64] This was the first public slap to Lyautey and his method (and especially to the "sacrosanct" notion of the combined use of military and political action) by the French government. Clearly the method had failed to prevent the Riffi attack or the French collapse and for this the marshal was held accountable.

Although Lyautey apologists would later blame Paris politicians and soldiers for denying Lyautey the men and equipment he needed for victory against Abd el-Krim, the numbers were always on Lyautey's side. As Daniel Rivet has shown, it was Lyautey's political "indecisiveness" (les flottements de Lyautey), Abd el-Krim's military skills, and the protectorate's own failure as an instrument of conquest and rule rather than metropolitan stinginess that determined the outcome on the Ouergha. During the course of a single season Moroccans both inside and outside of the war zone and from the highest to the lowest in Moroccan society began to detach themselves from the protectorate—sometimes openly, most often silently—in anticipation of the end of French rule. Most disturbing from the French point of view were the signs of separation among the empire's elite, from the bourgeoisie of Fez to the grands caïds of the Atlas, who had always been the most favored of the protectorate. All of this demonstrated in no uncertain terms the fragility of the house that Lyautey had built.[65]

Not surprisingly Lyautey was kept on the sidelines of the negotiations with Spain during the Madrid conference (17 June-25 July), which produced the terms for a peace offer to Abd el-Krim. According to a joint memorandum of 18 July, which Primo de Rivera considered the centerpiece of the six separate Franco-Spanish accords, the Rif would be granted autonomy "compatible with international treaties." If the negotiations failed—and in the end they did, for Abd el-Krim refused to agree to anything less than full independence for the Rif—France and Spain bound themselves to simultaneous military action. This proposed "new regime" in the Rif was nothing that Lyautey could have accepted without deep reserve, but the gravity of the crisis had brushed him and his concerns aside.[66]

Worse was to come. Marshal Philippe Pétain, the generalissimo of France's armies and vice president of the Supreme War Council, never an admirer of Lyautey nor his method, arrived in Morocco on 17 July for a ten-day tour of inspection. In addition to examining the military situation up close—for Ouezzane, Fez, and Taza still remained under the Riffi gun—Pétain defined the new command responsibilities between Naulin and Lyautey and oversaw the plans for future military operations. He also travelled to the Spanish zone to meet with Primo de Rivera, inaugurating at the highest level the political and military collaboration with Spain that had been forged in Madrid.[67]

By virtue of his "high authority" Pétain signalled a "new phase" in the Rif conflict as well as a change in French policy.[68] The conclusions of his report to the government, made public in early August, proclaimed the "brutal fact" that French armies had been attacked by "the most powerful and best-armed enemy that we have ever encountered throughout the course of our colonial operations." Pétain praised the "sacrificial mission" of the advance posts and acknowledged the "overwhelming task" of the troops along the northern front, "submerged in a rising tide of insurrection," who had fought "without respite" to save the endangered posts as well as to protect Fez and the road to Algeria. With somewhat less conviction he saluted Lyautey as a "great leader" who "in spite of his age and the burdens of a rugged colonial career" (Lyautey was only two years older than Pétain) had succeeded in defending his "work of civilization" against this "onslaught of barbarians."[69]

With all the confidence of an organizer of victory Pétain promised that plans were under way to "push back" the enemy, to reestablish French authority, and to set up "a solid organization," ensuring that nothing like this would ever happen again. At the same time he noted that Abd el-Krim had failed to achieve his major political objectives—Fez and Taza were still safely out of his reach—and, although Pétain knew better, that the Moroccan "interior" had remained "completely faithful" to France.[70]

With no positive response from Abd el-Krim on the terms for peace the French government authorized Pétain on 17 August to assume the overall direction of military operations in Morocco. Pétain had already made it clear to Painlevé and the cabinet that he intended to drive back Abd el-Krim's forces "step-by-step," restoring French control among the dissident tribes, and then, once the region around Taza was secure, to strike at the "heart of the Rif." For this effort, which no one could consider modest, Pétain received the promise of military reinforcements; he also counted on the full cooperation of the Spanish army, already engaged in operations with the French in the west around Ouezzane.[71]

Lyautey and Naulin had proposed an August offensive against the Tsoul and Branès tribes to clear the area west and northwest of Taza and a September attack on the Beni Zeroual to restore the French situation north of the Ouergha. Pétain considered this plan "inadequate" because its goals were "exclusively political," that is, solely concerned with reestablishing French authority among the tribes formerly under French control. According to Pétain, it in no way constituted "a direct threat" to the power of Abd el-Krim and the Rif tribes and would lead to "serious, costly, and long" French military efforts in the future.[72] As a result, he rejected it. Assured of government support, Pétain pushed French policy from the narrow confines of restoring the security of the northern front by a piecemeal action on the tribes to a broad Franco-Spanish coalition for military victory in the Rif.

Before returning to Rabat, Pétain had a second meeting with Primo de Rivera at Algeciras where he presented his plan for a combined Franco-Spanish offensive in the north. Primo countered with his own project for an amphibious landing at Alhucemas Bay west of Melilla that would put a Spanish army within artillery shot of Abd el-Krim's headquarters at Ajdir. Once Ajdir was in Spanish hands, Primo said he was willing to transfer some of his troops to Melilla to participate in joint operations with France. Although Pétain was only cautiously optimistic about Primo's proposals and Primo not wildly enthusiastic about Pétain's program, this became the agreed-upon Franco-Spanish order of battle.[73]

In Rabat on 22 August Pétain conferred with Lyautey on matters military and political, making clear his judgment of the limitations of Lyautey's own proposals, then proceeded to Fez to study the situation at the front and draw up his own plans. When finalized, they called for an advance against the Tsoul and Branès tribes at the end of August as well as a "double attack" north of Fez against the Riffi bastions of Teroual-Tafrant and Taounat, political action on the Beni Zeroual and the M'Tioua tribes, and the reestablishment of the most important posts north of the Ouergha by mid-September. In comparison with Lyautey's plans Pétain's offensive north of Fez was in his own words "simplified and restricted to only those actions which would bring about durable results." Another projected offensive north of Taza along the upper Msoun River, planned by Pétain for the end of September and in early October, would bring the French deep into the Rif, perhaps as far as a line along the Kert River, a possible point of departure for a final Franco-Spanish advance.[74]

In the end Lyautey approved Pétain's plan and, when he was called to Paris for consultations in late August, even defended it from hostile critics.[75] By that time, however, the transfer of military power had been completed. When Lyautey left Morocco on 26 August, he announced officially that Pétain would henceforth direct all military operations and all of Morocco's troops, thus unifying the command that had been split between Lyautey and Naulin. Despite persistent press speculation that Lyautey's days as resident general were numbered and that a civilian resident would soon be appointed to take his place, Paris asserted that Lyautey's political mission remained untouched.[76] That was untrue. Lyautey returned to Morocco on 12 September, but only to pack his bags. His public letter of resignation, dated a dozen days later, was tinged with bitterness. As he saw it, the Rif question had opened "new problems," which, as he noted in a separate and confidential letter, all related to Spain's concept of its role in the protectorate and how that affected French security. To solve them it was necessary to have a "new man" in the prime of life and bolstered by the "full confidence" of the government.[77] At this point he had neither the youth nor the political backing.

Later, in a private letter to Foreign Minister Aristide Briand, Lyautey made it clear that Pétain's entire military setup in Morocco—its organization, its doctrines, its methods, its programs—differed wholly from everything that he had practiced throughout his colonial career. "Rightly or wrongly, I have no confidence in their effectiveness." One last time he railed against plans that he considered "heavy," "slow," "unadapted to the country," and "very burdensome" for the French budget. His way, he insisted, aimed at quick, decisive results at less cost through the "simultaneous and more intense use of political action."[78] Not that it made any difference. Lyautey's advice on matters Moroccan was no longer wanted. At age seventy-one he was ending a colonial career of thirty years with his lifework in shambles.

Unaffected by Lyautey's fall, Pétain pursued the war in the Rif according to "his method," his own organizational skills, and his "profound knowledge" of the resources of the French army.[79] Employing what he had been given in new men and equipment and working in concert with the Spanish (who landed successfully near Alhucemas Bay on 8 September, then moved on Ajdir), Pétain "reconquered" the French positions all along the "former front" by mid-September.[80] And with this dramatic French advance came the tribes: first the Tsoul, then the Branès, finally the Beni Zeroual.[81] To be sure, Pétain's general offensive had not penetrated the Rif heartland—that would come in October—and neither vanquished nor captured Abd el-Krim. But the French zone of the protectorate was now secure.[82] At the beginning of November Pétain gave the military command back to Naulin and returned to France, proclaiming his mission completed: "Abd el-Krim is surrounded. He is no longer to be feared. The military action is finished. I hand the baton over to the political experts."[83]

Abd el-Krim's surrender in May 1926 and exile to Réunion marked the close of the Rif "adventure."[84] Although France had emerged victorious, nothing would be quite the same again, for the rebellion had exposed the shortcomings of the Lyautey method in the most public, dramatic, and undeniable of ways. Despite fourteen years of pacification and indirect rule, Moroccans continued to resent and resist the French presence. After all these years of "living together," the military commander at Fez noted with real disappointment, a gulf still existed between Moroccans and Frenchmen. The Rif rebellion had made it even wider.[85]

Conclusion

■ ■ ■ ■

In France Lyautey's reputation is secure. His tomb in Les Invalides is only steps away from Napoleon Bonaparte's and his statue in a quiet Paris garden on Place Denys-Cochin is dedicated to all Frenchmen, civilians as well as soldiers, who died overseas for France.[1] In truth, Lyautey's eclipse after the Rif rebellion was only temporary—in 1931 he presided over the grandiose Paris Colonial Exposition—for he had furnished France with a practice for colonial conquest and rule that matched the ideology of the civilizing mission. Whether his method of pacification and indirect rule worked or not was irrelevant. Frenchmen were unwilling to give it up even at gunpoint. Lyautey's justification (even celebration) of colonial wars that resulted in peace, prosperity, and progress—in some ways a Gallic response to Rudyard Kipling's wise and weary "White Man's Burden" of 1899—continued to mark French imperialism into the 1960s. Lyautey's words, fit for the raised metal and carved stone of memorials and public buildings as well as the "colonial discourse" of the Académie Française (where Lyautey's effort in Morocco was hailed as "so boldly civilizing and French"), described a French colonialism with a very human face.[2]

The words, however, never became flesh. In Morocco, the ultimate testing ground of the Lyautey method, pacification came everywhere through armed and bitter contests with resistant townsmen and tribesmen. Pacification was war, not peace. Politics and economics did little to pacify the people of Morocco's cities or the tribes of the Middle Atlas until they were subdued by the threat or the use of force. And the military collaboration with the *caïds* of southern Morocco, an experiment in pacification by indirect means, actually increased the French military burden in men, materiel, and money, drawing troops into a region where Lyautey would have preferred not to go. Without doubt Lyautey and his commanders in the field tried to combine political and economic tactics with the use of force.

But even the famous "Berber policy" and the *politique des grands caïds,* hailed as victories for peaceful penetration, were really forced on Lyautey by the circumstances of never-ending war on all fronts and actually weakened the partnership with the sultan and the Makhzen that Lyautey said he prized above all else. More important, they failed to stop the resistance to France.

Indirect rule also never came to pass. To be sure, the Lyautey method of colonial rule was more than a con game. Lyautey took it seriously, trying to make Moroccans both instruments and shields of French rule. But indirect rule failed in large part because of Franco-Moroccan cultural difference—what he called the dissimilarity in "mentalities" and "work habits"—and racial distance. Frenchmen, Lyautey admitted, had direct rule in their bones and were impatient and authoritarian by nature. Few tasks were ever completed under the "mere supervision" of a French officer. And too many Frenchmen, like those on the municipal commission of Rabat, tended to regard Moroccans "as an inferior race, as a negligible quantity."[3] In addition, wherever Frenchmen (like Lyautey himself) pressed the protectorate mission of political, social, and economic "modernization" with vigor, indirect rule foundered. Since all of this was calculated by the French yardstick and implemented according to French standards, it resulted, as Daniel Rivet has shown, in the creation of an all-powerful, centralized colonial state, a "modern Leviathan" that was directed by Frenchmen in the role of the "good tyrant."[4] Thus, despite Lyautey's 1920 complaint that there was too little indirect rule throughout the protectorate (especially at the very top) and his determination to give "a new direction *(un sérieux coup de barre)* to our native policy and to the participation of Muslims in public affairs," the realities of the colonial situation made indirect rule almost impossible to realize.[5] In fact, it was only "successful" with the most compliant of partners and with the most energetic and headstrong counselors as their guides. As the evidence from Casablanca and the Chaouïa shows, this was indirect rule directed.

Lyautey assumed that through his method Frenchmen would transform themselves and France as well as the colonial world overseas. Their impact on Morocco and Moroccans is difficult to measure. Morocco was undoubtedly changed, for the French brought a revolution of one sort or another with them wherever they went, but not without the resentment and resistance of a people pulled, pushed, and seldom consulted. When Lyautey died in July 1934, Sultan Mohammed Ben Youssef, Moulay Youssef's third son (hand-picked by the French to succeed his father in 1927), made it clear that he did not want the body of "the creator of modern Morocco" returned to Rabat for burial. The *grand vizir* fretted aloud that this might well provoke anti-French agitation by "nationalist elements" and open up a "new era of difficulties." And notables in Rabat and Fez "systematically" refused to discuss the subject, letting the French guess at the intensity of their displeasure. Despite this lack of enthusiasm, Lyautey was laid to rest in the gardens of the residency in a simple Moroccan-style sepulcher with a green-tiled roof.[6] After independence Lyautey came home to France. Today in Rabat a Garage Lyautey on Avenue Mohammed V alone bears his name and in Casablanca the heroic equestrian statue that once graced Place Lyautey (now Place des Nations-Unies) is safely tucked behind the ornamental grille of the French consulate. All of this hints at the ambiguity of Lyautey's legacy. By his method he had hoped to overcome Morocco's resistance to France and to build a firm Franco-Moroccan partnership. In this he was unsuccessful.

NOTES

Preface

1. See "Discours prononcé à l'occasion du transfert aux Invalides des cendres du maréchal Lyautey," 10 May 1961, in Charles de Gaulle, *Discours et messages*, 5 vols. (Paris: Plon, 1970), 3:315-17.

Chapter 1

1. On the Lyautey family history, see André Le Révérend, *Lyautey* (Paris: Fayard, 1983), 11-25.
2. Lyautey to Antonin de Margerie, 2 May 1881, in André Le Révérend, *Un Lyautey inconnu: Correspondance et journal inédits (1874-1934)* (Paris: Librairie Académique Perrin, 1980), 96.
3. Lyautey, "Notes de voyage en Algérie," 12 and 13 February 1878, in Le Révérend, *Un Lyautey inconnu*, 52.
4. Lyautey, "Notes de voyage en Algérie," 12 February 1878, in Le Révérend, *Un Lyautey inconnu*, 51; André Le Révérend, *Lyautey écrivain* (Gap: Éditions Ophrys, 1976), 56.
5. Lyautey, "Notes de voyage en Algérie," 29 February 1878, in Le Révérend, *Un Lyautey inconnu*, 59.
6. Lyautey, "Notes de voyage en Algérie," 2 March 1878, in Le Révérend, *Un Lyautey inconnu*, 59.
7. Lyautey, "Notes de voyage en Algérie," 9 February and 2 March 1878, in Le Révérend, *Un Lyautey inconnu*, 48, 59.
8. Lyautey to de Margerie, 18 November 1880, in Le Révérend, *Un Lyautey inconnu*, 70.
9. Lyautey to his father, 14 December 1880, in Le Révérend, *Un Lyautey inconnu*, 77.
10. Lyautey to his father, 14 December 1880, in Le Révérend, *Un Lyautey inconnu*, 74. On the Bureaux Arabes, see Kenneth J. Perkins, *Qaids, Captains, and Colons: French Military Administration in the Colonial Maghrib, 1844-1934* (New York: Africana Publishing Company, 1981).
11. Lyautey to his father, 14 December 1880, in Le Révérend, *Un Lyautey inconnu*, 74.
12. Lyautey to Joseph de la Bouillerie, December 1880, in Le Révérend, *Un Lyautey inconnu*, 80-81.
13. Lyautey to his father, 14 December 1880, in Le Révérend, *Un Lyautey inconnu*, 75.
14. Lyautey to his father, 10 September 1882, in Le Révérend, *Un Lyautey inconnu*, 131.
15. Lyautey to his father, 23 March 1881, in Le Révérend, *Un Lyautey inconnu*, 87.
16. Lyautey to de Margerie, 2 May 1881, in Le Révérend, *Un Lyautey inconnu*, 95.
17. Lyautey to his father, June 1881 and Lyautey to his mother, 1 July 1881, both in Le Révérend, *Un Lyautey inconnu*, 98, 100.

18. Lyautey to his mother, 1 and 29 July 1881, in Le Réverend, *Un Lyautey inconnu,* 101, 109.
19. Lyautey to his father, 10 September 1882, in Le Révérend, *Un Lyautey inconnu,* 125.
20. Lyautey to his father, 10 July 1881 and Lyautey to de Margerie, 20 April 1882, both in Le Révérend, *Un Lyautey inconnu,* 104, 116.
21. Lyautey to his father, 10 July 1881, in Le Révérend, *Un Lyautey inconnu,* 107. On the Bou Amama revolt, see Ross E. Dunn, *Resistance in the Desert: Moroccan Responses to French Imperialism, 1881-1912* (Madison: University of Wisconsin Press, 1977), 140-43.
22. Lyautey to his father, 10 July 1881, in Le Révérend, *Un Lyautey inconnu,* 107.
23. Le Révérend, *Lyautey,* 121-22.
24. Lyautey notes, 26 April 1886, quoted in Le Révérend, *Lyautey,* 122-23. Perhaps Lyautey's alleged homosexuality pushed him in this socially independent direction. See Douglas Porch, *The Conquest of Morocco* (New York: Alfred A. Knopf, 1983), 85-86 and Daniel Rivet, *Lyautey et l'institution du protectorat français au Maroc,* 3 vols. (Paris: L'Harmattan, 1988), 3:300.
25. [Louis-Hubert-Gonzalve Lyautey], "Du rôle social de l'officier," *Revue des deux mondes,* March-April 1891, 443-45. On de Mun who was a key figure in the growth of social Catholicism and in the *ralliement,* the political movement to reconcile Catholics to the Third Republic, see Benjamin F. Martin, *Count Albert de Mun: Paladin of the Third Republic* (Chapel Hill: University of North Carolina Press, 1978). On the army, see Raoul Girardet, *La société militaire dans la France contemporaine, 1815-1939* (Paris: Plon, 1953) and Douglas Porch, *The March to the Marne: The French Army, 1871-1914* (Cambridge: Cambridge University Press, 1981).
26. [Lyautey], "Du rôle social de l'officier," 443, 445-46, 450-51, 454-57.
27. Le Révérend, *Lyautey,* 161-64.
28. Le Révérend, *Lyautey,* 168-69, 190-91.
29. Le Révérend, *Lyautey,* 192.
30. Porch, *The Conquest of Morocco,* 84; Le Révérend, *Lyautey,* 192-94; André Maurois, *Lyautey* (Paris: Plon, 1931), 35.
31. Lyautey to de Margerie, 4 February 1897, in Lyautey, *Lettres du Tonkin et de Madagascar (1894-1899),* 2 vols. (Paris: Armand Colin, 1920), 2:144 and Lyautey to his brother, 25 March 1896, in Lyautey, *Lettres du Tonkin et de Madagascar,* 1:340.
32. Lyautey to his sister, 16 October 1894, in Lyautey, *Lettres du Tonkin et de Madagascar,* 1:13.
33. Lyautey to his sister, 9 November 1894, in Lyautey, *Lettres du Tonkin et de Madagascar,* 1:57.
34. See Jean de Lanessan, *La colonisation française en Indo-Chine* (Paris: Félix Alcan, 1895) and *Principes de colonisation* (Paris: Félix Alcan, 1897). On the debate over matters of colonial doctrine, see Raymond F. Betts, *Assimilation and Association in French Colonial Theory, 1890-1914* (New York: Columbia University Press, 1961).
35. Lyautey to his sister, 16 November 1894, in Lyautey, *Lettres du Tonkin et de Madagascar,* 1:71. Also see, Pascal Venier, "Lyautey et l'idée de protectorat de 1894 à 1902: Genèse d'une doctrine coloniale," *Revue française d'histoire d'outre-mer* 78, no. 293 (1991):499-517.
36. See J. Kim Munholland, "'Collaboration Strategy' and the French Pacification of Tonkin, 1885-1897," *Historical Journal* 24, no. 3 (1981):629-50.
37. Lyautey to his brother, 5 February 1895 and Lyautey to de Margerie, 7 March 1895, both in Lyautey, *Lettres du Tonkin et de Madagascar,* 1:112-15, 159-60.
38. Douglas Porch, *The French Foreign Legion: A Complete History of the Legendary Fighting Force* (New York: HarperCollins, 1991), 240-44; Lyautey to de Margerie, 7 March 1895, in Lyautey, *Lettres du Tonkin et de Madagascar,* 1:159.
39. Lyautey to de Margerie, 29 April 1895, in Lyautey, *Lettres du Tonkin et de Madagascar,* 1:189.

40. Lyautey to his sister, 9 February 1895, in Lyautey, *Lettres du Tonkin et de Madagascar,* 1:122.
41. Lyautey to his sister, 20 February 1895, in Lyautey, *Lettres du Tonkin et de Madagascar,* 1:142.
42. Lyautey to de Margerie, 29 April 1895, in Lyautey, *Lettres du Tonkin et de Madagascar,* 1:189-90.
43. Lyautey to his sister, 30 September 1895, in Lyautey, *Lettres du Tonkin et de Madagascar,* 1:237-38. On Gallieni in Tonkin, see Marc Michel, *Gallieni* (Paris: Fayard, 1989), 143-72 and Joseph-Simon Gallieni, *Trois colonnes au Tonkin, 1894-1895* (Paris: Librairie Militaire R. Chapelot et Cie., 1899) and Gallieni, *Gallieni au Tonkin (1892-1896) par lui-même* (Paris: Berger-Levrault, 1941).
44. Quoted in Le Révérend, *Lyautey,* 223.
45. Quoted in Le Révérend, *Lyautey,* 225.
46. Quoted in Le Révérend, *Lyautey,* 226.
47. Lyautey to his brother, 30 December 1895, in Lyautey, *Lettres du Tonkin et de Madagascar,* 1:267.
48. Lyautey to his brother, 16-18 March 1896, in Lyautey, *Lettres du Tonkin et de Madagascar,* 1:334.
49. Lyautey to his sister, 15 December 1895, in Lyautey, *Lettres du Tonkin et de Madagascar,* 1:261.
50. "At twenty the unknown is pure joy. At forty it is pain; you cannot forever keep starting your life over again." Lyautey to his sister, 23 December 1894, in Lyautey, *Lettres du Tonkin et de Madagascar,* 1:85.
51. Lyautey to de Margerie, 15 August 1896, in Lyautey, *Lettres du Tonkin et de Madagascar,* 2:44. Also see, Lyautey to Gustave Michelot, 6 January 1896 and Lyautey to Madame de Guerle, 10 June 1896, both in Le Révérend, *Un Lyautey inconnu,* 201-03.
52. Lyautey had earlier written Gallieni: "Wherever you are, whatever you want me to do, I will always and everywhere be at your command." Lyautey to de Margerie, 4 February 1897, in Lyautey, *Lettres du Tonkin et de Madagascar,* 2:117.
53. Lyautey to his sister, 21 November 1896, quoted in Le Révérend, *Lyautey,* 244.
54. Lyautey to his sister, February 1897, quoted in Le Révérend, *Lyautey,* 245-46.
55. Lyautey journal, 23 April 1896, in Lyautey, *Lettres du Tonkin et de Madagascar,* 2:23. On Chailley-Bert, whose writings on empire powerfully influenced Lyautey, see Stuart Michael Persell, "Joseph Chailley-Bert and the Importance of the Union coloniale française," *Historical Journal* 17, no. 1 (March 1974):176-84.
56. Lyautey to de Margerie, 4 February 1897, in Lyautey, *Lettres du Tonkin et de Madagascar,* 2:137.
57. Lyautey to de Margerie, 2 July 1895; Lyautey to Baroness d'A., 19 October 1895, both in Lyautey, *Lettres du Tonkin et de Madagascar,* 1:223, 255.
58. Lyautey to de Margerie, 20 September 1896, in Lyautey, *Lettres du Tonkin et de Madagascar,* 2:93.
59. Lyautey to his sister, 20 February 1897, in Lyautey, *Lettres du Tonkin et de Madagascar,* 2:151.
60. Lyautey to de Margerie, 4 February 1897, in Lyautey, *Lettres du Tonkin et de Madagascar,* 2:142.
61. Lyautey to his sister, 20 February 1897, in Lyautey, *Lettres du Tonkin et de Madagascar,* 2:151. Also see, Lyautey to de Margerie, 4 February 1897, in Lyautey, *Lettres du Tonkin et de Madagascar,* 2:137.
62. Lyautey to de Margerie, 4 February 1897, in Lyautey, *Lettres du Tonkin et de Madagascar,* 2:142. On Lyautey's admiration for the colonial Frenchman, also see, Lyautey to Henry Bérenger, 12 February 1897 and Lyautey to Eugène-Melchior de Vogüé, 26 February 1897, both in Lyautey, *Lettres du Tonkin et de Madagascar,* 2:148-49, 158.

63. Le Révérend, *Lyautey*, 233.
64. Le Révérend, *Lyautey*, 236-37. Also see, Lyautey to Henry Bérenger, 10 May 1898, in Lyautey, *Les plus belles lettres de Lyautey*, ed. Pierre Lyautey (Paris: Calmann-Lévy, 1962), 53.
65. Lyautey to Max Leclerc, 29 January 1897, in Lyautey, *Lettres du Tonkin et de Madagascar*, 2:114.
66. Lyautey to de Margerie, 21 August 1896 and 4 February 1897; Lyautey to his sister, 6 September 1896, all in Lyautey, *Lettres du Tonkin et de Madagascar*, 2:51-53, 91, 120-21. On Pennequin, see Munholland, "'Collaboration Strategy,'" 641, 643-45 and R. Couturier and P. Feuillet, "La politique du général Pennequin en Indochine, 1888-1913: De la pacification du nord-ouest du Tonkin aux projets d'armée indigène," Mémoire de Maîtrise, Université de Paris VII, 1983.
67. Lyautey to de Margerie, 4 February 1897, in Lyautey, *Lettres du Tonkin et de Madagascar*, 2:129-30.
68. Le Révérend, *Lyautey*, 250-51, 256-57. On Gallieni in Madagascar, see Michel, *Gallieni*, 175-234. Also see, Joseph-Simon Gallieni, *La pacification de Madagascar (opérations d'octobre 1896 à mars 1899)* (Paris: Librairie Militaire R. Chapelot et Cie, 1900); Gallieni, *Neuf ans à Madagascar* (Paris: Hachette et Cie., 1908); and Gallieni, *Lettres de Madagascar, 1896-1905* (Paris: Société d'Éditions Géographiques, Maritimes et Coloniales, 1928).
69. On the traditionalist, nationalist, xenophobic "rising of the red shawls" and Gallieni's policy toward the Merina elite, see Stephen D. K. Ellis, "The Political Elite of Imerina and the Revolt of the *Menalamba*: The Creation of a Colonial Myth in Madagascar, 1895-1898," *Journal of African History* 21, no. 2 (1980):219-34 and Ellis, *The Rising of the Red Shawls: A Revolt in Madagascar, 1895-1899* (Cambridge: Cambridge University Press, 1985).
70. According to Ellis, Gallieni used faked evidence of a conspiracy between *menalamba* leaders and Tananarive politicians to cover his earlier actions and Lyautey went along with this fraudulent reconstruction of history. See Ellis, "The Political Elite of Imerina and the Revolt of the *Menelamba*," 223-25 and Ellis, *The Rising of the Red Shawls*, 130-31.
71. Lyautey to Max Leclerc, 21 September 1897, in Lyautey, *Lettres du Tonkin et de Madagascar*, 2:212.
72. Lyautey to Max Leclerc, 21 September 1897, in Lyautey, *Lettres du Tonkin et de Madagascar*, 2:209.
73. Lyautey to his sister, 25 November 1897, in Lyautey, *Lettres du Tonkin et de Madagascar*, 2:219-20. The poet was actually Shakespeare (Lyautey had jotted only "Sh." in his notebook) and he had mistranslated the line from *Troilus and Cressida*, which read "joy's soul lies in the doing." See Le Révérend, *Lyautey*, 257. For Lyautey on "l'action créatrice de vie," see Lyautey to Louise Baignères, 9 September 1897, in Le Révérend, *Un Lyautey inconnu*, 207.
74. Le Révérend, *Lyautey*, 253.
75. Le Révérend, *Lyautey*, 254. Also see, Pascal Venier, "Un Lyautey malgache: Ankazobé, 1897-1899: Contribution à la biographie critique d'Hubert Lyautey," Mémoire de Maîtrise, Institut d'Histoire des pays d'Outre-Mer, Université de Provence, Aix-Marseille I, 1987.
76. Lyautey to Gallieni, 18 February 1898, in Lyautey, *Lettres du Tonkin et de Madagascar*, 2:233.
77. Lyautey to Max Lazard, 26 March 1898, in Le Révérend, *Un Lyautey inconnu*, 212.
78. Lyautey, *Lettres du Tonkin et de Madagascar*, 2:271. For the method in Gallieni's own words, see Gallieni, *Trois colonnes au Tonkin*, 153-61.
79. Lyautey, "Du rôle colonial de l'armée," *Revue des deux mondes*, 15 January 1900, 308-10. He also referred to the colonial ideal as a "mixed regime," for it would be a civil

and military combination. See his speech to the Réunion des voyageurs français, 19 February 1900, in Lyautey, *Paroles d'action: Madagascar, Sud-Oranais, Oran, Maroc (1900-1926),* with a preface by Louis Barthou. (Paris: Armand Colin, 1927), 5.

80. Lyautey, "Du rôle colonial de l'armée," 310-11, 316.
81. Lyautey, "Du rôle colonial de l'armée," 311.
82. Lyautey, "Du rôle colonial de l'armée," 312, 314-17.
83. Lyautey, "Du rôle colonial de l'armée," 315.
84. Lyautey, "Du rôle colonial de l'armée," 309, 318, 323, 328. On colonial war as a "means" to achieve peace and life as well as warfare that alone "produced life" *(la guerre productrice de vie),* see Lyautey to Paul Desjardins, 5 May 1896, in Lyautey, *Choix de Lettres, 1882-1919,* with a foreward by Paul de Ponton d'Amécourt. (Paris: Armand Colin, 1947), 107 and Lyautey to Baignères, 9 September 1897, in Le Révérend, *Un Lyautey inconnu,* 207.
85. Venier, "Un Lyautey malgache," 35.
86. Lyautey, "Du rôle colonial de l'armée," 324-27. On the creation of *La Coloniale,* see Anthony Clayton, *France, Soldiers and Africa* (London: Brassey's Defence Publishers, 1988), 6-7, 314-16.
87. See Stuart Michael Persell, *The French Colonial Lobby, 1889-1938* (Stanford: Hoover Institution Press, 1983) which traces the fortunes of the two leading colonial groups, the Comité de l'Afrique Française (founded in 1890) and the Union Coloniale Française (founded in 1893). Also see, Marc Lagana, *Le parti colonial français: Éléments d'histoire* (Sillery, Québec: Presses de l'Université du Québec, 1990) and James J. Cooke, *New French Imperialism, 1880-1910: The Third Republic and Colonial Expansion* (Hamden, Conn.: Archon Books, 1973). In November 1899 Lyautey joined the Société de Géographie Commerciale de Paris with Gallieni as his sponsor and in December he became a member of the Union Coloniale Française, sponsored by its president, Marseille businessman and republican politician Jules Charles-Roux, and its secretary-general, Joseph Chailley-Bert.
88. Lyautey to de Vogüé, 1 August 1900 and Lyautey to his sister, 3 August 1900, both in Lyautey, *Lettres du sud de Madagascar, 1900-1902* (Paris: Armand Colin, 1935), 8, 13.
89. Gallieni, "Arrêté créant le Commandement Supérieur du Sud," 12 September 1900, in Lyautey to de Vogüé, 20 September 1900; Lyautey to General Raoul Donop, 8 January 1901; and Lyautey to de Vogüé, 7 November 1900, all in Lyautey, *Lettres du sud de Madagascar,* 19-20, 39-43, 54.
90. Lyautey to his sister, 17 November 1900, in Lyautey, *Lettres du sud de Madagascar,* 43. On Gallieni's forty-sixth birthday he noted simply in his daybook: "I am forty-six years old." See Michel, *Gallieni,* 154.
91. Lyautey to Gallieni, 10 December 1900, in Lyautey, *Lettres du sud de Madagascar,* 50-51.
92. Lyautey to de Vogüé, 26 June 1901, in Lyautey, *Lettres du sud de Madagascar,* 119.
93. Lyautey to Gallieni, 25 June 1902, in Lyautey, *Lettres du sud de Madagascar,* 251, 256.
94. Lyautey to Gallieni, "La situation du cercle de Fort-Dauphin à la date du 15 juillet 1901," in Lyautey to his sister, 15 July 1901, *Lettres du sud de Madagascar,* 142.
95. Lyautey to de Vogüé, 8 July 1901, in Lyautey, *Lettres du sud de Madagascar,* 135.
96. Lyautey to his sister, 9 July 1901, in Lyautey, *Lettres du sud de Madagascar,* 136.
97. Lyautey to his sister, 19 and 20 July 1901, in Lyautey, *Lettres du sud de Madagascar,* 164.
98. Lyautey to Gallieni, 25 June 1902, in Lyautey, *Lettres du sud de Madagascar,* 266-72.
99. Lyautey, *Dans le sud de Madagascar: Pénétration militaire, situation politique et économique, 1900-1902* (Paris: Henri Charles-Lavauzelle, 1903), 5. Lyautey dedicated his 1920 *Lettres du Tonkin et de Madagascar* to Gallieni's memory, hoping, he said, to rekindle enthusiasm for the empire and colonial service through the "lessons and examples of that great man of action whose figure dominates all these letters, General Gallieni." Lyautey, *Lettres du Tonkin et de Madagascar,* 1:vii. Appropriately, Lyautey

printed "The Colonial Role of the Army" as the conclusion to these two volumes of letters. Lyautey, *Lettres du Tonkin et de Madagascar,* 2:273-97.
100. Lyautey to Gallieni, 25 June 1902, in Lyautey, *Lettres du sud de Madagascar,* 256, 296, 302.
101. Lyautey to Gallieni, 8 December 1901, in Lyautey, *Lettres du sud de Madagascar,* 204-05; Lyautey to Leclerc, March 1903, in Lyautey, *Choix de lettres,* 210-13.
102. Lyautey to Joseph Chailley-Bert, 21 May 1903, in Le Révérend, *Un Lyautey inconnu,* 229.

Chapter 2

1. Lyautey to Gallieni, 14 November 1903, in Lyautey, *Vers le Maroc: Lettres du Sud-Oranais, 1903-1906* (Paris: Armand Colin, 1937), 12-13. Lyautey's appointment was announced in September; he arrived at Aïn Sefra in October. On Jonnart, see Jean Du Sault, "Une réussite française en Afrique du Nord: Charles Jonnart," *Revue des deux mondes,* 15 October 1953, 607-25.
2. Lyautey to Gallieni, 14 November 1903, in Lyautey, *Vers le Maroc,* 14. On Taghit and El Moungar, see Dunn, *Resistance in the Desert,* 196-99 and Porch, *The Conquest of Morocco,* 64-73.
3. On precolonial Morocco, see Edmund Burke, III, *Prelude to Protectorate in Morocco: Precolonial Protest and Resistance, 1860-1912* (Chicago: University of Chicago Press, 1976), Ross E. Dunn, *Resistance in the Desert: Moroccan Responses to French Imperialism, 1881-1912* (Madison: University of Wisconsin Press, 1977), and Douglas Porch, *The Conquest of Morocco* (New York: Alfred A. Knopf, 1983).
4. See Burke, *Prelude to Protectorate,* 41-67 and Dunn, *Resistance in the Desert,* 176-203.
5. On Étienne, see Cooke, *New French Imperialism,* Lagana, *Le parti colonial français,* and Persell, *The French Colonial Lobby.*
6. On Delcassé, see Christoper M. Andrew, *Théophile Delcassé and the Making of the Entente Cordiale: A Reappraisal of French Foreign Policy, 1898-1905* (London: Macmillan and St. Martin's Press, 1968).
7. Lyautey to Gallieni, 14 November 1903 and Lyautey to François Charles-Roux, 19 December 1904, both in Lyautey, *Vers le Maroc,* 14, 118.
8. Lyautey, "Aperçu sur la situation de la frontière de la Subdivision d'Aïn Sefra," October 1903 and Lyautey, "Programme d'action que se propose d'appliquer le général commandant la Subdivision d'Aïn Sefra," November 1903, both in Lyautey, *Vers le Maroc,* 15-18, 20-21. On Lyautey's military organization at Aïn Sefra, see Captain Édouard Arnaud, "Étude d'organisation militaire saharienne," in Arnaud and Maurice Cortier, *Nos confins sahariens: Étude d'organisation militaire* (Paris: Larose, 1908), 49-58. Also see, Dunn, *Resistance in the Desert,* 204-10 and Porch, *The Conquest of Morocco,* 122-36.
9. Lyautey, "Aperçu sur la situation de la frontière" and "Programme d'action," both in Lyautey, *Vers le Maroc,* 17, 25-26. For the 1901-1902 accords, see Ministère des Affaires Étrangères, *Documents diplomatiques: Affaires du Maroc, 1901-1912,* 6 vols. (Paris: Imprimerie Nationale, 1905-12), 1:16-18, 34-41.
10. Lyautey, "Aperçu sur la situation de la frontière" and "Programme d'action," and Lyautey to Étienne, 17 February 1904, all in Lyautey, *Vers le Maroc,* 18-19, 27, 37; Dunn, *Resistance in the Desert,* 143.
11. Lyautey, "Programme d'action;" Lyautey to Max Leclerc, 29 April 1904; Lyautey to Étienne, 26 May 1904; and Lyautey to Chailley, 26 May 1904, all in Lyautey, *Vers le Maroc,* 27, 46, 64, 66. Lyautey's reference was to Evelyn Baring, first Earl of Cromer, England's proconsul in Egypt.
12. See Burke, *Prelude to Protectorate,* 68-75.
13. Lyautey to Étienne, 24 June and 7 July 1904 and Lyautey to his sister, 6 July 1904, all in Lyautey, *Vers le Maroc,* 76-81.

14. Lyautey to de Vogüé, 17 July 1904, in Lyautey, *Vers le Maroc,* 81.
15. Carl Vincent Confer, "Divided Counsels in French Imperialism: The Ras el Aïn Incident in 1904," *Journal of Modern History* 18, no. 1 (March 1946):55-57. Also see, Georges Saint-René Taillandier, *Les origines du Maroc français: Récit d'une mission, 1901-1906* (Paris: Plon, 1930), 194-200.
16. Lyautey to Major Henrÿs, 31 July 1904, in Lyautey, *Vers le Maroc,* 81.
17. Lyautey to Henrÿs, 31 July 1904 and Lyautey to Étienne, 31 July 1904, both in Lyautey, *Vers le Maroc,* 81, 83-85. Also see, Lyautey to Reibell, 31 July 1904, in Lyautey, *Lyautey devant le Maroc: Lettres inédites du général Lyautey au colonel Reibell, 1903-1908,* ed. Jean Brunon (Marseille: Vert et Rouge [Revue de la Légion Étrangère], n.d.), 18.
18. Lyautey to Étienne, 6 August 1904, in Lyautey, *Vers le Maroc,* 87.
19. Lyautey to Étienne, 8 August 1904, in Lyautey, *Vers le Maroc,* 92-93. Also see, Lyautey to Reibell, 8 August 1904, in Lyautey, *Lyautey devant le Maroc,* 18-20.
20. Lyautey to Max Leclerc, 14 August 1904; Lyautey to Étienne, 14 August 1904; and Lyautey to Henrÿs, 18 August 1904, all in Lyautey, *Vers le Maroc,* 95-98. For the telegram, see Lyautey's comments at the École des Sciences Politiques, 21 December 1912, in Lyautey, *Parles d'action,* 77.
21. Lyautey to Jonnart, 23 August 1904 and "Projet de note au sujet de l'organisation de la frontière algéro-marocaine établie pour M. Jonnart, gouverneur général de l'Algérie, par le général Lyautey, et destinée à servir de base pour les entretiens du gouverneur général et du ministre des affaires étrangères," 15 September 1904, both in Lyautey, *Vers le Maroc,* 100-01, 108.
22. *Journal Officiel de la République française* (Paris: Imprimerie Nationale, 1904-25), 8 and 10 November 1904, 2336-38, 2379-81. (Hereafter cited as *Journal Officiel.*)
23. Maurice Paléologue, *Un grand tournant de la politique mondiale (1904-1906)* (Paris: Librairie Plon, 1934), 210.
24. Lyautey to François Charles-Roux, 19 December 1904, in Lyautey, *Vers le Maroc,* 119.
25. Lyautey to de Vogüé, 2 January 1905; Lyautey to Major Charles Reibell, 6 January 1905; and Lyautey to Max Leclerc, 15 May 1905, all in Lyautey, *Vers le Maroc,* 144, 164, 181.
26. On the Makhzen resistance to France, see Burke, *Prelude to Protectorate,* 68-98. On Delcassé and the "first" Moroccan crisis, see Andrews, *Delcassé,* 268-301.
27. Lyautey to Étienne, May 1905, in Lyautey, *Vers le Maroc,* 184.
28. Lyautey to Jonnart, 4 June 1905, in Lyautey, *Vers le Maroc,* 192-93.
29. Lyautey to Joseph Chailley, 20 June 1905, in Lyautey, *Vers le Maroc,* 209-10. Also see, Lyautey to Raymond Aynard, 25 June 1905 and Lyautey to Jonnart, 13 July 1905, both in Lyautey, *Vers le Maroc,* 216, 224-27.
30. Lyautey to General Louis Herson, 9 February 1906 and Lyautey to Jonnart, 2 March 1906, both in Lyautey, *Vers le Maroc,* 245-46, 252, 254.
31. Lyautey to Étienne, 2 March 1906, in Lyautey, *Vers le Maroc,* 255-56.
32. See Burke, *Prelude to Protectorate,* 85-88.
33. Lyautey to de Vogüé, 9 May 1906, in Lyautey, *Vers le Maroc,* 270-71.
34. Lyautey to his sister, 28 May 1906 and Lyautey to de Vogüé, 31 May 1906, both in Lyautey, *Vers le Maroc,* 278, 280.
35. Lyautey to Regnault, 17 July 1906; Lyautey to his sister, 28 September 1906; and Lyautey to Jonnart, 30 September 1906 and October 1906, all in Lyautey, *Vers le Maroc,* 289-91, 294-95, 297; Dunn, *Resistance in the Desert,* 213-26.
36. Lyautey to his sister, 28 September 1906 and Lyautey to General Armand Servière, 15 October 1906, both in Lyautey, *Vers le Maroc,* 291, 303-06.
37. Lyautey to Jonnart, October 1906, in Lyautey, *Vers le Maroc,* 298-99.
38. Lyautey to Jonnart, 3 October 1906, in Lyautey, *Vers le Maroc,* 300.
39. Lyautey to Colonel Jules Laquière, 13 October 1906, in Lyautey, *Vers le Maroc,* 301-03.
40. Lyautey to his sister, 18 October 1906, in Lyautey, *Vers le Maroc,* 307.

41. Lyautey to Jonnart, 18 October 1906, in Lyautey, *Vers le Maroc,* 309.
42. Dunn, *Resistance in the Desert,* 221. Also see, Minister of War Georges Picquart to General Armand Servière, commanding the 19th Army Corps at Algiers, 16 October 1907 and Servière to Picquart, 20 November 1907, both in Service Historique de l'Armée de Terre, Archives du Maroc, Série 3H, carton 72, Correspondance avec le 19ème Corps d'Armée du 21 août au 31 décembre 1907. (Hereafter cited as SHAT, Maroc, 3H, carton number, dossier and/or sous-dossier name.) The published guide to these archives is Arnaud de Menditte and Jean Nicot, *Répertoire des archives du Maroc* (Série 3H, 1877-1960), vol. 1 (Château de Vincennes: Service Historique de l'Armée de Terre, 1982).
43. Lyautey to Jonnart, 18 May 1907, in Lyautey, *Les plus belles lettres de Lyautey,* 81; Le Révérend, *Lyautey,* 327.
44. Lyautey to Jonnart, 18 May 1907, in Lyautey, *Les plus belles lettres de Lyautey,* 78-84.
45. Lyautey to de Vogüé, 23 May 1907, in Lyautey, *Choix de lettres,* 261.
46. Picquart to Servière, 16 October 1907.
47. Lyautey to Reibell, 4 July 1907, in Lyautey, *Lyautey devant le Maroc,* 33; Picquart to Servière, 16 October 1907 and Servière to Picquart, 20 November 1907, both in SHAT, Maroc 3H, 72, Correspondance avec le 19ème Corps d'Armée du 21 août au 31 décembre 1907.
48. See Burke, *Prelude to Protectorate,* 93-98 and Porch, *The Conquest of Morocco,* 147-59.
49. Burke, *Prelude to Protectorate,* 98, 110-11.
50. On the Hafid rising, see Burke, *Prelude to Protectorate,* 99-127.
51. Lyautey to Colonel Henri Gouraud, 2 September 1907, in Lyautey, *Les plus belles lettres de Lyautey,* 87-88 and Lyautey to de Vogüé, 27 September 1907, in Lyautey, *Choix de lettres,* 263-64. Also see, Lyautey to Victor Barrucand, n.d., quoted in Le Révérend, *Lyautey,* 328-29.
52. In July 1906 Eugène Regnault replaced Saint-René Taillandier as head of the Tangier legation. On basic principles Regnault and Lyautey were "in complete accord." See Lyautey to Joseph Chailley, 10 July 1906 and Lyautey to the Comtesse Jean de Castellane, 29 September 1906, both in Lyautey, *Vers le Maroc,* 287, 293.
53. Lyautey to de Vogüé, 17 and 20 October 1907, in Lyautey, "Lettres de Rabat (1907)," *Revue des deux mondes,* 15 July 1921, 295-96, 298-99. Also see, Lyautey to de Vogüé, 5 and 11 October 1907, in Lyautey, "Lettres de Rabat," 275, 288-89.
54. Lyautey to Reibell, 12 September 1907, in Lyautey, *Lyautey devant le Maroc,* 34.
55. Lyautey to Reibell, 2 and 25 November 1907, in Lyautey, *Lyautey devant le Maroc,* 36 and Lyautey to Regnault, 20 November 1907, in Lyautey, *Les plus belles lettres de Lyautey,* 90-91.
56. Lyautey to de Margerie, 7 January 1908, in Lyautey, *Choix de lettres,* 266. On the Beni Snassen campaign, see Lucien-Louis Boullé, *La France et les Beni-Snassen: Campagne du général Lyautey* (Paris: Henri Charles-Lavauzelle 1909), 43-65 and Porch, *The Conquest of Morocco,* 188-92.
57. Lyautey to de Vogüé, 1 January 1908, in Lyautey, *Les plus belles lettres de Lyautey,* 94.
58. Le Révérend, *Lyautey,* 333-34.
59. Lyautey to Chailley, 18 January 1908, in Lyautey, *Choix de lettres,* 268.
60. Lyautey to de Mun, 27 January 1908, in Lyautey, *Choix de lettres,* 270-71.
61. Lyautey to de Mun, 27 January 1908, in Lyautey, *Choix de lettres,* 271-72.
62. See Dunn, *Resistance in the Desert,* 213-16.
63. See Porch, *The Conquest of Morocco,* 184-88.
64. Dunn, *Resistance in the Desert,* 232-34.
65. Dunn, *Resistance in the Desert,* 234-36 and Porch, *The Conquest of Morocco,* 192-99.
66. See Burke, *Prelude to Protectorate,* 128-52.
67. Lyautey to de Mun, 29 April 1909, in Le Révérend, *Un Lyautey inconnu,* 240-41 and Lyautey to General Raoul Le Mouton de Boisdeffre, 25 September 1909, quoted in Le Révérend, *Lyautey,* 337.

68. Lyautey to Jonnart, 24 July 1910, in Le Révérend, *Un Lyautey inconnu*, 243.
69. See Burke, *Prelude to Protectorate*, 163-71 and Porch, *The Conquest of Morocco*, 213-35. Also see, Colonel Paul Azan, *L'Expédition de Fez*, with an introduction by Marshal Lyautey and a preface by General Moinier. (Paris: Berger-Levrault, 1924) and Jean-Claude Allain, *Agadir, 1911: Une crise impérialiste en Europe pour la conquête du Maroc* (Paris: Publications de la Sorbonne, 1976).
70. Lyautey to Chailley-Bert, 7 November 1911, in Le Révérend, *Un Lyautey inconnu*, 245.
71. Lyautey to Chailley-Bert, 7 November 1911, in Le Révérend, *Un Lyautey inconnu*, 245.
72. Moinier to the minister of war, 7 August 1911 and Moinier to the chargé d'affaires de France au Maroc à Tanger [Regnault], 7 August 1911, both in Lyautey Papers, Archives Nationales (AN), Paris, No. 81: Documents fondamentaux sur la politique indigène.
73. The text of the Treaty of Fez is printed in *L'Afrique française* 22, no. 6 (June 1912):219-220. Also see, Président du Conseil, Ministre des Affaires Étrangères Raymond Poincaré to Président de la République Armand Fallières, 27 April 1912, printed in *L'Afrique française* 22, no. 5 (May 1912):183.
74. See Henry Marchat, "Les origines diplomatiques du 'Maroc espagnol' (1880-1912)," in *Revue de l'Occident musulman et de la Méditerranée* 7, no. 1 (1970):101-70 and Graham H. Stuart, *The International City of Tangier* (Stanford: Stanford University Press, 1955).
75. See Burke, *Prelude to Protectorate*, 180-87; Porch, *The Conquest of Morocco*, 236-47; and Rivet, *Lyautey et l'institution du protectorat français au Maroc*, 1:126-32.
76. Raymond Poincaré, *Au service de la France: Neuf années de souvenirs*, 11 vols. (Paris: Plon Nourrit et Cie., 1926-33), 1:97-100. Also see, Rivet, *Lyautey et l'institution du protectorat français au Maroc*, 1:148-51.
77. Poincaré to Fallières, 27 April 1912 and Decree of the President of the French Republic, 27 April 1912, both in *L'Afrique française* 22, no. 5 (May 1912):183. On Lyautey's authority as resident general, see Decree of the President of the French Republic, 11 June 1912, in *L'Afrique française* 22, no. 6 (June 1912):218.

Chapter 3

1. See Burke, *Prelude to Protectorate*, 188-90 and Rivet, *Lyautey et l'institution du protectorat français au Maroc*, 1:132-35.
2. See Burke, *Prelude to Protectorate*, 199-207 and Rivet, *Lyautey et l'institution du protectorat français au Maroc*, 1:125, 136-44.
3. Lyautey to his sister, 12 May 1912, in Lyautey, *Choix de lettres*, 286.
4. Procès-verbal du Conseil de politique indigène, 14 April 1925, quoted in Rivet, *Lyautey et l'institution du protectorat français au Maroc*, 1:160.
5. Lyautey to his sister, 26 May 1912, in Lyautey, *Choix de lettres*, 287-88; *L'Afrique française* 22, no. 6 (June 1912):214; Lyautey, 26 and 27 May 1912, in Lyautey, *Lyautey l'Africain, 1912-1925: Textes et lettres du maréchal Lyautey*, ed. Pierre Lyautey. 4 vols. (Paris: Plon, 1953-57), 1:7-9.
6. *L'Afrique française* 22, no. 6 (June 1912):215.
7. *L'Afrique française* 22, no. 6 (June 1912):215.
8. Lyautey, 27, 28, 29, 30, 31 May and 22 June 1912, in Lyautey, *Lyautey l'Africain*, 1:9-14, 17-18.
9. *L'Afrique française* 22, no. 6 (June 1912):216-17. Also see, Rivet, *Lyautey et l'institution du protectorat français au Maroc*, 1:213-14.
10. Lyautey to de Mun, 16 June 1912, in Lyautey, *Choix de lettres*, 288-90. Also see, Burke, *Prelude to Protectorate*, 187-88.
11. *L'Afrique française* 22, no. 6 (June 1912):216. Also see, Burke, *Prelude to Protectorate*, 193-95.

12. Lyautey to de Mun, 16 June 1912, in Lyautey, *Choix de lettres,* 290.

13. *L'Afrique française* 22, no. 6 (June 1912):218.

14. Lyautey to de Mun, 16 June 1912, in Lyautey, *Choix de lettres,* 291. Abd el-Kader had led the Algerian resistance to France in the 1830s and 1840s.

15. Lyautey to Saint-Aulaire, 24 June 1912, quoted in Rivet, *Lyautey et l'institution du protectorat français au Maroc,* 1:161. Also see, Lyautey to Emmanuel Rousseau, 9 July 1912 and Lyautey to de Mun, 20 July 1912, both quoted in Rivet, *Lyautey et l'institution du protectorat français au Maroc,* 1:161-62.

16. See Rivet, *Lyautey et l'institution du protectorat français au Maroc,* 1:107.

17. *L'Afrique française* 22, no. 6 (June 1912):218-19. Also see, Lyautey, 10 June 1912, in Lyautey, *Lyautey l'Africain,* 1:182-84.

18. *L'Afrique française* 22, no. 6 (June 1912):219.

19. Lyautey to Poincaré, 15 June 1912, in Lyautey Papers, AN, No. 81: Documents fondamentaux sur la politique indigène.

20. Henri Gaillard, "La réorganisation du gouvernement marocain," *Renseignements coloniaux et documents,* no. 6, p. 154, supplement to *L'Afrique française* 26, no. 6 (June 1916).

21. *L'Afrique française* 22, no. 9 (September 1912):368 and Lyautey, 22 October 1912, in Lyautey, *Lyautey l'Africain,* 1:48.

22. *L'Afrique française* 22, no. 9 (September 1912):348.

23. *L'Afrique française* 22, no. 9 (September 1912):368.

24. *L'Afrique française* 22, no. 9 (September 1912):349.

25. *L'Afrique française* 22, no. 9 (September 1912):348-49.

26. *L'Afrique française* 22, no. 9 (September 1912):347-48.

27. *L'Afrique française* 22, no. 6 (June 1912):218-19.

28. See Burke, *Prelude to Protectorate,* 202.

29. Lyautey, 11, 21, 22, 28 August and 4 September 1912, in Lyautey, *Lyautey l'Africain,* 1:27-29, 31-34. Lyautey's move on Marrakesh was made without the approval of the government in Paris. See Rivet, *Lyautey et l'institution du protectorat français au Maroc,* 1:142-43.

30. See Mangin's obituary by General Henri Gouraud in *L'Afrique française* 35, no. 5 (May 1925):209-14.

31. Porch, *The Conquest of Morocco,* 266-67. Also see, *L'Afrique française* 22, no. 9 (September 1912):360-61.

32. Lyautey, "Opérations militaires du 15 août à la prise de Marrakech" and 14 September 1912, both in Lyautey, *Lyautey l'Africain,* 1:38, 64. Also see, *L'Afrique française* 22, no. 10 (October 1912):394-98.

33. Lyautey, 6 October 1912, in Lyautey, *Lyautey l'Africain,* 1:43.

34. Lyautey, 6 October 1912, in Lyautey, *Lyautey l'Africain,* 1:42-43.

35. Lyautey, 14 and 18 September 1912, both in Lyautey, *Lyautey l'Africain,* 1:38, 40-41.

36. Lyautey to de Mun, 10 October 1912, in Lyautey, *Choix de lettres,* 300.

37. Lyautey to Gouraud, 25 September 1912, in Lyautey, "Une oeuvre, une amitié: Correspondance inédite Lyautey-Gouraud, 1912-1913," *Revue historique de l'Armée* 8, no. 2 (June 1952): 17.

38. Lyautey to de Mun, 10 October 1912, in Lyautey, *Choix de lettres,* 299-300. On Lyautey and the sultan, see Rivet, *Lyautey et l'institution du protectorat français au Maroc,* 1:171-75 and 2:130-40.

39. See Rivet, *Lyautey et l'institution du protectorat français au Maroc,* 1:165-200.

40. Alan Scham, *Lyautey in Morocco: Protectorate Administration, 1912-1925* (Berkeley and Los Angeles: University of California Press, 1970), 57. Also see, Rivet, *Lyautey et l'institution du protectorat français au Maroc,* 1:175-81.

41. See Scham, *Lyautey in Morocco,* 60-69.

42. See Scham, *Lyautey in Morocco,* 58-60.

43. See Rivet, *Lyautey et l'institution du protectorat français au Maroc*, 3:192-93.
44. On the *officiers de renseignements*, see Rivet, *Lyautey et l'institution du protectorat français au Maroc*, 2:45-55; Robin Bidwell, *Morocco under Colonial Rule: French Administration of Tribal Areas, 1912-1956* (London: Frank Cass, 1973); Kenneth J. Perkins, *Qaids, Captains, and Colons: French Military Administration in the Colonial Maghrib, 1844-1934* (New York: Africana Publishing Company, 1981); Jean-Dominique Carrère, *Missionnaires en burnous bleu: Au Service des Renseignements durant l'épopée marocaine* (Limoges: Charles-Lavauzelle, 1973); and Marc Méraud, *Histoire des A.I.: Le Service des Affaires Indigènes du Maroc*, with a preface by André Martel. Vol. 2 of *Histoire des Goums marocains* (Paris: La Koumia, 1990). In July 1925 there were 273 *officiers de renseignements* and over 80 *bureaux de renseignements*. The Service des Renseignements was renamed the Service des Affaires Indigènes in 1926.
45. See *Renseignements coloniaux et documents*, no. 8, pp. 314-15, supplement to *L'Afrique française* 23, no. 8 (August 1913) and Roger Gruner, *Du Maroc traditionnel au Maroc moderne: Le Contrôle Civil au Maroc, 1912-1956* (Paris: Nouvelles Éditions Latines, 1984), 26, 209-10.
46. Lyautey to the *chefs des Services Municipaux*, 4 May 1914, in Joseph Goulven, *Traité d'économie et de législation marocaines*, with a preface by Louis Marin. 2 vols. (Paris: Librairie des Sciences Économiques et Sociales Marcel Rivière, 1921), 1:195. (Paris: Librairie des Sciences Économiques et Sociales Marcel Rivière, 1921), 1:195.
47. Lyautey to regional commanders, 27 August 1917, in Lyautey, *Lyautey l'Africain*, 3:277. On the tasks of the *contrôleurs civils*, see Scham, *Lyautey in Morocco*, 71-74.
48. Lyautey to the Ministry of Foreign Affairs, 31 October 1917, quoted in Gruner, *Du Maroc traditionnel au Maroc moderne*, 21-22.
49. See Lyautey to regional commanders, 27 August 1917, in Lyautey, *Lyautey l'Africain*, 3:273-75; Lyautey, "Note sur les Contrôles Civils," 16 October 1920, in Lyautey, *Lyautey l'Africain*, 4:41-42; and Perkins, *Qaids, Captains, and Colons*, 199-200.
50. Lyautey to Adolphe Messimy, 28 June 1914, quoted in Rivet, *Lyautey et l'institution du protectorat français au Maroc*, 1:157. Gouraud was at Fez, Henrÿs at Meknès, Ernest Blondlat at Rabat, and Jean Brulard at Marrakesh.
51. Rivet, *Lyautey et l'institution du protectorat français au Maroc*, 1:157. For the military team over time, see ibid., 3:191-92.
52. Réginald Kann, *Le protectorat marocain* (Paris: Berger-Levrault, 1921), 76-77. For the expansion of the civil team and its work on government and the economy, see Rivet, *Lyautey et l'institution du protectorat français au Maroc*, 1:219-57.
53. *L'Afrique française* 22, no. 12 (December 1912):473.
54. See Rivet, *Lyautey et l'institution du protectorat français au Maroc*, 1:125, 158.
55. See Porch, "Bugeaud, Galliéni, Lyautey: The Development of French Colonial Warfare," in *Makers of Modern Strategy from Machiavelli to the Nuclear Age*, ed. Peter Paret (Princeton: Princeton University Press, 1986), 394-95 and Porch, *The Conquest of Morocco*.
56. Lyautey to de Mun, 10 October 1912, in Lyautey, *Choix de lettres*, 295-96.

Chapter 4

1. Résidence Générale de la République française au Maroc, Bureau Politique and Direction des Affaires Indigènes et du Service des Renseignements, *Rapport mensuel du Protectorat*, February 1913, 7. (Hereafter cited as *Rapport mensuel*.)
2. After the Beni Mtir decapitated the bodies of two European soldiers in January 1913, Reibell authorized the decapitation of about twenty dead and dying tribesmen. He was reprimanded by Lyautey and forced to leave Morocco. See Rivet, *Lyautey et l'institution du protectorat français au Maroc*, 1:215.

3. *Rapport mensuel,* February 1913, 5; *L'Afrique française* 23, no. 3 (March 1913):118.

4. "Rapport succinct du colonel Henrÿs, commandant le Cercle des Beni M'Tir sur les événements qui se sont déroulés dans le cercle du 16 mars au 24 mars 1913," 31 March 1913, SHAT, Maroc, 3H, 582, Colonne Henrÿs, 1913.

5. Henrÿs to Dalbiez, 30 March 1913, SHAT, Maroc, 3H, 901, Région de Meknès, 1913.

6. For the same reason Henrÿs later rejected Lyautey's suggestion to open negotiations with the Beni Mtir diehards. The initiative for any negotiations had to come from them, he insisted, "and them alone." Henrÿs to Lyautey, 20 May 1913, SHAT, Maroc, 3H, 901, Région de Meknès, 1913.

7. *Rapport mensuel,* April 1913, 1; June 1913, 1 and *L'Afrique française* 23, no. 4 (April 1913):142-43; 23, no. 5 (May 1913):195; 23, no. 6 (June 1913):218; 23, no. 7 (July 1913):275.

8. *Rapport mensuel,* April 1913, 1. Also see, *L'Afrique française* 23, no. 3 (March 1913): 117-18.

9. Franchet d'Espérey to Simon, 6 March 1913, SHAT, Maroc, 3H, 583, Cercle du Tadla, Oued Zem, 1913.

10. Lyautey to Minister of War Eugène Étienne, 2 August 1913, 2, SHAT, Maroc, 3H, 583, Opérations du Tadla, 1913; *L'Afrique française* 23, no. 4 (April 1913):141-42.

11. Lyautey to Franchet d'Espérey, 18 March 1913, SHAT, Maroc, 3H, 583, Cercle du Tadla, Oued Zem, 1913.

12. Lyautey to Mangin, 28 March 1913, in Lyautey to Étienne, 2 August 1913, SHAT, Maroc, 3H, 583, Opérations du Tadla, 1913.

13. Lyautey to Mangin, 25 April 1913, in Lyautey to Étienne, 2 August 1913 and Lyautey to Étienne, 2 August 1913, 3-7, both in SHAT, Maroc, 3H, 583, Opérations du Tadla, 1913; Lyautey to the Ministry of Foreign Affairs, 25 April 1913, SHAT, Maroc, 3H, 583, Cercle du Tadla, Oued Zem, 1913. Also see, *L'Afrique française* 23, no. 4 (April 1913): 141-42; 23, no. 7 (July 1913):278.

14. Lyautey to Étienne, 2 August 1913, 7-8, SHAT, Maroc, 3H, 583, Opérations du Tadla, 1913. For Mangin's battle record, see Mangin, "Journal de marche et opérations de la colonne Mangin au Tadla du 17 mars au 13 juin 1913," 13 June 1913, SHAT, Maroc, 3H, 583, Opérations du Tadla, 1913. Also see, *L'Afrique française* 23, no. 5 (May 1913):195. The French referred to the Berbers of the High Atlas and the Moroccan south collectively as the Chleuh.

15. Lyautey to Mangin, 2 May 1913, SHAT, Maroc, 3H, 583, Cercle du Tadla, Oued Zem, 1913.

16. Lyautey to Mangin, 11 May 1913 and Mangin to Lyautey, 13 May 1913, both in SHAT, Maroc, 3H, 583, Cercle du Tadla, Oued Zem, 1913.

17. Lyautey to Mangin, 11 May 1913, SHAT, Maroc, 583, Cercle du Tadla, Oued Zem, 1913; Lyautey to Mangin, 17 May 1913, in Lyautey to Étienne, 2 August 1913 and Lyautey to Étienne, 2 August 1913, 8-9, both in SHAT, Maroc, 583, Opérations du Tadla, 1913.

18. "Instructions pour le colonel Mangin," 24 May 1913, SHAT, Maroc, 3H, 583, Cercle du Tadla, Oued Zem, 1913.

19. Lyautey, "Instructions pour le colonel Mangin," 24 May 1913, SHAT, Maroc, 3H, 583, Cercle du Tadla, Oued Zem, 1913; "Renseignements sur les notabilités indigènes: Tadla," SHAT, Maroc, 3H, 584, Opérations en pays Zaïan, Colonne du Tadla, 1914; Lyautey to the minister of war, 2 August 1913, 11-12, SHAT, Maroc, 3H, 583, Opérations du Tadla, 1913; *L'Afrique française* 23, no. 7 (July 1913):278.

20. Mangin to Lyautey, 3 June 1913, in Lyautey to Étienne, 2 August 1913, SHAT, Maroc, 3H, 583, Opérations du Tadla, 1913.

21. Lyautey to Mangin, 4 June 1913 and Lyautey to the Ministry of Foreign Affairs, 4 June 1913, both in Lyautey to Étienne, 2 August 1913, SHAT, Maroc, 3H, 583, Opérations du Tadla, 1913; Lyautey to Étienne, 2 August 1913, 12-14, SHAT, Maroc, 3H, 583, Opérations du Tadla, 1913.

22. Lyautey to Étienne, 2 August 1913, 14-16 and Mangin, "Journal de marche et opérations de la colonne Mangin," both in SHAT, Maroc, 3H, 583, Opérations du Tadla, 1913. For the public version of El Ksiba, see *L'Afrique française* 23, no. 6 (June 1913):217-18.

23. *Rapport mensuel*, June 1913, 1.

24. Lyautey to Étienne, 2 August 1913, 17-19, SHAT, Maroc, 3H, 583, Opérations du Tadla, 1913.

25. *L'Afrique française* 23, no. 7 (July 1913):276-80. This reproduces the transcript of the Chamber session for 20 June 1913.

26. *L'Afrique française* 23, no. 7 (July 1913):275, 278-79. Lieutenant Colonel Noël Garnier-Duplessis was appointed commander of the newly created Cercle du Tadla. For contrasting assessments of the Tadla situation by Lyautey and Mangin, see Lyautey to Étienne, 2 August 1913, 19-24 and "Rapport d'opérations du Colonel Charles Mangin, Tadla (21 mars-21 juin 1913)," 24 June 1913, both in SHAT, Maroc, 3H, 583, Opérations du Tadla, 1913. Also see the anonymous article, "La campagne du Tadla," *Revue de Paris* 20, no. 5 (September-October 1913):417-48, which reports the Tadla campaign in dramatic and persuasive terms from the Mangin viewpoint.

27. *Rapport mensuel*, April 1913, 2.

28. Lyautey to Étienne, 2 August 1913, 17-18, 22, SHAT, Maroc, 3H, 583, Opérations du Tadla, 1913; Lyautey to de Mun, 10 October 1912, in Lyautey, *Choix de lettres*, 296-97.

29. *Rapport mensuel*, July 1913, 1.

30. *Rapport mensuel*, November 1913, 1, 7, 12; *L'Afrique française* 24, no. 1 (January 1914):23.

31. René de Segonzac, *Au coeur de l'Atlas: Mission au Maroc, 1904-1905* (Paris: Émile Larose, 1910), 55, 57.

32. *L'Afrique française* 24, no. 2 (February 1914):83-84, quoting Henry Gerlier in *Le Temps*, 10 February 1914.

33. Captain Maurice Le Glay, "Le Maroc central à la fin de 1913: Ali Amahouch et les Berbères," January 1914, 1-8, BGA, PA, Mission scientifique et la Section sociologique.

34. *Rapport mensuel*, April 1914, 1.

35. Lyautey to Henrÿs, 2 May 1914, SHAT, Maroc, 3H, 902, Opérations Zaïans, Directives et ordres du Commissaire Résident Général, 1914; *Rapport mensuel*, April 1914, 1-2; June 1914, 2.

36. *L'Afrique française* 24, no. 6 (June 1914):265-66. The taking of Taza is detailed in *L'Afrique française* 24, no. 5 (May 1914):202-05; 24, no. 6 (June 1914):260-65.

37. Lyautey, "Ordre général no. 82," 17 May 1914, in *L'Afrique française* 24, no. 6 (June 1914):265. Also see, Lyautey, "Ordre général no. 90," 28 July 1914, in *L'Afrique française* 25, no. 4 (April 1915):53-54 for a summary of the Taza operations.

38. *L'Afrique française* 24, no. 6 (June 1914):265.

39. Jacques Ladreit de Lacharrière, "A la colonne de Khenifra," *L'Afrique française* 24, no. 7 (July 1914):285.

40. "La politique berbère et l'action chez les Zaïan," *L'Afrique française* 24, no. 6 (June 1914):258.

41. See the ethnographic charts in Henrÿs to Dalbiez, 30 March 1913, SHAT, Maroc, 3H, 901, Région de Meknès, 1913 and "Renseignements sur les tribus," SHAT, Maroc, 3H, 1030, Rapports d'opérations, 1915-1916. Also see, Ladreit de Lacharrière, "A la colonne de Khenifra," 285. On Moha ou Hammou, see René de Segonzac, "Les Zaïan," *Renseignements coloniaux et documents*, no. 12, pp. 237-42, supplement to *L'Afrique française* 27, no. 12 (December 1917).

42. Lyautey to Henrÿs, 2 May 1914, SHAT, Maroc, 3H, 902, Opérations Zaïans, Directives et ordres du Commissaire Résident Général, 1914; Henrÿs to Lyautey, 14 May 1914, SHAT, Maroc, 3H, 904, Commandement général du Nord, Opérations Zaïans, 9 May-30 June 1914; Lyautey, "Ordre général no. 89," 27 July 1914, in *L'Afrique française* 25,

no. 4 (April 1915):51. On Mohamed Aguebli, see Lieutenant Colonel Henri Claudel to Lyautey, 24 August 1913, SHAT, Maroc, 3H, 582, Cercle des Beni M'Tir, Opérations 1913 and "Note au sujet de la situation politique actuelle dans le Cercle des Beni M'Tir," 5 December 1913, SHAT, Maroc, 3H, 901, Région de Meknès, 1913, Cercle des Beni M'Tir. On the feuding between Aguebli and Moha ou Hammou, see de Segonzac, "Les Zaïans," *Renseignements coloniaux et documents,* no. 12, p. 241, supplement to *L'Afrique française* 27, no. 12 (December 1917).

43. Lyautey to Henrÿs, 2 May 1914, SHAT, Maroc, 3H, 902, Opérations Zaïans, Directives et ordres du Commissaire Résident Général, 1914; Lyautey, "Programme pour l'action militaire et politique au Maroc occidental en 1914," 1 May 1914, in Lyautey, *Lyautey l'Africain,* 2:67.

44. Henrÿs to Lyautey, 14 May 1914, SHAT, 3H, Maroc, 902, Opérations Zaïans, Ordres, rapports, comptes-rendus du Général Commandant Général du Nord, 1914.

45. Henrÿs to Lyautey, 14 May 1914, SHAT, 3H, Maroc, 904, Commandement général du Nord, Opérations Zaïans, 9 May-30 June 1914.

46. Henrÿs to the commanders of the Groupe Mobile du Tadla and the Subdivision de Meknès, 20 May 1914, SHAT, Maroc, 3H, 902, Opérations Zaïans, Ordres, rapports, comptes-rendus du Général Commandant Général du Nord, 1914.

47. Henrÿs to Lyautey, 14 and 18 May 1914, both in SHAT, Maroc, 3H, 904, Commandement général du Nord, Opérations Zaïans, 9 May-30 June 1914.

48. *L'Afrique française* 24, no. 6 (June 1914):259.

49. Henrÿs to Lyautey, 31 May 1914, SHAT, Maroc, 3H, 904, Commandement général du Nord, Opérations Zaïans, 9 May-30 June 1914.

50. Lyautey, "Ordre général no. 89," 27 July 1914, in *L'Afrique française* 25, no. 4 (April 1915):51-52; *Rapport mensuel,* June 1914, 2, 12; Ladreit de Lacharrière, "A la colonne de Khenifra," 287; "La manoeuvre de Khenifra et la prise de possession du pays Zaïan," *L'Afrique française* 24, no. 7 (July 1914):312; *L'Afrique française* 24, no. 6 (June 1914):265.

51. Henrÿs to Lyautey, 10 June 1914, SHAT, Maroc, 3H, 902, Opérations Zaïans, Télégrammes Général Henrÿs au Résident Général.

52. Henrÿs to Lyautey, 10 and 11 June 1914, SHAT, Maroc, 3H, 902, Opérations Zaïan, Télégrammes Général Henrÿs au Résident Général; Lyautey, "Ordre général no. 89," 27 July 1914, in *L'Afrique française* 25, no. 4 (April 1915):51; Ladreit de Lacharrière, "A la colonne de Khenifra," 287-89; "La manoeuvre de Khenifra," 311-13; *L'Afrique française* 24, no. 6 (June 1914):265. Also see, "Opérations en pays Zaïan, Colonne Claudel, Rapport d'opérations pour la période du 10 au 20 juin inclus," 26 June 1914, SHAT, Maroc, 3H, 903, Zaïans, 1914, Journaux de marche des trois colonnes.

53. Henrÿs to Lyautey, 12 June 1914, SHAT, Maroc, 3H, 902, Opérations Zaïans, Télégrammes Général Henrÿs au Résident Général; Lyautey, "Ordre général no. 89," 27 July 1914, in *L'Afrique française* 25, no. 4 (April 1915):51; Ladreit de Lacharrière, "A la colonne de Khenifra," 289-90; "La manoeuvre de Khenifra," 313.

54. Henrÿs to Lyautey, 13 June 1914, SHAT, Maroc, 3H, 904, Commandement général du Nord, Opérations Zaïans, 9 May-30 June 1914.

55. Henrÿs to Lyautey, 15 June 1914, SHAT, Maroc, 3H, 902, Opérations Zaïans, Télégrammes Général Henrÿs au Résident Général; Lyautey, "Ordre général no. 89," 27 July 1914, in *L'Afrique française* 25, no. 4 (April 1915):51; Ladreit de Lacharrière, "A la colonne de Khenifra," 290; "La manoeuvre de Khenifra," 313-14.

56. Henrÿs, "Résultats politiques et militaires des opérations du 10 au 20 juin," SHAT, Maroc, 3H, 902, Opérations Zaïans, Ordres, rapports, comptes-rendus du Général Commandant Général du Nord, 1914 and Henrÿs to Lyautey, 17 June 1914, SHAT, Maroc, 3H, 902, Opérations Zaïans, Télégrammes Général Henrÿs au Résident Général.

57. *L'Afrique française* 24, no. 7 (July 1914):300-01. Also see, Henrÿs to Lyautey, 18 and 21 June 1914, SHAT, Maroc, 3H, 902, Opérations Zaïans, Télégrammes Général Henrÿs au Résident Général.

58. Henrÿs to base commanders, 23 June 1914, SHAT, Maroc, 3H, 904, Commandement général du Nord, Opérations Zaïans, 9 May-30 June 1914.

59. On Laoust's mission with Henrÿs, see Henrÿs to Lyautey, 6 June 1914, Henrÿs to the colonel commanding the Subdivision de Meknès, 8 June 1914, and Henrÿs to Garnier-Duplessis, 23 June 1914, all in SHAT, Maroc, 3H, 904, Commandement général du Nord, Opérations Zaïans, 9 May-30 June 1914. For Lyautey's detailed reports to Paris on the Zaïan occupation, see Lyautey to Minister of Foreign Affairs Gaston Doumergue, 9 June 1914 and Lyautey to Minister of Foreign Affairs René Viviani, 30 June 1914, both in Lyautey, *Lyautey l'Africain*, 2:185-203.

60. Henrÿs to Lyautey, 30 June and 3 July 1914, SHAT, Maroc, 3H, 902, Opérations Zaïans, Télégrammes Général Henrÿs au Résident Général; *Rapport mensuel*, June 1914, 2, 15-16; *L'Afrique française* 24, no. 7 (July 1914):300-01.

61. Henrÿs to Lyautey, 4, 5, and 6 July 1914, all in SHAT, Maroc, 3H, 902, Opérations Zaïans, Télégrammes Général Henrÿs au Résident Général; *Rapport mensuel*, June 1914, 2 and July 1914, 9; *L'Afrique française* 24, no. 7 (July 1914):301.

62. Henrÿs to Lyautey, 28 June 1914 and Henrÿs, "Rapport d'ensemble sur l'organisation militaire, administrative, et politique du front berbère," n.d. [June 1914], both in SHAT, Maroc, 3H, 902, Opérations Zaïans, Ordres, rapports, comptes-rendus du Général Commandant Général du Nord, 1914; *Rapport mensuel*, July 1914, 8-9.

63. Henrÿs, "Rapport d'ensemble sur l'organisation militaire, administrative, et politique du front berbère;" *Rapport mensuel*, July 1914, 8-9.

64. Henrÿs, "Rapport d'ensemble sur l'organisation militaire, administrative, et politique du front berbère."

65. Henrÿs to Lyautey, 6 July 1914, SHAT, Maroc, 3H, 904, Commandement général du Nord, Opérations Zaïans, 1 July-16 September 1914. On Moha's family tree, traced back to the reign of Sultan Moulay Ismaïl, see de Segonzac, "Les Zaïans," *Renseignements coloniaux et documents*, no. 12, pp. 237-42, supplement to *L'Afrique française* 27, no. 12 (December 1917).

66. Henrÿs to Lyautey, 28 June 1914 and "Rapport d'ensemble sur l'organisation militaire, administrative, et politique du front berbère," both in SHAT, Maroc, 3H, 902, Opérations Zaïans, Ordres, rapports, comptes-rendus du Général Commandant Général du Nord, 1914.

67. Henrÿs to Lyautey, 6 July 1914, SHAT, Maroc, 3H, 904, Commandement général du Nord, Opérations Zaïans, 1 July-16 September 1914; *L'Afrique française* 24, no. 6 (June 1914):257-58. For the dahir on the administration of the Berber tribes (11-15 September 1914), see *L'Afrique française* 25, no. 3 (March 1915):81. The "Berber policy" launched French administrators and social scientists into the investigation of the Berber tribes to generate information for the political supervision of the Berber populations. See *L'Afrique française* 25, no. 5 (May 1915):150-51.

68. Henrÿs, "Instructions politiques," 6 June 1914, SHAT, Maroc, 3H, 904, Commandement général du Nord, Opérations Zaïans, 9 May-30 June 1914.

69. Henrÿs to Lyautey, 6 July 1914, SHAT, Maroc, 3H, 904, Commandement général du Nord, Opérations Zaïans, 1 July-16 September 1914.

70. Henrÿs, "Note de service," 16 June 1914, SHAT, Maroc, 3H, 902, Opérations Zaïans, Ordres, rapports, comptes-rendus du Général Commandant Général du Nord, 1914.

71. Henrÿs, "Instructions politiques," 6 June 1914, SHAT, Maroc, 3H, 904, Commandement général du Nord, Opérations Zaïans, 9 May-30 June 1914.

72. Henrÿs to Lyautey, 28 June 1914, SHAT, Maroc, 3H, 902, Opérations Zaïans, Ordres, rapports, comptes-rendus du Général Commandant Général du Nord, 1914; Henrÿs to Lyautey, 6, 11, 12, 18, 22, 24, 26, 27 July 1914, SHAT, Maroc, 3H, 902, Opérations Zaïans, Télégrammes Général Henrÿs au Résident Général; "Rapport d'opérations des troupes d'occupation en pays Zaïan, 20 juin au 17 juillet 1914," 20 and "Rapport

d'opérations des troupes d'occupation en pays Zaïan, 17 juillet au 1er août 1914," 2-4, 7-8, both in SHAT, Maroc, 3H, 902, Opérations Zaïan, Rapports d'opérations du Général Commandant les Opérations Zaïans; Henrÿs, "Situation politique à la date du 15 juillet," 17 July 1914, SHAT, Maroc, 3H, 904, Commandement Général du Nord, Opérations Zaïans, 1er juillet-16 septembre 1914.

73. See Lyautey to Minister of War Adolphe Messimy, 22 August 1914 and Lyautey to regional commanders, 9 September 1914, both in Lyautey, *Lyautey l'Africain*, 2:241-57, 265-68. In July 1914 there were forty-eight battalions in western Morocco, twelve battalions in eastern Morocco; thirty-one of the forty-eight and six of the twelve were sent to France, leaving seventeen in the west and six in the east. See *L'Afrique française* 25, no. 4 (April 1915):60.

74. For a detailed account of these attacks, see "Rapport d'opérations des troupes d'occupation en pays Zaïan, 1er au 15 août 1914" and "Journal de marche, 16 août au 1er septembre 1914," both in SHAT, Maroc, 3H, 902, Opérations Zaïans, Rapports d'opérations du Général Commandant les Opérations Zaïans.

75. Lyautey, "Ordre général no. 100," 18 August 1914, in *L'Afrique française* 25, no. 4 (April 1915):58; *L'Afrique française* 25, nos. 6-7 (June-July, 1915):169-70.

76. "Journal de marche, 16 août au 1er septembre 1914," SHAT, Maroc, 3H, 902, Opérations Zaïans, Rapports d'opérations du Général Commandant les Opérations Zaïans.

77. Lyautey, "Ordre général no. 102," 21 August 1914, in *L'Afrique française* 25, no. 4 (April 1915):63.

78. "Rapport du Général Henrÿs, Commandant Général des Régions Fez, Meknès, sur le combat du 13 novembre à El Herri, près Khénifra," 26 November 1914, 1, SHAT, Maroc, 3H, 585, Affaire d'El Herri, 13 novembre 1914, Rapport du Général Henrÿs et pièces annexes; *L'Afrique française* 25, no. 4 (April 1915):64.

79. "Rapport du Général Henrÿs sur le combat du 13 novembre," 2-4.

80. "Rapport du Général Henrÿs sur le combat du 13 novembre," 4-5; Henrÿs to Lyautey, 22 December 1914 and Colonel Charles Scal to Henrÿs, 20 December 1914, both in Lyautey to Minister of War Alexandre Millerand, 2 January 1915, and Lyautey to Minister of War Alexandre Millerand, 16 December 1914, 10, both in SHAT, Maroc, 3H, 585, Affaire d'El Herri, 13 November 1914; Laverdure, Ordre d'opération, 12 November 1914, SHAT, Maroc, 3H, 585, Affaire d'El Herri, 13 November 1914, Rapport du Général Henrÿs et pièces annexes.

81. "Rapport du Général Henrÿs sur le combat du 13 novembre," 7-9.

82. "Rapport du Général Henrÿs sur le combat du 13 novembre," 9-12; *Rapport mensuel*, November 1914, 6-7; Lyautey, "Ordre général no. 112," 5 December 1914, in *L'Afrique française* 25, no. 4 (April 1915):66; *L'Afrique française* 25, no. 4 (April 1915):64. Also see, Jean Pichon, *Le Maroc au début de la guerre mondiale: El-Herri (vendredi, 13 novembre 1914)*, with a preface by General Henrÿs (Paris: Charles-Lavauzelle et Cie., 1936).

83. Croll to Lyautey and Henrÿs, 13 November 1914, SHAT, Maroc, 3H, 902, Opérations Zaïans, 1914: Ordres, rapports, comptes-rendus des commandants de colonne, Questions politiques et divers. The following day Croll sent a more detailed account of the events of the 13th. See Croll to Henrÿs, 14 November 1914, SHAT, Maroc, 3H, 902, Opérations Zaïans, 1914: Ordres, rapports, comptes-rendus des commandants de colonne, Questions politiques et divers.

84. *Rapport mensuel*, November 1914, 7.

85. Henrÿs, "Rapport d'opérations du 13 au 30 novembre 1914," 30 November 1914, SHAT, Maroc, 3H, 902, Opérations Zaïans, 1914, Ordres, rapports, comptes-rendus des commandants de colonne.

86. Henrÿs to Lyautey, 15 November 1914, SHAT, Maroc, 3H, 903, Opérations Zaïans: Affaire de Khénifra, Télégrammes du Résident Général au Général Henrÿs et du Général Henrÿs au Résident Général.

87. Henrÿs, "Rapport d'opérations du 13 au 30 novembre 1914;" *Rapport mensuel,* November 1914, 2, 7; Lyautey, "Ordre général no. 112," 5 December 1914, in *L'Afrique française* 25, no. 4 (April 1915):66.

88. "Rapport du Général Henrÿs sur le combat du 13 novembre," 12-14; Henrÿs, "Rapport d'opérations du 13 au 30 novembre 1914." The seven bodies (all of French officers, including that of Colonel Laverdure) were exchanged for Moha ou Hammou's two wives. See Henrÿs to Lyautey, 24 November 1914, in Henrÿs, "Rapport d'opérations du 13 au 30 novembre 1914."

89. Lyautey to Henrÿs, 23 November 1914, SHAT, Maroc, 3H, 903, Opérations Zaïans: Affaire de Khénifra, Télégrammes du Résident au Général Henrÿs et du Général Henrÿs au Résident Général.

90. Henrÿs, "Rapport du Général Henrÿs sur le combat du 13 novembre," 4-5; Henrÿs to Lyautey, 22 December 1914, in Lyautey to Millerand, 2 January 1915, SHAT, Maroc, 3H, 585, Affaire d'El Herri, 13 novembre 1914.

91. Henrÿs, "Rapport du Général Henrÿs sur le combat du 13 novembre," 5-7.

92. Lyautey to Millerand, 16 December 1914, 1, 4-10, SHAT, Maroc, 3H, 585, Affaire d'El Herri, 13 novembre 1914. Lyautey cited the writings of Pierre Khorat, Captain Charles Cornet, journalist Louis Botte and the speeches of Denys Cochin in the Chamber of Deputies as evidence of the existence and impact of this school, but these men were certainly not of the same mind. For example, Khorat (who was really Major Ibos of the colonial infantry), while candidly describing the problems of pacification and the disputes over colonial policy, was at heart a partisan of the Lyautey approach. See Khorat, "En colonne au Maroc: Impressions d'un témoin," *Revue des deux mondes,* 1 August 1911, 519-53; 15 September 1911, 363-96; 1 November 1911, 51-81. Also see, Khorat, "Petite garnison marocaine," *Revue des deux mondes,* 1 July 1912, 53-82 and "Scènes de la pacification marocaine," *Revue des deux mondes,* 1 October 1913, 645-82; 1 November 1913, 109-46; 1 December 1913, 630-70. See Cornet, *A la conquête du Maroc sud avec la colonne Mangin, 1912-1913* (Paris: Plon-Nourrit et Cie., 1914); Louis Botte, "Au Maroc: La conquête du pays berbère," *Revue de Paris* 21, no. 2 (March-April 1914):645-72; and for Cochin, France, Assemblée nationale, Annales de la Chambre des députés, *Débats parlementaires,* 10 and 24 March 1914, 1693, 2175-76.

93. Lyautey to Millerand, 16 December 1914, 11-14, SHAT, Maroc, 3H, 585, Affaire d'El Herri, 13 novembre 1914. Henrÿs was promoted to the rank of brigadier general, Garnier-Duplessis was raised to the rank of officer of the Legion of Honor, and Croll was promoted to the rank of *chef de bataillon.* See Lyautey, "Ordre général no. 111," 28 November 1914, in *L'Afrique française* 25, no. 4 (April 1915):66. When Millerand allowed the croix de guerre to be awarded to soldiers on the Moroccan "front" in 1915, Henrÿs received the first one, Croll the second. See Lyautey, "Aux officiers et sous-officiers de bataillons partant pour la France et en revenant," 8 August 1915, in Lyautey, *Paroles d'action,* 142-43.

94. *Rapport mensuel,* November 1914, 2, 7.

95. Lyautey to Millerand, 16 December 1914, 15. Also see, Lyautey to his sister, 5 December 1914, in Lyautey, *Choix de lettres,* 310-11. Only later would *L'Afrique française* admit that El Herri numbered "among the costliest colonial catastrophes" of the African conquest. *L'Afrique française* 25, nos. 6-7 (June-July 1915):160.

96. Henrÿs, "Rapport du Général Henrÿs sur le combat du 13 novembre 1914," 15-16; Lyautey to Millerand, 16 December 1914, 15-16.

97. Lyautey to Millerand, 16 December 1914, 16-17.

98. Lyautey to Millerand, 16 December 1914, 19-21.

99. *Rapport mensuel,* November 1914, 7, 9-12; Henrÿs, "Rapport du Général Henrÿs sur le combat du 13 novembre," 16.

100. *Rapport mensuel,* December 1914, 1. On the sultan at Constantinople and German propaganda in Morocco, see Lyautey to Millerand, 16 December 1914, 18-19.

101. Henrÿs, "Rapport du Général Henrÿs sur le combat du 13 novembre," 18.
102. Henrÿs to Lyautey, 25 November 1914, SHAT, Maroc, 3H, 903, Opérations Zaïans, Affaire de Khénifra, Télégrammes du Résident Général au Général Henrÿs et du Général Henrÿs au Résident Général; Henrÿs to Lyautey, 1 December 1914, SHAT, Maroc, 3H, 902, Opérations Zaïans, Ordres, rapports, comptes-rendus du Général Commandant Général du Nord, 1914; L'Afrique française 25, nos. 6-7 (June-July 1915):163.
103. Henrÿs to Garnier-Duplessis, 27 November 1914, SHAT, Maroc, 3H, 585, Affaire d'El Herri, 13 novembre 1914.
104. Rapport mensuel, January 1915, 1; L'Afrique française 25, no. 4 (April 1915):65.
105. "Rapport du Colonel Charles Scal sur l'opération combinée exécutée le 3 mars dans la région Foum Teguet, Djebel Tarat par les groupes mobiles Dérigoin et Duplessis," 19 March 1915, SHAT, Maroc, 3H, 908, Opérations Tadla-Zaïan, Ordres, rapports et compte-rendus, 1915; L'Afrique française 25, no. 4 (April 1915):112-13.
106. Henrÿs, "Situation politique du commandement général à la date du 10 mars 1915," 5-6, SHAT, Maroc, 3H, 1030, Rapports d'opérations, 1915-16.
107. Henrÿs, "Situation politique du commandement général à la date du 10 mars 1915," 7, SHAT, Maroc, 3H, 1030, Rapports d'opérations, 1915-16. According to Rivet, the refusal of Berber leaders to negotiate with Henrÿs doomed Lyautey's ambitious plans for the creation of "large 'native' commands" in the Middle Atlas within the Makhzen system. Thus, Henrÿs's Berber policy was at least in part a response to failure. See Rivet, Lyautey et l'institution du protectorat français au Maroc, 1:198-99.
108. Henrÿs, "Situation politique du commandement général à la date du 25 mai 1915," 25 May 1915, SHAT, Maroc, 3H, 1030, Rapports d'opérations, 1915-16; "Journal des marches et opérations de la colonne Tadla-Zaïan du 14 au 23 mai 1915," 27 May 1915, SHAT, Maroc, 3H, 908, Opérations Tadla-Zaïan, 1915, Journaux de marche de la Subdivision Tadla-Zaïan; L'Afrique française 25, nos. 6-7 (June-July 1915):164-65, 181. Lyautey later shared in the honors. At Khénifra in October he received the Médaille Militaire and the croix de guerre. See L'Afrique française 25, nos. 10-12 (October-December, 1915):299.
109. Garnier-Duplessis to Lyautey, 14 November 1915, SHAT, Maroc, 3H, 908, Opérations Tadla-Zaïan, Liaison entre les groupes mobiles du Tadla et des Beni M'Guild; Garnier-Duplessis, "Rapport d'opérations sur la journée du 11 novembre 1915," 29 November 1915, SHAT, Maroc, 3H, 908, Opérations Tadla-Zaïan, Ordres, rapports et comptes-rendus; L'Afrique française 25, nos. 10-12 (October-December 1915):299-300.
110. Garnier-Duplessis, "Rapport d'opérations pour la journée du 19 novembre 1915," 1 December 1915, SHAT, Maroc, 3H, 908, Opérations Tadla-Zaïan, Liaison entre les groupes mobiles du Tadla et des Beni M'Guild; L'Afrique française 25, nos. 10-12 (October-December 1915):298, 300.
111. L'Afrique française 25, nos. 10-12 (October-December, 1915):298; 26, nos. 1-2 (January-February 1916):13, 15-16; 26, no. 3 (March 1916):74, 78-79; "Rapport du Chef de bataillon Paul Colombat sur les opérations des 19 et 20 janvier 1916," 20 January 1916 and "Rapport du Chef de bataillon Colombat sur le combat du 23 janvier 1916," 24 January 1916, both in SHAT, Maroc, 3H, 1030, Rapports d'opérations, 1915-1916. The new chef de guerre was Miami Ould El Hadj Haddou, a nephew of Moha ou Hammou. See L'Afrique française 26, no. 5 (May 1916):173.
112. L'Afrique française 26, no. 7 (July 1916):248; 26, nos. 8-9 (August-September 1916):292. On Beni Mellal, also see SHAT, Maroc, 3H, 588, Tadla, 1916.
113. Colonel Poeymirau, commandant la Région de Meknès, to Lieutenant-Colonel Colombat, commandant le Cercle des Beni M'Guild à Aïn Leuh, 25 November 1916; Colombat to Chef du Poste du Service des Renseignements à Timhadit, 5 December 1916; Général de Division Henri Gouraud, Commissaire Résident Général de France

au Maroc, to Poeymirau, 13 March 1917; Poeymirau, "Instruction générale pour la campagne de 1917: plan d'action militaire," 29 March 1917, all in SHAT, Maroc, 3H, 1030, Colonnes 1917, Ordres préparatoires et renseignements divers; Lyautey to Gouraud, 7 June 1917, in Lyautey, *Lyautey l'Africain*, 3:237; *L'Afrique française* 27, nos. 5-6 (May-June 1917):188, 192; 27, nos. 7-8 (July-August 1917):281. For details on the activities of the mobile groups, see SHAT, Maroc, 3H, 1030, Colonnes 1917, Exécution and *L'Afrique française* 27, nos. 7-8 (July-August 1917):281-85. On the establishment of El Bekrit, see René de Segonzac's account in *L'Afrique française* 27, nos. 5-6 (May-June 1917):188-91.

114. Lyautey to Diplomatie/Guerre, Paris, 12 October 1917, SHAT, Maroc, 3H, 1030, Colonnes 1917, Ordres préparatoires et renseignements divers; *L'Afrique française* 27, nos. 9-11 (September-November 1917):333. On the road building in the Middle Atlas, see "Directives établies à la suite de la conférence tenue à Rabat avec le Général Poeymirau et le Lieutenant-Colonel Doury," 23 August 1917, SHAT, Maroc, 3H, 1030, Colonnes 1917, Ordres préparatoires et renseignements divers. There were also French inroads in the Tadla. On 10 October Colonel Jean Théveney's mobile group occupied Rhorm El Alem (which was fifteen kilometers southeast of Kasbah Tadla on the way to El Ksiba) and established a permanent post. Denied access to the plain, to Kasbah Tadla, and to the El Ksiba road, the Chleuh "reacted violently." They attacked the post during the night of 12-13 October and again at dawn on 15 October in "furious assaults" that ended in hand-to-hand combat. The French remained at Rhorm El Alem, but the fight cost them forty-three dead and fifty-five wounded. See Théveney, commandant le Territoire Tadla-Zaïan, to Lyautey, 10 February 1918, SHAT, Maroc, 3H, 590, Tadla-Zaïan, Opérations 1918; *L'Afrique française* 27, nos. 9-11 (September-November 1917):333-34.

115. Lyautey to Diplomatie/Guerre, 12 October 1917, SHAT, Maroc, 3H, 1030, Colonnes 1917, Ordres préparatoires et renseignements divers.

116. *L'Afrique française* 28, nos. 7-8 (July-August 1918):198, 202-03, 209-10; 28, nos. 9-10 (September-October 1918):295-96.

117. On the reasons for occupying Tafilalet, see Captain Henri Berriau, "Contribution à l'étude de la Région Sud-Ouest," 8 March 1911, BGA, PA, Notes sur diverses régions du Maroc.

118. Directeur du Service des Renseignements Henri Berriau to Doury, 3 December 1917, SHAT, Maroc, 3H, 590, Territoire de Bou Denib, Tafilalet: Opérations 1918, Directives Lyautey.

119. Lyautey to Doury, 20 February 1918, SHAT, Maroc, 3H, 590, Territoire de Bou Denib, Tafilalet: Opérations 1918, Directives Lyautey. Also see, *L'Afrique française* 28, nos. 9-10 (September-October 1918):289-292.

120. Lyautey to Poeymirau, 12 August 1918 and Lyautey to Région Marrakech, 13 August 1918, both in SHAT, Maroc, 3H, 590, Territoire de Bou Denib, Tafilalet: Opérations 1918, Directives Lyautey; *L'Afrique française* 28, nos. 9-10 (September-October 1918):291-92. In his official battle report Doury listed 238 dead and 68 wounded. See Lyautey to Premier and Minister of War Georges Clemenceau, 2 September 1918, SHAT, Maroc, 3H, 590, Territoire de Bou Denib, Tafilalet: Opérations 1918, Combat de Gaouz.

121. Lyautey to Doury, 14 August 1918, SHAT, Maroc, 3H, 590, Territoire de Bou Denib, Tafilalet: Opérations 1918, Directives de Lyautey; *L'Afrique française* 28, nos. 9-10 (September-October 1918):292.

122. Lyautey to Poeymirau, 16 August 1918 and Lyautey to the governor-general of Algeria, 23 August 1918, both in SHAT, Maroc, 3H, 590, Territoire de Bou Denib, Tafilalet: Opérations 1918, Directives de Lyautey.

123. Lyautey to Doury, 8 September 1918, SHAT, Maroc, 3H, 590, Territoire de Bou Denib, Tafilalet: Opérations 1918, Directives Lyautey.

124. Lyautey to Poeymirau, 9 September 1918, SHAT, Maroc, 3H, 590, Territoire de Bou Denib, Tafilalet: Opérations 1918, Directives de Lyautey.

125. Lyautey to Poeymirau, 17 October 1918, SHAT, Maroc, 3H, 590, Territoire de Bou Denib, Tafilalet: Opérations 1918, Directives de Lyautey. Also see, Poeymirau, "Compte-rendu des opérations au Tafilalet du 8 septembre au 18 octobre 1918," SHAT, Maroc, 3H, 590, Territoire de Bou Denib, Tafilalet: Opérations 1918; L'Afrique française 29, nos. 1-2 (January-February 1919):24-25.

126. Lyautey to Général, Commandant-en-Chef, Afrique-Nord in Algiers, 23 December 1918 and 17 January 1919, and Lyautey to the governor-general of Algeria, 2 February 1919, all in SHAT, Maroc, 3H, 590, Territoire de Bou Denib, Tafilalet: Opérations 1918, Télégrammes officiels: Tafilalet, 1917-1919; L'Afrique française 29, nos. 1-2 (January-February 1919):26-27. Although the crisis in the Tafilalet was over in early 1919, Lyautey warned that a new fire could flame up "at any moment." See "Rapport du Commissaire Résident-Général Commandant-en-chef sur la situation politique et militaire du Maroc au 15 juin 1919," 19 June 1919, 12, SHAT, Maroc, 3H, 591, Projets, Directives, 1919.

127. Lyautey to Poeymirau, 15 and 23 September 1918, both in SHAT, Maroc, 3H, 590, Territoire de Bou Denib, Tafilalet: Opérations 1918, Directives de Lyautey; Lyautey to Minister of War General Pierre Roques, 1 May 1916, in Lyautey Papers, AN, No. 610: Personnel du Maroc. Midelt was relieved on 6 February, Itzer on 8 February, and Ksabi (Kasbah El Makhzen) on 26 February 1919. L'Afrique française 29, nos. 1-2 (January-February 1919):28; 29, nos. 3-4 (March-April, 1919):100-101.

128. Colonel Jean Théveney, "Rapport d'opérations, Colonne de Khénifra, janvier 1918," SHAT, Maroc, 3H, 590, Tadla-Zaïan: Opérations 1918; L'Afrique française 28, nos. 4-5-6 (April-May-June 1918):136.

129. Poeymirau to Territoire Tadla, 4 June 1918 and Poeymirau to Lyautey, 12 June 1918, both in SHAT, Maroc, 3H, 590, Subdivision de Meknès: Opérations 1918. Also see, L'Afrique française 28, nos. 7-8 (July-August 1918):197-98. On the Zaïan family feud, see Rivet, Lyautey et l'institution du protectorat français au Maroc, 2:83-84.

130. L'Afrique française 30, nos. 7-8 (July-August 1920):241-42.

131. Poeymirau, "Rapport sur les opérations du Groupe Mobile de Meknès en pays Zaïan (avril-mai 1920)," SHAT, Maroc, 3H, 1031, Rapports sur les opérations du Groupe Mobile de Meknès en pays Zaïan.

132. Poeymirau, "Rapport sur les opérations du Groupe Mobile de Meknès en pays Zaïan (avril-mai 1920)," SHAT, Maroc, 3H, 1031, Rapports sur les opérations du Groupe Mobile de Meknès en pays Zaïan; L'Afrique française 30, nos. 7-8 (July-August 1920):242-44.

133. L'Afrique française 30, nos. 7-8 (July-August 1920):244-45; Bulletin Officiel 10, no. 431 (25 January 1921):137 and no. 453 (28 June 1921):1024-25. To the east and northeast 4,600 tents of the Beni Mguild had yet to submit and to the south and southwest 3,800 tents of "diverse tribes," joined with the Zaïan but not part of their confederation (such as the Aït Ischak, Aït Ichkern, and Aït Ihand), also remained untouched. L'Afrique française 30, nos. 7-8 (July-August 1920):245.

134. L'Afrique française 31, no. 5 (May 1921):156. Also see, de Segonzac, "Les Zaïans," Renseignements coloniaux et documents, no. 12, p. 241, supplement to L'Afrique française 27, no. 12 (December 1917). The ultimate conquest was ending up between the covers of a children's book. See G. Bernié, Moha ou Hamou, guerrier berbère (Casablanca: G. Gauthey, 1945).

135. Théveney, "Opérations de la Région de Bekrit, Automne 1921," SHAT, Maroc, 3H, 1032, Rapports spéciaux sur les combats de 1921; L'Afrique française 31, no. 7 (July 1921):218-19 and 31, no. 9 (September 1921):297-98.

136. Renseignements coloniaux et documents, no. 9, p. 246, supplement to L'Afrique française 32, no. 9 (September 1922).

137. See Lyautey to Poeymirau, 14 December 1921, SHAT, Maroc, 3H, 1032, 1921: Ordres divers, Rapports spéciaux sur les combats de 1921 and *Renseignements coloniaux et documents*, no. 9, p. 241, supplement to *L'Afrique française* 32, no. 9 (September 1922). Lyautey's plan called for a "pacified Morocco" budget for 1924, which meant sharply reduced costs and troop strength. The hope was to reduce the army from the postwar highs (91,778 in 1920, 94,734 in 1921, 85,951 in 1922, 78,000 in 1923) to 50,000. In the military zones the troops would be concentrated in a small number of "nerve centers" linked to posts on the periphery by modern automobile roads. In the civil zones an increased number of native police *(mokhazenis)* would help to keep the peace. See "Les Opérations militaires au Maroc en 1922," an extract from Raoul Calary de Lamazière's report on the war budget to the French Chamber, *Renseignements coloniaux et documents*, no. 12, p. 339, supplement to *L'Afrique française* 32, no. 12 (December 1922). Calary doubted that Lyautey could keep to his proposed pacification schedule and he turned out to be correct.

138. Lyautey, "Ordre général no. 316," 30 May 1922, *Renseignements coloniaux et documents*, no. 9, pp. 246-47, supplement to *L'Afrique française* 32, no. 9 (September 1922).

139. *Renseignements coloniaux et documents*, no. 9, pp. 245-46, supplement to *L'Afrique française* 32, no. 9 (September 1922); Lieutenant Kasdir, "Les Opérations du groupe mobile du Tadla en 1922," *Renseignements coloniaux et documents*, no. 5, pp. 150-51, supplement to *L'Afrique française* 33, no. 5 (May 1923). Also see, SHAT, Maroc, 3H, 1033, Opérations au Tadla et en Haute Moulouya, 1922.

140. *Renseignements coloniaux et documents*, no. 9, pp. 245-46, supplement to *L'Afrique française* 32, no. 9 (September 1922); Kasdir, "Les Opérations du groupe mobile du Tadla," 154-55.

141. *Rapport mensuel*, March 1924, II.

142. *Renseignements coloniaux et documents*, no. 3, p. 67, supplement to *L'Afrique française*, 30, no. 3 (March 1920), quoting Lyautey's introduction to Dr. Paul Chatinières, *Dans le Grand Atlas marocain: Extraits du carnet de route d'un médecin d'assistance médicale indigène, 1912-1916* (Paris: Plon-Nourrit et Cie., 1919).

143. As Daniel Rivet has shown, however, there were many forms of Moroccan resistance to the French, each determined by geography, history, ethnicity, economics, religious sentiments, way of life, and, most important, attitudes toward outsiders, including other Moroccans. This makes it difficult to speak of a national (or patriotic) Moroccan resistance or even a universal rejection of the foreigner, for in many cases an accommodation with the French was used for personal, family, clan, group, or tribal advantage. See Rivet, *Lyautey et l'institution du protectorat français au Maroc*, 2:87-117.

Chapter 5

1. See Lyautey to Président du Conseil Georges Clemenceau, 15 June 1919, in Lyautey, *Lyautey l'Africain*, 4:13-15.

2. See Colonel Léopold Justinard, *Le caïd Goundafi: Un grand chef berbère*, with a preface by Marshal Juin (Casablanca: Éditions Atlantides, 1951), 113-14.

3. On the "greatest" of the *grands caïds*, Thami el-Glaouï, who figured so prominently in the last years of French rule, see Rivet, *Lyautey et l'institution du protectorat français au Maroc*, 2:177-85.

4. Jacques Ladreit de Lacharrière, "Dans le Sud et l'Ouest du Maroc, Mission Ladreit de Lacharrière: Rapport au Comité du Maroc," *Renseignements coloniaux et documents*, no. 2, p. 31, supplement to *L'Afrique française* 22, no. 2 (February 1912).

5. Ladreit de Lacharrière, "Dans le Sud et l'Ouest du Maroc," 35-36. For a time Haïda had also been a German protégé. See René de Segonzac, "El Hiba, fils de Ma El Ainin,"

Renseignements coloniaux et documents, no. 3, p. 65, supplement to *L'Afrique française* 27, no. 3 (March 1917).

6. See General Maurice de Lamothe to Lyautey, 14 June 1917, SHAT, Maroc, 3H, 589, Marrakech, 1917, 1. On el-Hiba's jihad, see Burke, *Prelude to Protectorate,* 199-209.
7. De Segonzac, "El Hiba, fils de Ma El Ainin," 65-66.
8. *L'Afrique française* 23, no. 7 (July 1913):276; 23, no. 9 (September 1913):338; 23, no. 10 (October 1913):359; 23, no. 11 (November 1913):395.
9. *L'Afrique française* 23, no. 12 (December 1913):447.
10. *L'Afrique française* 24, no. 1 (January 1914):22.
11. *L'Afrique française* 24, no. 3 (March 1914):132.
12. Chef du Service des Renseignements à la Région de Marrakech en mission Lieutenant-Colonel Maurice de Lamothe to Lyautey, 10 July 1914, in Ministère des Affaires Étrangères, Nantes, Archives Diplomatiques, Maroc, Archives du Protectorat, 1912-1956, Région de Marrakech, carton 627, Vallée du Sous, Ras El Oued, 1912-15. (Hereafter cited as MAE, Nantes, Maroc, region, carton number, dossier and/or chemise name.)
13. *Rapport mensuel,* September 1914, 9.
14. *Rapport mensuel,* September 1914, 9-10.
15. *Rapport mensuel,* September 1914, 10.
16. *Rapport mensuel,* September 1914, 2, 10-11.
17. *Rapport mensuel,* October 1914, 8.
18. *Rapport mensuel,* October 1914, 8.
19. *Rapport mensuel,* November 1914, 10-11.
20. *Rapport mensuel,* December 1914, 8.
21. *Rapport mensuel,* December 1914, 2; Lyautey, "Exposé général de la situation du Maroc depuis la mobilisation," December 1914, in Lyautey, *Lyautey l'Africain,* 2:316.
22. *Rapport mensuel,* January 1915, 10; February 1915, 9.
23. *Rapport mensuel,* February 1915, 9.
24. *Rapport mensuel,* February 1915, 2, 7, 9; *L'Afrique française* 25, no. 4 (April 1915):65. Also see, de Segonzac, "El Hiba, fils de Ma El Ainin," 68.
25. *Rapport mensuel,* April 1915, 9-11.
26. *L'Afrique française* 25, nos. 6-7 (June-July 1915):181.
27. See Lyautey, "Ordre général no. 2," 25 February 1915, in *L'Afrique française* 25, no. 4 (April 1915):69.
28. Justinard, *Le caïd Goundafi,* 112-13. On the rivalry and distrust among the Makhzen *caïds* and the tribes of the south, see Léopold Justinard, "Notre action dans le Sous," *Renseignements coloniaux et documents,* no. 12, p. 549, supplement to *L'Afrique française* 36, no. 12 (December 1926).
29. *Rapport mensuel,* September 1915, 14; *L'Afrique française* 25, nos. 10-12 (October-December 1915):301.
30. *Rapport mensuel,* September 1915, 15; *L'Afrique française* 25, nos. 10-12 (October-December 1915):301.
31. *L'Afrique française* 25, nos. 10-12 (October-December 1915):302.
32. *Rapport mensuel,* September 1915, 15.
33. De Lamothe to Lyautey, 14 June 1917, 2-3, SHAT, Maroc, 3H, 589, Marrakech, 1917; "Les confins de la région de Marrakech en août 1922," *L'Afrique française* 32, no. 9 (September 1922):397. Justinard was thirty-eight years old in 1916. Graduated from St. Cyr in 1899, he served as a lieutenant in the 3ème Tirailleurs Algériens. In 1911 he was assigned to the French military mission in Morocco. Promoted captain in 1912, he fought in France in 1914 with the 306ème Régiment d'Infanterie, then in 1915 with the Tirailleurs Marocains. Wounded four times in combat, he joined the Service des Renseignements in 1916 and was assigned to the Région de Marrakech.

34. De Lamothe to Lyautey, 14 June 1917, 3, SHAT, Maroc, 3H, 589, Marrakech, 1917; De Lamothe to Justinard, "Ordre de mission," 14 October 1916, in Justinard, *Le caïd Goundafi*, 262-65.

35. De Lamothe to Justinard, "Ordre de mission," 14 October 1916, in Justinard, *Le caïd Goundafi*, 262-63.

36. De Lamothe to Justinard, "Ordre de mission," 14 October 1916, in Justinard, *Le caïd Goundafi*, 263-64.

37. Justinard, "Notre action dans le Sous," 550 and Justinard, *Le caïd Goundafi*, 129-40. Also see, de Segonzac, "El Hiba, fils de Ma El Ainin," part 2, *Renseignements coloniaux et documents*, no. 4, pp. 90-92, supplement to *L'Afrique française* 27, no. 4 (April 1917).

38. De Lamothe to Lyautey, 31 December 1916, in MAE, Nantes, Maroc, Région de Marrakech, 629, Dernière Harka du Pacha Haïda.

39. De Lamothe to Lyautey, 14 June 1917, 3-4, SHAT, Maroc, 3H, 589, Marrakech, 1917; *Rapport mensuel*, January 1917, 16. "Les Confins sud de la région de Marrakech en août 1922," *L'Afrique française* 32, no. 9 (September 1922):397.

40. De Lamothe to Lyautey, 14 June 1917, 4-5, SHAT, Maroc, 3H, 589, Marrakech, 1917; *Rapport mensuel*, January 1917, 16; Justinard, *Le caïd Goundafi*, 141; de Segonzac, "El Hiba, fils de Ma El Ainin," part 2, 92-93. Also see Justinard's account of Haïda's death in "Rapport mensuel pour la période du 15 décembre au 15 janvier," 21 January 1917, in MAE, Nantes, Maroc, Région de Marrakech, 629, Dernière Harka du Pacha Haïda.

41. *Bulletin Officiel* 6, no. 247 (16 July 1917):797.

42. De Lamothe to Lyautey, 14 June 1917, 5, SHAT, Maroc, 3H, 589, Marrakech, 1917; *Rapport mensuel*, January 1917, 11, 16-17; Justinard, *Le caïd Goundafi*, 141-43.

43. *L'Afrique française* 27, nos. 1-2 (January-February, 1917):18.

44. De Lamothe to Lyautey, 14 June 1917, 5-6, SHAT, Maroc, 3H, 589, Marrakech, 1917; Justinard, "Notre action dans le Sous," 551; *L'Afrique française* 27, no. 3 (March 1917):90.

45. Gouraud to de Lamothe, 10 February 1917, in MAE, Nantes, Maroc, Région de Marrakech, 629, Colonne du Sous, 1917; de Lamothe to Lyautey, 14 June 1917, 5, SHAT, Maroc, 3H, 589, Marrakech, 1917.

46. De Lamothe to Lyautey, 14 June 1917, 6 and Lyautey to Minister of War Paul Painlevé, 11 August 1917, both in SHAT, Maroc, 3H, 589, Marrakech, 1917.

47. De Lamothe to Lyautey, 14 June 1917, 7, SHAT, Maroc, 3H, 589, Marrakech, 1917; Justinard, *Le caïd Goundafi*, 146-47.

48. De Lamothe to Lyautey, 14 June 1917, 9, SHAT, Maroc, 3H, 589, Marrakech, 1917.

49. De Lamothe to Lyautey, 14 June 1917, 9 and Lyautey to Minister of War Paul Painlevé, 11 August 1917, both in SHAT, Maroc, 3H, 589, Marrakech, 1917; Lyautey to Diplomatie-Guerre, 26 April 1917, SHAT, Maroc, 3H, 94, Situation politique et militaire du Maroc, 1 janvier 1917-31 décembre 1917; Journal de marche, SHAT, Maroc, 3H, 1066, Colonne du Souss, 1917; *L'Afrique française* 27, no. 4 (April 1917):144, nos. 5-6 (May-June 1917):185; Justinard, *Le caïd Goundafi*, 148-55. On the battle at Ouijjane, see *L'Afrique française* 27, nos. 5-6 (May-June 1917):187-88. For a general account of the Sous column, see Henry Dugard [Louis Thomas], *La conquête du Maroc: La colonne du Sous (janvier-juin 1917)* (Paris: Perrin et Cie., 1918).

50. De Lamothe to Lyautey, 14 June 1917, 21 and Lyautey to Painlevé, 11 August 1917, both in SHAT, Maroc, 3H, 589, Marrakech, 1917; *L'Afrique française* 27, nos. 5-6 (May-June 1917):192; 29, nos. 7-8 (July-August 1919):230. On the career of el-Hiba, see René de Segonzac, "El Hiba, fils de Ma El Ainin," parts 1 and 2, *Renseignements coloniaux et documents*, no. 3, pp. 62-69, supplement to *L'Afrique française* 27, no. 3 (March 1917) and *Renseignements coloniaux et documents*, no. 4, pp. 90-94, supplement to *L'Afrique française* 27, no. 4 (April 1917).

51. De Lamothe to Lyautey, 14 June 1917, 23, SHAT, Maroc, 3H, 589, Marrakech, 1917.

52. De Lamothe to Lyautey, 14 June 1917, 23-24, SHAT, Maroc, 3H, 589, Marrakech, 1917. On el-Goundafi's croix de guerre, see *Bulletin Officiel* 7, no. 278 (18 February 1918):172-73. Justinard became the foremost French expert on the Berber tribes of the Sous. See Justinard, *Manuel de berbère marocain (dialecte chleuh)* (Paris: Gilmoto, [1916]); *Manuel de berbère marocain (dialecte rifain)* (Paris: Geuthner, 1926); "Poèmes chleuhs recueillis au Sous," *Revue du monde musulman* 60 (1925):63-107; "Notes d'histoire et littérature berbères," *Hespéris* 5 (1925):227-38 and 8 (1928):333-56; "Notes sur l'histoire du Sous au XIXème siècle," *Hespéris* 5 (1925):265-76 and 6 (1926):351-64; *Les Aït Ba Amran*, vol. 8, part 1 of Mission scientifique du Maroc and Direction Générale des Affaires Indigènes et Service des Renseignements, *Villes et tribus du Maroc: Documents et renseignements* (Paris: Honoré Champion, 1930); "Notes sur l'histoire du Sous au XVIème siècle," in Direction Générale des Affaires Indigènes, *Les Archives marocaines* 29 (Paris: Honoré Champion, 1933); "Folklore des berbères marocains," *Hommes et mondes* 16, no. 63 (October 1951):82-90.

53. De Lamothe to Lyautey, 14 June 1917, 24, SHAT, Maroc, 3H, 589, Marrakech, 1917. Houmad was removed as pasha of Taroudant in 1926.

54. De Lamothe to Lyautey, 14 June 1917, 22, 25-26, SHAT, Maroc, 3H, 589, Marrakech, 1917.

55. Lyautey to Painlevé, 11 August 1917, SHAT, Maroc, 3H, 589, Marrakech, 1917.

56. Captain R. Delmas-Fort, "Étude sur les tribus Chtoukas du Souss," CHEAM report, May 1947, 66; "Les Confins sud de la région de Marrakech en août 1922," *L'Afrique française* 32, no. 9 (September 1922):398-400; Justinard, *Le caïd Goundafi*, 159. On el-Goundafi at Tiznit, see Justinard, *Le caïd Goundafi*, 157-97 and Justinard, "Notre action dans le Sous," 551-53. Justinard believed that el-Goundafi was poorly treated by the French administration, including Lyautey, and unceremoniously dropped when he was no longer useful. El-Goundafi died at Marrakesh in 1928. For his work in the Sous Justinard was promoted to *chef de bataillon* and made an officer of the Legion of Honor. He was seriously wounded in an airplane accident during the Rif War. From 1931 until his retirement in 1937 (in the medina at Salé) Justinard directed the Section Sociologique of the Direction des Affaires Indigènes in Rabat.

57. Justinard, "Notre action dans le Sous," 548; Justinard, *Le caïd Goundafi*, 126.

58. Justinard, "Notre action dans le Sous," 551.

59. On the evolution of the *politique des grands caïds*, see Colonel Marie-Joseph de Mas-Latrie, "La politique des grands caïds au Maroc," *Revue militaire française* 100, no. 111 (1 September 1930):359-94.

Chapter 6

1. Guillaume de Tarde, "L'Urbanisme en Afrique du Nord," in Congrès international de l'urbanisme aux colonies et dans les pays de latitude intertropical, *L'Urbanisme aux colonies et dans les pays tropicaux*, ed. Jean Royer, 2 vols. (La Charité-sur-Loire and Paris: Delayance, 1932-35), 1:29. Also see, Henri de la Casinière, *Les municipalités marocaines: Leur développement, leur législation* (Casablanca: Imprimerie de la Vigie Marocaine, 1924), 88 and Paul-Louis Rivière, *Précis de législation marocaine* (Paris: Recueil Sirey, 1927), 58-59. Separation was not a one-way street. Moroccans also desired some distance between themselves and their French "protectors." See Rivet, *Lyautey et l'institution du protectorat français au Maroc*, 3:157. On Lyautey's "urbanism," see Rivet, *Lyautey et l'institution du protectorat français au Maroc*, 3:147-60 and Gwendolyn Wright, *The Politics of Design in French Colonial Urbanism* (Chicago: University of Chicago Press, 1991).

2. Henri Prost, "Le développement de l'urbanisme dans le protectorat du Maroc de 1914 à 1923," in *L'Urbanisme aux colonies*, 1:68.

3. On the Hassan tower, see Jacques Caillé, *La mosquée de Hassan à Rabat* (Paris: Arts et Métiers Graphiques, 1954).

4. Lyautey to de Vogüé, 10 October 1907, in Lyautey, "Lettres de Rabat," 286. For the history of Muslim Rabat, see Janet L. Abu-Lughod, *Rabat: Urban Apartheid in Morocco* (Princeton: Princeton University Press, 1980) and Jacques Caillé, *La ville de Rabat jusqu'au protectorat français: Histoire et archéologie*, 3 vols. (Paris: Vanoest Éditions d'Art et d'Histoire, 1949), which includes maps and photographs.

5. Lyautey, "A l'Université des Annales," 10 December 1926, in Lyautey, *Paroles d'action*, 451. Of the four "twin cities" only in Rabat was there a European community of any appreciable size. The building of Fez's European city only began in earnest in 1926 after the Rif war. See Mohamed Yakhlef, "La municipalité de Fez à l'époque du protectorat (1912-1956)," 3 vols. (Thèse de doctorat d'état en histoire contemporaine du Maroc, Université Libre de Bruxelles, 1990), 1:198.

6. On Prost in Morocco, see Wright, *The Politics of Design in French Colonial Urbanism*. For a summary of Prost's career, see Jean Royer, "Henri Prost, urbaniste," *Urbanisme* 34, no. 88 (1965):2-31.

7. For example, see the summary of street, sewer, and sanitation projects in Captain Robert Normand, "Rabat: Les débuts d'une municipalité au Maroc," *Renseignements coloniaux et documents*, no. 1, pp. 18-20, supplement to *L'Afrique française* 24, no. 1 (January 1914).

8. See Lyautey, "Directives pour la création de Rabat," 5 December 1913, in Lyautey, *Lyautey l'Africain*, 1:179-180. On Rabat's "interior" and "exterior" walls, see Abu-Lughod, *Rabat*, 114-17.

9. Mission scientifique du Maroc et Direction Générale des Affaires Indigènes et Service des Renseignements. *Villes et tribus du Maroc: Documents et renseignements*, 11 vols. (Paris: Éditions Ernest Leroux, 1915-32), 4:26-28; Abu-Lughod, *Rabat*, 157-60.

10. Prost, "Le développement de l'urbanisme," in *L'Urbanisme aux colonies*, 1:66.

11. Jules Borély, Lyautey's director of the Service des Beaux-Arts et des Monuments Historiques, later denounced the architectural style as "pseudo-Moroccan." He called for a new architecture for Rabat, based on a return to classic Oriental forms and proportions, bereft of "vain bourgeois decoration." See Borély, "Rabat, ville française," in *De Rabat-Salé et sa région: Guide touristique, historique* (Casablanca: Syndicat d'Initiative, 1931), 34-36. For a description of the new city and the protectorate's public architecture in 1922, see *Rabat-Salé et la région: Guide du voyageur, du touriste, et de l'artiste pour les villes de Rabat, de Salé et leur hinterland* (Rabat: Comité d'Initiative et de Tourisme de la Région de Rabat-Salé, [1922]).

12. Prost, "Le développement de l'urbanisme," in *L'Urbanisme aux colonies*, 1:70.

13. De Tarde, "L'Urbanisme en Afrique du Nord," in *L'Urbanisme aux colonies*, 1:31.

14. *Encyclopédie de l'Islam* 54 (circa 1936):1162, cited in Abu-Lughod, *Rabat*, 150.

15. Abu-Lughod, *Rabat*, 162, 195, and throughout chapters 8 and 9; De la Casinière, *Les municipalités marocaines*, 108-09. For the status of the Prost plan about 1922, see Abu-Lughod, *Rabat*, 196-201. For a positive evaluation of the methods and accomplishments of urban planning in Morocco, see De la Casinière, *Les municipalités marocaines*, 81-110.

16. Normand, "Rabat," 13. On the old order of things in Rabat, see *Villes et tribus du Maroc*, 4:29-31.

17. Normand, "Rabat," 16-17.

18. Normand, "Rabat," 16; Scham, *Lyautey in Morocco*, 76-78, 82.

19. Ville de Rabat, "Procès-verbal de la délibération de la Commission municipale du 3 novembre 1917," in Bibliothèque Générale et Archives, Rabat, Protectorate Archives, File Box: Municipalitiés, Dossier: Rabat, Commissions municipales: 1912-1925, Chemise: 1917 (hereafter cited as BGA, PA, file box name or number, dossier, chemise); Normand, "Rabat," 16. Born in Rabat in 1857, Bargach was named customs officer *(amin el-diouana)*

of Rabat in 1885. Under Sultan Abd el-Aziz he was appointed *khalifa* of Rabat, then pasha of Tangier, a post that he held for four years. Bargach returned to Rabat as both *khalifa* and customs officer until he was named *caïd* of the city. See Ville de Rabat, "Procès-verbal de la délibération de la Commission municipale du 3 novembre 1917," in BGA, PA, Municipalités, Rabat, Commissions municipales: 1912-1925, 1917.

20. Normand, "Rabat," 16-17; Scham, *Lyautey in Morocco*, 84-85.

21. *Villes et tribus du Maroc*, 4:33.

22. Lyautey, "Arrêté," 5 June 1912, in BGA, PA, Municipalités, Rabat, Commissions municipales: 1912-1925, 1912-1913 and Lyautey to Moinier, 18 June 1912, SHAT, 3H, 331, Administration Indigène, Personnel du Service des Renseignements.

23. Lyautey, "Arrêté," 21 October 1912, in BGA, PA, Municipalités, Rabat, Commissions municipales: 1912-1925, 1912-1913.

24. "Dahir portant création de Commissions municipales à Casablanca et à Rabat," 27 June 1913, in BGA, PA, Municipalités, Rabat, Commissions municipales: 1912 à 1925, 1912-1913; De la Casinière, *Les municipalités marocaines*, 8-10. By 1917 only the representatives of the departments of finance, public works, and health and the *mohtaseb* were de jure members of the commission; by 1923 they attended meetings only as technical consultants without voting rights. See De la Casinière, *Les municipalités marocaines*, 15. On Lyautey's policy of association with the urban elite, see Rivet, *Lyautey et l'institution du protectorat français au Maroc*, 2:156-60.

25. Scham, *Lyautey in Morocco*, 84-85.

26. See Comité national du centenaire de la naissance du maréchal Lyautey, *Livre d'or du centenaire de la naissance du maréchal Lyautey* (Casablanca: L'Office Marocain de Diffusion, [1954]), 198.

27. "Arrêté viziriel du 5 juillet 1913 portant nomination des membres de la Commission municipale de Rabat," in BGA, PA, Municipalités, Rabat, Commissions municipales: 1912-1925, 1912-1913. These population statistics are from the census of August 1913 where the total European population of Rabat was listed as 4,093. See Normand, "Rabat," 30.

28. See "Dahir du 5 juillet 1914 portant à huit le nombre des membres notables français de la Commission municipale de Rabat," *Bulletin Officiel du Protectorat de la République française au Maroc* 3, no. 90 (17 July 1914):587 (hereafter *Bulletin Officiel*). The membership of the commission was increased to twenty-four in 1920—twelve Frenchmen, twelve Moroccans (ten Muslims, two Jews)—then to thirty in 1923. See "Arrêté viziriel du 14 avril 1920 fixant le nombre des membres de la Commission municipale mixte de Rabat," *Bulletin Officiel* 9, no. 392 (27 April 1920):702 and "Arrêté viziriel du 13 janvier 1923 portant designation des notables de la ville de Rabat appelés à faire partie de la Commission municipale mixte de cette ville en 1923," *Bulletin Officiel* 12, no. 535 (23 January 1923):102.

29. For the names and occupations of the French and Moroccan members of the Rabat municipal commission, see the appropriate "Arrêté viziriel portant nomination des membres de la Commission municipale de Rabat" in *Bulletin Officiel* 2, no. 37 (11 July 1913):232-33; 3, no. 90 (17 July 1914):590; 5, no. 181 (10 April 1916):414; 6, no. 243 (18 June 1917):670; 9, no. 392 (27 April 1920):702-03; 10, no. 457 (26 July 1921):1158-59; 10, no. 479 (27 December 1921):2002; 12, no. 535 (23 January 1923):102; 13, no. 594 (11 March 1924):493; and 14, no. 642 (10 February 1925):218-19.

30. Chef des Services Municipaux René Brunet, "Feuille de Renseignements: Abderrahman Ben El Hadj Mohamed Ben Ahmed Bargach," 1935, BGA, PA, Région Civile du Gharb, Rabat, Ville de Rabat. Abderrahman Bargach was born in Rabat in 1872, the son of a wealthy merchant who had made several trips to Europe for the Makhzen. Well-considered, talented, and the heir to a great fortune, he was pasha of Casablanca at age twenty. After success in that city and postings to Marrakesh (as secretary to the Makhzen) and Mogador (as pasha), he was appointed *caïd* of Rabat in 1917.

31. Chef des Services Municipaux Jean Courtin, "Feuille de Renseignements: Si Abdennebi Souissi," 11 April 1922 and Courtin, "Feuille de Renseignements: Si El Hadj Abdelaziz Ben M'Hammed Souissi," 29 July 1929, both in BGA, PA, Région Civile du Gharb, Rabat, Ville de Rabat.

32. Chef des Services Municipaux Jean Courtin, "Feuille de Renseignements: Si Ahmed Zebdi," 29 July 1929 and Chef de la Région, "Note," 1935, both in BGA, PA, Région Civile du Gharb, Rabat, Ville de Rabat.

33. Chef des Services Municipaux René Brunet, "Fiche de Renseignements: Si Mohammed Ghennam," 1935, BGA, PA, Région Civile du Gharb, Rabat, Ville de Rabat.

34. Consul de France à Rabat Louis Rais to Lyautey, 10 March 1914, in BGA, PA, Municipalités, Rabat, Commissions municipales: 1912-1925, 1914.

35. Normand, "Rabat," 18.

36. "Dahir du 8 avril 1917 sur l'organisation municipale," Bulletin Officiel 6, no. 236 (30 April 1917):486-89; De la Casinière, Les municipalités marocaines, 12-21; Paul Decroux, La vie municipale au Maroc (Lyon: Bosc Frères, M. et L. Riou, 1932), 29, 33-36, 55, 60-62.

37. Normand, "Rabat," 14; Scham, Lyautey in Morocco, 54, 78-79.

38. Normand, "Rabat," 14, 32. For the protectorate subsidies to Rabat's municipal budget from 1913 to 1918, see De la Casinière, Les municipalités marocaines, 32.

39. Joseph Court, "Note au sujet des propositions budgétaires des municipalités pour 1917," n.d. and "Note sur les budgets municipaux," 14 January 1918; Directeur des Affaires Civiles Guillaume de Tarde to Sécrétaire Général du Protectorat Lallier du Coudray, 14 February 1918, all in BGA, PA, Municipalités, Rabat, Budgets municipaux: 1914-1920, Notes de principes; De la Casinière, Les municipalités marocaines, 34-35, 57. On the history and reform of the gate and market taxes, see De la Casinière, Les municipalités marocaines, 50-65.

40. Ville de Rabat, "Réunion de la Commission municipale du 17 février 1917" and Ville de Rabat, "Commission municipale, Séance du 13 décembre 1917," both in BGA, PA, Municipalités, Rabat, Commissions municipales: 1912-1925, 1917; de Tarde to Lallier du Coudray, 14 February 1918, in BGA, PA, Municipalités, Rabat, Budgets municipaux: 1914-1920, Notes de principes. Well into the 1930s Rabat required an annual subsidy to balance its budget. See Decroux, La vie municipale au Maroc, 277.

41. L'Écho du Maroc, 20 November 1920.

42. Ville de Rabat, "Réunion de la Commission municipale du 17 février 1917," in BGA, PA, Municipalités, Rabat, Commissions municipales: 1912-1925, 1917. On the fiscal perimeters, see Decroux, La vie municipale au Maroc, 36-39.

43. Ville de Rabat, "Procès-verbal de la séance du 17 décembre 1917," in BGA, PA, Municipalités, Rabat, Commissions municipales: 1912-1925, 1917.

44. Ville de Rabat, "Procès-verbal de la séance du 2 février 1918," in BGA, PA, Municipalités, Rabat, Commissions municipales: 1912-1925, 1918.

45. L'Écho du Maroc, 30 November 1920.

46. Ville de Rabat, "Extrait du registre des déliberations de la Commission municipale, séance plénière du 21 octobre 1922," in BGA, PA, Municipalités, Rabat, Commissions municipales: 1912-1925, 1922; La Vigie marocaine, 24 October 1922.

47. Commission municipale de la Ville de Rabat, "Séance plénière du 31 décembre 1924," in BGA, PA, Municipalités, Rabat, Commissions municipales: 1912-1925, 1924.

48. Commission municipale de Rabat, "Séance du 18 juin 1925," 7, and Commission municipale de Rabat, "Procès-verbal de la séance du 26 novembre 1925," 23, both in BGA, PA, Municipalités, Rabat, Commissions municipales: 1912-1925, 1925.

49. Commission municipale de Rabat, "Procès-verbal de la séance du 26 novembre 1925," 27, in BGA, PA, Municipalités, Rabat, Commissions municipales: 1912-1925, 1925.

50. See Decroux, La vie municipale au Maroc, 365-72.

51. Normand, "Rabat," 20-22. Also see, "Compte-rendu des séances du Conseil du Gouvernement des 6 et 7 juin 1913," in Bulletin Officiel 2, no. 33 (13 June 1913):174.

52. Normand, "Rabat," 22-23.
53. Normand, "Rabat," 23; De la Casinière, *Les municipalités marocaines*, 128-30; Ville de Rabat, "Séance de la Commission Municipale de Rabat du 30 mai 1916," in BGA, PA, Municipalités, Rabat, Commissions municipales: 1912-1925, 1916. For the status of the water question in 1916, see Lucien Roussel, "Rabat en 1916," *Revue du monde musulman* 35 (1917-18):21-25.
54. See "Arrêté viziriel du 19 janvier 1919 déclarant d'utilité publique les travaux d'adduction et de distribution à Rabat des eaux d'Aïn Attig et d'Aïn Reboula," *Bulletin Officiel* 6, no. 276 (4 February 1918):90 and "Arrêté viziriel du 29 juin 1918 déclarant d'utilité publique les travaux à exécuter par la Société Marocaine de Distribution d'Eau, de Gaz, et d'Électricité pour l'amener à Rabat des eaux d'Aïn Reboula," *Bulletin Officiel* 6, no. 303 (12 August 1918):779.
55. Petit, "La question de l'eau douce," *L'Écho du Maroc*, 15 December 1920.
56. Petit, "La question de l'eau douce," *L'Écho du Maroc*, 15 December 1920 and "Le barrage du Bou-Regreg," *L'Écho du Maroc*, 17 December 1920.
57. Services Généraux du Protectorat, *Rapport trimestriel d'ensemble*, January-February-March 1923, A-4.
58. See Will D. Swearingen, *Moroccan Mirages: Agrarian Dreams and Deceptions, 1912-1986* (Princeton: Princeton University Press, 1987), 166.
59. Ville de Rabat, "Séances de la Commission municipale de Rabat," 3, 5, and 6 July and 18 September 1916, in BGA, PA, Municipalités, Rabat, Commissions municipales: 1912-1925, 1916; De la Casinière, *Les municipalités marocaines*, 147.
60. Ville de Rabat, "Séance de la Commission municipale de Rabat du 18 septembre 1916," in BGA, PA, Municipalités, Rabat, Commissions municipales: 1912-1925, 1916.
61. Ville de Rabat, "Séance de la Commission municipale de Rabat du 18 septembre 1916," in BGA, PA, Municipalités, Rabat, Commissions municipales: 1912-1925, 1916; De la Casinière, *Les municipalités marocaines*, 147.
62. Ville de Rabat, "Séance de la Commission municipale du 24 février 1919," in BGA, PA, Municipalités, Rabat, Commissions municipales: 1912-1925, 1919; De la Casinière, *Les municipalités marocaines*, 147-48.
63. Ville de Rabat, "Séance de la Commission municipale du 24 février 1919," in BGA, PA, Municipalités, Rabat, Commissions municipales: 1912-1925, 1919.
64. Ville de Rabat, "Procès-verbal de la réunion de la Commission municipale (section française), 7 juillet 1919," in BGA, PA, Municipalités, Rabat, Commissions municipales: 1912-1925, 1919.
65. *L'Écho du Maroc*, 14, 15, and 19 August 1920.
66. *L'Écho du Maroc*, 28 August 1920.
67. *L'Écho du Maroc*, 4, 5, 14, and 16 December 1920. On Lyautey's rocky relations with the urban colonial community and close ties to "big capital" after the First World War, see Rivet, *Lyautey et l'institution du protectorat français au Maroc*, 3:52-62, 85-89.
68. *L'Écho du Maroc*, 30 November 1920.
69. *L'Écho du Maroc*, 21 December 1920.
70. Ville de Rabat, "Session extraordinaire, 15 novembre 1921," in BGA, PA, Municipalités, Rabat, Commissions municipales: 1912-1925, 1921. Rabat never measured up to nor broke loose from the plan. In 1952 the city had a total population of 170,000 and covered an area equal to that of Lyon, which had a population of nearly 600,000 inhabitants. See Agence Havas marocaine, Guide touristique Havas, Le Maroc, 2nd ed. (Casablanca: Havas, 1952), 72.
71. Ville de Rabat, "Session extraordinaire, 15 novembre 1921," in BGA, PA, Municipalités, Commissions municipales: 1912-1925, 1921.
72. De la Casinière, *Les municipalités marocaines*, 148, 155-57.
73. *Bulletin Officiel* 3, no. 90 (17 July 1914):570.

74. Ville de Rabat, "Procès-verbal de la séance du 2 février 1918" and "Séance du 26 décembre 1918," both in BGA, PA, Municipalités, Rabat, Commissions municipales: 1912-1925, 1918. Also see, *L'Écho du Maroc,* 23 September 1919 and 23 December 1920.
75. *Bulletin Officiel* 5, no. 176 (6 March 1916):276-77; *Rapport mensuel,* April 1923, i.
76. Ville de Rabat, "Commission municipale, Session Extraordinaire, 25 novembre 1921," in BGA, PA, Municipalités, Rabat, Commissions municipales: 1912-1925, 1921.
77. Henri Gerlier and Georges Guerard, *Rabat-Salé et la région* (Rabat: n.p., [1917]), 7-10, 31, 37.
78. Ville de Rabat, "Séance du 24 octobre 1919," in BGA, PA, Municipalités, Rabat, Commissions municipales: 1912-1925, 1919. On the crisis, see *L'Écho du Maroc,* 16, 17, 19, and 22 October 1919 and Lyautey to Minister of Foreign Affairs Stéphen Pichon, 21 October 1919, in Lyautey, *Lyautey l'Africain,* 4:50-53.
79. *L'Écho du Maroc,* 25 and 27 October 1919. Also see Rivet, *Lyautey et l'institution du protectorat français au Maroc,* 3:56-57, 119-24.
80. *L'Écho du Maroc,* 25 and 28 November 1919.
81. This was particularly true after February 1919 when newspaper correspondents were permitted to attend the commission sessions. See Ville de Rabat, "Séance de la Commission municipale du 24 février 1919," in BGA, PA, Municipalités, Rabat, Commissions municipales: 1912-1925, 1919.
82. Commission municipale de Rabat, "Séance du 26 décembre 1918," in BGA, PA, Municipalités, Rabat, Commissions municipales: 1912-1925, 1918; Normand, "Rabat," 27. On the persistent French effort to demolish the El-Gza gate, see Ville de Rabat, "Séance du 22 juin 1922," in BGA, PA, Municipalités, Rabat, Commissions municipales: 1912-1925, 1922. The significant resident European population in the *medina* (which seemed uninterested in moving) also demanded the same city services as Europeans residing in the new city. This was both difficult and expensive. It prevented, for example, the creation of a wholly Moroccan police force for the *medina*. Europeans refused to recognize the authority of the traditional native night watchmen or even uniformed Moroccan policemen. As long as there were Europeans in the *medina*, European policemen had to be there as well. Ville de Rabat, "Extrait du registre des délibérations de la Commission municipale (séance plénière du 21 octobre 1922)," 6-8, in BGA, PA, Municipalités, Rabat, Commissions municipales: 1912-1925, 1922.
83. Ville de Rabat, Commission municipale, "Séance du 26 décembre 1918," in BGA, PA, Municipalités, Rabat, Commissions municipales: 1912-1925, 1918. Also see, Ville de Rabat, "Séance de la Commission municipale du 13 avril 1918," in BGA, PA, Municipalités, Rabat, Commissions municipales: 1912-1925, 1918.
84. Ville de Rabat, Commission municipale, "Séance du 26 décembre 1918" and "Séance de la Commission municipale du 6 juillet 1918," both in BGA, PA, Municipalités, Rabat, Commissions municipales: 1912-1925, 1918.
85. Ville de Rabat, Commission municipale, "Séance du 26 décembre 1918," BGA, PA, Municipalités, Rabat, Commissions municipales: 1912-1925, 1918.
86. Ville de Rabat, Commission municipale, "Séance du 26 décembre 1918," in BGA, PA, Municipalités, Rabat, Commissions municipales: 1912-1925, 1918.
87. Ville de Rabat, Commission municipale, "Séance du 26 décembre 1918," in BGA, PA, Municipalités, Rabat, Commissions municipales: 1912-1925, 1918.
88. Ville de Rabat, Commission municipale, "Séance du 26 décembre 1918," in BGA, PA, Municipalités, Rabat, Commissions municipales: 1912-1925, 1918.
89. Ville de Rabat, Commission municipale, "Séance du 26 décembre 1918," in BGA, PA, Municipalités, Rabat, Commissions municipales: 1912-1925, 1918.
90. Ville de Rabat, Commission municipale, "Séance du 26 décembre 1918," in BGA, PA, Municipalités, Rabat, Commissions municipales: 1912-1925, 1918.

91. Ville de Rabat, Commission municipale, "Séance du 26 décembre 1918," in BGA, PA, Municipalités, Rabat, Commissions municipales: 1912-1925, 1918.
92. L'Écho du Maroc, 22 September, 18 and 29 October 1919.
93. "Extrait du Procès-verbal de la séance de la Commission municipale de Rabat du 28 juillet 1917" and Commission municipale de Rabat, "Séance du 3 septembre 1917," both in BGA, PA, Municipalités, Rabat, Commissions municipales: 1912-1925, 1917; Lyautey, "Réception de la colonie française," 14 July 1917, in Lyautey, Paroles d'action, 226.
94. Commission municipale de la Ville de Rabat, "Séance du 18 décembre 1923 (section française)" and Commission municipale de Rabat, "Séance du 18 juin 1925," 20, both in BGA, PA, Municipalités, Rabat, Commissions municipales: 1912-1925, 1923 and 1925. In the end, both the Avenue and the Place were named for Lyautey.
95. Commission municipale de la Ville de Rabat, "Séance plénière du 12 avril 1924," 30-33, in BGA, PA, Municipalités, Rabat, Commissions municipales: 1912-1925, 1924.
96. Commission municipale de la Ville de Rabat, "Séance plénière du 6 juillet 1924," 21, in BGA, PA, Municipalités, Rabat, Commissions municipales: 1912-1925, 1924.
97. Commission municipale de Rabat, "Séance du 18 juin 1925," 18-19, in BGA, PA, Municipalités, Rabat, Commissions municipales: 1912-1925, 1925.
98. See "A la réunion des chambres représentatives françaises: chambres de commerce et chambres d'agriculture," 24 November 1919, in Lyautey, Paroles d'action, 300.

Chapter 7

1. Colonel Antoine Targe, commandant la Subdivision de Casablanca, to Lyautey, 30 November 1914, BGA, PA, 24 (Casablanca-Ville), Casablanca-Ville, Ben Kirane. On the Muslim personalities in Casablanca in 1914, see Villes et tribus du Maroc, 1:59-60.
2. Between 1907 and 1912 Casablanca's population increased from 25,000 to 47,000, an average annual increase of 4,400. The 1913 census put the population at 60,000, triple the previous annual increases. See Joseph Goulven, "Casablanca, la commerçante," Renseignements coloniaux et documents, no. 2, pp. 75-81, supplement to L'Afrique française 24, no. 2 (February 1914). On the history of Casablanca, see André Adam, Casablanca: Essai sur la transformation de la société marocaine au contact de l'Occident, 2 vols. (Paris: Centre National de la Recherche Scientifique, 1968) and Adam, Histoire de Casablanca, des origines à 1914 (Gap: Éditions Ophrys, 1968).
3. Lyautey, "Réception offerte à M. Paul Deschanel, président de la Chambre des Députés," 3 May 1914, in Lyautey, Paroles d'action, 104.
4. Ministre de France au Maroc Regnault to Moinier, commandant le Corps de Débarquement à Casablanca, 25 August 1910, SHAT, Maroc, 3H, 331, Lettres du Ministre de France à Tanger.
5. Moinier to Chargé de France à Tanger Robert de Billy, 21 November 1910, SHAT, Maroc, 3H, 330, Service des Renseignements, 1909-1911.
6. Moinier to de Billy, 21 November 1910.
7. Moinier to Minister of War Adolphe Messimy, 6 January 1912, SHAT, Maroc, 3H, 330, Service des Renseignements, 1909-1911.
8. See Villes et tribus du Maroc, 1:59, 76.
9. Targe to Lyautey, 23 October 1914, BGA, PA, 24, Casablanca-Ville, El Hadj Omar Tazi, Pacha de Casablanca.
10. Chef de Bataillon Georges Tribalet, Chef du Service des Renseignements de la Subdivision de Casablanca, to Lyautey, 21 October 1914, BGA, PA, 24, Casablanca-Ville, Omar Tazi.
11. Tribalet to Lyautey, 21 October 1914.

12. Tribalet to Lyautey, 21 October 1914; Targe to Lyautey, 23 October 1914.
13. Targe to Lyautey, 23 October 1914; Tribalet to Lyautey, 21 October 1914.
14. Targe to Lyautey, 23 October 1914.
15. Lyautey to Targe, 5 November 1914, BGA, PA, 24, Casablanca-Ville, Relations entre le Pacha et le Cadhi de Casablanca, 1915. This document is misfiled.
16. Targe to Lyautey, 30 November 1914.
17. Targe to Lyautey, 30 November 1914.
18. Targe to Lyautey, 30 November 1914.
19. Tribalet to Lyautey, 21 October 1914.
20. Targe to Lyautey, 23 October 1914.
21. Colonel Jean Calmel, commandant la Région de Casablanca, to Lyautey, 10 September 1917, BGA, PA, 24, Casablanca-Ville, Omar Tazi.
22. Tribalet to Lyautey, 21 October 1914.
23. Tribalet to Lyautey, 21 October 1914.
24. Rivet, *Lyautey et l'institution du protectorat français au Maroc,* 1:89.
25. Lyautey to Chef des Services Municipaux de Casablanca Alfred Collieaux, 7 December 1914, BGA, PA, 24, Casablanca-Ville, Omar Tazi; Tribalet to Lyautey, 7 December 1914, BGA, PA, 24, Casablanca-Ville, Omar Tazi; Captain Louis Coustillière [Subdivision de Casablanca] to Lyautey, 6 December 1914, BGA, PA, 24, Casablanca-Ville, Omar Tazi; Colonel Henri Berriau, Chef du Cabinet Politique, to Subdivision Casablanca, 7 December 1914, BGA, PA, 24, Casablanca-Ville, Omar Tazi.
26. Le Commissaire, Chef de la Sûreté Pierre Carrieu, "Rapport à M. le Colonel Commandant la Subdivision à Casablanca," 9 December 1914, BGA, PA, 27, Guerre, 1914-1918: Suspects, Surveillance, Propagande, Divers.
27. Lyautey to Collieaux, 7 December 1914.
28. Carrieu, "Rapport à M. le Colonel Commandant la Subdivision à Casablanca," 22 December 1914, BGA, PA, 24, Casablanca-Ville, Omar Tazi; Collieaux to Targe, 18 January 1915, BGA, PA, 24, Casablanca-Ville, Relations entre le Pacha et le Cadhi de Casablanca.
29. Targe to Secrétariat Général du Gouvernement Chérifien, Cabinet Politique, 13 January 1915, BGA, PA, 24, Casablanca-Ville, Ben Kirane; "Notice individuelle: Si Abdelkrim Ould Bou Azza Ben Msik," n.d. [1914], BGA, PA, 24, Casablanca-Ville, Ben Kirane.
30. "Notice individuelle: Si Abdelkrim Ben Ahmed el-Heddaoui," n.d. [1914], BGA, PA, 24, Casablanca-Ville, Remplacement de l'amin du Mostafad et du khalifa du Pacha de Casablanca; Targe to Secrétariat Général, 13 January 1915.
31. "Notice individuelle: Si Abdelkrim Ould Bou Azza Ben Msik;" Targe to Secrétariat Général, 13 January 1915; Collieaux to Targe, 18 January 1915.
32. Région de Casablanca, "Feuille de Renseignements concernant Si El Hadj Omar Tazi, Pacha de Casablanca," n.d., BGA, PA, 24, Casablanca-Ville, Omar Tazi; nomination sheet proposing Omar Tazi for the rank of *grand officier* of the Order of Ouissam Alaouite Chérifien in Calmel to Lyautey, 10 September 1917, BGA, PA, 24, Casablanca-Ville, Omar Tazi.
33. Tribalet to Rabat, n.d. [early 1916], BGA, PA, 24, Casablanca-Ville, Omar Tazi; Calmel to Lyautey, 10 September 1917, BGA, PA, 24, Casablanca-Ville, Omar Tazi; "Note, Objet: Politique indigène," 7 September 1918, BGA, PA, 24, Casablanca-Ville, Omar Tazi; Lyautey to Région Casablanca, 9 September 1918, BGA, PA, 24, Casablanca-Ville, Omar Tazi; Lyautey to Région Casablanca, 12 September 1918, BGA, PA, 24, Ville-Casablanca, Abdellatif Tazi, Pacha de Casablanca.
34. Région de Casablanca, "Feuillet de renseignements et de notes concernant Si Hadj Omar Ben Abdelkrim Tazi," n.d., BGA, PA, 24, Casablanca-Ville, Omar Tazi.
35. Targe to Lyautey, 16 January 1915, BGA, PA, 24, Casablanca-Ville, Relations entre le Pacha et le Cadhi de Casablanca.

36. "Feuillet de renseignements et de notes concernant Moulay Ahmed el-Belghiti," n.d. [1917], BGA, PA, 24, Casablanca-Ville, Cadi de Casablanca: Si Ahmed Ben El Mahmoun el-Belghiti. On the judicial organization of Morocco under the French, see Scham, *Lyautey in Morocco*, 162-90.

37. Targe to Lyautey, 16 January 1915; Collieaux to Targe, 18 January 1915, BGA, PA, 24, Casablanca-Ville, Relations entre le Pacha et le Cadhi de Casablanca, 1915. El-Araki was el-Belghiti's predecessor as *cadi*.

38. Tazi to Targe, 13 January 1915, BGA, PA, 24, Casablanca-Ville, Relations entre le Pacha et le Cadhi de Casablanca.

39. Targe to Collieaux, 16 January 1915, BGA, PA, 24, Casablanca-Ville, Relations entre le Pacha et le Cadhi de Casablanca; Targe to Lyautey, 16 January 1915, BGA, PA, 24, Casablanca-Ville, Relations entre le Pacha et le Cadhi de Casablanca.

40. Collieaux to Targe, 18 January 1915, BGA, PA, 24, Casablanca-Ville, Relations entre le Pacha et le Cadhi de Casablanca.

41. Lyautey to Targe, 19 February 1915, BGA, PA, 24, Casablanca-Ville, Relations entre le Pacha et le Cadhi de Casablanca.

42. Collieaux to Targe, 18 January 1915.

43. Collieaux to Targe, 18 January 1915.

44. Collieaux to Lyautey, 1 July 1915, BGA, PA, 24, Casablanca-Ville, el-Belghiti; Pétition des Indigènes de Casablanca to General Jean Calmel, commandant la Subdivision de Casablanca, 26 June 1918, BGA, PA, 24, Casablanca-Ville, el-Belghiti; Calmel to Lyautey, 11 December 1918, BGA, PA, 24, Casablanca-Ville, el-Belghiti.

45. Tazi to Calmel, 6 July 1918, BGA, PA, 24, Casablanca-Ville, el-Belghiti.

46. Tazi to Calmel, 6 July 1918; Calmel to Lyautey, 9 July 1918, BGA, PA, 24, Casablanca-Ville, el-Belghiti; Résidence Générale, Rabat to Calmel, 16 July 1918, BGA, PA, 24, Casablanca-Ville, el-Belghiti; Calmel to Lyautey, 13 August 1918, BGA, PA, 24, Casablanca-Ville, el-Belghiti; Calmel to Lyautey, 11 December 1918, BGA, PA, 24, Casablanca-Ville, el-Belghiti.

47. Collieaux to Lyautey, 1 July 1915.

48. Calmel to Lyautey, 5 July 1915, BGA, PA, 24, Casablanca-Ville, el-Belghiti.

49. Calmel to Lyautey, 9 July 1918; Calmel to Lyautey, 11 December 1918.

50. Calmel to Lyautey, 5 July 1915; Lyautey [Saint-Aulaire] to Calmel, 30 July 1915, BGA, PA, 24, Casablanca-Ville, el-Belghiti.

51. Calmel to Lyautey, 9 July 1918; Calmel to Lyautey, 13 August 1918; Calmel to Lyautey, 11 December 1918.

52. Conseiller du Gouvernement Chérifien Raoul Marc to Commissaire du Gouvernement près les Juridictions Chérifiennes Louis Martin, 4 April 1919, BGA, PA, 24, Casablanca-Ville, el-Belghiti. In 1923 el-Belghiti was appointed *cadi* of Meknès.

53. Lyautey to Région Casablanca, 12 September 1918, BGA, PA, 24, Casablanca-Ville, Abdellatif Tazi, Pacha de Casablanca.

54. Contrôleur Civil Frédéric Weisgerber, Chef de la Circonscription des Doukkala, Mazagan, "Feuille de Renseignements: Si Abdellatif Tazi," n.d., BGA, PA, 24, Casablanca-Ville, Abdellatif Tazi; "Note pour M. Le Directeur des Affaires Indigènes et du Service des Renseignements," 1 April 1919, BGA, PA, 24, Casablanca-Ville, Abdellatif Tazi; Martin to Calmel, 12 April 1919, BGA, PA, 24, Casablanca-Ville, Abdellatif Tazi. In 1918 the peseta hassani was worth about one franc.

55. "Feuillet de Renseignements et de Notes concernant Si Hadj Omar Ben Abdelkrim Tazi," n.d., BGA, PA, 24, Casablanca-Ville, Omar Tazi.

56. Tazi to Calmel, 6 January 1919, BGA, PA, 24, Casablanca-Ville, Abdellatif Tazi.

57. Calmel's notation on Tazi to Calmel, 6 January 1919.

58. Martin to Calmel, 12 April 1919; "Note pour M. le Directeur des Affaires Indigènes et du Service des Renseignements," 1 April 1919.

59. Contrôleur Civil chargé des Affaires Indigènes à Casablanca Joseph Charrier to Secrétaire Général du Protectorat Pierre de Sorbier de Pougnadoresse, "Rapport sur la politique indigène dans la Région Civile de la Chaouïa," No. 15 (15 April 1921), BGA, PA, 24, Casablanca-Ville, Politique Indigène: Rapports de M. Charrier.

60. Délégué à la Résidence Générale de la République française Urbain Blanc to Contrôleur Civil, Chef de la Région Civile de la Chaouïa à Casablanca Alexandre Laurent, 10 April 1921, BGA, PA, 24, Casablanca-Ville, Abdellatif Tazi.

61. Marc to Lyautey, 30 May 1921 in Lyautey to Laurent, 31 May 1921, BGA, PA, 24, Casablanca-Ville, Assainissement du Maghzen de Casablanca.

62. Lyautey to Laurent, 20 April 1921, BGA, PA, 24, Casablanca-Ville, Assainissement du Maghzen de Casablanca.

63. Tazi to Major André Leclerc, Chef du Bureau Régional de Renseignements, 19 and 21 March 1917, BGA, PA, 24, Casablanca-Ville, Mohammed Ben Bouazza, Khalifa du Pacha de Casablanca.

64. Région [Casablanca] to Lyautey, 27 March 1917, BGA, PA, 24, Casablanca-Ville, Mohammed Ben Bouazza.

65. "Feuille de Renseignements et de Notes concernant Si Mohamed Ben Bouazza Ben el-Hejjamia," n.d., BGA, PA, 24, Casablanca-Ville, Mohammed Ben Bouazza.

66. Lyautey to Calmel, 25 April 1919, BGA, PA, 24, Casablanca-Ville, Si Mohamed Ben Taieb el-Bedraoui.

67. Also dismissed was Adel Si Mohammed Ben Hadj Ahmed Messaoudi. Marc to Lyautey, 30 May 1921 in Lyautey to Laurent, 31 May 1921, BGA, PA, 24, Casablanca-Ville, Assainissement du Maghzen de Casablanca.

68. "Notes Annuelles: Boubeker Chantoufi Es Slaoui," 16 January 1923, BGA, PA, 29, Casablanca-Banlieue, Cadhi Si Boubeker Bouchentouf.

69. Blanc to Laurent, 19 July 1920, BGA, PA, 29, Casablanca-Banlieue, Boubeker Bouchentouf.

70. "Notes Annuelles: Boubeker Chantoufi Es Slaoui."

71. Lyautey to Laurent, 20 April 1921, BGA, PA, 24, Casablanca-Ville, Assainissement du Maghzen de Casablanca.

72. Charrier, "Rapport sur la politique . . . ," no. 16 (26 April 1921), BGA, PA, 24, Casablanca-Ville, Politique Indigène: Rapports de M. Charrier.

73. Charrier, "Rapport sur la politique . . . ," no. 16 (26 April 1921).

74. "Feuillet de Renseignements et de Notes concernant Moulay Ahmed Ben Mansour," n.d., BGA, PA, 24, Casablanca-Ville, Moulay Ahmed Ben Mansour.

75. Caïd Moulay Ahmed Ben Mansour, Khalifa du Pacha de Casablanca, to Charrier, 12 April 1921, BGA, PA, 24, Casablanca-Ville, Ben Mansour.

76. Ben Mansour to Charrier, 12 April 1921.

77. Ben Mansour to Charrier, 12 April 1921.

78. Ben Mansour to Charrier, 12 April 1921.

79. Ben Mansour to Charrier, 12 April 1921.

80. Charrier to Lyautey, 26 April 1921, BGA, PA, 24, Casablanca-Ville, Ben Mansour.

81. Charrier, "Rapport sur la politique . . . ," no. 16 (26 April 1921).

82. Charrier, "Rapport sur la politique . . . ," no. 16 (26 April 1921).

83. Lyautey to Marc, 3 May 1921, BGA, PA, 24, Casablanca-Ville, Ben Mansour.

84. Lyautey to Laurent, 7 May 1921, BGA, PA, 24, Casablanca-Ville, Ben Mansour.

85. Charrier, "Rapport sur la politique . . . ," no. 18 (15 June 1921).

86. "Hadj Djilali Ben Guendaoui," 26 April 1921, BGA, PA, 24, Casablanca-Ville, Notables Divers: Feuilles de Renseignements.

87. Feuille de Renseignements: Hadj Djilali Bel Guendaoui, Khalifa du Pacha, 13 December 1921, BGA, PA, Région Civile de la Chaouïa, Casablanca.

88. Contrôleur en Chef de la Région Civile de la Chaouïa Alexandre Laurent to de Sorbier, 5 July 1921 (draft) and Feuille de Renseignements concernant Si Ahmed Ben Sayah el-Abdellaoui, 4 July 1921, both in BGA, PA, 24, Casablanca-Ville, Si Ahmed Ben Sayah.

89. Blanc to Laurent, 22 August 1921, BGA, PA, 24, Casablanca-Ville, Si Ali Bel Hadj Kairouani; Laurent to Blanc, 24 August 1921, BGA, PA, 24, Casablanca-Ville, Kairouani.

90. Laurent to Blanc, 24 August 1921; Feuille de Renseignements: Si Ali Bel Hadj Kairouani, 24 August 1921 (attached to above).

91. Laurent to de Sorbier, 24 January 1922 (draft); and Laurent to de Sorbier, 9 November 1922, both in BGA, PA, 24, Casablanca-Ville, Kairouani.

92. Laurent, nomination form for the Ordre du Ouissam Alaouite Chérifien, 20 April 1922; and Laurent to de Sorbier, 24 April 1922, both in BGA, PA, 24, Casablanca-Ville, El Hadj Djilali Ben Guendaoui.

93. Charrier, "Rapport sur la politique . . . ," no. 17 (15 May 1921).

94. Le Conseiller du Gouvernement Chérifien to Secrétaire Général du Protectorat Georges Duvernoy, 28 October 1927, BGA, PA, 27, Personnel européen: Notes et Avancement, Bertrand. The *commissaires du gouvernement près les juridictions chérifiennes,* attached to the Contrôle Civil, were supervisory officers who, somewhat like public prosecutors, oversaw the justice meted out in the pasha's courts. See "Dahir réglementant la juridiction des Pachas et Caïds," *Bulletin Officiel* 7, no. 306 (2 September 1918):838-39; "Dahir du 25 octobre 1918 nommant les Commissaires du Gouvernement près les Tribunaux des Pachas de Rabat, Salé, Casablanca, et Mazagan," *Bulletin Official* 7, no. 315 (4 November 1918):1106; Scham, *Lyautey in Morocco,* 181-86 and Rivet, *Lyautey et l'institution du protectorat français au Maroc,* 3:193.

95. Laurent to de Sorbier, 24 January 1922 (draft), BGA, PA, 24, Casablanca-Ville, Kairouani.

96. Untitled report on the relationship between Pasha Ben Mansour and Commissaire du Gouvernement près les Juridictions Chérifiennes Jean Peyrou, 20 December 1921, BGA, PA, 24, Casablanca-Ville, Ben Mansour.

97. Untitled report on the relationship between Pasha Ben Mansour and Commissaire du Gouvernement Peyrou, 20 December 1921.

98. Untitled report on the relationship between Pasha Ben Mansour and Commissaire du Gouvernement Peyrou, 20 December 1921.

99. Charrier, "Rapport sur la politique . . . ," no. 17 (15 May 1921).

100. Lyautey to Minister of Foreign Affairs Stéphen Pichon, 2 March 1918, BGA, PA, Administration Civile, Service du Personnel, Contrôles Civils; Nominations, promotions, mutations, 1913 à 1924; Affaires divers, 1919.

101. Untitled report on the relationship between Pasha Ben Mansour and Commissaire du Gouvernement Peyrou, 20 December 1921.

102. Commissaire du Gouvernement près le Tribunal du Pacha, Contrôleur des Juridictions Chérifiennes et des Habous Jean Peyrou to Conseiller du Gouvernement Chérifien Raoul Marc, 31 December 1921, BGA, PA, 24, Casablanca-Ville, Personnel au service du Pacha de Casablanca.

103. Marc to Peyrou, 20 January 1922, BGA, PA, 24, Casablanca-Ville, Personnel au service du Pacha de Casablanca.

104. Laurent's notation, 28 July 1921, on Commissaire du Gouvernement près le Tribunal du Pacha de Casablanca, Contrôleur des Juridictions Chérifiennes et des Habous Gabriel Beaujolin to Marc, 25 July 1921, BGA, PA, Région Civile de la Chaouïa, Casablanca, Cadi Si Mohammed Ben Allalech Chraïbi.

105. Marc to Laurent, 2 June 1921, BGA, PA, Région Civile de la Chaouïa, Casablanca, Chraïbi; Feuille de Renseignements: Si Allal Ben Mohamed Chraïbi, 13 December 1921 and Feuille de Notes Annuelles: Si Allal Chraïbi, 23 January 1923, both in BGA, PA, Région Civile de la Chaouïa, Casablanca, Chraïbi.

106. Beaujolin to Marc, 25 July 1921, BGA, PA, Région Civile de la Chaouïa, Casablanca, Chraïbi.

107. Beaujolin to Laurent, 22 July 1921; and Beaujolin to Marc, 25 July 1921, both in BGA, PA, Région Civile de la Chaouïa, Casablanca, Chraïbi.

108. Beaujolin to Laurent, 22 July 1921.
109. Beaujolin to Marc, 25 July 1921.
110. Charrier's note, 26 July 1921, in Beaujolin to Marc, 25 July 1921. On this matter as an example of the difficulty of making the protectorate work, see Rivet, *Lyautey et l'institution du protectorat français au Maroc,* 3:198-99, 201.
111. Feuille de Renseignements: Si Allal Ben Mohamed Chraïbi, 13 December 1921.
112. Feuille de Notes Annuelles: Si Allal Chraïbi, 23 January 1923.
113. For the Chraïbi-Bou Chentoufi dispute, see Laurent to Marc, 6 October 1924, and Contrôleur Civil, Chef de la Circonscription de Chaouïa-Nord Louis Watin to Marc, 31 January 1925.
114. For the candidates and the financial arrangements, see the minutes of the Conseil de Politique Indigène, 14 February, 16 March, and 20 March 1922, in Lyautey Papers, AN, no. 560, Conseil de Politique Indigène, procès-verbaux, 1921-22. Also see, Rivet, *Lyautey et l'institution du protectorat français au Maroc,* 2:140.
115. Pasha Si Mohammed Ben Abdelouahad to Laurent, 3 April 1922, BGA, PA, Région Civile de la Chaouïa, Casablanca, 1er Khalifa: Si Abderrahmane Ben Bouazza.
116. Laurent to de Sorbier, 3 April 1922, BGA, PA, Région Civile de la Chaouïa, Casablanca, Ben Bouazza.
117. Feuille de Renseignements: Si Abderrahmane Ben Bouazza, 26 April 1921; Feuille de Notes Annuelles (1922): Si Abderrahmane Ben Bouazza, 23 January 1923, both in BGA, PA, Région Civile de la Chaouïa, Casablanca, Ben Bouazza.
118. Proposal for rank of Chevalier du Ouissam Alaouite, 29 October 1924, BGA, PA, Région Civile de la Chaouïa, Casablanca, Ben Bouazza.
119. Pasha Si Mohammed Ben Abdelouahad to Laurent, 12 May 1922, BGA, PA, Région Civile de la Chaouïa, Casablanca, 2ème Khalifa: Si El-Ghali Ben Larbi el-Mernissi.
120. Laurent to Lyautey, 16 May 1922, BGA, PA, Région Civile de la Chaouïa, Casablanca, el-Mernissi.
121. "Note au sujet de la nomination d'un deuxième khalifa du pacha de Casablanca," n.d., in de Sorbier to Laurent, 17 June 1922, BGA, PA, Région Civile de la Chaouïa, Casablanca, el-Mernissi.
122. Feuille de Notes Annuelles (1922): Si El-Ghali Ben el-Arbi el-Mernissi, 23 January 1923, BGA, PA, Région Civile de la Chaouïa, Casablanca, el-Mernissi.
123. Pacha Si Mohammed Ben Abdelouahed to Laurent, April 1924, BGA, PA, Région Civile de la Chaouïa, Casablanca, el-Mernissi.
124. Pasha Si Mohammed Ben Abdelouahad, "Note," 28 April 1924, BGA, PA, Région Civile de la Chaouïa, Casablanca, el-Mernissi.
125. *Rapport mensuel,* December 1923, 12.
126. Pasha Si Mohammed Ben Abdelouahad, "Note," 29 April 1924, BGA, PA, Région Civile de la Chaouïa, Casablanca, el-Mernissi.
127. Chef des Services Municipaux de Casablanca to Laurent, 30 April 1924; and de Sorbier to Laurent, 14 October 1924, both in BGA, PA, Région Civile de la Chaouïa, Casablanca, el-Mernissi.
128. "Compte-rendu de la mission du Chef du Contrôle de la Justice de la Chraâ Octave Pesle to Conseiller du Gouvernement Chérifien Auguste Gérardin," n.d., in Ministre Plénipotentiaire, Délégué à la Résidence Générale de la République française Jean Hellu to Contrôleur Civil, Chef de la Région de la Chaouïa Émile Orthlieb, 30 June 1934, BGA, PA, 27, Personnel européen: Notes et avancement jusqu'à 1936, M. Bertrand.
129. See "Note de M. Henri Gaillard sur le Contrôle Civil," [1916] and Lyautey, "Observations au sujet de la Note de M. Gaillard sur le Contrôle," [1916], both in Lyautey to Secrétaire Général du Protectorat Lallier du Coudray, 27 April 1916, BGA, PA, Administration Civile, Service du Personnel, Contrôles Civils; Notes et Rapports.

Chapter 8

1. On the rebellious Chaouïa peasantry, see Burke, *Prelude to Protectorate*, 95-96.
2. Contrôleur Civil Pierre Coudert, Chef du Contrôle Civil de Chaouïa-Sud to Secrétaire Général du Protectorat Georges Duvernoy, n.d. [November 1926], in BGA, PA, 29, Caïd Lahcen.
3. Huot, "Note," 20 April 1908, in "Note succincte sur le Caïd Tounsi Ben el-Bahloul des Oulad Bouziri," n.d. [1915-1916], BGA, PA, Région Civile du Gharb, Oulad Bou Ziri, Caïd Tounsi Ben el-Bahloul, Notes annuelles et feuilles de renseignements. The Oulad Bou Ziri were in the Chaouïa, not the Gharb, but the tribal files are located in the cartons of the Région Civile du Gharb.
4. "Note succincte sur le Caïd Tounsi" and Captain Jules Maitrat, Contrôleur en Chef, Contrôle Civil de Settat, "Note annuelle," 1914 (10 January 1915), BGA, PA, Région Civile du Gharb, Oulad Bou Ziri, Caïd Tounsi, Notes annuelles.
5. Forey, commandant la Colonne Mobile des Mzamza, to General Charles Moinier, commandant le Corps de Débarquement à Casablanca, 16 March 1910, BGA, PA, Région Civile du Gharb, Oulad Bou Ziri, Caïd Tounsi, Succession Tounsi.
6. "Notes des années précédentes, 1911-1921," BGA, PA, Région Civile du Gharb, Oulad Bou Ziri, Caïd Tounsi, Notes annuelles.
7. Lyautey to Général, commandant la Région de la Chaouïa, 6 December 1912, BGA, PA, Région Civile du Gharb, Oulad Bou Ziri, Caïd Tounsi, Punitions et récompenses.
8. Maitrat, "Notes annuelles," 1914 (10 January 1915), 1915 (20 January 1916), 1916 (12 January 1917), BGA, PA, Région Civile du Gharb, Oulad Bou Ziri, Caïd Tounsi, Notes annuelles.
9. Maitrat, "Note annuelle," 1914 (10 January 1915); Rey, Chef du Contrôle de Chaouïa-Sud, "Note annuelle," 1917 (30 November 1917) and Rey, "Note annuelle," 1917 in "Notes des années précédentes, 1911-1921," both in BGA, PA, Région Civile du Gharb, Oulad Bou Ziri, Caïd Tounsi, Notes annuelles.
10. Caïd Si Tounsi Ben Bahloul de la tribu des Oulad Bou Ziri to Calmel, 22 May 1918, BGA, PA, Région Civile du Gharb, Oulad Bou Ziri, Caïd Tounsi, Renseignements divers.
11. Coudert to Calmel, 22 May 1918; Calmel to Coudert, 28 May 1918; Calmel to Tounsi, n.d., all in BGA, PA, Région Civile du Gharb, Oulad Bou Ziri, Caïd Tounsi, Renseignements divers.
12. Coudert, "Note annuelle," 1922 (5 January 1923), BGA, PA, Région Civile du Gharb, Oulad Bou Ziri, Caïd Tounsi, Notes annuelles.
13. "Note succincte sur le Caïd Tounsi" and Frédéric Weisgerber, Contrôleur de la Circonscription de Settat, "Note annuelle," 1917 (6 February 1917), BGA, PA, Région Civile du Gharb, Oulad Bou Ziri, Caïd Tounsi, Notes annuelles.
14. Coudert, "Notes annuelles," 1918 (31 December 1918) and 1919 (21 February 1920), BGA, PA, Région Civile du Gharb, Oulad Bou Ziri, Caïd Tounsi, Notes annuelles.
15. "Note succincte sur le Caïd Tounsi."
16. Contrôleur Civil Coudert, Chef du Contrôle Civil de Chaouïa-Sud et des Services Municipaux de Settat to Contrôleur, Chef de la Région Civile de Casablanca Alexandre Laurent, 11 June 1920 et Directeur des Affaires Civiles Louis Sicot to Coudert, 10 July 1920, both in BGA, PA, Région Civile du Gharb, Oulad Bou Ziri, Caïd Tounsi, Punitions et récompenses.
17. Coudert, "Note annuelle," 1922 (5 January 1923).
18. Coudert, "Note annuelle," 1922 (5 January 1923).
19. Coudert to Secrétaire Général du Protectorat Pierre de Sorbier de Pougnadoresse, 21 December 1923, BGA, PA, Région Civile du Gharb, Oulad Bou Ziri, Caïd Tounsi, Succession Tounsi.
20. Coudert to de Sorbier, 21 December 1923.

21. Coudert to de Sorbier, 21 December 1923.
22. Coudert to de Sorbier, 21 December 1923.
23. Coudert to de Sorbier, 21 December 1923.
24. Coudert to de Sorbier, 21 December 1923.
25. Coudert to de Sorbier, 21 December 1923. The French civil-military regional administration divided Morocco into *régions, territoires, cercles, circonscriptions, annexes,* and *postes.* See Scham, *Lyautey in Morocco,* 69-70.
26. Coudert to Laurent, 6 October 1923, BGA, PA, Région Civile du Gharb, Oulad Bou Ziri, Caïd Tounsi, Succession Tounsi.
27. Coudert to Laurent, 6 October 1923.
28. Coudert to Laurent, 6 October 1923.
29. Laurent to Lyautey, 10 January 1924, BGA, PA, Région Civile du Gharb, Oulad Bou Ziri, Caïd Tounsi, Succession Tounsi.
30. Tounsi's successor as *caïd* of the Oulad Bou Ziri was his brother and the *khalifa* of the tribe, Si Selham Ben el-Bahloul.
31. Capitain Jules Maitrat, Contrôleur en Chef, Contrôle Civil de Settat, "Note annuelle," 1914 (10 January 1915); Frédéric Weisgerber, Contrôleur de la Circonscription de Settat, "Note annuelle," 1916 (8 February 1917); Chef de Bataillon François Rey, Chef du Contrôle de Chaouïa-Sud, "Note annuelle," 1917 (30 November 1917); Pierre Coudert, Chef du Contrôle de Chaouïa-Sud, "Note annuelle," 1922 (5 January 1923), all in BGA, PA, 29ter, Chaouïa-Sud: Settat-Banlieue, Mzamza: Caïd Si Boubeker Ben El Hadj el-Maâti, Notes annuelles et feuilles de renseignements. On El Hadj el-Maâti, see C. Barrouquère-Claret, *Settat, centre historique de la Chaouïa* (Paris: Émile Larose, 1919), 50-58. For Abd el-Hafid's efforts to keep the *caïdat* from el-Maâti's heirs and otherwise meddle in their affairs, see General Charles Moinier to Ministre de France au Maroc Eugène Regnault, 23 January 1911, SHAT, 3H, 330, Service des Renseignements, 1909-11.
32. Pierre Collomb, Contrôleur en Chef, Contrôle Civil de Settat, "Note annuelle," 1914 (25 December 1914), BGA, PA, 29ter, Chaouïa-Sud: Settat-Banlieue, Mzamza: Caïd Boubeker, Notes annuelles.
33. Maitrat, "Note annuelle," 1914 (10 January 1915); Weisgerber, "Note annuelle," 1916 (8 February 1917); Coudert, "Note annuelle," 1919 (21 February 1920), all in BGA, PA, 29ter, Chaouïa-Sud: Settat-Banlieue, Mzamza: Caïd Boubeker, Notes annuelles.
34. Rey, "Note annuelle," 1917 (30 November 1917).
35. Coudert, "Note annuelle," 1919 (21 February 1920); Weisgerber, "Note annuelle," 1916 (8 February 1917); and Rey, "Note annuelle," 1917 (30 November 1917).
36. "Note annuelle," 1921, n.d. and Coudert, "Note annuelle," 1922 (5 January 1923), both in BGA, PA, 29ter, Chaouïa-Sud: Settat-Banlieue, Mzamza: Caïd Boubeker, Notes annuelles.
37. Coudert to de Sorbier, 2 February 1923, BGA, PA, 29ter, Chaouïa-Sud: Settat-Banlieue, Mzamza: Caïd Boubeker, Renseignements divers.
38. Coudert, "Note annuelle," 1922 (5 January 1923).
39. Coudert to de Sorbier, 2 February 1923.
40. Coudert to Laurent, 30 October 1926, BGA, PA, 29ter, Chaouïa-Sud: Settat-Banlieue, Mzamza: Caïd Boubeker, Succession du Caïd Boubeker.
41. Coudert to Laurent, 30 October 1926.
42. Coudert to Laurent, 30 October 1926.
43. Coudert to Laurent, 30 October 1926.
44. Laurent to Steeg, 3 November 1926 and Secrétaire Général du Protectorat Georges Duvernoy to Laurent, 7 January 1927, both in BGA, PA, 29ter Chaouïa-Sud: Settat-Banlieue, Mzamza: Caïd Boubeker, Succession du Caïd Boubeker. Si Mohamed el-Merini, Casablanca's first *khalifa,* had wanted the post of pasha of Settat, but he was passed over.

45. Coudert to Duvernoy, n.d. [November 1926].
46. Coudert to Duvernoy, n.d. [November 1926].
47. Laurent to Directeur du Service des Renseignements, 26 November 1926, BGA, PA, 29, Caïd Lahcen.
48. In 1909 their numbers were tallied as follows:

Mlal	2,372 tents
Beni Brahim	1,042
Oulad Mrah	3,241
Oulad Chebana	674
Achache	3,019
TOTAL	10,348

See Chef de Bataillon Jules Mouveaux, commandant le Détachement Régional des Achache, to Moinier, 2 July 1909, BGA, PA, 29, Mzab/Mlal, Caïd Lahsseine Ben Larbi Ben Cherqui, Decès et succession du Caïd Larbi Ben Cherki.
49. Lieutenant Colonel Delagrange, commandant la Colonne Mobile à Kasbah Ben Ahmed, "Notice concernant le Caïd Si Larbi Ben Cherki, *caïd* de la tribu des Mzab," 27 July 1908, BGA, PA, 29, Mzab/Mlal, Caïd Lahsseine Ben Larbi Ben Cherqui, Notes annuelles et feuilles de renseignements. Also see, Paul Azan, *Souvenirs de Casablanca,* with a preface by General d'Amade (Paris: Librairie Hachette et Cie., 1911).
50. Delagrange, "Notice concernant le Caïd Si Larbi Ben Cherki."
51. Delagrange, "Notice concernant le Caïd Si Larbi Ben Cherki."
52. Azan, *Souvenirs de Casablanca,* 394-95.
53. Captain Maitrat, ffons. Contrôleur en Chef to Colonel Jean Calmel, commandant la Région à Casablanca, 8 May 1916, BGA, PA, 29, Mzab/Mlal, Caïd Lahsseine, Renseignements divers. Larbi's cross was awarded posthumously. On Larbi Ben Cherki also see, *Villes et tribus du Maroc,* 2:165-67.
54. Mouveaux to Moinier, 2 July 1909.
55. Mouveaux to Moinier, 2 July 1909.
56. Mouveaux to Moinier, 24 July 1909, BGA, PA, 29, Mzab/Mlal, Caïd Lahsseine, Decès et succession du Caïd Larbi.
57. Moinier to Mouveaux, 26 July 1909 and Moinier to Chargé d'Affaires de France à Tanger, 26 July 1909, both in BGA, PA, 29, Mzab/Mlal, Caïd Lahsseine, Decès et succession du Caïd Larbi.
58. Mouveaux to Moinier, 29 July 1909, BGA, PA, 29, Mzab/Mlal, Caïd Lahsseine, Decès et succession du Caïd Larbi.
59. Mouveaux to Moinier, 2 August 1909, BGA, PA, 29, Mzab/Mlal, Caïd Lahsseine, Decès et succession du Caïd Larbi.
60. Octave Peyssonnel, Chef de l'Annexe de Ben Ahmed, "Note annuelle," 1917 (28 November 1917), BGA, PA, 29, Mzab/Mlal, Caïd Lahsseine, Notes annuelles.
61. Restier, "Note annuelle," 1912 (16 August 1912), BGA, PA, 29, Mzab/Mlal, Caïd Lahsseine, Notes annuelles.
62. Lapasset, Chef du Bureau de Renseignements de Ben Ahmed, "Note annuelle," 1911 (15 December 1911), BGA, PA, 29, Mzab/Mlal, Caïd Lahsseine, Notes annuelles.
63. Lapasset, "Note annuelle," 1912 (26 July 1912) and Jacquet, Chef du Bureau de Renseignements de Ben Ahmed, "Note annuelle," 1913 (23 December 1913), both in BGA, PA, 29, Mzab/Mlal, Caïd Lahsseine, Notes annuelles.
64. Maitrat, Contrôleur en Chef de la Circonscription Civile de Settat, "Notes annuelles," 1914 (16 January 1915) and 1915 (20 January 1916), BGA, PA, 29, Mzab/Mlal, Caïd Lahsseine, Notes annuelles.
65. De Féraudy, Chef du Bureau du Contrôle Civil de Ben Ahmed to Maitrat, 3 May 1916, BGA, PA, 29, Mzab/Mlal, Caïd Lahsseine, Renseignements divers.
66. Maitrat to Calmel, 8 May 1916.

67. Maitrat to Calmel, 8 May 1916.
68. Maitrat to Calmel, 8 May 1916.
69. Calmel to Lyautey, 18 May 1916, BGA, PA, 29, Mzab/Mlal, Caïd Lahsseine, Renseignements divers.
70. De Féraudy, Chef du Bureau de Renseignements de Ben Ahmed, "Note annuelle," 1916 (15 December 1916), BGA, PA, 29, Mzab/Mlal, Caïd Lahsseine, Notes annuelles.
71. De Féraudy to Maitrat, 13 June 1916, BGA, PA, 29, Mzab/Mlal, Caïd Lahsseine, Renseignements divers.
72. Calmel to Maitrat, 17 June 1916, BGA, PA, 29, Caïd Lahsseine, Renseignements divers.
73. Lyautey to Calmel, 22 September 1917, BGA, PA, 29, Mzab/Mlal, Caïd Lahsseine, Renseignements divers.
74. De Féraudy, "Note annuelle," 1917 (6 February 1917), BGA, PA, 29, Mzab/Mlal, Caïd Lahsseine, Notes annuelles.
75. Le Contrôleur Civil Suppléant Peyssonnel, Chef de l'Annexe de Ben-Ahmed to Chef du Contrôle Civil de la Chaouïa-Centre à Ber-Rechid Captain Émile Riottot, 12 October 1917, BGA, PA, 29, Mzab/Mlal, Caïd Lahsseine, Renseignements divers.
76. Riottot, Chef du Contrôle Civil de Chaouïa-Centre to Colonel Jean Calmel, commandant la Région de Casablanca, 19 October 1917, BGA, PA, 29, Mzab/Mlal, Caïd Lahsseine, Renseignements divers.
77. Calmel to Lyautey, 5 November 1917, BGA, PA, 29, Mzab/Mlal, Caïd Lahsseine, Renseignements divers and Peyssonnel, "Note annuelle," 1917 (28 November 1917), BGA, PA, 29, Mzab/Mlal, Caïd Lahsseine, Notes annuelles.
78. Lyautey to Calmel, 10 November 1917 and Calmel to Lyautey, 4 February 1918, both in BGA, PA, 29, Mzab/Mlal, Caïd Lahsseine, Renseignements divers. Also see, Peyssonnel to Calmel, 28 January 1918, BGA, PA, 29, Mzab/Mlal, Caïd Lahsseine, Renseignements divers.
79. Calmel to Riottot, 4 March 1918 and Peyssonnel to Riottot, 10 March 1918, both in BGA, PA, 29, Mzab/Mlal, Caïd Lahsseine, Renseignements divers.
80. Calmel to Riottot, 4 March 1918.
81. "Note annuelle," 1918, BGA, PA, 29, Mzab/Mlal, Caïd Lahsseine, Notes annuelles.
82. Croix-Marie, "Note annuelle," 1919 [December 1919], BGA, PA, 29, Mzab/Mlal, Caïd Lahsseine, Notes annuelles.
83. Croix-Marie, "Note annuelle," 1919 [December 1919] and Coudert, "Note annuelle," 1920 (6 March 1920), BGA, PA, 29, Mzab/Mlal, Caïd Lahsseine, Notes annuelles.
84. Croix-Marie, "Note annuelle," 1920 (December 1920), BGA, PA, 29, Mzab/Mlal, Caïd Lahsseine, Notes annuelles.
85. Croix-Marie, "Note annuelle," 1921 (2 November 1921), BGA, PA, 29, Mzab/Mlal, Caïd Lahsseine, Notes annuelles.
86. Contrôleur Civil Coudert, Chef du Contrôle de Chaouïa-Sud, "Note annuelle," 1921 (12 November 1921), BGA, PA, 29, Mzab/Mlal, Caïd Lahsseine, Notes annuelles.
87. "Note annuelle," 1922 (December 1922), BGA, PA, 29, Mzab/Mlal, Caïd Lahsseine, Notes annuelles.
88. Coudert, "Note annuelle," 1922 (12 January 1923), BGA, PA, 29, Mzab/Mlal, Caïd Lahsseine, Notes annuelles.
89. Laurent to Directeur du Service des Renseignements, 26 November 1926, BGA, PA, 29, Caïd Lahcen.
90. Contrôleur Civil Georges Rousseau, Chef de l'Annexe de Boucheron, "Note annuelle," 1914 (15 January 1915), BGA, PA, 29ter, Chaouïa-Nord: Annexe de Boucheron, M'dakra: Caïd Abdelqader Ben El Hadj el-Maâti Ould Fardjia, Notes annuelles.
91. Captain Pierre Nancy, Chef du Bureau de Renseignements de Boucheron, "Note annuelle," 1910 (20 July 1910), BGA, PA, 29ter, Chaouïa-Nord: Annexe de Boucheron, M'dakra: Caïd Abdelqader, Notes annuelles.

92. Nancy, "Note annuelle," 1910 (20 July 1910), and "Notes du Capitaine Nancy, 1910" in Gabriel Beaujolin, Chef de l'Annexe de Boucheron, "Résumé des notes anciennes données au Caïd Si Abdelkader Ben El Hadj el-Maâti Ould Farjia, de la tribu des Ouled Cebbah et Ouled Ali," 24 February 1923, in BGA, PA, 29ter, Chaouïa-Nord: Annexe de Boucheron, M'dakra: Caïd Abdelqader, Notes annuelles.
93. "Notes du Capitaine Nancy, 1910," in "Résumé des notes anciennes."
94. Rousseau, "Note annuelle," 15 January 1915, in "Résumé des notes anciennes."
95. Contard, Chef de l'Annexe de Boucheron, "Notes annuelles," [1915], 1 February 1917, and 22 October 1917, in "Résumé des notes anciennes."
96. Contard, "Note annuelle," 1 February 1917, in "Résumé des notes anciennes."
97. Contard, "Note annuelle," [1915], in "Résumé des notes anciennes."
98. Bergé to Contard, 25 August 1917, BGA, PA, 29ter, Chaouïa-Nord: Annexe de Boucheron, M'dakra: Caïd Abdelqader, Réclamations successives instruites contre ce chef indigène.
99. Contard to Bergé, 29 November 1917, BGA, PA, 29ter, Chaouïa-Nord: Annexe de Boucheron, M'dakra: Caïd Abdelqader, Réclamations successives.
100. Metour, "Note annuelle," 5 November 1918, in "Résumé des notes anciennes."
101. Beaujolin, Chef de l'Annexe de Boucheron, "Note annuelle," 1922 [December 1922], in "Résumé des notes anciennes."
102. Beaujolin, "Note annuelle," 1922 [December 1922]," in "Résumé des notes anciennes;" Contrôleur Civil Louis Watin, Chef de la Circonscription de Chaouïa-Nord to Contrôleur Civil Alexandre Laurent, Chef de la Région de la Chaouïa, 13 August 1923, 29ter, Chaouïa-Nord: Annexe de Boucheron, M'dakra: Caïd Abdelqader, Réclamations successives.
103. Watin to Délégué à la Résidence Générale Urbain Blanc, [September-December 1923], BGA, PA, 29ter, Chaouïa-Nord: Annexe de Boucheron, M'dakra: Caïd Abdelqader, Réclamations successives.

Chapter 9

1. See Shannon E. Fleming, "North Africa and the Middle East," in *Spain in the Twentieth-Century World: Essays on Spanish Diplomacy, 1898-1978*, ed. James W. Cortada (Westport, Conn.: Greenwood Press, 1980), 125. The Spanish army counted 8,000 dead—including its commander, General Manuel Fernández Silvestre—and over 5,000 wounded. Two hundred prisoners and 114 pieces of heavy artillery were left in Riffian hands. The best overall accounts of the Rif war are David S. Woolman, *Rebels in the Rif: Abd el Krim and the Rif Rebellion* (Stanford: Stanford University Press, 1968) and C. Richard Pennell, *A Country with a Government and a Flag: The Rif War in Morocco, 1921-1926* (Wisbech, England: Middle East and North African Studies Press, 1986).
2. Lyautey to Wladimir d'Ormesson, 16 August 1921, in Le Révérend, *Lyautey*, 420. On Spanish policy, see C. Richard Pennell. "The Responsibility for Anual: The Failure of Spanish Policy in the Moroccan Protectorate, 1912-21," *European Studies Review* 12 (1982):67-86. In February 1921 by vote of the French cabinet (and the persistence of Premier Louis Barthou, a Lyautey admirer) Lyautey had been "elevated to the dignity" of marshal of France.
3. Contrôleur Civil Le Faye, 26 August and 27 September 1921, BGA, PA, Municipalités, Région du Gharb, Rapports politiques de Mechra Bel Ksiri; Contrôleur Civil Marc de Mazières, 27 August 1921, BGA, PA, Municipalités, Région du Gharb, Rapports politiques de Petitjean.
4. *Rapport mensuel*, July 1921, 1-2.
5. *Rapport mensuel*, August 1921, 1-2, 5.

6. *Rapport mensuel*, September 1921, 1, 5.
7. *Rapport mensuel*, October 1921, 1-3. For Lyautey's account of Franco-Spanish relations in Morocco, see Lyautey, "Note privée pour le commandant [Pierre] de Cuverville," 4 March 1924, SHAT, Maroc, 3H, 100, Collaboration franco-espagnole, 1925.
8. Rivet, *Lyautey et l'institution du protectorat français au Maroc*, 3:270-74.
9. *Rapport mensuel*, November 1921, i-ii and December 1921, ii-iii.
10. *Rapport mensuel*, May 1922, ii; June 1922, ii-iii; and July 1922, i-ii. On the difficult and fragile process of the consolidation of the Rif state, see Pennell, *A Country with a Government and a Flag*, 97-122.
11. *Rapport mensuel*, July 1922, i; September 1922, iii-iv; October 1922, ii-iii; December 1922, ii-iii. Also see, Rapport politique mensuel (Région de Fez), December 1922, in BGA, PA, Municipalités, Région du Gharb, Rapports et télégrammes émanant de diverses régions.
12. *Rapport mensuel*, April 1923, i-iii and May 1923, ii.
13. *Rapport mensuel*, August 1923, i-ii, 4 and September 1923, ii, 3. Also see, Rapport politique mensuel (Région de Fez), July and August 1923 in BGA, PA, Municipalités, Région du Gharb, Rapports et télégrammes émanant de diverses régions.
14. *Rapport mensuel*, December 1923, i-ii, 2-3. Also see, Rapport politique mensuel, (Région de Fez), December 1923, 1-3 in BGA, PA, Municipalités, Région du Gharb, Rapports et télégrammes émanant de diverses régions.
15. Shannon E. Fleming, *Primo de Rivera and Abd-el-Krim: The Struggle in Spanish Morocco, 1923-1927* (New York: Garland, 1991), 98-99, 103-04.
16. Fleming, *Primo de Rivera and Abd-el-Krim*, 111, 115-19; Robert Montagne, "La crise nationaliste au Maroc," CHEAM lecture, 18 December 1941.
17. Fleming, *Primo de Rivera and Abd-el-Krim*, 144-45, 194-95. Also see, Lyautey to Diplomatie, Paris, 18 July 1924, in SHAT, Maroc, 3H, 134, Zone espagnole.
18. Lyautey to Ministry of Foreign Affairs, 27 February 1924, in Hubert-Jacques, *L'Aventure riffaine et ses dessous politiques* (Paris: Éditions Bossard, 1927), 55-56.
19. Rapport politique mensuel (Région de Fez), March 1924, in BGA, PA, Municipalités, Région du Gharb, Rapports et télégrammes émanant de diverses régions; *Rapport mensuel*, February 1924, ii, 6 and March 1924, 5, 8.
20. Rapport politique mensuel (Région de Fez), April and May 1924, both in BGA, PA, Municipalités, Région du Gharb, Rapports et télégrammes émanant de diverses régions; *Rapport mensuel*, April 1924, ii, 8-10 and May 1924, ii, 6-7.
21. Rapport politique mensuel (Région de Fez), May 1924, in BGA, PA, Municipalités, Région du Gharb, Rapports et télégrammes émanant de diverses régions.
22. *Rapport mensuel*, May 1924, iv.
23. Rapport politique mensuel (Région de Fez), June 1924, in BGA, PA, Municipalités, Région du Gharb, Rapports et télégrammes émanant de diverses régions.
24. Rapport politique mensuel (Région de Fez), June 1924, in BGA, PA, Municipalités, Région du Gharb, Rapports et télégrammes émanant de diverses régions.
25. Rapport politique mensuel (Région de Fez), July 1924, in BGA, PA, Municipalités, Région du Gharb, Rapports et télégrammes émanant de diverses régions; *Rapport mensuel*, July 1924, i-ii, 7-8.
26. *Rapport mensuel*, June 1924, 9; July 1924, i.
27. *Rapport mensuel*, September 1924, 1-4; Rapport politique mensuel (Région de Fez), September 1924, 4, in BGA, PA, Municipalités, Région du Gharb, Rapports et télégrammes émanant de diverses régions.
28. *Rapport mensuel*, October 1924, i, 2, 8.
29. Lyautey, "Note d'ensemble sur la situation politique et militaire du Maroc au 20 décembre 1924," cited in Rivet, *Lyautey et l'institution du protectorat français au Maroc*, 3: 277.

30. Lyautey, "Note d'ensemble sur la situation politique et militaire du Maroc au 20 décembre 1924 et sur les mesures qu'elle comporte," in Lyautey, *Lyautey l'Africain*, 4:267-68.
31. Lyautey to the minister of foreign affairs, 22 March 1924, in SHAT, Maroc, 3H, 100, Collaboration franco-espagnole, 1925.
32. *Rapport mensuel*, January 1925, i, iii, 1 and February 1925, i-ii, 1.
33. *Rapport mensuel*, April 1925, 1.
34. De Chambrun, "Rapport d'Opérations (avril-mai 1925)," 2-4, SHAT, Maroc, 3H, 598, Région de Fez, Commandement du Front Nord and Lyautey to Ministry of Foreign Affairs, 17 April 1925, SHAT, Maroc, 3H, 101, Opérations du Rif, 1925.
35. *Rapport mensuel*, April 1925, ii, 1-3, 8.
36. Lyautey to Ministry of Foreign Affairs, 25 April 1925, SHAT, Maroc, 3H, 101, Opérations du Rif, 1925.
37. Lyautey to Ministry of Foreign Affairs, 29 April 1925, SHAT, Maroc, 3H, 101, Opérations du Rif, 1925.
38. Lyautey to Ministry of Foreign Affairs, 29 April 1925, SHAT, Maroc, 3H, 101, Opérations du Rif, 1925.
39. *Rapport mensuel*, April 1925, i-ii.
40. Lyautey to Ministry of Foreign Affairs, 30 April and 3 May 1925, SHAT, Maroc, 3H, 101, Opérations du Rif, 1925; Lyautey to Minister of Foreign Affairs Aristide Briand, 13 May 1925, in Lyautey, *Lyautey l'Africain*, 4:305.
41. Lyautey, "Instructions," 12 May 1925, in Lyautey, *Lyautey l'Africain*, 4:299; *Rapport mensuel*, April 1925, 1, 4.
42. De Chambrun, "Rapport d'Opérations," 6-7 and *Rapport mensuel*, April 1925, 2, 8.
43. Lyautey to Ministry of Foreign Affairs, 3 May 1925, SHAT, Maroc, 3H, 101, Opérations du Rif, 1925. Also see, Lyautey to Painlevé, 30 May 1925, in Lyautey, *Lyautey l'Africain*, 4:316.
44. Lyautey to Ministry of Foreign Affairs, 4 May 1925, SHAT, Maroc, 3H, 101, Opérations du Rif, 1925.
45. *Rapport mensuel*, May and June 1925, i. Months earlier Lyautey had sharply criticized Spain for using poison gas. See Daniel Rivet, "Le commandement français et ses réactions vis-à- vis du mouvement rifain, 1924-1926," in *Abd el-Krim et la république du Rif*. [Actes du Colloque international d'études historiques et sociologiques, 18-20 January 1973] (Paris: Maspero, 1976), 103.
46. René Thierry, "L'Agression des Rifains contre le Maroc français," *L'Afrique française* 35, no. 5 (May 1925):255.
47. On Louis Malvy's visit to Spain (14-23 May), see Woolman, *Rebels in the Rif*, 179-80.
48. De Chambrun, "Rapport d'Opérations," 9. The casualty figures supplied to the Senate commissions on the army and foreign affairs in early June were 318 dead, 1,115 wounded, and 195 missing for a total of 1,628. See Thierry, "L'Agression des Rifains," *L'Afrique française* 35, no. 6 (June 1925):308. For a summary of the operations of the three mobile groups under de Chambrun's command, see René Thierry, "L'Agression des Rifains," *L'Afrique française* 35, no. 5 (May 1925):254-57 and no. 6 (June 1925):305-06.
49. Lyautey, "Ordre général No. 527," 28 May 1925, *Bulletin Officiel* 14, no. 658 (2 June 1925):944. As part of France's postwar budget reductions, the number of regular troops in Morocco was reduced from 75,500 in 1922 to 54,500 in 1924. Ministère de la Guerre, État-Major de l'Armée, Section d'Études (Afrique, Orient, Colonies), "Note sur l'agression riffaine," 20 May 1925, 10, SHAT, Maroc, 3H, 107, Notes diverses sur les opérations. On the financial crisis of 1924, see Stephen A. Schuker, *The End of French Predominance in Europe: The Financial Crisis of 1924 and the Adoption of the Dawes Plan* (Chapel Hill: University of North Carolina Press, 1976).

50. Lyautey to Ministry of Foreign Affairs, 23 May 1925, SHAT, Maroc, 3H, 101, Opérations du Rif, 1925; *Rapport mensuel,* May-June, 1925, 3. Daugan was seconded by General Gaston Billotte, responsible for military and operational questions, and de Chambrun, responsible for political and territorial matters. The northern front was divided into three sectors under the individual command of General Paul Colombat and Colonels Henri Freydenberg and Albert Cambay. In the early days of June the center sector was expanded to put all the access roads to Fez under a single commander; Billotte was given that command.

51. "Note sur l'agression riffaine," 20 May 1925, 16-17.

52. Thierry, "L'Agression des Rifains," *L'Afrique française* 35, no. 6 (June 1925):305.

53. Lyautey to Ministry of Foreign Affairs, 6 June 1925, SHAT, Maroc, 3H, 101, Opérations du Rif, 1925 and Lyautey to Président du Conseil, Ministre de la Guerre Paul Painlevé, 6 June 1925, SHAT, Maroc, 3II, 100, Ordres d'opérations divers. On the June fighting, see Thierry, "L'Agression des Rifains," *L'Afrique française* 35, no. 6 (June 1925):305-06 and no. 7 (July 1925):354-56.

54. *Bulletin Officiel* 14, no. 662 (30 June 1925):1114. On Painlevé in Morocco (10-14 June), see Thierry, "L'Agression des Rifains," *L'Afrique française* 35, no. 6 (June 1925):308-10.

55. Thierry, "L'Agression des Rifains," *L'Afrique française* 35, no. 6 (June 1925):311-12 and no. 8 (August 1925):411.

56. See "Note sur l'agression riffaine," 20 May 1925. Protectorate authorities carefully tracked the global impact of the Rif war in the *Bulletin mensuel.*

57. See Édouard Bonnefous, *Cartel des gauches et union nationale, 1924-1929,* vol. 4 of *Histoire politique de la troisième république* (Paris: Presses Universitaires de France, 1960), 53, 83-6. On the French left, see Georges Oved, *La gauche française et le nationalisme marocain, 1905-1955,* 2 vols. (Paris: L'Harmattan, 1984) and David H. Slavin, "The French Left and the Rif War, 1924-25: Racism and the Limits of Internationalism," *Journal of Contemporary History* 26, no. 1 (January 1991):5-32.

58. Lyautey to Painlevé, 17 May and 14 June 1925, in Lyautey, *Lyautey l'Africain,* 4:305-06, 330-31; *Rapport mensuel,* May and June, 1925, 1.

59. Lyautey to Ministry of War, 5 July 1925, SHAT, Maroc, 3H, 101, Opérations du Rif, 1925. On the Taza situation, see Thierry, "L'Agression des Rifains," *L'Afrique française* 35, no. 7 (July 1925):355-57.

60. Rapport politique mensuel (Région de Taza), July 1925, BGA, PA, Rapports politiques mensuels, May-September 1925.

61. Lyautey to Ministry of War, 5 July 1925, SHAT, Maroc, 3H, 101, Opérations du Rif, 1925.

62. Lyautey to Ministry of War, 7 July 1925, SHAT, Maroc, 3H, 101, Opérations du Rif, 1925. On the French at Bab Taza and Kifane, see Thierry, "L'Agression des Rifains," *L'Afrique française* 35, no. 7 (July 1925):357.

63. *Rapport mensuel,* July and August 1925, 7. In mid-June Painlevé first mentioned publicly that a general who had won his spurs in the Great War and also had experience in Africa might be given the "entire responsibility" for military operations in Morocco. See Thierry, "L'Agression des Rifains," *L'Afrique française* 35, no. 6 (June 1925):312. In the restructured command, Daugan was named Naulin's deputy. Thierry, "L'Agression des Rifains," *L'Afrique française* 35, no. 8 (August 1925):400.

64. *Bulletin Officiel* 14, no. 665 (21 July 1925):1242. See Lyautey to Painlevé, 7 and 16 June 1925, in Lyautey, *Lyautey l'Africain,* 4:322-23, 331-33 and Lyautey to Ministry of Foreign Affairs, 9 and 15 July 1925, SHAT, Maroc, 3H, 101, Opérations du Rif, 1925. Naulin was not a senior commander and had only limited colonial experience: Two years in Morocco and twelve months in Syria. See Thierry, "L'Agression des Rifains," *L'Afrique française* 35, no. 7 (July 1925):360.

65. Rivet, *Lyautey et l'institution du protectorat français au Maroc,* 3:286-96.

66. See Fleming, *Primo de Rivera and Abd-el-Krim*, 249-55, 262-63. The "complete text" of the peace terms was made public by Painlevé in a speech on 3 October. See Thierry, "L'Agression des Rifains," *L'Afrique française* 35, no. 10 (October 1925):529-30.

67. On the Pétain trip, see Thierry, "L'Agression des Rifains," *L'Afrique française* 35, no. 7 (July 1925):362 and no. 8 (August 1925):400-01. On the July fighting, see Thierry, "L'Agression des Rifains," *L'Afrique française* 35, no. 7 (July 1925):360-61 and no. 8 (August 1925):401-03.

68. Naulin, "Ordre," 25 July 1925, in Thierry, "L'Agression des Rifains," *L'Afrique française* 35, no. 8 (August 1925):400.

69. Thierry, "L'Agression des Rifains," *L'Afrique française* 35, no. 8 (August 1925):401. For the still precarious French military situation along the northern front after mid-July, see Daugan, "Note," 20 July 1925, SHAT, Maroc, 3H, 597, Provenant de la Région de Fez.

70. Thierry, "L'Agression des Rifains," *L'Afrique française* 35, no. 8 (August 1925):401.

71. Pétain to Painlevé, 20 October 1925, SHAT, Maroc, 3H, 100, Rapport Pétain sur l'affaire du Riff.

72. Pétain to Painlevé, 20 October 1925.

73. Pétain to Painlevé, 20 October 1925. Also see, Fleming, *Primo de Rivera and Abd-el-Krim*, 270-71.

74. Pétain to Painlevé, 20 October 1925.

75. Pétain to Painlevé, 20 October 1925.

76. Thierry, "L'Agression des Rifains," *L'Afrique française* 35, no. 9 (September 1925):464-65.

77. *L'Afrique française* 35, no. 10 (October 1925):487. For the letters, see Lyautey, *Paroles d'action*, 420-25. Lyautey's successor was Théodore Steeg, a member of the Radical-Socialist party who had served as governor-general of Algeria from 1921-25.

78. Lyautey to Briand, 10 October 1925, in Lyautey, *Lyautey l'Africain*, 4:377-78. Lyautey left Morocco for France for the last time on 10 October.

79. Thierry, "L'Agression des Rifains," *L'Afrique française* 35, no. 9 (September 1925):465.

80. On the Alhucemas landing, which Fleming calls "one of the most ambitious Spanish military undertakings since the Great Armada of 1588," see Fleming, *Primo de Rivera and Abd-el-Krim*, 263-99.

81. Thierry, "L'Agression des Rifains," *L'Afrique française* 35, no. 9 (September 1925):466. For the criticism that the offensive against the Beni Zeroual had not gone far enough and thus delayed the confederation's submission, see *Rapport mensuel*, September 1925, 4.

82. Thierry, "L'Agression des Rifains," *L'Afrique française* 35, no. 10 (October 1925):535-38.

83. Thierry, "L'Agression des Rifains," *L'Afrique française* 35, no. 11 (November 1925):597.

84. For the end of the Rif war, see Fleming, *Primo de Rivera and Abd-el-Krim*, 322-60; Pennell, *A Country with a Government and a Flag*, 196-226; and Woolman, *Rebels in the Rif*, 197-214.

85. Colonel Charles Noguès, interim commander of the Région de Fez, to Resident General Théodore Steeg, 15 March 1926, SHAT, Maroc, 3H, 936, Action politique, Fès, 1926.

Conclusion

1. To commemorate the centenary of Lyautey's birth the Conseil Municipal de Paris proposed to erect a statue on an island in the Bois de Vincennes, not far from the location of the 1931 Colonial Exposition, Lyautey's last hurrah. When architects complained that the obscure locale was better suited to a monument to the head of a fisherman's union than to a marshal of France, the project was shelved. See *Le Figaro,*

4 March and 5 April 1955. On the fiftieth anniversary of Lyautey's death, a statue was finally erected on Place Denys-Cochin. See Lyautey, *Le rôle social de l'officier* (Paris: Éditions Albatros, 1989), 139.

2. On Lyautey, the Colonial Exposition, and Greater France, see Herman Lebovics, *True France: The Wars over Cultural Identity, 1900-1945* (Ithaca: Cornell University Press, 1992). On the Académie Française, see *L'Afrique française* 35, no. 10 (October 1925):489. In *The Casablanca Connection: French Colonial Policy, 1936-1943* (Chapel Hill: University of North Carolina Press, 1984) I showed how Lyautey's legacy was used to French advantage at crucial moments of a political and economic world crisis.

3. See Lyautey, "Politique de protectorat," 18 November 1920, in Lyautey, *Lyautey l'Africain,* 4:30. Also see, Rivet, *Lyautey et l'institution du protectorat français au Maroc,* 3:197-202, 230-33.

4. See Rivet, *Lyautey et l'institution du protectorat français au Maroc,* 3:195-97, 203-12. In July 1914 there were 1,569 civil servants in Morocco; in 1925 there were 6,731. Rivet, *Lyautey et l'institution du protectorat français au Maroc,* 3:196. On Lyautey and the theme of modernization in French imperialism, see Barnett Singer, "Lyautey: An Interpretation of the Man and French Imperialism," *Journal of Contemporary History* 26, no. 1 (January 1991):131-57.

5. See Lyautey, "Politique de protectorat," 18 November 1920, in Lyautey, *Lyautey l'Africain,* 4:25.

6. Direction des Affaires Indigènes, "Note au sujet de l'inhumation du corps du maréchal Lyautey au Maroc et les répercussions possibles sur l'opinion indigène," 4 September 1934, BGA, PA, Maréchal Lyautey, Opposition des jeunes nationalistes au transfert des cendres du maréchal and Direction des Affaires Indigènes, "Bulletin des renseignements," 5 November 1935, BGA, PA, Maréchal Lyautey, Cérémonie des translation des cendres du maréchal au mausolé de Rabat. Also see, Jacques Ladreit de Lacharrière, "Le tombeau du maréchal Lyautey," *L'Afrique française* 44, no. 9 (September 1934):508-11 and Jules Borély, *Le tombeau de Lyautey* (Paris: Éditions de Cluny, 1937). On the burial ceremonies at Rabat on 30 October 1935, see *L'Afrique française* 45, no. 11 (November 1935):652-57. Also see, Résidence Générale de France au Maroc, *Translation au Maroc des cendres du Maréchal Lyautey, 20-30 octobre 1935* (Rabat: Résidence Générale de France au Maroc, [1935]).

BIBLIOGRAPHY

Manuscript Sources
Private Papers and Official Archives

France

Archives Nationales, Paris (Cited as AN)
    Lyautey Papers
    81: Documents fondamentaux sur la politique indigène.
    560: Renseignements et questions indigènes, 1921 à 1923.

Centre des Hautes Études sur l'Afrique et l'Asie Modernes, Paris (Cited as CHEAM)
    Delmas-Fort, Captain R. "Étude sur les tribus Chtoukas du Souss." CHEAM report, May 1947.
    Montagne, Robert. "La crise nationaliste au Maroc." CHEAM lecture, 18 December 1941.

Ministère des Affaires Étrangères, Paris (Cited as MAE) Archives Diplomatiques, Maroc, 1917-1938

Ministère des Affaires Étrangères, Nantes (Cited as MAE, Nantes) Archives Diplomatiques, Maroc; Archives du Protectorat, 1912-1956

Service Historique de l'Armée de Terre, Vincennes (Cited as SHAT) Archives du Maroc, Série 3H, 1877-1960[1]
    72: Occupation d'Oujda, colonne des Beni Snassen, frontière algéro-marocaine, 1904-1908.
    94: Situation politique et militaire, 1914-1918.
    100: Situation dans le Rif, 1925; Collaboration franco-espagnole, 1925.
    101: Opérations du Rif, 1925.
    107: Opérations du Rif, 1925.
    134: Zone espagnole et le Rif, 1922-1925.
    330: Relations avec le Maghzen, 1909-1912; Services municipaux, 1909-1913.
    331: Administration indigène, 1908-1912; Personnel du Service des Renseignements, 1908-1912.
    582: Opérations dans la région de Meknès, dans le cercle des Beni M'Tir, 1913.
    583: Opérations dans les régions du Tadla et de Oued Zem, 1913.
    584: Opérations en pays Zaïan, 1914.
    585: Opérations en pays Zaïan, 1914.
    588: Opérations dans la région du Tadla-Zaïan, 1915-1916.
    589: Colonne du Sous, 1917.
    590: Opérations dans les Territoires du Tadla-Zaïan et de Bou Denib, 1918.
    591: Commandement supérieur des troupes du Maroc: Directives et rapports d'opérations, 1919.

---

[1] The published guide to these archives is Arnaud de Menditte et Jean Nicot, *Répertoire des archives du Maroc*, vol. 1 (Château de Vincennes: Service Historique de l'Armée de Terre, 1982).

597: Campagne du Rif, 1925; Opérations et organisation du front Nord, 1924-1925.
871: Rapports politiques des cercles, 1925-1926.
901: Colonne Henrÿs chez les Beni M'Tir et chez les Zaïans, 1913.
902: Opérations chez les Zaïans, 1914.
903: Opérations chez les Zaïans, 1914.
904: Courrier expédié par le général Henrÿs, 1914.
908: Opérations de la subdivision du Tadla-Zaïans, 1915.
936: Directives et rapports d'action politique des troupes françaises, 1925-1926.
1030: Opérations de la Région de Meknès, 1913-1919; Renseignements sur les tribus de la Région de Meknès, 1915-1916.
1031: Opérations de la Région de Meknès, 1920.
1032: Opérations de la Région de Meknès, 1921.
1033: Opérations du Tadla et de la Haute Moulouya, 1922.
1066: Colonne du Sous, 1917.

Morocco
Bibliothèque Générale et Archives, Rabat (Cited as BGA) Protectorate Archives (Cited as PA)
Archives de la Mission scientifique et de la Section sociologique
Administration Civile, Service du Personnel, Contrôles Civils
Contrôle des Municipalités
Maréchal Lyautey
Municipalités: Rabat
Rapports politiques mensuels
Région Civile de la Chaouïa
    24: Casablanca-Ville
    27: Casablanca-Ville
    29: Casablanca-Banlieue
    29ter: Chaouïa-Nord, Chaouïa-Sud
Région Civile du Gharb

Government Documents and Official Publications

France
Assemblée Nationale, Annales de la Chambre des députés. *Débats parlementaires.* Paris: Imprimerie Nationale, 1912-25.
État-Major de l'Armée. *Les opérations militaires au Maroc.* Paris: Imprimerie Nationale, 1931.
Journal Officiel de la République française. Paris: Imprimerie Nationale, 1904-25. (Cited as *Journal Officiel*)
Ministère des Affaires Étrangères. *Documents diplomatiques: Affaires du Maroc, 1901-1912.* 6 vols. Paris: Imprimerie Nationale, 1905-12.

Morocco
Bulletin Officiel du Protectorat de la République française au Maroc. Rabat: Imprimerie Nationale, 1912-25. (Cited as *Bulletin Officiel*)
Mission scientifique du Maroc and Direction Générale des Affaires Indigènes et Service des Renseignements. *Villes et tribus du Maroc: Documents et renseignements.* 11 vols. Paris: Éditions Ernest Leroux and Honoré Champion, 1915-32.
Résidence Générale de France au Maroc. *Translation au Maroc des cendres du Maréchal Lyautey, 20-30 octobre 1935.* Rabat: Résidence Générale de France au Maroc, [1935].

Résidence Générale de la République française au Maroc. Bureau Politique and Direction des Affaires Indigènes et du Service des Renseignements. *Rapport mensuel du Protectorat.* Rabat, 1912-25. (Cited as *Rapport mensuel*)

Résidence Générale de la République française au Maroc. *La renaissance du Maroc; Dix ans de protectorat, 1912-1922.* Rabat: Résidence Générale de la République française au Maroc, [1922].

Books

Abu-Lughod, Janet L. *Rabat: Urban Apartheid in Morocco.* Princeton: Princeton University Press, 1980.

Adam, André. *Casablanca: Essai sur la transformation de la société marocaine au contact de l'Occident.* 2 vols. Paris: Centre National de la Recherche Scientifique, 1968.

————.*Histoire de Casablanca, des origines à 1914.* Gap: Éditions Ophrys, 1968.

Agence Havas marocaine. Guide touristique Havas. *Le Maroc.* 2nd ed. Casablanca: Havas, 1952.

Allain, Jean-Claude. *Agadir, 1911: Une crise impérialiste en Europe pour la conquête du Maroc.* Paris: Publications de la Sorbonne, 1976.

Amade, Albert-Gérard-Léo, comte d'. *La campagne de 1908-1909 en Chaouïa: Rapport du général d'Amade.* Paris: R. Chapelot, 1911.

Andrew, Christopher M. *Théophile Delcassé and the Making of the Entente Cordiale: A Reappraisal of French Foreign Policy, 1898-1905.* London: Macmillan and St. Martin's Press, 1968.

Ayache, Germain. *Les origines de la guerre du Rif.* Paris and Rabat: Publications de la Sorbonne and Société Marocaine des Éditeurs Réunis, 1981.

Azan, Paul-Jean-Louis. *L'Expédition de Fez.* With an introduction by Marshal Lyautey and a preface by General Moinier. Paris: Berger-Levrault, 1924.

————.*La frontière algéro-marocaine au début de 1907.* Tonnerre: Imprimerie Bailly, C. Puyfagès, successeur, 1907.

————.*Souvenirs de Casablanca.* With a preface by General d'Amade. Paris: Librairie Hachette et Cie., 1911.

Barlow, Ima Christina. *The Agadir Crisis.* Chapel Hill: University of North Carolina Press, 1940.

Barrouquère-Claret, C. *Settat, centre historique de la Chaouïa.* Paris: Émile Larose, 1919.

Barthou, Louis. *La bataille du Maroc.* Paris: Éditions Champion, 1919.

Bernard, Augustin. *Les confins algéro-marocains.* Paris: Éditions Larose, 1911.

Bernié, G. *Moha ou Hamou, guerrier berbère.* Casablanca: G. Gauthey, 1945.

Berque, Jacques. *Le Maghreb entre deux guerres.* Paris: Éditions du Seuil, 1962.

Betts, Raymond F. *Assimilation and Association in French Colonial Theory, 1890-1914.* New York: Columbia University Press, 1961.

Bidwell, Robin Leonard. *Morocco under Colonial Rule: French Administration of Tribal Areas, 1912-1956.* London: Frank Cass, 1973.

Boisboissel, Yves-Marie-Jacques-Guillaume de. *Dans l'ombre de Lyautey.* With a preface by Marshal Lyautey. Paris: Éditions André Bonne, 1954.

Bonnefous, Édouard. *Cartel des gauches et union nationale, 1924-1929.* Vol. 4 of *Histoire politique de la troisième république.* Paris: Presses Universitaires de France, 1960.

Borély, Jules. *Le tombeau de Lyautey.* Paris: Éditions de Cluny, 1937.

Boullé, Lucien-Louis. *La France et les Beni-Snassen: Campagne du général Lyautey.* Paris: Henri Charles-Lavauzelle, 1909.

Burke, Edmund III. *Prelude to Protectorate in Morocco: Precolonial Protest and Resistance, 1860-1912.* Chicago: University of Chicago Press, 1976.

Caillé, Jacques. *La mosquée de Hassan à Rabat.* Paris: Arts et Métiers Graphiques, 1954.
———. *La ville de Rabat jusqu'au protectorat français: Histoire et archéologie.* 3 vols. Paris: Vanoest Éditions d'Art et d'Histoire, 1949.
Carrère, Jean-Dominique. *Missionnaires en burnous bleu: Au Service de Renseignements durant l'épopée marocaine.* Limoges: Charles-Lavauzelle, 1973.
Casinière, Henri de la. *Les municipalités marocaines: Leur développement, leur législation.* Casablanca: Imprimerie de la Vigie Marocaine, 1924.
Catroux, General Georges. *Lyautey le Marocain.* Paris: Hachette, 1952.
Chatinières, Dr. Paul. *Dans le Grand Atlas marocain: Extraits du carnet de route d'un médecin d'assistance médicale indigène, 1912-1916.* With an introduction by Marshal Lyautey. Paris: Plon-Nourrit et Cie., 1919.
Clayton, Anthony. *France, Soldiers and Africa.* London: Brassey's Defence Publishers, 1988.
Cohen, William B. *Rulers of Empire: The French Colonial Service in Africa.* Stanford: Hoover Institution Press, 1971.
Colliez, André. *Notre protectorat marocain: La première étape, 1912-1930.* Paris: Librairie des Sciences Politiques et Sociales Marcel Rivière, 1930.
Comité national du centenaire de la naissance du maréchal Lyautey. *Livre d'or du centenaire de la naissance du maréchal Lyautey.* Casablanca: L'Office Marocain de Diffusion, [1954].
Cooke, James J. *New French Imperialism, 1880-1910: The Third Republic and Colonial Expansion.* Hamden, Conn.: Archon Books, 1973.
Cornet, Charles-Joseph-Alexandre. *A la conquête du Maroc sud avec la colonne Mangin, 1912-1913.* Paris: Plon-Nourrit et Cie, 1914.
Decroux, Paul. *La vie municipale au Maroc.* Lyon: Bosc Frères, M. et L. Riou, 1932.
Dugard, Henry [Louis Thomas]. *La conquête du Maroc: La colonne du Sous (janvier-juin 1917).* Paris: Perrin et Cie., 1918.
Dunn, Ross E. *Resistance in the Desert: Moroccan Responses to French Imperialism, 1881-1912.* Madison: University of Wisconsin Press, 1977.
Durosoy, Maurice. *Avec Lyautey: Homme de guerre, homme de paix.* Paris: Nouvelles Éditions Latines, 1976.
———. *Lyautey, maréchal de France, 1854-1934.* Paris: Editions Lavauzelle, 1984.
Ellis, Stephen D. K. *The Rising of the Red Shawls: A Revolt in Madagascar, 1895-1899.* Cambridge: Cambridge University Press, 1985.
Espérandieu, Pierre. *Lyautey et le protectorat.* With a forward by Pierre Lyautey. Paris: Éditions R. Pichon et R. Durand-Auzias, 1947.
Fleming, Shannon E. *Primo de Rivera and Abd-el-Krim: The Struggle in Spanish Morocco, 1923-1927.* New York: Garland, 1991.
Gabrielli, Léon. *Abd-el-Krim et les événements du Rif, 1924-1926.* Notes et souvenirs recueillis et présentés par Roger Coindreau. With a preface by Marshal Lyautey. Casablanca: Éditions Atlantides, 1953.
Gaillard, Jean-Michel. *Jules Ferry.* Paris: Fayard, 1989.
Gallieni, Joseph-Simon. *Galliéni au Tonkin (1892-1896) par lui- même.* Paris: Berger-Levrault, 1941.
———. *Lettres de Madagascar, 1896-1905.* Paris: Société d'Éditions Géographiques, Maritimes et Coloniales, 1928.
———. *Neuf ans à Madagascar.* Paris: Hachette et Cie., 1908.
———. *La pacification de Madagascar (Opérations d'octobre 1896 à mars 1899).* Ouvrage rédigé d'après les archives de l'État- Major du Corps d'occupation par F. Hellot. Paris: Librairie Militaire R. Chapelot et Cie., 1900.
———. *Trois colonnes au Tonkin, 1894-1895.* Paris: Librairie Militaire R. Chapelot et Cie., 1899.
Gaulle, Charles de. *Discours et messages.* 5 vols. Paris: Plon, 1970.

Gerlier, Henri, and Georges Guerard. *Rabat-Salé et la région.* Rabat, n.p., [1917].

Girardet, Raoul. *La société militaire dans la France contemporaine, 1815-1939.* Paris: Plon, 1953.

Goulven, Joseph. *Traité d'économie et de législation marocaines.* With a preface by Louis Marin. 2 vols. Paris: Librairie des Sciences Économiques et Sociales Marcel Rivière, 1921.

Gouraud, Henri-Joseph-Eugène. *Au Maroc, 1911-1914: Souvenirs d'un Africain.* Paris: Plon, 1949.

———. *Lyautey.* Paris: Hachette, 1938.

Grasset, Alphonse-Louis. *A travers la Chaouïa avec le corps de débarquement de Casablanca, 1907-1908.* Paris: Hachette et Cie., 1911.

Gruner, Roger. *Du Maroc traditionnel au Maroc moderne: Le Contrôle Civil au Maroc, 1912-1956.* Paris: Nouvelles Éditions Latines, 1984.

Halstead, John P. *Rebirth of a Nation: The Origins and Rise of Moroccan Nationalism, 1912-1944.* Cambridge: Harvard University Press, 1967.

Hardy, Georges. *Le Maroc.* Vol. 3 of *Histoire des colonies françaises.* Paris: Plon, 1930.

———. *Portrait de Lyautey.* With a preface by Émile Vatin-Pérignon. Paris: Bloud & Gay, 1949.

Harris, Walter Burton. *France, Spain, and the Rif.* London: Edward Arnold and Company, 1927.

Hart, David M. *The Aith Waryaghar of the Moroccan Rif: An Ethnography and History.* Tucson: University of Arizona Press, 1976.

Hoisington, William A., Jr. *The Casablanca Connection: French Colonial Policy, 1936-1943.* Chapel Hill: University of North Carolina Press, 1984.

Horne, Alistair. *The Fall of Paris: The Siege and the Commune, 1870-1871.* New York: St. Martin's Press, 1966.

Howard, Michael E. *The Franco-Prussian War: The German Invasion of France, 1870-1871.* New York: Macmillan, 1961.

Hubert-Jacques. *L'Aventure riffaine et ses dessous politiques.* Paris: Éditions Bossard, 1927.

Julien, Charles-André. *Le Maroc face aux impérialismes, 1415-1956.* Paris: Éditions Jeune Afrique, 1978.

Justinard, Léopold-Victor. *Les Aït Ba Amran.* Vol. 8, part 1 of *Villes et tribus du Maroc: Documents et renseignements.* Paris: Honoré Champion, 1930.

———. *Le caïd Goundafi: Un grand chef berbère.* With a preface by Marshal Juin. Casablanca: Éditions Atlantides, 1951.

———. *Manuel de berbère marocain (dialecte chleuh).* Paris: Gilmoto, [1916].

———. *Manuel de berbère marocain (dialecte rifain).* Paris: Geuthner, 1926.

Kann, Réginald. *Le protectorat marocain.* Paris: Berger-Levrault, 1921.

Khoury, Philip S. *Syria and the French Mandate: The Politics of Arab Nationalism, 1920-1945.* Princeton: Princeton University Press, 1987.

Lagana, Marc. *Le parti colonial français: Éléments d'histoire.* Sillery, Québec: Presses de l'Université du Québec, 1990.

Lanessan, Jean-Marie-Antoine de. *La colonisation française en Indo-Chine.* Paris: Félix Alcan, 1895.

———. *Principes de colonisation.* Paris: Félix Alcan, 1897.

Laure, Auguste-Marie-Émile. *La victoire franco-espagnole dans le Rif.* Paris: Plon, 1927.

Lebovics, Herman. *True France: The Wars over Cultural Identity, 1900-1945.* Ithaca: Cornell University Press, 1992.

Le Glay, Maurice. *Chronique marocaine: Année 1911 jusqu'à l'arrivée des Français à Fez.* Paris: Berger-Levrault, 1933.

Le Révérend, André. *Lyautey.* Paris: Fayard, 1983.

———. *Lyautey écrivain.* Gap: Éditions Ophrys, 1976.

————. *Un Lyautey inconnu: Correspondance et journal inédits (1874-1934)*. Paris: Librairie Académique Perrin, 1980.

Lyautey, Louis-Hubert-Gonzalve. *Choix de lettres, 1882-1919*. With a foreward by Paul de Ponton d'Amécourt. Paris: Armand Colin, 1947.

————. *Dans le sud de Madagascar: Pénétration militaire, situation politique et économique, 1900-1902*. Paris: Henri Charles-Lavauzelle, 1903.

————. *Lettres du sud de Madagascar (1900-1902)*. Paris: Armand Colin, 1935.

————. *Lettres du Tonkin et de Madagascar (1894-1899)*. 2 vols. Paris: Armand Colin, 1920.

————. *Lyautey l'Africain, 1912-1925: Textes et lettres du maréchal Lyautey*. Edited by Pierre Lyautey. 4 vols. Paris: Plon, 1953-57.

————. *Lyautey devant le Maroc: Lettres inédites du général Lyautey au colonel Reibell, 1903-1908*. Edited by Jean Brunon. Marseille: Vert et Rouge [Revue de la Légion Étrangère], n.d.

————. *Paroles d'action: Madagascar, Sud-Oranais, Oran, Maroc (1900-1926)*. With a preface by Louis Barthou. Paris: Armand Colin, 1927.

————. *Les plus belles lettres de Lyautey*. Edited by Pierre Lyautey. Paris: Calmann-Lévy, 1962.

————. *Du rôle social de l'officier*. With a preface by General Juin. Paris: R. Julliard, 1946.

————. *Le rôle social de l'officier*. With a preface by General Weygand. Paris: Plon, 1935.

————. *Le rôle social de l'officier*. Paris: Éditions Albatros, 1989.

————. *Vers le Maroc: Lettres du Sud-Oranais, 1903-1906*. Paris: Armand Colin, 1937.

Mangin, Louis-Eugène. *Le général Mangin, 1866-1925*. Paris: F. Lanore, 1986.

Martin, Benjamin F. *Count Albert de Mun: Paladin of the Third Republic*. Chapel Hill: University of North Carolina Press, 1978.

Maurois, André. *Lyautey*. Paris: Plon, 1931.

Méraud, Marc. *Histoire des A.I.: Le Service des Affaires Indigènes du Maroc*. With an introduction by André Martel. Vol. 2 of *Histoire des Goums marocains*. Paris: La Koumia, 1990.

Michel, Marc. *Gallieni*. Paris: Fayard, 1989.

Oved, Georges. *La gauche française et le nationalisme marocain, 1905-1955*. 2 vols. Paris: L'Harmattan, 1984.

Paléologue, Georges-Maurice. *Un grand tournant de la politique mondiale, 1904-1906*, Paris: Librairie Plon, 1934.

Pennell, C. Richard. *A Country with a Government and a Flag: The Rif War in Morocco, 1921-1926*. Wisbech, England: Middle East and North African Studies Press, 1986.

Perkins, Kenneth J. *Qaids, Captains, and Colons: French Military Administration in the Colonial Maghrib, 1844-1934*. New York: Africana Publishing Company, 1981.

Persell, Stuart Michael. *The French Colonial Lobby, 1889-1938*. Stanford: Hoover Institution Press, 1983.

Pichon, Jean. *Le Maroc au début de la guerre mondiale: El-Herri (vendredi, 13 novembre 1914)*. With a preface by General Henrÿs. Paris: Charles-Lavauzelle et Cie., 1936.

Poincaré, Raymond. *Au service de la France: Neuf années de souvenirs*. 11 vols. Paris: Plon-Nourrit et Cie., 1926-33.

Porch, Douglas. *The Conquest of Morocco*. New York: Alfred A. Knopf, 1983.

————. *The French Foreign Legion: A Complete History of the Legendary Fighting Force*. New York: HarperCollins, 1991.

————. *The March to the Marne: the French Army, 1871-1914*. Cambridge: Cambridge University Press, 1981.

Power, Thomas F., Jr. *Jules Ferry and the Renaissance of French Imperialism*. New York: King's Crown Press, 1944.

Rabat-Salé et la région: Guide du voyageur, du touriste, et de l'artiste pour les villes de Rabat, de Salé et leur hinterland. Rabat: Comité d'Initiative et de Tourisme de la Région de Rabat-Salé, [1922].

Rivet, Daniel. *Lyautey et l'institution du protectorat français au Maroc, 1912-1925.* 3 vols. Paris: L'Harmattan, 1988.

Rivière, Paul-Louis. *Précis de législation marocaine.* Paris: Recueil Sirey, 1927.

Saint-Aulaire, Auguste-Félix-Charles de Beaupoil, comte de. *Confession d'un vieux diplomate.* Paris: Flammarion, 1953.

Saint-René Taillandier, Georges. *Les origines du Maroc français: Récit d'une mission, 1901-1906.* Paris: Plon, 1930.

Scham, Alan. *Lyautey in Morocco: Protectorate Administration, 1912-1925.* Berkeley and Los Angeles: University of California Press, 1970.

Schuker, Stephen A. *The End of French Predominance in Europe: The Financial Crisis of 1924 and the Adoption of the Dawes Plan.* Chapel Hill: University of North Carolina Press, 1976.

Segonzac, Édouard-Marie-René, marquis de. *Au coeur de l'Atlas: Mission au Maroc, 1904-1905.* Paris: Émile Larose, 1910.

Simon, Henri-Joseph. *Un officier d'Afrique: Le commandant Verlet-Hanus. Mission saharienne, pacification marocaine (1898-1912). Lettres et souvenirs inédits.* Paris: J. Peyronnet et Cie., 1930.

Spillmann, Georges. *Du protectorat à l'indépendance: Maroc, 1912-1955.* Paris: Plon, 1967.

Stuart, Graham H. *The International City of Tangier.* 2nd ed. Stanford: Stanford University Press, 1955.

Sullivan, Anthony T. *Thomas-Robert Bugeaud: France and Algeria, 1784-1849: Politics, Power, and the Good Society.* Hamden, Conn.: Archon Books, 1983.

Swearingen, Will D. *Moroccan Mirages: Agrarian Dreams and Deceptions, 1912-1986.* Princeton: Princeton University Press, 1987.

Trout, Frank E. *Morocco's Saharan Frontiers.* Geneva: Droz, 1969.

Woolman, David S. *Rebels in the Rif: Abd el-Krim and the Rif Rebellion.* Stanford: Stanford University Press, 1968.

Wright, Gwendolyn. *The Politics of Design in French Colonial Urbanism.* Chicago: University of Chicago Press, 1991.

Articles and Chapters in Books

Ageron, Charles-Robert. "La politique berbère du protectorat marocain de 1913 à 1934." *Revue d'histoire moderne et contemporaine* 18, no. 1 (January-March 1971):50-90.

Andrew, Christopher M., and Sydney Kanya-Forstner. "The French 'Colonial Party': Its Composition, Aims, and Influence, 1885-1914." *Historical Journal* 14, no. 1 (March 1971):99-128.

———. "The *Groupe Colonial* in the French Chamber of Deputies, 1892-1932." *Historical Journal* 17, no. 4 (1974):837-66.

Arnaud, Édouard. "Étude d'organisation militaire saharienne." In Arnaud and Maurice Cortier, *Nos confins sahariens: Étude d'organisation militaire,* 49-58. Paris: Larose, 1908.

Ayache, Germain. "Les implications internationales de la guerre du Rif, 1921-1926." *Hespéris-Tamuda* 15 (1974):181-224.

Borély, Jules. "Rabat, ville française." In *De Rabat-Salé et sa région: Guide touristique, historique,* 28-36. Casablanca: Syndicat d'Initiative, 1931.

Botte, Louis. "Au Maroc: La conquête du pays berbère." *Revue de Paris* 21, no. 2 (March-April 1914):645-72.

Burke, Edmund III. "A Comparative View of French Native Policy in Morocco and Syria, 1912-1925." *Middle Eastern Studies* 9, no. 2 (May 1973):175-86.

———. "The Image of the Moroccan State in French Ethnological Literature: A New Look at the Origin of Lyautey's Berber Policy." In *Arabs and Berbers: From Tribe to Nation in North Africa.* Edited by Ernest Gellner and Charles Micaud, 175-99. Lexington, Mass.: Heath, 1972.

"La campagne du Tadla." *Revue de Paris* 20, no. 5 (September- October 1913):417-48.

Confer, Carl Vincent. "Divided Counsels in French Imperialism: The Ras el Aïn Incident in 1904." *Journal of Modern History* 18, no. 1 (March 1946):48-61.

Cooke, James J. "Lyautey and Étienne: The Soldier and the Politician in the Penetration of Morocco, 1904-1906." *Military Affairs* 36, no. 1 (February 1972):14-18.

Du Sault, Jean. "Une réussite française en Afrique du Nord: Charles Jonnart." *Revue des deux mondes,* 15 October 1953, 607-25.

Ellis, Stephen D. K. "The Political Elite of Imerina and the Revolt of the *Menalamba*: The Creation of a Colonial Myth in Madagascar, 1895-1898." *Journal of African History* 21, no. 2 (1980):219-34.

Fleming, Shannon E. "North Africa and the Middle East." In *Spain in the Twentieth-Century World: Essays on Spanish Diplomacy, 1898-1978.* Edited by James W. Cortada, 121-54. Westport, Conn.: Greenwood Press, 1980.

Fleming, Shannon E. and Ann K. "Primo de Rivera and Spain's Moroccan Problem, 1923-1927." *Journal of Contemporary History* 12, no. 1 (January 1977):85-99.

Gershovich, Moshe. "Lyautey, Mangin and the Shaping of French Military Strategy in Morocco, 1912-1914." In *Proceedings of the Nineteenth Meeting of the French Colonial Historical Society, Providence, Rhode Island, May 1993.* Edited by James Pritchard, 173-86. Cleveland: French Colonial Historical Society, 1994.

Justinard, Léopold-Victor. "Folklore des berbères marocains." *Hommes et mondes* 16, no. 63 (October 1951):82-90.

———. "Notes d'histoire et littérature berbères." *Hespéris* 5 (1925):227-38 and 8 (1928):333-56.

———. "Notes sur l'histoire du Sous au XVIème siècle." In Direction Générale des Affaires Indigènes, *Les Archives marocaines.* Vol. 29. Paris: Honoré Champion, 1933.

———. "Notes sur l'histoire du Sous au XIXème siècle." *Hespéris* 5 (1925):265-76 and 6 (1926):351-64.

———. "Poèmes chleuhs recueillis au Sous." *Revue du monde musulman* 60 (1925):63-107.

Khorat, Pierre [Major Ibos]. "En colonne au Maroc: Impressions d'un témoin." Parts 1-3. *Revue des deux mondes,* 1 August 1911, 519-53; 15 September 1911, 363-96; 1 November 1911, 51-81.

———. "Petite garnison marocaine." *Revue des deux mondes,* 1 July 1912, 53-82.

———. "Scènes de la pacification marocaine." Parts 1-3. *Revue des deux mondes,* 1 October 1913, 645-82; 1 November 1913, 109-46; 1 December 1913, 630-70.

Lyautey, Louis-Hubert-Gonzalve. "Du rôle colonial de l'armée." *Revue des deux mondes,* 15 January 1900, 308-28.

———. "Lettres de Rabat (1907)." *Revue des deux mondes,* 15 July 1921, 273-304.

———. "Une oeuvre, une amitié: Correspondance inédite Lyautey- Gouraud, 1912-1913." *Revue historique de l'Armée* 8, no. 2 (June 1952):11-19.

———. "Voyage en Espagne (Octobre 1913)." *Revue des deux mondes,* 15 June 1935, 794-823.

[Lyautey, Louis-Hubert-Gonzalve]. "Du rôle social de l'officier." *Revue des deux mondes,* March-April 1891, 443-59.

Marchat, Henry. "Les origines diplomatiques du 'Maroc espagnol' (1880-1912)." *Revue de l'Occident musulman et de la Méditerranée* 7, no. 1 (1970):101-70.

Mas-Latrie, Marie-Joseph de. "La politique des grands caïds au Maroc." *Revue militaire française* 100, no. 111 (1 September 1930):359-94.

Matthew, Virgil L., Jr. "Joseph Simon Gallieni (1849-1916)." In *African Proconsuls: European Governors in Africa.* Edited by L. H. Gann and Peter Duignan, 80-108. New York: The Free Press, 1978.

Munholland, J. Kim. "'Collaboration Strategy' and the French Pacification of Tonkin, 1885-1897." *Historical Journal* 24, no. 3 (1981):629-50.

————. "Rival Approaches to Morocco: Delcassé, Lyautey and the Algerian-Moroccan Border, 1903-1905." *French Historical Studies* 5, no. 3 (Spring 1968):328-43.

Pennell, C. Richard. "The Responsibility for Anual: The Failure of Spanish Policy in the Moroccan Protectorate, 1912-21." *European Studies Review* 12, no. 1 (January 1982):67-86.

Persell, Stuart Michael. "Joseph Chailley-Bert and the Importance of the Union coloniale française." *Historical Journal* 17, no. 1 (March 1974):176-84.

Porch, Douglas. "Bugeaud, Galliéni, Lyautey: The Development of French Colonial Warfare." In *Makers of Modern Strategy from Machiavelli to the Nuclear Age*. Edited by Peter Paret, 376- 407. Princeton: Princeton University Press, 1986.

Prost, Henri. "Le développement de l'urbanisme dans le protectorat du Maroc, de 1914 à 1923." In Congrès international de l'urbanisme aux colonies et dans les pays de latitude intertropical, *L'Urbanisme aux colonies et dans les pays tropicaux*. Edited by Jean Royer. 2 vols. 1:59-80. La Charité-sur-Loire and Paris: Delayance, 1932-35.

Rivet, Daniel. "Le commandement français et ses réactions vis-à- vis du mouvement rifain, 1924-1926." In *Abd el-Krim et la république du Rif*. (Actes du Colloque international d'études historiques et sociologiques, 18-20 January 1973), 101-36. Paris: Maspero, 1976.

Roussel, Lucien. "Rabat en 1916." *Revue du monde musulman* 35 (1917-18):1-30.

Royer, Jean. "Henri Prost, urbaniste." *Urbanisme* 34, no. 88 (1965):2-31.

Singer, Barnett. "Lyautey: An Interpretation of the Man and French Imperialism." *Journal of Contemporary History* 26, no. 1 (January 1991):131-57.

Slavin, David H. "The French Left and the Rif War, 1924-25: Racism and the Limits of Internationalism." *Journal of Contemporary History* 26, no. 1 (January 1991):5-32.

Tarde, Guillaume de. "L'Urbanisme en Afrique du Nord." In Congrès international de l'urbanisme aux colonies et dans les pays de latitude intertropical, *L'Urbanisme aux colonies et dans les pays tropicaux*. Edited by Jean Royer. 2 vols. 1.27-31. La Charité-sur-Loire and Paris: Delayance, 1932-35.

Venier, Pascal. "Lyautey et l'idée de protectorat de 1894 à 1902: Genèse d'une doctrine coloniale." *Revue française d'histoire d'Outre-Mer* 78, no. 293 (1991):499-517.

Theses and Dissertations

Couturier, R. and P. Feuillet. "La politique du général Pennequin en Indochine, 1888-1913: De la pacification du nord-ouest du Tonkin aux projets d'armée indigène." Mémoire de Maîtrise, Université de Paris VII, 1983.

Venier, Pascal. "Un Lyautey malgache: Ankazobé, 1897-1899: Contribution à la biographie critique d'Hubert Lyautey." Mémoire de Maîtrise, Institut d'Histoire des pays d'outre- mer, Université de Provence, Aix-Marseille I, 1987.

Yakhlef, Mohamed. "La municipalité de Fez à l'époque du protectorat (1912-1956)." 3 vols. Thèse de doctorat d'état en histoire contemporaine du Maroc, Université Libre de Bruxelles, 1990.

Newspapers and Periodicals

L'Afrique française, 1912-1925.
L'Echo du Maroc, 1919-1920.

INDEX